ECONOMICS OF DISSENT

Main Currents in Modern Economics

Poverty as a Public Issue (editor)

Most Notorious Victory: Man in an Age of Automation

Permanent Poverty: An American Syndrome

Aspects of Poverty (editor)

BEN B. SELIGMAN

Economics of Dissent

FOREWORD BY CLARENCE E. AYRES

Quadrangle Books

Chicago 1968

Most of the essays in this book appeared in slightly different form in
various publications. Grateful acknowledgment is made to the following
sources for permission to reprint copyrighted materials:

America Illustrated (published by the United States Information Agency
in Polish and Russian) for "Wage Incentives in the Labor System"
(November 1964)

American Economic Review for "On the Question of Operationalism"
(March 1967)

Challenge for "The Search for a Working Theory" (May 1964) and
"Organized Labor and Education" (March 1964)

Commentary for "Man, Work, and the Automated Feast" (July 1962);
"Those Dark, Satanic Mills" (July 1964); "The High Cost of Eating"
(July 1967); "Tariffs and American Politics" (March 1962);
"Disarmament and the Economy" (May 1963); "Portrait of a Labor
Leader" (December 1945); and a portion of "On Writing Labor
History" (January 1960), all copyright the respective years by the
American Jewish Committee

Congress Bi-Weekly for "The Dwindling Great Society" (June 20, 1966)

Dissent for "The American Corporation: Ideology and Reality" (Summer
1964); "Merger and Monopoly in the United States" (Spring 1955);
"Ideology and Big Business" (Autumn 1957); "Courage and Economics
in Washington" (Winter 1962); "New Frontier Taxes" (Spring 1963);
"Can the United States Reconvert to Peace?" (Winter 1960);
and a portion of "Economic Annals of the 1950's" (Spring 1956
and Spring 1958)

Encyclopedia of Social Work for "On Economic Planning" (1965)

Enzyklopädisches Wörterbuch (Freiburg, Germany) for "The Character
of Western Economics"

Grolier, Inc., for "Collective Bargaining" from the *Encyclopedia
Americana*

Jewish Frontier for "On the Road to Socialism" (July 1952); "They
Came to Hollywood" (July 1953); a portion of "Economic Annals of
the 1950's" (February 1954); "Needle Trades Unionism" (September
1953); and "Images of Labor in America" (March 1962)

Labor and Nation for "Demobilization: 1918–1945" (October 1945)
and "Game Theory and Collective Bargaining" (January–March 1952)

Midstream for a portion of "New Views on Labor" (April 1967)

New Leader for "Price Conspiracy: The Case of General Electric"
(October 1, 1962); a portion of "New Views on Labor" (January 20
and April 27, 1964); and a portion of "On Writing Labor History"
(September 14, 1964), all copyright the respective years by the
American Labor Conference on International Affairs, Inc.

To Matthew and Renée

Foreword

For many years Ben Seligman has been leading a double life. He
has been a dedicated professional scholar. In this role he has
assimilated virtually the entire corpus of the economic literature
of the past century, and in his *Main Currents in Modern Economics* he has reduced it all to an orderly exposition. Not only is
this the most comprehensive study of modern economic literature
anyone has made; the skill with which Seligman has traced the
interweaving and intermingling of diverse intellectual currents
makes this book a model of organization and exposition to which
scholars will refer for many years.

But Ben Seligman has never been only a scholar. He has been
an active participant in the hurly-burly of contemporary American
life. As the essays in Parts Two, Three, and Four clearly attest,
he has played an active role in the most vital social and economic
controversies of our day, ranging from the economic bias of the
Constitution to the price-fixing conspiracy in the electrical industry
and the role of unions in the needle trades.

As a participant, Seligman has always been committed to reform
as against the *status quo,* to "labor" as against "capital," to "the
common man" as against "the establishment." This bias shows
clearly in the essay that opens this book. In tracing the tortuous
course economists have taken in "The Search for a Working
Theory," Seligman came inevitably to the work of Professor
Milton Friedman of the University of Chicago, the leader of the
"positivist school" and one of the most abstruse and dogmatic of
present-day economists. As the reader will see, Ben Seligman
epitomizes the human significance of Friedman's work by saying:

I shall not go into the technicalities involved, but merely observe that in his view poverty is simply a matter of choice made by the poor, since they are so utterly unwilling to undertake risk. Observations of this character are so outlandish in the light of contemporary sociological knowledge that they must be rejected out of hand.

As it happens, Professor Friedman does not take criticism lightly. He furiously resented this characterization of his views and wrote a protesting letter to the editor of *Challenge,* demanding that the letter be published in the most prominent possible place, and restating the disputed point. According to this restatement of the case, it seems that Seligman had erred in attributing to Friedman the supposition that non-risk-takers are the only unfortunates. There are, Friedman wrote, also "people who were willing to take risks, did so, and lost." Moreover, not all non-risk-takers are poor. They are just stationary. "People who are 'utterly unwilling to take risks' remain in their initial estate whether this be high or low!" (Friedman's exclamation point). In short, Harlem is populated in part by people who (though penniless) took the appalling risk of migrating from Alabama or Puerto Rico but failed to find Utopia, and also by people who, though thoroughly dissatisfied with a ghetto existence, stubbornly refuse to get out and organize a corporate conglomerate, being in this respect as timid as wealthy dowagers who crouch in their penthouse apartments and never venture out except to visit their banks or clip the coupons on their municipal bonds (on which they pay no income tax).

This is part of what Seligman means by identifying his position with "the economics of dissent," but not all. Many "orthodox" economists have been emotionally humane. John Stuart Mill is perhaps the prime example. Rigidly orthodox in his "principles," he dilutes his ink with tears as he discusses the probable future of "the laboring classes." I am sure that Ben Seligman's dissent applies just as much to the "principles" of economic scholasticism as to the injustices of what John Kenneth Galbraith calls the "technostructure." Indeed, dissent is the keynote that harmonizes the professional lucubrations of Part One with the humanitarian sentiments of Parts Two, Three, and Four.

Moreover, to understand what Ben Seligman is driving at the reader must remember that in every age the men who have left the deepest imprint on our thinking have been dissenters. Adam Smith was a dissenter. His *Inquiry into the Nature and Causes of the Wealth of Nations* was written to refute and denounce the "mercantile system" which had prevailed for three centuries before his time. It was a study of what we now call "economic development," in which Smith argued most convincingly that nations do not develop at each other's expense but rather all together, and that economic growth is only impeded by royal grants of monopoly and proceeds best when let alone.

John Maynard Keynes, by far the most influential economic writer of our own day, was also a dissenter. Keynes became convinced that the economics of laissez faire suffers from a fatal flaw: it does not assure the constant full employment that is essential to economic health and growth. Keynes thought that only deliberate public policies could maintain full employment.

But is this the terminus of dissent? By no means! Granted that laissez faire is a great improvement over the legalized monopoly of the Hudson's Bay Company and the East India Company, free trade still falls somewhat short of Utopia. The dogmas of the "free market" still challenge the iconoclasts, and Ben Seligman is one of these.

One of the things wrong with the free market is that it doesn't exist. Adam Smith himself recognized this, even though he rested his whole case on "the obvious and simple system" of free exchange. Everybody believes in free competition, and everybody tries to obtain some special advantage for himself. As Smith said, "People in the same trade seldom meet together, even for merriment and diversion, but the conversation ends in a conspiracy against the public, or in some contrivance to raise prices." Several of the essays in this collection deal with specific cases of this endemic disease of the market economy.

These are only shortcomings of what might still be regarded as the best conceivable system for "allocating scarce resources among alternative uses," as the textbooks say. But is it? On this decisive issue the better textbooks hedge a bit. This, they say, is the best conceivable system *given the prevailing distribution of property and income*. But what does this mean? Who has given what to whom?

The proudest boast ever made for the "market-organized" economy is that (in the language of John Bates Clark) "Free competition tends to give to labor what labor creates, to capitalists what capital creates, and to entrepreneurs what the coordinating function creates." Overlooking the hedge delicately suggested by the word "tends," we are still confronted by the question, "Who appointed, elected, or otherwise designated the capitalists?" Entrepreneurs, we know, are self-selected. Furthermore, theirs is a very risky occupation, for (unlike the rest of the population) they are continually confronted by "uncertainties" in which they may lose the fruits of previous coordinations and may even have to go to work. But capitalists are beholden only to the institutions of organized society.

To recognize that the resources of organized society are allocated by the institutions of organized society is not to sound the tocsin "To the barricades." But dissenting economists like Ben Seligman do insist on calling a spade a spade, and this constantly irritates the orthodox. Thus, in the passage quoted above to which Professor Friedman objected, Seligman refers to the poor. In his retort Professor Friedman puts this nasty word in quotation marks. In the lucubrations of economic "analysis" there is no such category. Indeed, even to mention the poor is enough to convict one of being a sociologist.

It is from this dogma—and all the sterilities of economic "analysis"—that Ben Seligman dissents. His is the direct, common-sense approach to a wide variety of economic problems: some simple and obvious, and some complex and subtle, but all capable of being resolved into essentially simple elements by the expository artistry of this great scholar.

I had thought, when I set out to write this note, that I would run through the roster of economic problems and situations with which the book deals. But this has proved impossible within the compass of an introductory note. Moreover, in each case Seligman's essay is so much more intelligible and attractive than my abridgement that it would be a disservice to the reader as well as the author for me to intrude between them. I can do no better than to urge the reader of these words to go straight on and read what Seligman has written. A liberal education as well as the most rewarding kind of pleasure reading will be found between these covers.

CLARENCE E. AYRES

Preface

One of the more pleasant egocentricities of academic life is to discover one's pieces, hitherto thought to be fleeting, cited on occasion by one's colleagues. Such egocentricities often threaten to become a peculiar form of narcissism, leading to the belief that it might be worthwhile to put together such pieces between a single set of covers, if only to make it easier to refer students to one or another article.

Yet there are, I believe, more important issues at stake. Much of the work in social science today manifests a strange *ad hoc* quality: the efforts of the economist seem unrelated to those of the sociologist; the investigations of the social psychologist appear completely distinct from the insights of the political scientist; the social worker refuses to listen to operations analysts; and none will pay heed to the philosopher or historian.

Why has this situation developed? It stems, I think, from the inordinate concern with "behavioristic" propositions in the social sciences. Unfortunately, such propositions all too often suffer from an overly stringent application of Occam's Razor, for they have sought to deal only with the observable and nothing else. Generalizations have been elucidated from bits and pieces of knowledge making it relatively easy to assert that certain behavior patterns, for example, are deviant because they violate or distort some implicit norm. It has not always been clear that there might be an interest or even theoretical usefulness in uncovering the etiology of human action; such concerns are obviously not measurable, and therefore not within the boundaries of behavioristic social science.

Further, since human behavior cannot be quantified too satisfactorily, the immeasurable is measured by rank orders of importance, thus imitating rarefied economic theory in which linear transformations are used to sneak cardinal utility in by the back door. The law of large numbers validates the models and ideal types, and if the labels are capitalized, so much the better. Somehow the exceptions and extremes are forgotten in the anxiety to get a paper published in a respectable professional journal which may be read at most by a few graduate students. George Stigler once remarked that if a so-called law in economics covered only one-third of the cases, it was good enough for him. I doubt that this is sufficient, for what is often of major importance may occur at either end of the distribution.

A sociologist once said that social science must always cross the path of history. It is a dictum honored mainly in the breach. Though social theory acknowledges the relevance of change, to the economist most of it is a matter of constructing elegant but nevertheless static models. There seems to be an incapacity among social scientists to deal with the *internal* elements of change, an incapacity that hinders the handling of crucial questions. I once listened to an eminent sociologist expounding eloquently on the application of Parsonian taxonomy to the underdeveloped countries. It was an elegant structure of order, integration, and self-regulation, but it remained a static scheme without much meaning for a Ghana or an India or a Senegal. One could not help wondering how Darwin might have been added to the scheme.

In economics, the notion that discourse might have something to do with the palpable *human relations* stemming from the fact of scarcity is seldom entertained. The inner logic of the science simply does not allow any trespass on other fields. Lionel Robbins, for example, has said that economics is completely neutral as to ends: it can discourse only on means. Here is the technicist impulse, the consequences of which are to do away with such problems as economic power, business cycles, income distribution, or the human use of human beings. Choice, says Robbins, is an abstract act of behavior on which no judgment can be expressed because no comment is allowed on how choice has been socially or culturally conditioned. Moreover, the truth of an economic proposition is to be distinguished from its empirical content since formal statements of relationships are said to be independent of statements of fact. Theory becomes a game in which propositions are manipulated in accordance with rules set forth in the premises. And, according to some economists, the premises need not even reflect anyone's conception of reality; they may be completely arbitrary. As one young economist remarked, "Premises are not statements of behavior; they are sets of variables."

When Professor J. G. Miller coined the term "behavioral" in 1949, he did so thinking this would lead to an ethically neutral social science. But this really is a fatuous notion. An ethically neutral social science is impossible. Moreover, neutrality of this sort carries its own ideological lumber, for it is to choose the status quo and to give up the search for relevance. As David Riesman has said, in such a situation the adaptive aspects are most likely to come to the forefront. Let me illustrate with a reference to a recent work on sociology in which the concept of maturity was defined as a state of mind that has come to terms with what exists. Why should not maturity be defined as a state of mind that has the capacity to dream of betterment, of perhaps a world without war, or a world of meaningful work?

Partial investigations unrelated to the totality of man's experience—so characteristic of today's social science—create only atomistic microcosms of society, and distorted ones at that. For it is patent that those elements included in the atomistic set conjoin other sets. Interactions spill over: the set is invariably subjected to external influences: it forms and reforms around the main currents of institutional behavior. It is the latter that is the proper province of the social sciences. The broader socio-economic pressures shape the core of experience, and when social science closes the door on them, it fails to convey the true nature of society. All too often the outcome is an overweening concern with so-called small systems that frequently results in a diminution of relevance and the concomitant and extraordinary compilation of data for its own sake, culminating in what Dwight Macdonald has described as a coefficient of comprehensibility that decreases in direct ratio to the mass and length of the study, with a standard deviation from the obvious, inversely related to the magnitude of the generalization. To illustrate the latter, how useful it is to be told, as in a paper on worker protest published a few years ago, that "the totality of theorizing about worker protest must be viewed as an interlocking structure of hypotheses and generalizations of varying scope and compass," or that the "formulation and expression of a complaint is dependent upon the prerequisite cognizance of aberration from some normative mode."

Today, even as in 1939, when Robert S. Lynd published his *Knowledge For What?*, we need acute and candid thinking in the social sciences and an awareness of the sources of our own presuppositions. We need the sort of expertise that recognizes the devilish complexity of our society. We need the kind of constructive thought that spares no one, least of all the social scientist. In a sense, what is required is perhaps best described as a humanistic purview. For if we speak for the values of democracy and equality of opportunity in an affluent society, then the continuing poverty of some thirty million Americans seems a more critical problem than the interacting Venn diagrams of a fictive sociological or economic model. If we are to study the behavior of humans in their setting, then the transitivity or intransitivity of a preference curve hardly seems relevant. To quote Professor John Kenneth Galbraith, the trouble is that the social scientist, like members of gangs, congregations, primitive tribes, and holders of diplomatic passports, wants to safeguard the boundary between himself and everyone else. The language of discourse within these tightly knit groups is such that one need not worry much about reality. Thus, economists in the upper reaches of the Galbraithian ladder can call for the elimination of unions, the enforcement of free competition, therapeutic deflation, and nullification of income taxes without straining the credulity of their colleagues or injuring their own reputations.

Yet social science, and economics particularly, cannot avoid a genuine concern with the human animal, that is, with his behavior as a political, social, and economic being. This, it would seem, implies leaving behind the premises and techniques of behaviorism and returning to the grim realities of the human situation: it should imply looking at man in his total setting. Only such an approach will provide the foundations for a viable social science and a viable economics.

These observations have consciously or unconsciously shaped the ideas expressed in the papers, articles, and reviews included in this volume. They were written over a span of twenty-five years: most of them appeared in a variety of journals, ranging from magazines of opinion such as *Dissent* and *The New Leader* to *Commentary,* to the other end of the spectrum—the *American Economic Review.* When it came to the arrangement of the articles, I discovered that they fell naturally into four categories: (1) premises and preconceptions in economics; (2) American institutions: business; (3) American institutions: government; and (4) American institutions: labor. Obviously, the political perspective that infuses many of the articles is identified with the viewpoint of the original place of publication. It is a perspective that accords with the humanistic thrust that I have urged is necessary in social science.

Publication of these articles has been urged upon me by many friends and associates. A few minor alterations have been made, deleting irrelevant material and changing tenses here and there. The editors of the various journals, among whom were Haig Babian, Norman Podhoretz, Shlomo Katz, John Gurley, Irving Howe, the late J. B. S. Hardman, and Nathan Glick, were always helpful. I thank them all for permission to reprint these assorted articles. A number of the pieces were discussed prior to publication with Professors Howard Quint, William Davis, Milton Cantor, and Stanley Young, and with Messrs. Wallace Markfield, Samuel J. Meyers, and Bertram Gottlieb. I trust they will now accept a belated expression of thanks for efforts that date back sometimes a decade or more.

BEN B. SELIGMAN

Amherst, Massachusetts
June 1968

Contents

PART ONE. PREMISES AND PRECONCEPTIONS

The Search for a Working Theory

In the beginning, economics was philosophy. That this is no longer the case may be an occasion for regret, depending on one's turn of mind. In any case, some loss in perspective did occur when economists decided upon the pursuit of the purely scientific, leaving the consideration of values and goals to the tender mercies of the philosopher and sociologist. Of course, the separation of the economist from his intellectual antecedents is part of the fission that has taken place in the work process generally since the eighteenth century; it is not unrelated to the desire to create a bona fide occupational category in which one could earn a fair livelihood.

Fundamentally, there are two kinds of economists—word economists (theory) and fact economists (numbers). Generally these two don't speak to each other, thus imitating the antics of the pure physicist and applied physicist of thirty years ago. The physicists have learned better since then; at least the need to build an atom bomb brought them within conversation range of each other. However, economists still suffer from a cultural lag. One seldom finds a fact economist conceding that a word economist really knows what goes on in the world, while the latter dissociates himself from practicality because the fact man's fingernails are apt to be too dirty from digging in the earth. Now, when the two are combined in the same personality, as is the situation with several distinguished professors, grave troubles may ensue, for the payoff all too often is a clinical case of intellectual indecision.

Let me document the argument. Professor Paul Samuelson opted for the "word" approach in his presidential address to the American Economic Association in December 1961. In it, he spoke at length in praise of the theoretical approach as opposed to *political* economy. He asserted that the inner logic of the science had little to do with the common sense view of the man in the street. In fact, he said, the good *political* economist was sure to be an indifferent theorist—or analyst—while the good analyst really did not have to bother about the state of the world.

This was a rather troublesome proposition for a good many in the audience, for to them Professor Samuelson had always embodied the best attributes of both. Nevertheless, Professor Samuelson went on to suggest that most of the genuinely great figures in the history of economic thought had been poor theorists because they were so deeply concerned with the public welfare.

Later, Professor Samuelson insisted that he was misunderstood. In the published version of his address he added a footnote to say that he was not really interested in logical elegance for the sake of elegance, but rather in the pursuit of truth wherever it might lead. The footnote was unconvincing; the damage had been done. He was indeed urging economists to turn their backs on the world of reality.

But one must also read his Stamp Memorial lecture given in England only a month prior to his presidential address. In it he said: (1) political economy is much too important to leave to non-economists; (2) business, far from being nobody's business, definitely was the economist's business; and (3) "What do they know of economics who political economy do not know?"

The theorist, then, if we read Samuelson properly, must have a speaking acquaintanceship with facts: numbers are parallel to words. (Of course, a good theory can help us select relevant facts, for theory essentially is a program for research.) We come then, finally, to the position that economics has a need for both facts and words. Words alone run the risk of being little more than subtle rationalizations for special pleading. One need but examine the pronouncements of some businessmen on the federal budget to become aware that economics can still be little more than a naive philosophy about how men earn their keep.

The latter approach was especially evident in American economics in the nineteenth century. Again, as Professor Samuelson once indicated, a quick perusal of the writings of Henry Carey or the two Walkers or Simon Newcomb reveals the following characteristics: (1) unbounded optimism and a belief in eternal harmony; (2) acceptance of Darwinian struggle as a description of man's behavior in society, all taking place under the benign benevolence of a noninterfering Deity; (3) a nationalist sentiment supporting a protectionist posture, and (4) an anti-intellectualist, antitheoretical, and predominantly conservative bias.

It was against this frame of mind that some of the younger economists rebelled shortly after the turn of the century. Thorstein Veblen and John R. Commons, and, later, Wesley C. Mitchell and John Maurice Clark, while stressing different facets of theory, were all quite critical of the dominant schools of thought. As a cohesive type of thinking, however, the style they exemplified appears to be all but extinct, except for an occasional economist *cum* sociologist, or such part-time dissenters from the mainstream as John Kenneth Galbraith and Gardiner Means. However, the announcement of the demise of this school may be premature, for the dissatisfaction with received doctrine appears to be spreading, at least enough to encourage a number of rebellious economists to form a rump group within the profession.

But the fact of the matter is that the conservative bent in American economics is difficult to uproot. Its tenacity is a remarkable cultural phenomenon, and today it is quite sophisticated. Moreover, one can observe a specific line of development, starting with John Bates Clark, nurtured by Frank H. Knight, and flowering in the neolibertarianism of Milton Friedman. It is hard, tough-minded, absolutist, filled with the formulas of game theory and other recondite notions—and dead wrong.

Consider the theoretical views of Professor Knight. In his definition of the field in which economics should function, Knight excludes technology and all other empirical details. Economics, he has insisted, is not a descriptive science, but rather a deductive discipline. It must necessarily be abstract, since it utilizes inferences drawn from certain premises and always has recourse to intuitive knowledge. But just how economic truth was to be secured through intuition was not made clear.

It is indeed difficult to conceive that any proposition in economics may be characterized as *a priori*. That is to say, we must be in a position to refute or affirm any statement made in economics, or sociology, or any of the social sciences. Carrying abstraction to an extreme, Knight would reduce all the factors of production to capital. He considers the ideas of land, labor, and capital, as distinct categories, to be superfluous, and he has argued that there is no substantial difference between permanent and nonpermanent resources. It was clear that this would only fudge any attempt to develop a coherent theory of distribution, and Knight was severely criticized for this by other economists.

Not unexpectedly, Knight's attitude toward labor has been quite hostile. Low wages were attributed to the disposition of workers to gamble recklessly with life and limb as well as income. This supposedly explained why their condition was so poor. More recently, he has objected to collective bargaining beyond the enterprise or plant level and has argued that any kind of bargaining is monopoly price setting. According to Knight, employers cannot afford highhanded action toward employees because other workers will know about it, and productive efficiency requires worker morale.

It is interesting to note that as far back as 1933 Knight thought it poor taste for economists to descend to the "public's level of thinking" in order to exert some influence on policy. There was a rather odd sort of snobbery in this remark, for he was referring to those economists who had left the campus to go to Washington. They should have stayed home, Knight intimated, to engage exclusively in problem solving. Yet, surely, discovering a way out of a great depression was a meaningful problem that demanded solution. To Knight, however, those economists who believed that the administrative tasks of government possessed their own worthwhile intellectual excitement were merely pandering to the tastes of the crowd.

This approach has been furthered with great subtlety and much theoretical refinement by Milton Friedman. Professor Friedman does not believe that values are necessary in a positive analysis of economic questions. But as Gunnar Myrdal has demonstrated, a belief in the existence of scientific knowledge in social science, independent of value systems, reflects a rather naive empiricism. Facts are ordered by concepts, and concepts are fundamentally expressions of human interest and a particular viewpoint; they can be described only as valuations. The latter are not arbitrary, for they stem from the society in which we live and work.

For Friedman, on the other hand, economics must be concerned solely with positive propositions and hypotheses. The validity of an hypothesis, he has contended, must be judged solely by its predictive powers. Direct verification is not essential to the procedure. And any consideration of the realism of one's assumptions in economic theory is irrelevant. Fortunately, most leading theorists are concerned that their assumptions concur with reality. As Professor Samuelson has said, an economic theory is a set of statements about observable reality. If it is not that, then it may be mathematics, but it is not economics.

Some of Friedman's more abstruse studies are concerned with the maximization of utility under conditions of risk. I shall not go into the technicalities involved, but merely observe that in his view poverty is simply a matter of choice made by the poor, since they are so utterly unwilling to undertake risk. Observations of this character are so outlandish in the light of contemporary sociological knowledge that they must be rejected out of hand.

There are many other oddities in Friedman's corpus. His strange history of the role of money; his equally odd "permanent income" hypothesis; and his insistence, with several minor modifications, that the quantity theory of money is sufficient to explain what does, in fact, happen in the economy, document a most singular view of economics. And seldom are political or sociological problems approached by Friedman other than in black and white terms. He would go so far as to apply legislated laissez faire to public education by limiting the government's role to financing and by abolishing compulsory aspects wherever possible, so that the law of the market might rule even in this critical area. Parents would be permitted to select their own schools and in no case would vocational training be provided by the authorities. Public education is to be limited solely to citizenship, which usually means whatever the writer wants it to mean.

Can we find countervailing voices in American economics? The answer is, *yes!* One can do no better than to start with the strongest of them—that of Thorstein Veblen. But to understand Veblen, he must be read, and read in his entirety. One cannot discuss Veblen by parroting his interpreters, as did one distinguished sociologist at a Veblen Centenary meeting in New York a few years ago. This social scientist announced that as a student he had been taught never to read a great writer in the original, but to read comments about him. That was supposedly more fruitful and took less time. However, he confessed that for the meeting he decided to read just a bit of Veblen's work. He expressed horror at its muddle-headedness. The trouble with Veblen was that he did not realize that in our economy the consumer is king. The response came from Walton Hamilton, who admitted that indeed the consumer was king, but that, like the monarchs of old, he was surrounded by courtiers, flatterers, and deceivers whose function it was to get his Royal Highness to do what they wanted him to.

Now, Veblen clearly was a man of his time, and in his work you will find some error that requires criticism. But if the short-comings, which are trivial, are put to one side, much remains to demonstrate that Veblen was not only of his time but of ours as well. He wrote when most of his contemporaries, both in and out of the academy, were convinced that mankind could only continue to make progress. But Veblen had a nightmare: he saw imbecilic institutions being perpetuated all about him. And one wonders, after our experience with two world wars and a depression, whether he does not speak to us more directly than he did to his contemporaries.

Veblen understood quite well the irrational components of human behavior and human nature. Our intellectual heritage has by far overestimated man's special and ever-increasing capacity to exercise reason. And when he came to examine the technical side of economics, he found that it was not an evolutionary science. The older economists held to an immutable model of economic man and they frequently confounded it with reality. Veblen argued that the model was cumbersome and contradicted reality. He pointed to monopoly and depression as areas that the standard economics of his time simply did not want to discuss.

With his conception of a dichotomy between business and industry, Veblen was able to focus on the manner in which the criteria of vendibility perverted the innate capacities of the industrial system. Credit (or the creation of a paper economy in which the pursuit of pecuniary rewards and the pursuit of money to make more money are carried on without regard to the underlying realities of the productive apparatus) became the subject of a most scathing analysis.

Veblen's approach was pragmatic and provisional—essentially the same as that which most scientists would respect today in that it points to the fallacies of scientism. He was always underscoring limitations and ridiculing the deification of ideas. He complained chronically; he criticized, deflated, satirized. He was concerned with the imperfections of society, and it may very well be that one lesson we can learn from Veblen stems from his perpetual dissatisfaction with the nature of society.

While "cranks" like Veblen are never satisfied with the way events are going, their Socratic questioning, their insistence that the Emperor has no clothes, may make us aware that the world indeed needs help if it is to survive.

Nowhere is the lack of a humanistic purview and the joy of playing with technique for its own sake displayed more openly than in the most recent stress in economic thinking, to wit, the mathematical approach. We are frequently told by the practitioners of this arcane art that they are quite aware of the limitations of the elegant models they construct, and that these models are only provisional. But the charges of the nonmathematical economists that the procedure is all too sterile can be substantiated by a careful examination of the literature.

An egregious example may be seen in one recent attempt to indicate that economic growth can be expressed mathematically by an equation in which Y, the national product, is set as a function of capital stock services, the rate of use of natural resources, employment of the labor force, society's fund of applied knowledge, and the cultural milieu in which the economy operates. Stated verbally, the expression makes some sense. But when the mathematical equation sets forth the last element as U, implying that the cultural background can be subjected to the mathematical operations of differentiation and integration, then we have simply approached the boundaries of intellectual aridity.

Of course, this sort of game playing makes it easy for the young economist to climb the ladder of his profession. To adopt the approaches of the humanist and the historian appears much too arduous a routine. It is so much easier to learn some cookbook mathematics, compute several coefficients of correlation and then get an easy *A* in your economics course. At a somewhat higher professional level, the result frequently is that the sensible person reads professional journals mainly for the book reviews and the obituaries. The net outcome is that professors help maintain the printing industry at a high level of efficiency.

Max Planck, the eminent physicist, once said that he found economics to be too difficult. Obviously, he was not referring to the mathematical content, which he could have mastered in about twenty-four hours. It was, rather, the need to know a huge body of facts, with a substantial background in history, psychology, and a comprehension of underlying social pressures. The economist has to be not only a mathematician, but as one British writer remarked, "a philosopher, a psychologist, an anthropologist, an historian, a geographer and a student of politics; a master of prose exposition; and a man of the world, with experience of practical business and finance, an understanding of the problems of administration and a good knowledge of four or five languages."

This implies that economics cannot avoid a genuine concern with the human animal—that is, with his behavior as a political, social, and economic being. It implies leaving behind the pure techniques in which the economist has such implicit faith these days, and returning to the grim realities of the human condition. It implies looking at man in his total setting. And it implies that we keep before us at all times Joan Robinson's motto: "The purpose of studying economics is not to acquire a set of ready-made answers to economic questions, but to learn how to avoid being deceived by economists."

1964

The Character of Western Economics

I

An increasing stress on technical analysis has been the predominant feature of recent Western economics. This has been emphasized by the extraordinary development of input-output studies, econometrics, operations research, game theory, linear programming, and certain aspects of contemporary welfare theory. In some of these approaches an effort has been made to outline concepts of behavior that would provide parameters of action for the particular economic model under consideration. Thus recent theory has spoken of man as a simulator, maximizer, minimizer, sequential decision-maker, or satisficer. The simulator, undecided what to do, resorts to a digital computer to help him arrive at a decision; the maximizer seeks the largest potential profit, much like the economic man of the nineteenth century; the minimizer is concerned with reducing risks and costs; and the satisficer is content with merely satisfactory results.

While none of these models is real by itself, taken together they seem to say something about the nature of economic behavior. More important, they reflect some awareness of the complexity of economic action, for in an evolving society neither firm nor household, neither capitalist nor worker are today what they were two or three decades ago. As Joseph A. Schumpeter once argued, the innovative entrepreneurial spirit undergoes erosion as the businessman is converted into an institutionalized manager for whom a table of organization is a categorical imperative. A significant part of current economic theory, however, has been captured by the more technical aspects of these developments, with the consequence that its practitioners appear to have forgotten that economics is a social science the viability of which depends not only on mathematics, but on psychology, anthropology, history, geography, technology, and political science as well.

Economics, it has been argued, is but one way of looking at the total complex of social behavior. In this sense, it is a branch of a general theory of social systems, and has as its primary task the study of those processes that are specifically economic, as well as the forms of behavior that stem from them. Traditionally, economists have focused their attention on the areas of production and distribution. But goods and services are not only commodities and performances; they are significantly related to the human actors who control them and who in turn are controlled. Further, the relationships which the actors establish among themselves are also economic. Overlooking these considerations may result in an undue emphasis on artifacts and may lead economists to evade the responsibility for including in their models the goals that people may pursue. Had this been achieved in the past, the more recent theoretical models would have provided more malleable behavior equations. As Jan Tinbergen has said, additional parameters of conduct are needed to analyze economic behavior. Were this available, utility surfaces and welfare propositions, for example, would not be based on assumptions of isolated preferences, for it would have been acknowledged that analytic concepts are rooted in social experience.

II

One effort to accomplish this purpose was undertaken by Abram Bergson in 1938. Bergson developed a general function which associated social welfare with the goods bought by all the individuals in a community. Such social welfare was explicitly based on value judgments that might be established by some higher authority. Indifference curves could then be worked up, said Bergson, to provide a social welfare function that might be maximized subject to the limitations of existing production possibilities. Of course, the difficulty here was knowing what the community really wanted, for there was no mechanism available to reach a public consensus. Furthermore, as Kenneth Arrow has demonstrated, social decision-making would require consistency in the array of preferences, majority action, the absence of external pressures, and choice based only on the alternatives available. Since a consistent rule for proceeding from individual preferences to a social preference could not be found, said Arrow, it was unlikely that economists could evolve a rigorous concept of social choice.

The welfare approach to social judgment was further compromised by Paul A. Samuelson, who defined the welfare function ordinally; that is, one had to speak of it in terms of merely better or worse, or as one in which the social attitude was one of utter indifference. While a welfare function might not be able necessarily to indicate which of two social situations was the best, it could reveal, presumably, for a limited set of situations, which would be better if a choice were at all possible. In examining the various theorems in this area of economic analysis, Samuelson found that prices were usually excluded; the relevant variables were applicable to either individuals or groups; assumptions of homogeneity were generally involved; all preference statements were ostensibly rational; assumptions of symmetry suggested conditions of equality; and welfare usually meant maximizing cardinal utility. None of these, suggested Samuelson, was realistic, nor did they escape the ethical overtones of interpersonal comparisons of utility.

So far as ordinary economics was concerned, however, standard market theory still appeared to many economists as the most satisfactory explanation for the transition from individual action to social performance. But this was so only in theoretical models since the real-life counterpart for such a theory was difficult to uncover. Even during the days when laissez-faire doctrine was in flower, in the nineteenth century, there was ample evidence of a mixed situation with frequent government intervention supplementing growing corporate control of markets. The consequence was that the model of the free market acquired a purely normative meaning by which the results of actual market behavior were adjudged to have serious shortcomings. It was seldom acknowledged that the supposed operations of natural law and individual freedom, which underpinned the theory of the free market, were rooted in the ideology of the Enlightenment and that they were bound to be emptied of meaning in an age of urbanism and industrialism. Today, for example, the survival of some individuals is predicated on the limitation of the freedom of others, as in the case of traffic regulations. And the law of eminent domain is an explicit acknowledgment that social purposes may override individual convenience.

The cornerstone of traditional market theory is the law of supply and demand, according to which prices vary directly with demand and inversely with supply. The analysis of the behavior of firms and the flow of international trade is generally drawn from this fundamental axiom. Yet as Lord Keynes revealed in his demonstration of the possibility of low-level equilibrium, output and prices may indeed move in consonance with each other; or a worker may reject increased hours despite higher earnings simply because his preference may have shifted to leisure time. Evidently there are situations in which the "law" is not immutable.

Furthermore, the law of supply and demand suggests that a businessman is always inspired by maximum profitability. Yet it is conceivable that his primary concern is, as W. J. Baumol asserts, sales maximization subject to a given minimum profit constraint. If this is the case, then that output which maximizes sales would be determined at some point greater than the profit-maximizing output. The major objective could very well be securing as large a share of the market as possible. The profit constraints could then be established at levels that would provide sufficient latitude to encompass higher costs. Once this view is adopted, the governing principle of supply and demand is subordinated to the pursuit of as wide a range of market penetration as might be allowed by law and competition. Such behavior is quite common, as illustrated by the practice of many large firms in the United States—Standard Oil of Indiana and Sears, Roebuck are cases in point.

Refinements of the theory of demand have been attempted, most notably by John R. Hicks, who supposed that consumers are able to choose between lists of goods in various combinations. This assumption was necessary in order to make ordinal valuations possible and so escape the philosophical limitation of cardinal utility. By employing the indifference curve approach, Hicks was able to analyze the effects of income and substitutability on consumer reactions, but he did so without regard to the patent fact that a large proportion of consumer outlays comprise fixed commitments. In essence, what the theory described was the relation of a reduced price for one good as contrasted with another, making the slope of the demand curve of the affected good somewhat negative. On the other hand, the lower price ostensibly provided additional income, leading to a possible shift to other goods. All this presumed a rationality that itself could be deemed to be uneconomic, since the cost involved in making minute calculations of alternatives could far exceed the gain in utility that the consumer might enjoy. Consumer behavior, in the final analysis, is culturally conditioned, an element that most economic theorists either ignore or merely say is given. Yet clearly this weakened perceptibly the usefulness of the law of supply and demand, since cultural motivations impelled consumers to make routine purchases from favorite establishments rather than rationally seek to reduce their outlays to a minimum.

The growth of modern industry, characterized by heavy capital investments, specific equipment, long periods of investment, and overhead costs, has also raised serious questions regarding the classical law of supply and demand. These problems were explored in a most incisive fashion by J. M. Clark, who began with the theory of demand as but a provisional statement of consumer behavior. Clark's analysis further implied that the principle of profit maximization was based on trial and error, with aggressive action undertaken by some firms and defensive responses by others. The competitive market was not a self-regulating device, said Clark, and it could not be because of the domination of overhead costs. Fixed capital had become so important an element in industry that firms tended to stay in business so long as wages and raw material costs could be recaptured. The outcome was excess capacity and cutthroat competition, unless stability was introduced via mutual agreement.

III

Nevertheless, the search for a theoretical approach that would provide criteria of efficient resource allocation continued without abatement. Characteristic examples were input-output analysis for macroeconomic purposes and linear programming, a method suitable to the microeconomic unit. Supplementing these techniques were econometrics and operations research. The former devised mathematical models of some economic entity in order to predict the future behavior of the economic variables contained in the model. The technique involved first specifying an equation, as in the rather simple statement that consumption is a linear function of national income. The second step required estimating the numerical values of the parameters, usually by calculating regression coefficients. After making these calculations, the econometrician attempted to verify his equations by checking against certain criteria. Once these steps were completed, the results might be projected into the future. Characteristic of econometric models are the isolation of endogenous variables, those the behavior of which is assumed to be induced by changes in the national income; autonomous variables, usually government expenditures; lagged variables, those the value of which is governed by time periods; and jointly determined variables. The presumption is that econometric analysis provides a sharper insight into qualitative and quantitative changes in the economy and allows for estimating levels of confidence in the mathematically calculated predictions.

Related to this technique, but intended to provide guidelines on a microeconomic level, is operations research, developed during World War II as a way of solving strategic and tactical problems. The central purpose of this analytical approach is to give the decision-maker a quantitative basis for selecting one of several possible choices. Basic to the method is the assumption that decisions can be rooted in rational calculation. Once the problem has been outlined, a mathematical model is constructed, employing calculus, linear algebra, or probability theory to represent the system being evaluated. When the solution has been worked out, the operations researcher can then specify the possibilities for the exercise of rational choice. The technique has been useful in establishing economical inventory levels and in such areas as queuing theory. But the presumption that it can be employed as a general guide for planning an entire economy seems premature. Operations research may be suitable for certain microeconomic problems, but its success decreases as the researcher moves to the higher and more complex arena of the total society. While it may solve traffic flow problems on a bridge crossing, operations research has not yet been able to say anything significant about such matters as growth in the general economy.

Input-output analysis, on the other hand, promises a more viable approach to the total economy. Developed by W. W. Leontief during the 1940's (although the basic idea goes back to a 1925 article written by Leontief on Soviet economic balances), the method provides large sets of economic equations capable of numerical solutions. An entire nation is visualized as one large accounting system, with a matrix showing output flows from one sector to all the others, as well as inputs to the various sectors. Outputs are distributed horizontally across the matrix, with inputs distributed vertically. Either value or quantity terms may be used. However, vertical totals for inputs are meaningless since tons and yards cannot be added. In this way, it becomes possible to write out an equation describing how much of a sector's output has gone to the others. Further, the value-added for each industry can be estimated, indicating each industry's own contribution to the national product over and above the value of the inputs drawn from other industries. In Leontief's original formulation it was assumed that the coefficients of production were fixed, on the ground that costs were strictly proportional to output. Consequently, the matrix could be constructed with homogeneous linear equations and there was no need to employ marginal productivity theory. In effect, what had been obtained was a general equilibrium system with the simplifying assumptions of static analysis. On the other hand, if some of the variables, particularly those relating to households, were thought to have been independently determined, then it became possible to estimate the level of activities required for full employment. This stemmed from the fact that given the flow of labor from households and the level of final demand, the required magnitudes for full employment in the input-output cells could be computed. In more recent analyses, the system is made "dynamic" by introducing income-creating forces, alternative production methods, and changes in investment.

Some economists have questioned the use of fixed coefficients since a change in any single one alters the equation in which it appears and forces a new solution of all the equations in the matrix. Changing coefficients, moreover, would provide a basis for evaluating the effects of new technology. A more serious criticism is that the input-output matrix is based on hindsight, that it represents only a convenient classification of past data. Even this is not fully damaging, because with high-speed computers experimental alterations can be made in the data to judge the consequences of movements in the variables.

A further illustration of the enthusiasm of Western economists for technical analysis is afforded by the rapid spread of linear, or more accurately, mathematical programming. This may have been a reflection of the frustration suffered as a result of ordinary theory's inability to supply computational methods. When it was discovered that certain practical problems, albeit on a microeconomic level, could be solved by linear programming, its future in the profession was assured. Linear programming, like operations research, to which it is affiliated, was a postwar development. Its specific formulation had its roots in the work of G. B. Dantzig for the U.S. Air Force on scheduling activities related to stockpiling, production, and inventories. But L. V. Kantorovich, a Soviet mathematician, had sketched some linear programming problems as far back as 1939, although there seems to have been no connection between his work and Dantzig's.

Formally, the central problem in linear programming is to maximize a linear function of a set of variables subject to certain constraints. Linearity presumes that proportionality exists between inputs and outputs, or, as an economist would say, that there are constant returns to scale. The ensuing model is an abstract analysis of the requirements for the most efficient least-cost allocation of resources at microeconomic levels. The mathematics itself is drawn from set theory and the theory of linear vector spaces, thus allowing the development of systems of inequalities. By breaking down the analysis in terms of the particular techniques available and specifying the constraints or limitations, it became possible to indicate what the firm might be able to do. In other words, the domain of the variables was bounded: only compact convex sets could be considered.

Typical problems amenable to the linear programming method are the case of an automobile plant wishing to establish the level of production it should set for automobile and truck assembly, given the capacity limits of its various departments; the construction of a least-cost diet containing a specified quantity of food elements; the blending of gasoline in a refinery; and the shipment of a standardized product from several warehouses to different locations.

Associated with the maximizing problem was the "dual" minimizing one. This involved the imputation of values to the inputs employed, so that corresponding to the maximization of profit was the minimization of cost. Thus resource allocation in linear programming became one aspect of the pricing problem; in effect, the solution of one was the solution of the other, leading enthusiasts to proclaim that linear programming methods were suitable for both capitalist firms and socialist systems—in fact, for any organization in which the decision-making process was centralized. The theory became a vindication of economic equilibrium under competitive conditions.

But the suggestion that programming techniques are analogues for the economy as a whole commits the fallacy of composition, for institutional constraints must be considered as well. Further, constant cost conditions do not apply to all firms or industries, and increasing returns could nullify a linear solution which might recommend a process less concentrated than would be desirable.

Some Western economists have argued that these methods do not provide a genuine *political* economy. It has been said that the significance and immanent meaning of economic theory may be studied most fruitfully by relating it to practical policy: useful theory emerges as pro and con statements in movements of social change or during times of crisis. If this is the case, then verbal meaning and practical goals are antecedent to logical validity or analytical elegance. Moreover, if economics is a science of social fact, one needs to check theory against real events. The problem of relevance, it has been argued, is that which makes the theory itself a way of perceiving economic reality. Without this perception, theory cannot guide empirical inquiry. A further difficulty stems from the normative elements that are often embedded in pure theory. Hence, economics must frequently have reference to value judgments, for at the very point where inquiry is initiated, where facts are ordered, there is a deep human urge to evaluate fundamental concepts. Thus it can be argued that the theory of the competitive economy, and its concomitant law of supply and demand, is essentially a prescriptive and normative construct.

Many of the mathematical and econometric models may be said to be mechanistic constructions using highly restricted premises and developing even fewer operational propositions. Such principles as are developed are expected to function in identical fashion under all circumstances. One difficulty stems from the use of homogeneous factors, to be sure a useful analytical device at the start. But once capital and labor are postulated as homogeneous, the economist often forgets his own *caveat* and treats economic affairs only in such terms. At times, taxonomy is confused with analysis; or it is asserted that only the internal validity of a model is needed to establish its usefulness; or the implications of a set of premises are traced in such manner as to arrive at conclusions which are tautologies to begin with. When the economist is concerned solely with mathematical model-building, say sociologically minded critics, he overlooks the fact that theory must be more than a sequence of such models.

IV

Many of these strictures were overcome in the theory of John Maynard Keynes. In essence, Keynes was the savior of private enterprise insofar as he demonstrated how limited government planning could maintain a modicum of equilibrium and eliminate some of the more egregious defects of capitalism without destroying it. Though businessmen considered Keynes too radical, he produced, in fact, the only usable economic theory since laissez faire ceased to be a meaningful slogan. The Keynesian theory countered traditional long-run equilibrium with an incisive short-run analysis that led directly to the theory of employment. And despite its seemingly static character, it was easily adapted to a study of economic dynamics through the introduction of time periods, lags, and expectations. With such an approach, the analysis of growth and capital accumulation could be readily vitalized.

Keynes's resort to a monetary framework for his general theory, in which money is no illusion but rather a central feature of economic behavior, enabled him to reduce a complex image of the economic system to a few social aggregates: consumption, saving, investment. He then related the actions of individuals and firms to these aggregates through such concepts as the multiplier, the marginal efficiency of capital, the marginal propensity to consume, and liquidity preferences. Fundamental to the system was a concern with aggregate demand, since this has a profound effect on the level of consumption and investment. Should aggregate demand fall below business expectations, and thereby fail to cover costs, the consequence, said Keynes, would be a fall in output and employment. Earlier economists had supposed that left to itself the economy would achieve full-employment equilibrium through adjustments in wage rates; but they had failed to recognize that reduced earnings implied a lower level of aggregate demand. The complete Keynesian system made investment a function of the marginal efficiency of capital and the rate of interest. A second equation related employment to income and investment. The marginal efficiency of capital was itself a function of expectations and capital cost. And the rate of interest was dependent on liquidity preference and the stock of money. Consequently, if liquidity preference fell, the rate of interest would drop, encouraging an expansion of investment, while income would be enhanced through the multiplier, which had been derived in the first place from the consumption function.

Keynesian theory thus pointed to the behavior of people as the motive force in the economic process. It was the action of people, rather than impersonal market drives, that created stocks and flows—the raw materials for economic analysis. The explanation of income movements could be framed in terms of individuals; it might even be possible to exercise the sort of control that would reduce cyclical changes in business activity. Economic relationships could be defined as the outcome of interpersonal and group relationships, and government action could be employed to influence and modify the behavior of economic groups.

The application of these ideas to long-run problems may be assayed in the theory of growth, to which Western economists in recent years have paid increasing attention. The key question here was the relation between the rate of output and the growth in the stock of capital, a problem native to both capitalism and socialism. Given an expansion of aggregate demand consonant with output, the ability of capital to adapt to new techniques, a constant ratio of replacement investment to the stock of capital, and a continuous investment of depreciation reserves, it would be possible even for a capitalist economy to maintain an "expansionary equilibrium." In a sense, it was necessary to account for added capital formation and the subsequent increase in the ability to produce. The problem appeared to be one of determining the magnitude of investment required to make the increase in income equal to the increase in productive capacity. But this implied a continuous expansion in investment, a somewhat moot proposition, according to some economists. Moreover, a capitalist economy always had to contend with the threat of excess capacity. In any case, the theory of growth suggested economic rules that would be applicable to capitalism and socialism. There were certain relationships between population growth, capital stock, and technique that any industrialized nation would have to establish to remain viable. The connection between social income and social surplus was equally important for both systems, and the rate of accumulation, or capital formation, was something that a planning authority could not easily ignore.

V

Western economics has also been concerned with the theory of capital. This has created more problems of definition than perhaps any other concept in the field of economics. In addition to establishing a clear notion of what capital is, *id est*, whether it be a collection of things used in production, or a fund of claims that give command over goods, economists have had to wrestle with problems of measurement, the nature of capital formation, the relation of capital to other factors of production, and the role of capital in distribution.

While most discussions of capital begin with Adam Smith's treatment, "Of the Nature, Accumulation, and Employment of

Stock," in Book II of the *Wealth of Nations*, there is sufficient anthropological evidence to suggest that capital markedly influenced economic behavior in preliterate societies. Smith's crude anthropology led him to speak of that "rude state of society in which there is no division of labor [and] it is not necessary that any stock should be accumulated. . . ." Yet even a primitive group would have to forgo alternative employments in order to provide hoes, nets, knives, canoes, and similar instruments which do in fact further production. Generally, this implied a rough division of labor, particularly when ritual and ceremony were involved in the preparation of a particular artifact. Where such "capital" could be accumulated, in the sense that some goods ordinarily used for consumption were diverted for productive purposes, it further implied an availability of surplus labor in excess of the subsistence needs of the group. It was a phenomenon somewhat like this that Raymond Firth observed in Polynesia. Moreover, it was evident that the use of primitive capital to produce a surplus of goods provided an economic foundation for political and social stratification, as was demonstrated by Paul Radin in his book *Primitive Religion* (1937).

Nevertheless, there were few purely theoretical discussions of capital until economics as a distinct science began to emerge. Not that the term was unused before Adam Smith wrote his great opus in 1776. The word "capital" was evidently introduced into England during the Renaissance by North Italian merchants who had learned their principles of double-entry bookkeeping from Luca di Pacioli, generally credited with the invention of accounting. This suggests its origin in the Latin *caput,* meaning head, but the connotation appears to have stressed the notion of importance, as in the phrase "a capital city." It was not long before the term was transferred to designate the principal or chief sum employed in a commercial enterprise, to which the Latin *capitalis* was applied. By the sixteenth and seventeenth centuries, "capital" became the term used to describe the contribution of various partners to a joint venture. As such, it was frequently found in the records of the English trading companies.

Commercial usage, consequently, provided the basis for Smith's concept of capital. Referring primarily to a sum of money placed into an enterprise and intended for conversion into material goods for either trading or manufacturing purposes, the notion assumed a double meaning—liquid funds and more or less illiquid material goods. While Smith spoke of "stock," it was in a sense comparable to the present notion of capital, especially when he conceived of it as a collection of unfinished goods which allowed the producer to span the interval of time between the inception of a productive process and the emergence of the final output. Fixed and circulating capital were given their characteristic definitions, with the former describing those goods that were used in production without changing hands while the latter consisted of goods sold. Smith, however, conceived of circulating capital in real terms, rather than money terms, as was the practice among some later writers.

Since accumulation or growth was a major preoccupation in eighteenth-century England, Smith was deeply concerned with such activities as would increase capital, hence his distinction between productive and unproductive labor (Book II, Chapter III). In essence, he urged his countrymen to engage only in such work as would assist in the task of accumulating capital; he deplored the unproductive use of resources in the pursuit of luxury. In contemporary terms, Smith advised that net investment be utilized for income-generating endeavors and to increase the stock of productive equipment. Nevertheless, the distinction between productive and unproductive labor created some difficulties, for it excluded from economic accounting the whole realm of services which, to a modern economist, is as productive as the fabrication of material goods. The dichotomy persisted throughout all of English classical theory and was adopted by Karl Marx to become the foundation of national income computation in the Soviet Union.

The optimistic purview on capital accumulation that may be discerned in Adam Smith was challenged by the more dour interpretation developed by David Ricardo, for whom the stationary state appeared to be an inescapable outcome. It appeared to Ricardo that with a production function governed by diminishing returns and with increased employment, wages, and rent, the price of food would rise, enforcing further increases in wage rates and downward pressure on the rate of profit. Classical economists continued to expound variants of this theory, despite the rapid increase in production stemming from the Industrial Revolution and its explosive spread of factories, canals, steamships, and railroads. At the same time, banks and intermediate financial institutions developed as channels for the investment of fluid capital, making the relationship of capital to investment increasingly complex. By the last quarter of the nineteenth century, the classical theory of capital seemed quite unsatisfactory as either a predictive or explanatory device. To John Stuart Mill, capital was simply a technological category; the pecuniary complications stemming from scarcity, monopoly, and accumulation did not appear as explicit elements in his analysis. On the other hand, there was the Marxian version of capital theory, essentially sociological in its implication, which viewed capital as an instrument of exploitation.

The marginal-utility economists consequently sought to escape the limitations and strictures of earlier theory. W. Stanley Jevons began with the classical version of capital but soon became aware of the distinction between equipment and wage-goods. For Jevons, capital was important because it supported a given number of employees during the time it took them to complete their productive tasks. That is, capital allowed for the expenditure of a quantity of wage-goods in advance. Involved in this conception was the fund notion of capital, for equipment or sunk capital was to Jevons not the really meaningful category. Insufficient finance could jeopardize the whole process, since capitalist production covered a given time span in his effort to connect the present and future.

These ideas were more fully explored by the Austrian marginal utility economists, and especially by Eugen von Böhm-Bawerk, who took capital theory as his special province. Somewhat earlier, Carl Menger, acknowledged as the founder of the Austrian school, spoke of capital as a fluid fund and referred to the power to employ capital at the proper moment in production, but he refused to accept Böhm-Bawerk's concept of time in capital theory. Friedrich von Wieser, the second of the Austrian marginal-utility triumvirate, discussed capital as a consequence of his theory of imputation (itself essentially a problem of distribution). Wieser argued that capital was continually used up in production and therefore its return had to be sufficient to restore the original sum as well as provide a surplus which was justified by its function as a cooperating factor. The present value of that factor was derived from the discounted sum of the products which a given capital good would yield in the future.

Neither Menger's nor Wieser's capital theories were satisfactory: it was left to Böhm-Bawerk to construct a seemingly more cohesive version. For him, capital was primarily a stock of goods to be used in production rather than a fluid fund. And in an effort to undermine the Marxian exploitation theory, capital, said Böhm-Bawerk, was by no means an historical category (which would have meant social conflict), but rather a theoretical construct that did not require sociological inquiry. With marginal utility as the starting point, the definition of capital was rooted in material goods rather than such considerations as rights and intangibles. It was necessary, he said, to begin with production as the transformation of matter for the purpose of creating things to satisfy wants. But effective production was roundabout, and capital comprised all the intermediate goods that were created in the various stages of this indirect process. Any economic order that utilized roundabout production was really "capitalistic"; thus Böhm-Bawerk, in characterizing economies, eliminated all elements but the economic-technical ones. The relationships between capitalists, workers, and landowners, in which the more sociologically minded economist might be interested, were displaced by the category of time. In Böhm-Bawerk's model, time was central: it was clearly implied by roundabout production and was influenced by the postponement of present consumption for the sake of the future.

Yet it could be argued that time eliminated capital as a distinct factor of production since its extension into the past made it a product of nature and labor. The time dimension was necessary for roundabout production and indeed for the period of production that it implied. Additional capital extended the production period and made the roundabout method more capitalistic—that is, more roundabout. Böhm was getting closer to a circular argument at this point: nevertheless, the idea of a period of production seemed to have some value in that it allowed him to relate the durability of capital goods to the rate of interest.

American economists, particularly, reacted sharply to these views. John Bates Clark, often described as the founder of pure economics in the United States, defined capital as a permanent, fluid fund of value which contrasted sharply with capital goods, which were neither permanent nor mobile. Since capital expressed itself in money terms, it could move readily from one form to the next. Clark was evidently searching for a macroeconomic concept that would refute Böhm-Bawerk's idea of the period of production. But he did not succeed in this endeavor, nor was he able to overcome the duality of circulating and fixed capital; and as set forth by Clark, the fund notion of capital acquired an almost mystical character.

The distinction between capital as fund and capital as equip-- ment underpinned the sharp disagreements between American and European marginal utility economists. The debate continued well into the 1930's. On the American side were Irving Fisher and Frank H. Knight; among the Europeans were Friedrich A. von Hayek, Fritz Machlup, and others. Fisher, who began with definitions of capital and income derived from accounting practice, gave somewhat more emphasis to the goods aspect than did his colleague. Yet in his concern with stocks and flows, the fund concept was acknowledged to be important. Capital was meaningful only insofar as it yielded an income, said Fisher. It was the latter that established the connection between the goods and fund definitions of capital; this was achieved through the capitalization of income at the current rate of interest in a sequence that proceeded fundamentally through four ratios: physical productivity, value productivity, physical return, and value return. The first two were quantity concepts; the latter two were value concepts.

Frank H. Knight, on the other hand, would have nothing to do with physical notions. For him, capitalism was an enterprise economy with production carried on by abstract units distinct from the persons who comprised them. He sought to simplify distribution and price theory by abolishing the tripartite distinction among the factors of production. Everything was converted into capital, which remained as the sole factor in an economy. Capital, after all, argued Knight, was only a generic term for all productive services. Hence, any separation between natural and artificial or permanent and nonpermanent resources was useless. For example, land was developed and maintained at a cost, and its value necessarily had to be compared with the values of other forms of capital. The return to the worker also was like a return to capital, and in fact, labor too was a form of capital.

Knight charged that the Austrians had adopted English classical ideas in their capital theory by asserting fixed proportions between capital and labor in their model and by converting the former into a linear function of a variable production period. This, he contended, failed to account for the simultaneous nature of the production process, for there was really no observable production period. Services were produced as they were consumed in a continuous stream. That there might be some lags between production and consumption was dismissed by Knight as a vague notion. Replacements of capital items were mere technical details that did not impede the perpetual flow of investment. And since capital was inherently immortal, the concept of an average durability of capital was devoid of meaning. Thus, Knight believed that he had severed the connection between time and capital which the Austrian economists had labored so long to establish.

These arguments did not go unanswered. Fritz Machlup demonstrated that without the idea of a production period, it would be difficult to sustain a theory of net investment or disinvestment. Nicholas Kaldor suggested that the degree of roundaboutness could be measured by the ratio of the initial cost of investment to its annual maintenance. Further, capital could be set off from other factors by virtue of its "augmentability." Kenneth Boulding demonstrated how capital could act as a bridge between input and output, so that the total capital required in a particular situation would depend upon revenue and the period of production.

The most damaging attack on Knight's conception of capital was leveled by Friedrich A. von Hayek, for whom it represented mythology and dimensionless metaphysics. Hayek was quite firm in rejecting any theory of capital which conceived of it as solely a fund. For him, capital was a stock of particular items that required maintenance, and the perpetual automatic renewal implied in Knight's notion of simultaneity was simply unrealistic. Capital was a nonpermanent factor; hence the need for continuous reproduction. It was this that made the position of capital in the time structure of production so significant, contended Hayek. Moreover, the supply of capital affected the choice of technique and required the economist to recognize variability in production functions.

The basic question in the theory of capital, argued Hayek, was: how do nonpermanent resources enable production to be maintained at a high level in order to yield a constant flow of income? Since capital was limited by definition to wasting assets, Hayek's analysis unfortunately was restricted to what others called circulating capital. The organization of production was then related to varying levels of output, again stressing the importance of the production function. Any stock of capital represented a contribution to future income. But as production continued through time, changes were bound to occur in the structure of production. And involved in this complicated procedure was the need to date equipment and connect it with the various stages of production. Yet Hayek did not indulge in mere definition: the theory of capital became an integral part of his business-cycle analysis in which breakdown stemmed from distortion in the structure of production.

The basis for a more satisfactory theory of capital had been provided by the Swedish economist Knut Wicksell, who sought to construct an analysis suitable for the long run. Short-run changes were later analyzed by Hayek. Beginning with marginal productivity, Wicksell focused upon capital accumulation and its effect on distribution. Clearly this was an important facet of capital, perhaps more significant than the entire preceding debate over definitions. Land and variable-factor proportions were crucial to Wicksell's analysis. At the same time it was evident that the function of time in his model was to relate the value of capital and its technical aspects. The capital composition of any society was simply the total number of saved-up units of labor and land multiplied by the time period during which such units were invested. Capital had both "height" and "width" and could be measured by the length of the average period of production required by the amount of capital employed. "Height" referred to the length of time it took for capital to mature; "width," to the proportion of input services required to replace used-up capital goods. An expansion of width, therefore, implied an increase in the kind of capital already in existence, while height referred to the adoption of new forms of capital. The common development, said Wicksell, was the utilization of width first; then, when saturation depressed the marginal productivity of capital, there would be a shift to different kinds of capital. To this imposing model, Wicksell added factors of saving and accumulation, which in turn were related to the rate of interest and, ultimately, to the business cycle. For example, Wicksell was aware that the accumulation of capital could be absorbed in part by an increase in real wages and that this would have an impact on the time structure of capital. The relationships were macroeconomic and the outcome was a theory in which capital, income, prices, and money were effectively integrated.

Nevertheless, each of these theories appeared to stress but one aspect of capital in preference to others. Sometimes capital was a stock of goods to maintain workers until the output had been sold; at other times it comprised a collection of goods in process, or what was called circulating capital. To some writers, capital consisted of durable assets with a definite life, so that the age structure of fixed capital seemed to have an overriding importance. To others, it was the maturing process, as with forests, that revealed most strikingly the element of capital, viz., the factor of time. In actuality, each was but a different manifestation of capital theory, for each described varying facets of the productive process. Or one might evade all of these issues by simply speaking of a rate of return on investment—an approach which essentially converts capital theory into interest theory. This has been done by Robert Solow, who, however, does seek to account for technical change.

Yet in all of these analyses the fundamental methodological consideration has been the relationship of things to things, a feature of bourgeois economics that had been attacked by Karl Marx as "commodity fetishism." The Marxian analysis spoke of capital as a relationship that was most sharply exposed by the labor theory of value. This relationship, set in an employer-employee context, was essentially exploitative. But the labor theory of value was clearly nonoperational: it could not explain price level changes; it dealt inadequately, if at all, with noncompeting labor groups; and it excluded services from the realm of value-creating categories, as was the case with Ricardo. Yet despite these strictures, the historian must observe that the theories of capital accumulation and the circulation of capital set forth in *Das Kapital* were remarkable performances. If these aspects of Marxian theory are examined dispassionately, then one realizes that the purpose of the analysis was to study man-made means of production and the social relations that governed their use. Since the latter were rooted in the wage relationship, capital had to be defined by alienation from tools and property.

Marx divided industries into those supplying new means of production, those which provided workers with subsistence, and the ones whose output consisted of luxury goods to satisfy the consumption of capitalists. The production of each was divisible into constant capital, variable capital, and surplus value. The first referred to the value of machinery and materials which was absorbed by production and added to the value of the product. That is to say, raw materials and depreciation represented the values transferred in the productive process. Variable capital, on the other hand, was the value of the labor power employed, but it was that portion of capital that yielded a surplus value. The three categories together comprised the value of output. Surplus value could be consumed or reinvested. If the latter took place, then the surplus value again became either variable or constant capital, in which case, part of the output was to be exchanged against goods of the other sectors.

This then was the circulation process in its simplest form. Consumer goods, fixed and circulating capital were put back as used, so that the value created during a given period was equal to the claims on consumption. But to Marx, accumulation was central to the capitalist process. Also involved were changes in the organic composition of capital or the relative proportions of constant and variable capital, which, because of the tendency for the constant element to increase, occasioned a fall in the rate of profit. Accumulation was governed by the available total of surplus value and it could have implied an increased demand for labor. But with a relative increase in constant capital, a larger volume of surplus value was to be extracted only by increased exploitation. This dour conclusion stemmed from an unwillingness on Marx's part to consider capital-saving forms of constant capital as a real possibility. It would seem feasible that a decline in the relative share of constant to total capital might develop which, together with increasing productivity, would be able to sustain the rate of profit over long periods. And in fact it appears that empirical evidence substantiates such a contingency so that capital, even in Marxian theoretical terms, can avoid the ultimate day of reckoning predicted in *Das Kapital*. The *reductio ad absurdum* of the original Marxist formulation was provided by Henryk Grossman, whose calculations showed that after several decades the quantity of surplus value that would be forthcoming could not possibly meet the system's requirements, since the average rate of profit on the monstrous sum of fixed investment would just barely allow for simple reproduction.

Nevertheless, the problems of accumulation that Marx had underscored could not be dismissed, and, in fact, recent writers, in their concern with economic growth, have paid increasing attention to it. For example, Sir Roy Harrod and Professor Evsey Domar have been concerned with the impact of accelerated accumulation and its relation to economic growth. To Harrod, the central question has been the expansion of income required to insure the full use of an ever-increasing quantity of capital, while Domar observed that investment exhibits a dual character in that it not only generates income but also increases productive capacity. Equilibrium therefore would have to shift continuously with the required rate of growth established by setting the rate of increase in productive capacity equal to the rate of increase in income. Although Domar expressed doubts that such equilibrium could be maintained, mainly because of the tendency for excess capacity to inhibit the necessary increment of investment, Harrod seemed more optimistic. A similar problem was explored by Mrs. Joan Robinson, in whose analysis the technical composition of capital played a more predominant role than in other recent theories. In her view, progress and growth could become uneven when the rate of technical progress was altered and accumulation failed to move in consonance with increases in productivity. It was this phenomenon that explained movements in the business cycle, she argued. The Robinsonian model sought to demonstrate that an expansion of output at a constant rate of profit depended on the rate of technical progress and the rate of increase in the labor force. The growth rate itself was the highest rate of capital accumulation that could be sustained at a constant rate of profit. But a higher rate of accumulation would increase the degree of mechanization and in the long run induce a lower rate of profit. Consequently, while capitalism can demonstrate economic progress, suggested Mrs. Robinson, it bears within it seeds of destruction. Accumulation must expand with output and the entrepreneurial spirit must not falter, for profit underpinned accumulation and, in the absence of adequate accumulation, difficulties would ensue.

Through this analysis, the purpose of which was to extend Keynes's theory to the long run, there ran several unmistakable Marxian threads.

Mrs. Robinson's analysis represented, from a methodological standpoint, an effort to employ some of the Marxian categories in genuinely creative ways. But this can hardly be said for those Western economists whose tacit approval of Soviet capital investment programs has been little more than a subtle rationalization for the centralized command economy of the Russians. The outstanding exponent of this school in the West has been Maurice Dobb of Cambridge, in whose model decisions on alternative investment possibilities were to be made by a Central Planning Board by simple inspection. The board had only to determine the ratio of productivity to the cost of a capital project and in this way develop a list of priorities which would enable it to plan investment over a long period of time. Despite a willingness in his later writings to consider market influences, as in the Yugoslavian model, Dobb continued to insist that capital intensive investments were essential in the early stages of economic development, although in no way did this accord with actual experience in the West. The objective, of course, was to insure that development would not deviate from the preferences of the central planners.

VI

Western economists have also been involved in analyzing interest, which today is a payment for the use of money. Many economists, however, prefer to think of it as that part of the return on investment which remains after deductions for handling charges, payments for the assumption of risk, and reimbursements necessary to maintain capital. In this same sense interest is a pure yield stemming from the use of capital. This rather sophisticated concept was unknown in pre-literate societies, although the practice of making gifts and returning them represents an approximation to the phenomenon of interest. However, primitive gift exchange appears to have been a matter of generous social behavior rather than an effort to secure payment for loans. On the other hand, more advanced agricultural societies evidently engaged in some crude lending-for-interest practices: surplus cattle was borrowed on occasion with an obligation to return something more, either in the form of the animal's progeny or a portion of some crop.

Early legal codes sought to regulate debtor-creditor relationships, as in ancient Babylonia, where the maximum rate of interest was set at 33⅓ percent a year for grain loans and 20 percent for loans in silver. In Greece, Solon's codification of earlier laws prohibited the enslavement of debtors, who frequently were unable to meet their obligations because of high interest rates. Although Plato had opposed ordinary interest charges, he thought that an extra return might be justifiably exacted when contractual payments were delayed. Aristotle's opposition to interest was even more intransigent: for him lending as a means of acquiring wealth was unnatural and abhorrent, since money was presumed to be barren. Yet his hostility was quite understandable in a society in which most borrowing was for consumption rather than for productive purposes.

Aristotle's attitude colored the thinking of Western society on interest for a millennium and a half. Roman law had appropriated Greek economic ideas, as happened in many other areas. The Council of Nicea, convened by Constantine, asserted that charging interest was an un-Christian practice. Bans on interest, or usury, as it was then called, found their way into Justinian's Code in the sixth century. In the fourteenth century, Pope Clement declared secular legislation which approved of usury to be null and void. During these periods the opportunity for the productive use of borrowed capital was limited: the more important loans were made to members of the nobility to pay for military adventures and high living. Royalty, however, was not averse to employing canonical prohibitions on usury to escape their obligations. This was bound to create conditions of great risk for lenders, who were then likely to extract even higher charges when loans were renewed.

After several centuries of relative quiet, trade began to revive in Europe during the eleventh and twelfth centuries. Merchants increasingly sought financial aid for their ventures, and by the fifteenth century there were enough active capitalists about to provide a viable basis for the growth of money institutions. The legitimation of interest was unavoidable. The Church itself had been active in business: its theorists, such as Aquinas and Antoninus, were able to rationalize interest as a payment necessary to reward opportunities forgone by the lender. During the Mercantilist era it was generally acknowledged that attempts to regulate interest were useless, since it merely drove the practice underground. In essence, since the Mercantilists, interest was a price for money and should be permitted to find its own level in the market in accordance with the laws of supply and demand. While Adam Smith had rejected most of the Mercantilist corpus, he accepted this precept which subsequently was embodied in classical economic doctrine. Later theorists argued that the regulation of interest could result in a rate too low to attract capital into risky enterprise. In an economy in which burgeoning capitalists sought fresh finance for expansion, such a view was understandable.

Western economists have expended much effort over the last 150 years to explain the origins and nature of interest. Among the various theories was that of Nassau Senior, who argued that the essence of interest as an element in cost was the pain of abstinence. That is to say, the postponement of consumption was disagreeable enough to require an added payment in order to encourage capital accumulation. Such an argument is sometimes offered today as well, but in a milieu in which capital accumulation is a function of large organizations, such as insurance companies and corporations, the abstinence theory has only limited application.

Böhm-Bawerk developed what was essentially a productivity theory of interest (although he would have rejected such a classification). He had posed the same question as did Karl Marx: why did capitalists, as mere owners of property, receive a surplus of goods? While Böhm-Bawerk conceded that interest was indeed a surplus payment, in no way, he argued, did it stem from exploitation, as the socialists had contended. The solution to the riddle, he said, lay in the notion of time, for interest was simply a measure of the difference between present and future. Although the present was generally valued more highly, man produced for the future because he knew that unmet needs would arise at various points in time yet to come. Hence, a premium or interest (which Böhm-Bawerk called an "agio") was required for the surrender of present goods. Of course, the time it would take to produce future goods—the period of production—would markedly influence the agio. Further, the marginal rate of interest, or what would have to be paid for an additional unit of borrowed capital, was limited by the yield of the last increment of capital employed in production.

While there were numerous other theories, based on such notions as command over capital, availability of capital, the demand for money per se, and the like, it was the time-preference theory advanced by the Austrians that appeared to offer a definitive reply to the contention of the socialists that interest, as a portion of surplus value, was merely a mechanism of exploitation. According to the Austrian economists, capitalists traded their present goods for future goods, particularly in transactions with labor, and in the course of this exchange secured interest. This focused attention on wealth as the center of economic analysis and suggested to Böhm-Bawerk a thoroughgoing rebuttal of Marxian theory, which had asserted that the bourgeois economists' argument was nothing more than a supercilious effort to explain the division of surplus value among different groups of capitalists.

1964

On Economic Planning

All economic societies have engaged in some measure of planning. This was true for the hydraulic civilizations of Asia, whose large waterworks were planned and built for irrigation and communication; it was true for the Romans planning bridges, aqueducts, and roads to sustain their political grasp of a vast empire; it was true for the mercantile nations of the seventeenth century employing economic plans as weapons in military and diplomatic maneuvers; and it was true for the United States in the nineteenth century when huge landholdings were distributed to foster a class of small independent farmers. In fact, in the United States a kind of vestigial planning may be found in Alexander Hamilton's program to encourage manufacturing through tariff protection. In retrospect, Hamilton's policy provided a basis for a particular form of government intervention that continued unabated until recent years. As business corporations grew and expanded, each inevitably developed its own private planned sector of economic activity. But the responsibility for a balanced and equitable use of resources did not extend beyond these partially planned spheres with the result that over-all allocation became haphazard, bringing with it no small degree of social conflict.

While individual business corporations in the United States engage in planning their own internal economies, they are fairly vocal in opposing any effort on the part of government to undertake broader schemes for coordinating the activity of various economic groups. They argue that the market economy provides the best mechanism for achieving such coordination, a view echoed in the writings of such conservative economists as Ludwig von Mises, Friedrich A. von Hayek, and Milton Friedman. Traditional market theory presupposes that there are no frictions or impediments in achieving quick adjustments to alterations in underlying economic conditions so that the response of buyers and sellers to variations in supply or demand would be rapid enough to clear the market at any given time. The assumption is that all economic participants possess full knowledge not only of the consequences of their own actions but of the actions of others as well. Hence, the argument concludes, a market economy obviates the need for planning.

The evidence of economic history strongly suggests that the attainment of equilibrium in this sense has been a rare achievement. Consequently, many economists, both socialist and non-socialist, have advocated coordination of economic activity through conscious effort. Prior to World War II, the initial concern was economic stabilization and a desire to avoid the sequence of prosperity and depression engendered by the disorder of the marketplace. After the war, and especially after the attainment of independent statehood by the former colonial areas in Asia and Africa, the major thrust in economic plans has been directed toward rapid economic growth.

It is generally agreed among advocates of economic planning that the objectives of stabilization and growth demand the displacement of the uncontrolled market, particularly as it affects capital accumulation and the allocation of resources for investment. Conscious effort, it is argued, must be made by an organ of society. Whether or not actual coercive force is employed, planning necessarily exhibits a collective or communal character requiring the subordination of individual demands to social need.

Even when voluntarism is a major component in economic plans, as is the case in the Scandinavian countries, decision-making necessarily shifts from the individual to the community.

Economic planning, therefore, may be defined as a scheme designed by a communal body that offers qualitative and quantitative guidelines for economic activity. By requiring or suggesting the kind of productive processes to be undertaken, an economic plan seeks to obtain the optimum use of resources and to achieve both stabilization and economic growth as dual goals of a single endeavor. Planning, however, is not necessarily synonymous with government intervention. The latter is frequently *ad hoc,* or at best partially planned. Even a specific economic policy may exhibit but few features of genuine planning. It may be argued, for example, that Hamilton's program for stimulating manufactures was more of an effort to underpin a special sector than it was overall economic planning.

Postwar reconstruction in Western Europe provided a powerful impetus to the idea of economic planning, but there were numerous precedents for such thinking—notably in Great Britain and Sweden. In Great Britain, the Depression impelled Lord Keynes to turn away from the neoclassical doctrines of his teachers and to urge that the government recognize its moral obligation to undertake measures that would eliminate unemployment. In Sweden, a remarkable group of young economists, including such noted writers as Gunnar Myrdal and Dag Hammarskjöld, debated the causes of excess capacity and unused resources and sought to establish useful criteria for overcoming the Depression. All facets of economic policy were included in their discussions— monetary policy, public works, fiscal programs, consumption measures, and so on. It was the postwar experience, however, that established the indubitable values of national economic planning. The economic performance of France, Holland, Sweden, and Norway served to diminish the fears of those who believed that planning necessarily implies the suppression of individual freedom.

THE UNITED STATES

The climate of opinion in the United States has generally been hostile to the notion of national planning. The pragmatic spirit of the American people appears to be antipathetic to the notion of planning. Government action of an *ad hoc* nature, addressed to particular interest groups and particular needs, provides the major framework of intervention in economic affairs in the United States, but seldom is a given course of action related to another in any integrated manner. Beginning with tariffs, sundry public works, and certain monetary controls, the federal government by force of circumstance has extended its participation in economic affairs until it now embraces fiscal controls, interest rate determination, housing, safety regulation, antitrust action, industrial relations, and, in situations of emergency such as war, the direct allocation of resources. These sorties into extramarket ventures are sporadic and often contradictory and they do not represent coordinated economic planning.

At best, the objective of such planning as exists in the United States is directed toward the goal of full employment, as expressed in the Employment Act of 1946. Implicit in this statute is the desire to increase the national product and achieve a more equitable distribution of output. The rather general character of these goals makes them palatable to all groups in society; the debate which has ensued over the years revolves only about specific proposals. Virtually everyone concedes that improvements in education and health are desirable and that ways to utilize more effectively the new technology ought to be evolved. However, there is considerable argument about the degree to which public services are denied their quota of resources and their efficacy in stimulating economic growth. Differences arise concerning the stress to be placed by public policy on consumption as opposed to investment. The resolution of such debates, of course, has considerable impact on actual decision-making as evidenced by the dispute in 1963 over tax reduction and tax reform. Thus, advocates of the policy to encourage consumption are apt to propose that the former be extended mainly to lower-income recipients; those who believe that demand flows out of the productive process itself tend to support investment measures.

The Employment Act was hailed in 1946 as the American version of economic planning. A more objective evaluation indicates that it by no means represents such a development. While the statute expresses the concern of the federal government with economic performance, there is no commitment per se to planning, nor is one intended. At best, the act provides for annual economic reports, which have varied in character and quality, and an indication by the Council of Economic Advisers of the probable direction of economic movement. Aside from these measures, statutory implementation is still within the province of the United States Congress.

Enthusiastic observers insist that the educational values of the Employment Act are worthwhile; at least members of Congress are exposed to intelligent discussions of economic issues. On the other hand, critics suggest that the act in its present form is outdated since it provides no clear guide for resolving the more recent dilemmas of economic policy; for example, the clash during the 1960's between liquidating the balance of payments deficit and the need for more rapid domestic growth. At the present juncture, however, it seems unlikely that there will be any substantive revision in the act's objectives; consequently, in order to assay the nature of economic planning in action and to evaluate its problems and difficulties, most students of the subject necessarily turn to the European experience.

EUROPE

Most Europeans do not view government ownership of particular industries as a threat to liberty. The attempt to fend off depressions and to extend the welfare state to the point where planning is an imperative is not thought to be incompatible with the pursuit of individual values. While it is as yet open to question how far planning undermines the private market economy, all groups in Western Europe agree that the essential element is to maintain a suitable balance between the private sector and the public sector for the benefit of each. Although they may disagree on the fundamental philosophy of planning, economists of both conservative and socialist persuasions generally agree on specific measures for financing the welfare state or on how to counteract a recession.

More conservative planners, while granting that the free market of the eighteenth century would be an anachronism under modern industrial conditions, tend to argue that planning is necessary only to provide a more viable institutional framework in which a maximum of unfettered economic activity may take place. Thus, legislation may be necessary to prevent monopoly or a progressive tax system may be installed to correct marked income inequality. None of this, in the last analysis, should impede competition. Socialist-oriented planners consider such a view as begging the question; competition by itself, they argue, will not assure rapid economic growth. This may be best achieved, they say, by purposeful planning that would avoid the chaotic consequences of a competitive market.

The postwar period provided a test for these contending views. There was no doubt but that the boom created by reconstruction and suppressed demand called attention to the need for coordinated planning. Immediately after the war, it was evident that any relaxation of controls, particularly of prices, would engender an intolerably chaotic situation. Consequently, there was no precipitate action in eliminating government controls such as that undertaken by President Truman in the United States in mid-1946. By 1957, progress in European reconstruction had been such that some countries began to experience just enough slackening in economic activity to arouse fears of an impending recession. However, the incipient downturn was halted with the creation of the Common Market, which resulted in a rather rapid economic advance. Furthermore, the Common Market itself impelled each of the six participating nations to evaluate their respective economic positions vis-à-vis their partners, thus establishing a basis for intelligent planning. Nevertheless, those European nations that have entered upon programs of conscious economic planning have been careful to avoid the impression of a "command economy." In France and Holland, both of which have central planning agencies, stress is placed on the concept of inducement planning. The central agency's function is simply to indicate general tendencies and the direction in which government, business, and labor ought to move.

Great Britain and Germany. Central planning, even when noncoercive, has not found favor in Great Britain and Germany. These countries adopted planning policies midway between those of France, Holland, and Sweden and that of the United States. Such a moderate approach involves the preparation of government budgets and the recommendation of fiscal programs designed to achieve the twin goals of growth and stability. Subsidies may be suggested for housing or urban redevelopment. Most important, all the proposals form part of a long-range forecast of economic development.

Britain has perhaps leaned closer to the United States position on economic planning than any of the other European countries. The home of laissez-faire policy, it has sought to rely as much as possible on the functioning of the free market. Yet this had not been entirely successful in the postwar era, for lagging economic growth and rising unemployment in recent years suggested that reliance on traditional habits of thought does not meet the needs of an age in which technology advances relentlessly. Consequently, the British established a National Economic Development Council, comprising representatives from government, management, and labor. Thus far NEDC has limited its analyses to long-range economic development, but it is hoped that it may exert a more direct influence on current policy.

Even in West Germany, where much has been made of the capacity to recover from devastation without government participation, there appears to be an increasing awareness that new conditions require a change in attitude. Growth was not as rapid in the early 1960's as it had previously been and with the Berlin Wall's elimination of the inflow of refugees, a tight labor market ensued that curtailed the competitive advantage of West German goods in foreign markets. This has raised for the Germans the specter of inflation, and no matter how strong the espousal of laissez faire, no German government can politically afford to allow prices to rise faster than output. It is more than likely that altered economic conditions will impel officials to intervene actively in the economic process. The willingness to undertake such action may not be unrelated to the fact that well over half of all investment in the postwar period was indeed influenced by the West German government to flow into areas where it was particularly required.

Sweden. The classic demonstration of successful noncoercive economic planning may be found in Sweden. In that country responsibility for planning is vested in the National Labor Market Board and its subsidiary bodies, the county labor boards. The uniqueness of the Swedish approach may be seen in its attempts to deal with rigidities in labor markets. With both labor and management represented on the boards, an effort is made to achieve such balance in the various labor markets as would best enhance economic growth. Forecasts are made of anticipated changes based mainly on expected shifts in employment. The necessary data for the analyses of labor markets are derived from information supplied by employers who are required to advise of any planned curtailment in production. Hence, labor surpluses can be quickly located.

The battery of control devices includes fiscal and monetary measures intended to influence investment in various parts of the Swedish economy. Construction permits are utilized to limit building whenever a labor shortage in certain localities threatens to force prices up. Obviously, the other side of the coin provides for the relaxation of building restrictions and additional financing whenever pockets of unemployment develop. Such new finance usually flows from the investment reserves built up during prosperous periods through earmarked taxes. These are not placed into the government's general fund, but held rather in special bank accounts to be used expressly for capital purposes when new investment is deemed essential. The government may itself undertake public works should these measures prove to be insufficient.

Flexibility in labor markets is achieved by encouraging unemployed workers to move to areas where they may be needed. This is done by offering eligible unemployed workers travel and moving allowances. Consequently, unemployment is kept at the rate of 1.5 percent of the work force, an extraordinarily low figure as compared with the United States or Great Britain. Most observers agree that these measures enable Sweden to cope with its labor market problems in a manner quite unusual for a Western economy.

The Netherlands. Economic planning in the Netherlands is achieved through the Central Planning Bureau, which, as a byproduct of its major function, has supplied economists with a remarkable series of studies. The Dutch economists' contributions to the theory and practice of planning has been outstanding, and much of this may be attributed to the efforts of Jan Tinbergen of the Netherlands School of Economics, whose incisive analyses demonstrate that a fusion of theory and practice is not impossible. For the Dutch, an "optimum" economy is one that most likely includes both private and public sectors and is neither completely centralized nor decentralized. Planning data must encompass physical and psychological characteristics as well as the operations of institutions, which need to be expressed in the plan in both quantitative and qualitative terms.

The logic of planning in the Netherlands requires the decision-maker to envisage current problems against a backdrop of pre-determined goals. With certain inducements available to direct economic activity into the desired channels, the plan is conceived as a blueprint for action. Since the planning is noncoercive, the program essentially is an attempt to delineate certain economic hopes and expectations. That is to say, the plan's goals will be fulfilled if the community heeds the directives implicit in its specifications. Unfulfilled goals represent deviations from the plan's perspectives and a rejection by the community of the economist's advice.

The Central Planning Bureau's projections are short-run in that their work consists primarily of year-to-year forecasts. These are drawn from a complex econometric model into which changes or parameter shifts are frequently introduced in order to accommodate the model to reality. The twenty-odd equations seek to explain the movement of an equal number of variables which express such entities as consumption, investment, prices, exports, imports, employment, taxes, transfer payments, and so on. The level of domestic prices is related to imports and wage rates while other elements, such as imports and wages, are considered to be independent variables affected by considerations external to the forecast model. Similarly, outlays for education and land improvement also represent independent variables. Aside from import prices, most of the independent variables are subject to government control; thus, it is in large measure the decision of the latter which influences the behavior of the model.

When the model suggests that the economy is moving in an undesirable direction, the planners will advise the government so that corrective steps may be taken. In addition, the econometric analysis can be employed to study the impact of the government's proposed measures. While Dutch economists are not entirely happy with the results of their work, there appears to be reasonable agreement that this is the manner in which noncoercive planning ought to be done. A satisfactory growth rate, which increased 30 percent from 1953 to 1960, was maintained. This was somewhat better than Sweden's 24 percent growth rate in the same period, although not as good as West Germany's 48 percent gain. The unemployment rate was kept to a low of around 1–2 percent of the work force and, in fact, in some years there were more job vacancies than unemployed workers. Whether these conditions can be attributed to planning or not is a moot question, since the high-pressure economies of Western Europe have exhibited certain features which may be attributed in large part to such considerations as the formation of the Common Market itself.

France. In contrast to the Dutch interest in short-term forecasts, the French *Commissariat du Plan de Modernisation et d'Equipement,* established in 1946, merely offers a target or goal every four years on the assumption that it constitutes a commitment for all Frenchmen, who consequently will act accordingly. This was the premise of the original Monnet Plan, whose originator, Jean Monnet, drew upon his observations of American wartime agencies. Understandably, the end of the war found France exhausted, and the extensive shortages of goods required direct allocation of strategic materials, limitation of consumption, and the rebuilding of industry. The *Commissariat* first concentrated on fuel, power, transport, steel, cement, and agricultural equipment; by 1950, the supply of these basic industries had caught up with demand. Similar planning was then applied to manufacturing, housing, and agriculture with rather remarkable success, so much so that investment, in constant prices, rose 38 percent between 1954 and 1958.

The *Commissariat* has a small staff that works through other organizations in an effort to minimize any obstacles that may develop. Attached to the Ministry of Finance and Economic Affairs, it gathers the necessary statistics, devises the various plans and transmits them to the Economic Council for submission to the French parliament. The planning program starts with a forecast of national income in which feasible growth rates are subjected to careful scrutiny; various features, such as the balance of payments and consumer expenditure, are then carefully evaluated. The result is a set of alternative models which presents reasonable targets for the twenty-five sector planning committees responsible for working out the necessary details. The areas covered by the sector committees include, in addition to the usual industry groupings, education, urban renewal, manpower, productivity, research, and regional planning. It is at the sector planning stage that negotiation and revision of the plans may take place, but it is the function of the *Commissariat* to assure consistency in the over-all planning effort.

Most authorities consider the French approach to planning fairly successful, and the economy has exhibited steady growth. The Third Plan, set forth in 1957, attained its official target without too much strain, although it required a 6.3 percent spurt in 1959–60 to overcome a lagging growth rate of 2.3 percent in 1958–59. Involved in the forces behind the rapid expansion of the later years was a high level of investment in government-controlled industries, such as transport and electric power, and in housing and public works. Low interest rate loans are employed to encourage private investment and some reliance is placed on "announcement effects," which tend to give the plan a self-fulfilling thrust.

SUMMARY

It appears evident that planning in the Western nations, in contrast to Soviet-type systems, reveals more of a trouble-shooting character than the latter's centralized coordination. Generally, economists, engineers, town planners, health experts, and demographers work out specific projects and suggest ways in which to direct private investment. The most extreme case is that of sectoral planning, as in France, which involves projections and recommendations that may or may not be accepted by the legislative authorities. The target planning of the Soviet Union and its satellites, based on enforceable directives for action, attempts to achieve the sort of coordination that most Western economists do not deem desirable, if only because a central agency is not apt to have intimate knowledge of local plant conditions. Yet it is clear that those responsible for the operations of a single plant or group of plants would know only their own plans and could at best but guess as to those of rivals, suppliers, and customers. Consequently, such plans are suffused with much risk and uncertainty, a condition that planning advocates insist can be mitigated by a central agency. The latter would gather information for the entire economy and in effect test the internal consistency of the various individual plans by checking them against available resources. This would require an evaluation of both the physical flow of goods and services provided by the productive system and the prices that would emerge. According to some economists this represents an impossibly superhuman task, necessitating the solution of millions of equations. Nevertheless, the statistical and mathematical methods developed in recent years known as input-output analysis and linear programming, together with the availability of high-speed electronic computers, promise the necessary analytical techniques for economic planning.

The extension of services under the welfare state may follow a process of cumulative causation, leading to economic planning. The intervention in economic life enforced by the sequence of crises after the First World War, coupled with the spread of large-scale enterprise, tends to create conditions of increasing complexity. The consequent need for coordination beyond the ordinary run of welfare measures appears to be impressing itself upon Western nations with increasing conviction.

1965

Man, Work, and the Automated Feast

Automation is said to have ancient beginnings. To be sure, the technology from which it stems goes back several centuries, at least. Automatic devices in the middle eighteenth century included a mechanical loom for the manufacture of figured silks; James Watt's steam engine utilized a fly-ball governor which controlled the speed at which his contrivance operated; and it has been suggested that automation's basic concept—the linkage of machines—is evident in the detachable harpoon head of the Eskimo. Yet to assert that automation is simply the latest link in a great chain of industrial history obscures what is patently a new phenomenon. In the old days, industrial change developed through fission: division of labor was the key to a huge pool of unskilled persons who in the main had been forced to migrate from farm to city. Today, it is precisely these unskilled, together with semi-skilled and even some of management's people, who are displaced and poured back into the pool. Furthermore, automation represents a marked acceleration of change with so cumulative a force that this alone spells a profound difference from what went on before.

Automation is already moving with a rapidity that threatens to tear apart existing social and organizational structures; according to some observers, it will even alter the habits of thought that men have up to now prided themselves on. Such a prospect is perhaps not surprising when we consider the cataclysmic results of the eighteenth century's Industrial Revolution: the changes then were so swift as to constitute a whole new phenomenon. And Marx and Weber and Sombart had shown convincingly how human and social transformation accompanied technological transformation.

Now, new industrial functions, new economic forms, new work habits, and new social headaches are being created in ways that signify a kind of dialectic leap. Even John Diebold, who claims to have invented the word "automation" and whose ebullient advocacy of computer technology has done much to spread the gospel, confesses: "I believe that [automation] marks a break with past trends, a qualitative departure from the more conventional advance of technology that began with jagged pieces of flint and progressed up to the steam engine."

Why is this so? Up to recent times, technology simply sought to substitute natural force for animal or human force. In the early days, primacy of place was given to windmills and waterfalls. Then came metallurgical discoveries; and the screw and the lathe made possible the machine, essentially a contrivance which man could watch in action. But man remained at the center of the whole business, essential to both operation and control, still more or less the maker and master of materials. With automation, man not only loses irrevocably his function as *homo faber;* he no longer even possesses the character of *animal laborans.* At best, he is a sometime supervisor of a flow process. Actual control is removed from him and given to an electronic contraption whose feedbacks and servomechanisms make it possible to produce goods and manipulate information in a continuous system, without human participation.

To realize what automation implies, we must examine the kinds of machines employed and see what they do to people and organizations. Essentially, today's scientific upheaval comprises four aspects: the conversion of industrial materials into a flow; the setting of uniform standards so that output can be treated as a flow; the utilization of electronic computers with built-in feedbacks to enable the exercise of automatic control; and the application of new energy sources to the whole process. Thus, raw materials, which represent the "input" of an industry, must be handled without human hands, as in a modern meat-packing plant. Production, at one time a series of discrete steps, is completely integrated by means of transfer machines. In some cases, computers tied to cams or templates can make the producing machine follow a predetermined pattern with greater accuracy and sharper tolerances than were dreamed possible in the heyday of the skilled machinist. Computers, into which all sorts of complex information can be fed by "programmers," automatically correct errors. A wide range of goods is now produced in this startling manner: chemicals, automobiles, steel, glassware, electric bulbs, television sets, beverages, and drugs, to name a few. Factories are able to function twenty-four hours a day, 365 days a year, while manpower needs are reduced dramatically. And with the development of nuclear energy for industrial power, manufacturers no longer need to be near their source of raw materials; they can set up their plants closer to markets, or—if they are seeking to escape the union organizer—in the most isolated of places. Yet one industry necessarily must relate itself more intimately with the next; a seamless web envelops all the entrepreneurs and their works.

There is no lack of Panglossian attempt to assuage our concern. In the long run, we are told (who lives that long?), natural economic forces will work out the necessary adjustments. A shorter work week might stem from automation, suggest some experts; but at the thought that men might work less than the ordained forty hours a week, all kinds of people, from the Secretary of Labor down, immediately explode with great cries of anguish. Or we are told that human desires are insatiable: demand will grow, enough to reabsorb men displaced by machines—which calls to mind an apocryphal conversation between Henry Ford II and Walter Reuther. "How," said Ford, as he revealed his automatic factory, "are these machines going to pay you dues, Walter?" "How," replied Reuther, "will they buy your autos?"

We are assured that more jobs will be created by new industry, that higher skills will be required, that economic stability will be guaranteed by automation. There are pitifully few facts available to support these euphoric hopes. More likely a vast trauma awaits us all, to use Irving Howe's phrase. Then why automate? The underlying motives were exposed with unaccustomed bluntness in one of the trade journals recently when an automation advocate wrote: "[Machines] don't call in sick; they don't talk back; they work early and late without overtime; they don't get tired; and last, but far from least, they don't line up at the cashier's window every week for a slice of the operating funds."

The automobile industry illustrates how an integrated set of machines can function. There the engine production line, for example, consists of a series of drilling, boring, and milling operations connected by transfer machines which move the engine blocks from one point to the next. Tolerances are checked automatically; if something is awry, the whole line is stopped by an electronic device. Or one can see an automatic assembly machine put the components of a television set on a printed board and then solder them into place. These are repetitive operations and their economic justification stems from the replacement market. There is not much of a style factor here and such model changes as do occur can be handled with relative ease. Yet even where variation in the product is essential, as in machine tools, the operation still can be made automatic.

The machine tool industry, mainly a congeries of small shops employing highly skilled labor, has notoriously resisted innovation. But since it is now so closely allied to Air Force and space technology, it has been impelled willy-nilly by the needs of the armed forces to the adoption of newer techniques. Formerly, a human operator worked from blueprints, controlling his equipment with a variety of jigs and templates. To avoid waste, and perhaps because he was concerned with craftsmanship, he worked slowly. But now, all the variables can be "programmed" into computers, and with the technique known as "numerical control" these electronic brains direct the same cutting tools, handle the same jigs and templates once operated by the machinist. Most important of all, this sort of automation is economically feasible for small lots in which there are changes in product design.

The key here is feedback, the simplest case of which is the home thermostat turning a furnace on and off in order to maintain a constant room temperature. In essence, signals are sent from one part of the automated line to another, correcting errors, shifting power loads, or modifying the speed of the line. No human need adjust gauges or read thermometers or press buttons. Feedback or servomechanisms do a better control job than humans, especially when many elements are involved. Whereas the human eye can follow the motion of a gauge at about two cycles a second, a servomechanism does about 100 a second. Now, marry feedback to a computer and automation is complete. The computers, really giant adding machines and calculators, receive information from the gauges and thermometers, analyze the data, and then transmit new instructions to other gauges and instruments.

Computers, whose basic concept goes back to Blaise Pascal, were developed in their electronic form during World War II to help guns hit their targets more efficiently. There are two basic types: the analog and digital computer. The former is a kind of electronic slide rule able to apply higher mathematics to problems of rates of change in various flows. However fast it might have been, for the engineer, mathematician, and operations researcher, it was not fast enough. So the digital computer was devised, a machine that employs the binary number system and consequently can only add and subtract. This is no impediment, for like an electronic abacus, the digital computer sends its impulses forward at an unbelievable speed, giving it a marked advantage over the analog machine. Moreover, digital computers have "memory" drums in which data can be stored for future use. The electrical pulses in a digital computer last less than one-millionth of a second. Information can be extracted from the memory drum in about ten-millionths of a second.

Of course, a considerable amount of human brain power is expended before the computer can be put to work. This is the science of programming. Instructions are written on a process sheet, then coded and entered on tape. That is, English is translated into machine language. The control unit of the system then "reads" the tape, gives forth with the appropriate electrical impulses, and sets the servomechanisms to work. One writer compared the operation to an old-fashioned player piano in which the punched holes in the roller actuate the hammers to bang out either the "Basin Street Blues" or a Beethoven sonata.

Lending a nightmarish quality to these developments is the current scientific talk about artificial intelligence. Machines, it is said, can be built to recognize certain patterns and can learn to plan simple tasks. While the computer may be something of a moron, awaiting instructions from a human Ph.D., the fact that an electrical contrivance can be made to learn anything is astonishing enough. If a heuristic or generalized solution is sufficient, then a thinking computer is no longer science fiction. Chess-playing machines are at least feasible: the only problem seems to be that they would have to review the outcomes of all possible plays and that might take centuries. Perhaps that is what makes them morons.

The names one often sees bandied about—PERT, ALGOL, COBOL, GECOM, SURE—are merely abbreviations for specific programming methods, each utilizing one or more computer installations constructed by Burroughs, Bendix, Rand, or IBM. PERT, for example—Program Evaluation and Review Technique —is based on the concept of a tree network with alternatives to be considered at each node of the tree. Since the computer works so much faster than the human mind and also uses stored information, it can review the accumulating cost of a flow process at each step and then direct the sequence of decisions along the critical or least-cost pathway. PERT originated in the Polaris Missile Project when it became essential to keep track of some 11,000 contractors and subcontractors. Again, military need provided the research motive. So complex can these matters become that the Defense Department had to work out a standardized pidgin English to coordinate programming.

It is sometimes said that the considerable investment in these systems precludes all but the largest firms from employing them. This is not so. Any number of consulting services are available for smaller concerns to meet data-processing needs, and some firms have set up cooperative research centers. Span, Inc., is one such co-op doing the bookkeeping for a number of insurance companies in Hartford; Tamcor maintains brokerage records in New York, and IBM, the biggest of them all, makes its equipment available to all comers through seventy locations around the country. In fact, the latter is now compiling tape libraries, dubbed by one journal "computer laundromats." Thus, the new technology is available to anyone who wants to make use of it.

All this must be worthwhile, for rental costs run from $12,000 a year up, and outright purchase of computer equipment can cost millions. Some $2 billion has been invested in computers by private companies since 1950, and this does not include what the government has spent. It is estimated that by 1970 computer sales will hit $500 million a year or about 2½ times present outlays. When the Pennsylvania Railroad automated its Conway, Pa., yards, it expected to recoup its $34 million cost within three years. At Ford, nine workers at three machines putting holes into crankshafts replaced thirty-nine workers at thirty-nine machines. A Philco plant reduced its work force by 25 percent by using printed circuitry. A computer engineer once remarked that he could cut one man off the payroll for every $5,000 spent on automated equipment. And finally, the initial cost of installing a computer system, according to Wassily Leontief, comes to no more than 6 percent of total plant investment. The value of new technology seems undeniable.

By now "Detroit" automation is quite well known. Automatic machines, linked by transfer equipment, move engine blocks through a complete manufacturing process, performing 530 precision cutting and drilling operations in 14.5 minutes as compared to nine hours in a conventional plant. The Chrysler Corporation's recent breakthrough on computer "balancing" of assembly lines, essentially a "combinatorial" problem, now defines each job so rigidly that little liberties like a worker's taking a few minutes out for a smoke become serious impediments to the smooth flow of cars. An automated power plant in Louisiana saved $175,000 in fuel, $100,000 in maintenance, $1.5 million in eliminating delays and mishaps, and $500,000 in labor. A Jones & Laughlin sheet-plate mill turns out strip at the speed of seventy miles an hour with no labor other than the supervision of engineers. Punch-card systems in a reversing roughing mill modify ingot shapes, and the computer even "remembers" what to do when the forms have to be changed. Foundry work, traditionally a hand operation, is now being tied to the computer. In petroleum and chemicals the story is almost ancient: as far back as 1949 catalytic cracking plants were turning out 41,000 barrels a day with instruments and only a few workers to watch gauges. In a Texaco refinery, the computer controls twenty-six flow rates, seventy-two temperatures, three pressure levels, and three gas combinations. General Electric uses segmented "automation," that is, batch production, for motors of varying models up to thirty horsepower. Ribbon machines make 800 electric bulb blanks a minute, running without end, and requiring only one worker who stands by to make an occasional adjustment.

Even in the office and retail store, one finds evidence of the new technology. Although office work has expanded tremendously since 1910 (today 17 percent of the labor force is found in the office as compared to 5 percent fifty years ago), it is precisely the enormous quantity of paper work and routine operation that makes automation feasible here. Banks, utilities, insurance companies, and government bureaus have eagerly made room for yards of the new equipment—so much faster is the computer than the old-fashioned bookkeeper and clerk. As a result, office work no longer is the growth industry it was— at least in terms of jobs. One California firm, studied by Mrs. Ida R. Hoos, put only two accounting operations on a computer and promptly eliminated 300 out of 3,200 office jobs and drastically altered the functions of some 980 others.

In retailing, automation starts with inventory and accounting records. Sales data are transmitted to control centers where billing, inventory, and credit information is stored. Bad credit risks are automatically checked and information returned to the sales clerk before the package can be wrapped. Sylvania and IBM have been working on automatic checkout counters for supermarkets—the number of cash registers would be reduced as well as the number of workers. Ferris wheels, conveyor belts, chutes, and slides, all controlled by electronic computers, deliver garments from receiving platforms to stockrooms and even return the merchandise to the ground floor if necessary. Eventually we will pay our traffic penalties to a computer: in Illinois, records of driver violations are stored in a computer and the fines are calculated by machine.

This, then, is the automated feast. Tasks are accomplished with unimaginable speed. Decisions are made by coded instructions and errors quickly detected. Facts are stored and extracted from memory drums. The machines learn and "perceive": they analyze stock market conditions; establish rocket flight patterns before the shot is fired into space; write television scripts that compare favorably with what is now available; compose music; translate; and play games. They combine high technical competence with just enough of an I.Q. to keep them tractable. They do precisely the kind of work to which junior executives and semi-skilled employees are usually assigned.

No slur is intended here, for in addition to the ordinary worker it is the middle manager, the backbone of the average corporation, who will be most affected by automation. He has a bleak future indeed, when computers relay information to each other, do all the scheduling, and control manufacturing from inception to the point at which the product is packaged and rolled into a box car. It is rather the archon of industry—as Edward Ziegler has dubbed him—who ultimately wins out, for with the elimination of both plant and office staff, this man at the very top gains even tighter control over the decision-making process. The sort of organizational looseness that prevailed prior to the advent of the computer is eliminated, and corporate structure becomes more formal, more "integrated," since with the computer there must be greater "cooperation." The number of links in the chain of command is reduced drastically; vice-presidents are soon out of a job. No less an authority than Herbert A. Simon of Carnegie Tech has said that by 1985 machines can dispense with all middle echelons in business. Production planning is handed over to the digital demon, while both the middle manager and the displaced worker drive taxicabs. The sociologist may very well ask, whither the American dream of status and success?

Quite often the computer engineer tries to build his own empire within the corporation. Fresh to the ways of business life, he has unabashedly played havoc with established relations. He and his programmer cohorts, cutting across all divisions, have often ignored and undermined the authority of department heads and vice-presidents. Many middle management people in automated companies now report that they are awaiting the ax or, if more fortunate, retirement. Bright young men leave for non-automated firms, hoping to reach the top elsewhere before the computer catches up with them. Sometimes the new elite does lose out: it has not been unknown for a computer installation to be yanked as a result of corporate internecine warfare.

Usually, though, archon and engineers are in complete accord. With the computer creating certain expectations, the firm must operate through a series of highly rigid sequences. Flexibility has been dispensed with, for the whole plant is now a single technical structure in which total performance must be "optimized." The engineer examines each step in the process solely in terms of efficiency—industrial logic of the most unremitting kind takes primacy of place. Under automation, the engineer or mathematician is *the* skilled man in the plant, while workers, those who remain and those who do not, are expected to adjust with equanimity to a situation for which they have had no responsibility. In fact, the engineer's attitude quite often is tough and hard, too much so for ordinary men: what the worker doesn't know, says he, won't hurt him. The scientists appreciate only "facts": the human problems of an industrial system frequently have little meaning for them. Unlike the organization men of the fifties, they are usually "inner directed," disturbers of the corporate peace, freebooters in pursuit of the idols of efficiency. Since the latter is measured by high profit and low cost, such scientific ruthlessness meets the approval of the archon. The latter really doesn't know what the scientist is doing: top management merely voices a faith based on payoff. Thus the programmer, who often assumes the aspect of a medieval alchemist, runs his own show, designing projects, cutting corporate red tape with abandon, and advising the industrial relations department that labor displacement is "none of your business." At best, the engineer can parrot some devotee of the conventional economic wisdom by repeating that automation creates new demand and new jobs, upgrades the worker and inspires everyone with its challenge. There must be a certain glory in the marvels of automation: but the men who once worked in the chemical plants, oil refineries, and steel mills are now out of sight and out of mind.

Between 1953 and 1960, a million and a half jobs disappeared. In one plant, studied by Floyd Mann of the University of Michigan, automation reduced the work force by half. In the electrical industry, output increased 21 percent between 1953 and 1961, while employment declined 10 percent. There was a loss of 80,000 production jobs in steel during the decade of the fifties. In the shift from aircraft to missiles, 200,000 jobs went down the technological drain. For the five-year period 1955–1960, production workers in automobile factories were down 21 percent. All this displacement occurred in an affluent society that had gone through four postwar recessions each of which left behind an increasingly hard-core residue of unemployment—3 percent in 1951–53; 4 percent in 1955–57; and 5 percent in 1959–60.

Full employment for the next ten years means creating twelve million new jobs—25,000 a week, or almost double the number of new openings in the 1947–57 decade. Extending the period to 1961, we find that output rose 65 percent while the number of production and maintenance jobs declined. True, white collar workers increased 7 percent, but now automation is making them just as insecure. If we assume that demand in the sixties will expand at the same rate as it did in 1947–57, then output by 1970 may very well be 50 percent greater. However, if the present rate of productivity is maintained, then the number of required man-hours will have increased by 12 percent, providing only seventy-five million jobs at the end of the decade. Thus, about eight million persons, 10 percent of the labor force, will have no work. And this is a moderate forecast, for should the secular growth rate fall below 3 percent per annum, as is conceivable, output will have gone up about 40 percent. Add to this the effects of automation, and the job increase by 1970 may be only two million, leaving a residue of perhaps ten million persons without jobs.

Is this so weird a tale? The ever optimistic Bureau of Labor Statistics' chief, Ewan Clague, recently admitted to an Arden House conclave that 200,000 jobs a year would be lost through "disemployment by automation." He found that in 70 percent of manufacturing industries such "disemployment" comprised four-fifths of the jobs lost. And his estimate did not include computer displacement among white collar workers.

The unions now know what automation can do to them. No matter how strong the security clause in a collective bargaining agreement, the serious drop in membership for most internationals is a harbinger of approaching catastrophe. Further, it is so much easier now for plants to escape to communities where unionism seems to represent little threat. And in such towns, management does not worry about a labor supply, for under automation what need is there for workers? There are also related problems for the unions: What happens to seniority? How about pension rights? Can traditional unionism with its roots in craft concepts cope with an industry whose shape has assumed the form of a process? Is the programmer a part of the bargaining unit? Or does his role in decision-making place him in management's ranks? And how effective is the strike when a handful of engineers can operate the whole works? This last question was answered in Port Arthur, Texas, where about 3,700 production workers walked off the job at an oil refinery, leaving 600 white collar employees and supervisors behind to run the plant at 65 percent of capacity. One labor relations man was reported to have said: "Maybe they ought to have removed a couple of transistors."

Some have argued that the displaced can be directed to jobs in the service and white collar fields. What jobs? Automation, as we have already noted, has been moving into these fields in the last three years just as rapidly as elsewhere. In 1960, at the Census Bureau, fifty technicians plus a battery of computers did the work that it had taken over 4,000 statisticians to do in 1950. The little black code numbers now appearing on blank checks inform us that our accounts are debited, credited, and cleared by a scanning device hooked into a computer. It is poor consolation, moreover, to be told that employment adjustments will be made via the A & P route—attrition and pregnancy—for this is an admission that there really are no jobs for those who want to work.

The notion that all who have been displaced by machines will quickly find new employment is a cheerful thought, something like whistling while walking through a cemetery. Some years ago, such cheerfulness was quite common, even among labor leaders. Walter Reuther's early speeches all but embraced the computer, so high was the regard for technology, so powerful the belief in growth and progress. The Joint Economic Committee's 1955 report on automation urged laissez faire, for no serious problems were envisioned. In the short space of seven years, hesitation and doubts have cropped up. There is no longer the ancient and well-regarded optimism that more machines mean expanded employment elsewhere or that automation will upgrade workers. It is evident, rather, that the new technology enforces a deterioration of skills for the great mass of workers and offers only the social junk pile for the unskilled and untutored.

What is the solution? Frankly, there is none, at least none of a definitive character. The numerous suggestions for dealing with the pressing problems that stem from automation are all piecemeal, pecking at a spot here and a point there. No amount of federal fiscal tinkering will meet the immediate needs of those who are attached to a dying industry. Economic growth, while essential, will not of itself put to work again the idle coal miner, ex-machinist, and troubled bookkeeper whose jobs have vanished like the first atom bomb tower. Administration economists believe that automated unemployment can be solved by turning on ordinary Keynesian tap valves; it's all a matter of failing effective demand, they assert. There seems little awareness in important circles that the American economy is undergoing deep-rooted and subtle structural changes and that it will take massive economic and social therapy to assuage the hurt.

The AFL-CIO has been advocating a series of measures, including meaningful retraining programs especially for workers over forty, area redevelopment, better unemployment insurance, an improved national placement service, special help to relocate the "disemployed," higher pensions, and even shorter hours. But will we—American management, American unions, Congress, the administration—really expend the necessary hard thought? Don Michael doubts it, for it is unlikely, says he, that ". . . our style of pragmatic making-do and frantic crash programs can radically change in the next few years. . . ." It is hard to disagree.

Consider the retraining effort. A case of too little, if not too late, it is hardly a roaring success. In West Virginia, the federal pilot scheme plus the state's own twenty-two-month-old program have been able to uncover new jobs for only half the 3,000 "graduates." Most of the others simply returned to the ranks of the unemployed. In Pennsylvania, 1,760 persons enrolled in retraining courses in 1957. Of these, 884 completed their re-education, 741 obtained new jobs. The state had a half million unemployed at the time.

Where private enterprise undertakes some corrective steps, it is usually found that a labor union had been doing the prodding, as in the meat-packing industry. Yet when 433 workers were laid off in Armour's Oklahoma City plant, only sixty could qualify for retraining and those who did secure new employment had to accept a lower rate of pay. Some firms are genuinely disturbed about the effects of automation. For example, U. S. Industries, a manufacturer of electronic equipment, and the machinists' union have agreed upon a jointly managed fund to study the entire question. The company's president, John Snyder, at least acknowledges that each one of his machines sends sixty workers scurrying to the unemployment insurance offices. Incidentally, one of U. S. Industries' contributions is the invention of automatic equipment to train displaced workers for typing and similar tasks.

There have been other experiments in adjustment. Some take the form of liberal severance-pay allowances. One of the earliest such schemes, though not related to automation per se, was the famous 1936 Washington Agreement between the railroad companies and the unions. Displaced workers receive 60 percent of their average pay as severance compensation for periods as long as five years whenever mergers occur. In cases of relocation, moving expenses are paid and losses resulting from forced sales of homes reimbursed. More recently, another generous plan was agreed upon by TWA and its navigators, who, if replaced by automatic instruments, will receive $25,000 plus $400 a month for three years as severance. In addition, the now foot-loose navigators will be given free lifetime travel passes on the airline. Thus they will have at least acquired mobility and will be able to search for jobs in all corners of the globe. Yet such measures offer no genuine solution: they are mere palliatives, for they fail to confront the fundamental question—what does a man do with his time, either during the temporary period of affluence, or when the windfall resources will have given out, or for that matter, even when he has not been detached from industry?

Not every arrangement exhibits a handsome concern for the displaced. In the coal fields a contemptible alliance between John L. Lewis and the operators cast adrift almost 300,000 miners. The coal industry, caught between the grinders of competitive fuels and high operating costs, was thoroughly run-down by the mid-forties. Deciding not to worry any more about the unemployed at the pits, Lewis acquiesced in rapid technological change. Output per day rose from 6.4 tons in 1949 to 14.4 tons in 1961; one ton of coal now requires less than half the labor it did a decade ago. At the Paradise, Kentucky, coal field an automatic shovel larger than the Statue of Liberty strips 200 tons of material in one scoop. In Harvey Swados' words, Lewis decided to trust to time and mortality to resolve the problem of the unemployed. And so the coal industry no longer suffers from economic decay. With a return on investment of 7.5 percent, it compares favorably with steel and oil. To hasten the day when his union can depend upon a healthy industry for its forty-cent per ton royalty, Lewis directed the mine workers to invest in sundry mine operations and even lent $35 million to Cyrus Eaton, whose interests include peace movements as well as coal. Of course, it would have been troublesome to apprise the membership of these transactions, so all the deals were carried through with great secrecy, only to be smoked out last year in a Tennessee lawsuit. At a recent convention of the union, an innocent delegate who suggested that perhaps something might be done for the unemployed was " . . . verbally torn to pieces by a buckshot charge of oratory from John L. Lewis himself." Declining dues are amply compensated for by investment returns in banks, mines, railroads, and power plants. Meanwhile, 300,000 miners continue to rot in the idle towns of Pennsylvania and West Virginia.

This sort of cooperation could set a strange trend if other unions were to adopt the Lewis formula. One that did is Harry Bridges' West Coast Longshoremen's International. Several years ago, the ILWU signed an agreement with the Shipping Association that was hailed as a reply to automation. Indeed, the retirement benefits are quite munificent and the pay scale increased somewhat, but at the same time the employers were given the go-ahead signal to install a whole range of technological improvements which will virtually exclude entire blocs of workers not yet ready to retire. Moreover, the new work rules, extracted by the employers as a price for the higher pay and the liberalized pensions, have intensified work loads on the docks virtually to the human breaking point.

Thus, one comes back to an immediate step, which though not by any means a "solution," nevertheless offers a practicable way for mitigating some of the effects of automation—the shorter work week. Mere mention of this is apt to send a shudder down the backs of administration economists and devotees of the conventional wisdom. Expressing their horror at the thought that man should have even more leisure than he now enjoys, the latter urge that a shorter work week means less production and higher costs. And in the present context of growthmanship, this is unthinkable. Arthur Goldberg, whose grasp of legal subtleties contrasts sharply with his simplistic formulations of economic issues, warned the International Ladies' Garment Workers' Union recently that fewer hours per week would ". . . impair adversely our present stable price structure [and] make our goods less competitive both at home and abroad. . . ." The enormous productive capacity of America's industry was conveniently forgotten, a capacity so enhanced by automation that it can more than compensate for the alleged loss of output. And this is to say nothing about the quality and content of contemporary "production"—

that would require another essay. The point to observe now is the curious inner tension of an industrial system whose fundamental Puritan outlook demands an incessant, unremitting outpouring of goods (for what?) while at the same time it imposes dreary idleness and dismal futures on those to whom the cornucopia is directed. We may well ask, what is the feedback in this insane circle?

But to return to the shorter work week—a cursory review of its history would demonstrate how completely reasonable it is. Prior to 1860, the rule was dawn to dusk with as much as seventy-two hours as the weekly standard. Demands for a shorter span were met with the contention that twelve hours a day, six days a week had been divinely ordained in order to strengthen worker morality. Three decades later the work week had been shortened by twelve hours. In 1910, the average ranged from fifty-one to fifty-five hours, and at that time a work force of thirty-four million produced a gross national product of about $37 billion. The work week continued to shrink: in 1920, it was forty-eight hours; in 1929, forty-four hours; and since 1946, forty hours. By 1955, the labor force had almost doubled while GNP increased ten-fold as compared to 1910. And all the time the work week kept declining, about thirteen hours in a forty-five year span, or roughly fifteen minutes a year.

Was anyone hurt? Did productivity lag? Has technology been impeded? The Depression years aside, whatever unemployment did occur would have been unquestionably greater without the steady drop in hours. A continuation of this secular decline would cut back the normal work week by one hour every four years. According to one estimate, this might create about a million jobs a year which, together with the normal increase in job openings, could really begin to cut into the displacement caused by automation. When Harry van Arsdale of the New York electricians' union obtained a five-hour day, he was savagely flayed for selfishness and lack of patriotism. Even the labor movement felt embarrassed. Van Arsdale insisted that he was only seeking to "spread the work." Now it seems, according to Theodore Kheel, the industry's arbitrator, that well over 1,000 new jobs will be made available as a result of the union's action.

What has happened in agriculture presents, in a sense, an object lesson we ought to heed. As W. H. Ferry remarked in a perceptive paper on affluence and plenty, the farm is technology's most notorious victory. Here abundance has become an economic catastrophe. So advanced is our agricultural establishment that even the 10 percent of the labor force it now employs is too much. Farm output increased 77 percent between 1910 and 1954, while land used for crops went up only 15 percent. During the same period, labor on farms as measured by man-hours dropped over 30 percent. This suggests an almost threefold rise in productivity. According to the late John D. Black, a leading farm expert, the major element in this change unquestionably was the substitution of machine power for muscle power. Yet the economic and political thrust of our system is such that 70 to 80 percent of the federal government's spending on agriculture goes to counteract the price impact of an ever-accumulating surplus.

The parallel between farm and industry is startling. There is enough grain in storage to feed everyone from Maine to Hawaii, but some fifty million Americans barely manage to subsist, even today. The steel industry functions at 65 percent of capacity, or thereabouts, while thousands of able-bodied men are shoved aside by automation. Strategic curtailment of production is employed, like the farm parity program, to distort the genuine capacity of our economy. Technology, rather than man, becomes the central focus of existence, and at the same time that it destroys, for example, the belief in the family farm, it seemingly ought to compel a desiccated concept of resource allocation and optimum production to retire in favor of a philosophy of distribution. But we really have no adequate social theory to deal with the latter. The ideas of a Galbraith, a C. Wright Mills, a Paul Goodman, or a Harvey Swados deal only with aspects of the problem. We wait to be told what is happening to us, what we need to do. And even then we shall not listen.

It is of course a common cliché that scientific advances have outrun our capacity to deal with them. Technology, the practical and material basis of life, has acquired a tidal force of its own which threatens to inundate human thought. Moreover, modern technology, as evidenced by automation, manifests no orderly growth. Its leads and lags, its uneven development, create new power centers that result in unaccustomed strains. To be sure, this has happened before, but always at immense human cost. It is this that the high priests of automation fail to grasp, while those of us who are merely bystanders can only hope that society will eventually catch up with the engineers and scientists and archons of industry who see only a handsome profit in what the machine can do.

1962

Those Dark, Satanic Mills

To a generation reared on classical economic history, it was something of a shock to be told a few years ago that the agony of the Industrial Revolution was a myth. Earlier historians such as Engels, the Hammonds, the Webbs, G. D. H. Cole, and the elder Toynbee had vividly depicted the havoc wrought by a burgeoning middle class determined to forge its destiny out of coal, cotton, and the machine. Thus, the Hammonds, *doyens* of English economic historians, taught that the Industrial Revolution brought confusion to the settled ways of free-born Englishmen that we are still seeking to compose, power that we are still seeking to subdue. Cole's mountainous compilation of facts revealed that severe deprivations in material existence were the common lot of more than half of all England in those days. And Toynbee also forcefully reminded us that industrialism can produce wealth without producing well-being.

In 1954, however, a group of economic theorists and historians of a Whig-like persuasion published a series of studies, *Capitalism and the Historians,* to prove that all this was largely fiction. Their intent was to correct the exaggerations they found in the earlier historians and to demonstrate that capitalism, even in its early traumatic days, had improved the condition of the laboring classes. Friedrich Hayek, for example, argued that the capitalists had applied their earnings on a large scale to provide means of production for workers who could not otherwise have produced their own sustenance. Indeed, the altruism of the capitalist was responsible for palpable advances in the standard of life for everyone. Evidence to support this interpretation was supplied by Sir John Clapham, T. S. Ashton, and W. H. Hutt. The classical view which looked with dismay upon the Industrial Revolution as an upheaval that scattered its social debris all over England was replaced by a supposedly empirical circumspection. Misery and political reaction were only by-products of a "take-off" into sustained economic growth. That the enclosures destroyed village after village was of no great moment, for the entire process had allowed a larger population to be better fed, and the social tension it bred was merely an accident of rising food prices. The new, conservative view of the Industrial Revolution gained a good deal of currency in the following years even among liberals who might have been expected to question it.

Now comes a young, brilliant English writer, E. P. Thompson, lecturer at Leeds University, with a tenacious drive for truth and a knowledge of historical sources vastly superior to that of the Hayeks and the Hutts, to assure us of the fact that the Industrial Revolution *was* a human catastrophe. Disturbed by the complacency and narrowness of the revisionist position, Thompson in his *The Making of the English Working Class* (1964) restores the balance of historical truth with extraordinary skill and with a fervor that makes the Ashtons and the Claphams seem like desiccated compilers of figures.

First of all he demonstrates that the statistical evidence employed to sustain the revisionist thesis is completely muddled. Clapham had totaled county wage averages and from them had derived a national average—a patent arithmetical absurdity. Also, this calculation obscured the fact that 60 percent of the workers were in counties with earnings well below the national "average." More importantly, Thompson draws upon a much more concrete awareness of the actualities of political as well as social life in the late eighteenth and nineteenth centuries. As he so rightly observes, it is possible for the statistical measures and human existence to run in opposite directions. (Witness the writing of contemporary commentators who do not wish to be bothered about poverty in the United States because it affects only one-fifth of the population.) Thompson's feeling for the debased quality of experience created by the new, mass society makes his observations on the economic situation of the time unusually trenchant:

> The condition of the majority was bad in 1790; it remained bad in 1830 (and forty years is a long time). . . . there were undoubted increases in real wages among organized workers during the burst of trade union activity between 1832–34; but the period of good trade between 1833 and 1837 was accompanied by the smashing of the trade unions by the concerted efforts of Government, magistrates, and employers . . . even in the mid-40's the plight of very large groups of workers remains desperate . . . This does not look very much like a "success story."

The traditional village economy in the countryside collapsed under the pressure of those who wanted sheep runs. "The cottager without legal proof of rights was rarely compensated. The cottager who was able to establish his claim was left with a parcel of land inadequate for subsistence and a disproportionate share of the very high enclosure costs." The enclosures were a plain case of class robbery, says Thompson, motivated by a greed for high rents: they had little to do with a wish to feed a growing industrial population. The new instruments of production transformed the social as well as natural landscape. Skilled artisans were replaced by ordinary workers and ordinary workers by machines. The dubious measurements of the revisionist historians made wages seem high in the first half of the nineteenth century, but, as Thompson shows, the indexes of urban wages were based on the earnings of skilled workers, ignoring the great mass of unskilled and unemployed. And working conditions everywhere grew worse than before.

While Thompson bases a good deal of his history on sound statistical and economic analysis, its major thrust is political, for the character of the Industrial Revolution cannot be understood outside of its political context. Together with the economic exploitation that went hand-in-hand with frighteningly depersonalized social relationships, there was bred a new climate of repression. A casual word of doubt about the wisdom of the Crown might be reported by a hundred spies and suffice to send the speaker to jail for years. A penny pamphlet in defense of freedom brought charges of high treason. Beneath all this was the system of Old Corruption by which Parliament remained firmly in the hands of the landed aristocracy: their rule, sustained by the complaisant approval of wealthy merchants and manufacturers as well as an emerging white-collar class, was stupid enough to bring England to the edge of Revolution. Meanwhile, noblemen dipped into the public coffers at will for imaginary services to the state. Decade after decade, venality continued unabated, mainly because most of the populace, aside from literate artisans and workers, was indifferent. The Industrial Revolution had made them prosperous and they did not wish to call the system into question. Thus, while the throne was occupied by inert idiots, hereditary gentlemen and their commercial companions were able to maintain control of the society and the empire.

Hence, it was not surprising that the old regime soon encountered opposition from the dispossessed classes and their spokesmen. How working-class protest was created and fostered forms a large part of Mr. Thompson's story. Attracted by the example of the French Jacobins, English artisans almost immediately began the fight in behalf of social justice and effective law, and for their pains they were just as immediately hounded, jailed, and hanged. Indeed, it was not so much the Reign of Terror across the Channel that threw the propertied classes into a panic, but rather the demands of "working men in villages and towns over the whole country claiming *general* rights for themselves." Working-class impulses, given strong voice by Tom Paine, began to shape themselves into class consciousness, and by 1795, according to Thompson, a deep cleavage between the classes had appeared. Any possible national alliance between an impatient bourgeoisie and an emerging proletariat was shattered before it could start. A mutual fear impelled the middle classes and the landowners to lock arms in a common corruption. Thompson tells this story with full awareness of its dramatic tensions. His cast of characters is no mere collection of shadows but is made up of genuine people driven by greed and power at the top, indignation and fear at the bottom.

Though widely supported, especially in the countryside, radicalism was unable to develop real offensive strength. Yet there were ardent, articulate defenders of its principles and it became a powerful tradition in British political life, even though it had to stay underground. For many years its major spokesman was William Cobbett, a great political pamphleteer, who was sickened alike by the incomparable scandals of royalty, the corruption of the merchant class, the prostituted press, the gouging and squeezing of factory worker and peasant. For exposing brutality in the army, Cobbett was fined two thousand pounds and sentenced to two years in jail. In the first quarter of the nineteenth century the authorities grew so fearful of criticism that they resorted to spies and hoked-up evidence on a scale unknown before in England.

The early worker movements were desperate but politically naïve affairs—Luddite armies to break machines, Cato Street conspiracies to assassinate the Cabinet (in this one spies supplied the guns), correspondence societies to propagandize the hinterlands, illegal trade unions to protect ancient crafts, and even a millennarian search for heavenly salvation to escape the spreading oppressiveness of industry. Let us not judge these hungry men harshly, says Thompson. Relief and reform could come only with constitutional advances, which were unlikely when the governing powers refused to concede that working men had the right to human existence, much less to a political one.

From all this turmoil there evolved an important workingman's culture that neither Tory nor Whig nor middle-class reformer could continue to ignore or suppress. The worker had learned how harsh political strife could be and from this experience had forged his own brand of radicalism. As his ideology developed he focused on the freedom to speak and assemble as primary rights of man. He sought to reclaim the dignity that the machine had destroyed. There seems little doubt, as Thompson says, that the Reform Bill of 1832 turned aside imminent revolution. But the workers were to gain nothing from this strange piece of legislation, for the "reformed" Commons at once launched an effective counter-attack. Throughout the rest of the century, England's two societies remained in a state of unending tension.

Thompson's account is blunt and courageous: he reads the facts as they are given in the record and they are usually far from pleasant. He has rescued the past from the hands of those who for ideological reasons would obscure its true significance and in doing so he has told us much about ourselves. And is this not what the good historian must do? For the indifference of nobility and bourgeois to the fate of those crushed by the nineteenth century's industrial upheaval is more than matched by the self-satisfaction of the affluent who today turn away from the nameless troubles of workers displaced by computers. Thompson's book has been called controversial, but perhaps only because so many have forgotten how explosive England was during the Regency and the early reign of Victoria. Without any reservation, *The Making of the English Working Class* is the most important study of those days since the classic work of the Hammonds.

1964

The Implications of Technology

The development of technology has been one of man's most pervasive pursuits. He has always sought to manipulate and control his environment in order to satisfy his needs. In this sense technology is simply organized skill. Of course, technology has been but one part of his heritage; there also were language, social organization, philosophy, religion. All have affected one another, and all have made man what he is, even while man was himself creating them. Yet the most significant set of interactions has been that between technology and social organization, for it has determined the manner in which material objects are to be used.

Technology has thus reflected a practical manipulative activity, not a contemplative one. It seldom has been the product of idle curiosity, for it has been used to give man control over nature—or over other men. In large measure, it has been ". . . the story of the clever people to pass on . . . backbreaking work to others less clever than themselves. . . ." Kindly historians have noted how technology reduces the struggle for existence by altering the physical environment. Those who are perhaps more critical may have serious questions to pose, for technology has been employed all too often in modes not necessarily inherent in the machine process. When this took place, the ultimate function of technology was lost to view and transformed into unending, senseless activity and a "plundering of life."

Modern technology is clearly the phenomenon of Western culture. Although the detachable harpoon head of the Eskimo, the bow and arrow of Neolithic man, and the hand loom of ancient Mesopotamia were all artifacts of technology, they did not display the predominant features of modern technique in which complex machines and motive power stemming from sources other than man have molded work and thought. In ancient times men could control their technology and shape their philosophy by the heavens. The capacity to do that today is moot.

Before the rise of the West, technology involved almost exclusively the use of tools. These instruments, generally small in size, were extensions of the hand, and they made the opposable thumb more powerful than it ever could be in a pure state of nature. But man himself supplied the power. Yet the hand's very flexibility made tools ill suited to a machine-like process unless they could be torn from the grip of humans. The hand could not work endlessly or with high precision, for, despite the possibilities of limited "automatic" action, hands and arms cannot rotate perpetually. The natural processes of fatigue prevented man from becoming a robot.

Here the machine became a truly revolutionary device, so specialized that it could be made automatic, rotating without pause, as long as energy was fed into its driving mechanism. The striking feature about machines in the twentieth century, however, has been precisely their flexibility, their all-purpose character. Although a hundred years ago the drive was to create single-purpose equipment (and indeed this drive is still prevalent in our own technology), there is a decided tendency now to have an increasing variety of work done by a single or closely related bank of machines. Modular machine tools and numerical control, and indeed the computer itself, demonstrate enough capacity to engage in manifold tasks to suggest that, at least in the sense of flexibility, the machine is again becoming a kind of tool.

In examining the historical record, we must note that technology enabled the English bourgeoisie to break away from the tutelage of the aristocracy. The latter's mentality always had been framed by the natural turn and rhythm of the seasons and a sometime concern for the welfare of its villeins. The era of the middle class, however, was one of utter callousness. Poverty was too intense to be recognized, and, as in present-day America, the prosperous members of society quickly learned to keep it out of sight and out of mind. The poor were subhuman, appendages to the machine, and poverty simply guaranteed their proper behavior. The middle-class merchant-manufacturer could in no way afford the luxury of an aristocratic purview. His vision was long run, employing abstinence as a way of completing economic ventures that might not mature for a number of years. Capital had to be carefully husbanded, for failure meant humiliation and debasement before one's peers. As Morse Peckham suggests, the aristocrat did not mind failure: what he regretted was uncertainty—a quality of mind and behavior that the bourgeois accepted.

Technology thus entered into the economic faith of the middle class, for it assured its members that the scientist and the engineer would be harnessed to achievement. The philosophy of natural law, with its stress on order, suited the bourgeois very well; the destiny of man, that is, middle-class man, was guided by a Provident Unseen Hand. Thus, while the capacities of technology were pushed to the utmost, a new morality was created. Such was the beneficence under which ". . . only the middle classes had the gall to use every propaganda instrument in their power to persuade the miserable working classes that their standard of living would automatically rise, and to attempt to train them to postpone that gratification to the lives of their great-grandchildren, long after their own lives had ended." Middle-class men were practical and successful. Considering the values of the age, they were deemed to be right.

There was, of course, no smoothness, no linearity in the development of technology. Much of what occurred seemed to possess the quality of happenstance. Yet it all moved with a force to be explained primarily by social and economic considerations. For example, the automobile arrived when it did because a *nouveau riche, fin de siècle* society was prepared for a vehicle of marked prestige. The internal combustion engine was not the necessary condition for the innovation of the automobile, for electric and steam motors, it must be recalled, were quite common in the early days of the auto. Indeed, the first locomotives might have become automobiles, if the rich of the early nineteenth century had been as fascinated by horseless carriages as were their descendants. Evidently, more than profitable opportunity is involved in innovation.

In other instances, there is a curious social pressure to innovate because it is fashionable. Industrialists in the United States have always been ready to scrap a machine, no matter how good, as long as there is a new one to replace it. Henry Ford, for example, threw out equipment as soon as he discovered more advanced replacements. Maintenance and repair seemed less profitable than acquiring other labor-saving gadgets. In part this phenomenon stemmed from relatively flimsy construction and in part from the breakneck pace at which American factories operated, compared, for example, to British plants: but the major motivation appears to have been an impulse to display something new to visitors and rivals. And this impulse was strengthened by the expectation that a better machine or a better mouse trap would always be available to further the game of oneupmanship in industrial competition. This process happens frequently with automation, in which control of production often is shifted to the computer, whether economically feasible or not, simply because rival companies have installed the new hardware.

Such practices can lead to venerating the machine as if it were a religious icon. The phenomenon is not new: in the eighteenth century, various mechanics and scientific societies manifested their abiding faith in the machine with offers of reward for novel devices. And of course the state had always expressed a close interest in technology, dating back to the hydraulic societies of Asia, in which large water works were maintained for irrigation and communication. One may add, too, the temples and pyramids of Egypt, the hanging gardens of Babylon, the bridges and aqueducts of the Romans, and the Manhattan Project of wartime America. In fact, it has been in the waging of war that the state has had the greatest need of the technologist. The public career of da Vinci was matched by that of the Flemish fortification expert Stevinus, whose service to the Dutch Republic in the sixteenth century was invaluable. Lavoisier's work on gunpowder helped to make the armies of the French Revolution almost invincible. States helped also with the patent system, which seems to have started in the North Italian cities in the latter half of the fifteenth century. Undeniably, grants of monopoly, which were what patents implied, were important incentives.

The closeness of the state, war, and technology has been emphasized in our own time by that most terrible of all weapons, the thermonuclear bomb, the cost of which could have been borne only by government resources. Sonic detecting instruments, radar, anti-aircraft control, proximity fuses, linear programming, a mathematical technique for inventory housekeeping, and the computer itself were developed under the pressures of war. Only the state can shoot satellites into the atmosphere and pay for the exploration of space. It is not surprising that a substantial part of the federal budget is now regularly allocated to "research and development." The scientific community is virtually dependent on government largesse: in 1961, more than three-fourths of electronic scientists and engineers were engaged in projects paid for by the federal government.

It is improbable that the state can or will relax its interest in technology, for the latter unquestionably supports its power. Often it is a matter of the highest "security" as in the present-day United States. When the Byzantine Empire discovered "Greek fire," a compound of sulphur, pitch, and naphtha first used successfully to repel an Arab attack in the eighth century, it kept the invention to itself for 400 years. During those centuries, the Byzantines developed all sorts of devices to apply the fire more efficiently.

Throughout the ages—from the Greek fire to huge stone throwers, gunpowder, metals for cannon, bridges, the semaphore telegraph, and mass production in arsenals—technology and the machine have served the gods of war. As Lewis Mumford has said, "At every stage in its modern development, it was war rather than industry and trade that showed in complete outline the main features that characterize the machine." Interchangeable parts, a basic principle for the modern assembly line, were devised by the Frenchman Le Blanc in 1785 and the American Whitney in 1800, primarily for weaponry. Not until the 1860's was interchangeability applied to nonmilitary machines like the reaper. And the disciplined mass army became the model for the discipline of the factory; the faceless uniformity of the military matched to perfection the men on the production line.

In modern history, the rate of technological change has greatly accelerated. Minor differences aside, Europe in 1000 A.D. was not unlike mainland Greece in Alexander's day from a material point of view. Muscle power, supplemented by animals, was the primary source of energy for over a millennium and a half. Water and the power of the winds were not harnessed until the fifteenth and sixteenth centuries. Then came an overwhelming surge, reaching its climax in the eighteenth century, and within less than 200 years industry and urbanization displaced agriculture as society's chief preoccupation, while the machine came to dominate the life of man. If the speed at which we can cross the earth's surface is a reflection of the rate of invention and innovation, then clearly the pace has been intensified. Between 1829 and the present, the automobile, the railroad, and the jet airplane have added more to man's ability to move than was achieved in all the aeons that went before it. It took the crowned heads of Europe about three days to get to London for the funeral of Edward VII in 1910; the death of President Kennedy brought dignitaries to Washington from the six continents in less than twenty-four hours.

If the ability to kill large masses of people in war is a rough index of rapid technological change, then surely there has been exponential growth between the fifteenth century and the hydrogen bomb. Or, as Kenneth Boulding has noted, it took less than a decade to rebuild Europe and Japan, as contrasted to decades in the past, or centuries after the fall of Rome. Acceleration in technology feeds upon itself, devouring earlier techniques and machines in great gulps. Quick obsolescence has become a datum of industrial endeavor. UNIVAC I, the world's first data-processing computer, was retired to a museum by the United States Census Bureau in 1963 (after operating continuously for but twelve years) because it was much too slow and too small compared to up-to-date equipment. Enshrined in Washington's spanking new Museum of Science and Technology, it is as archaic as the wood-burning locomotives stored in other Smithsonian buildings.

The acceleration thesis, developed most forcibly by the sociologist Hornell Hart, has been challenged on occasion. But the counterarguments, which merely tally patents on file, are not persuasive. Granted that innovation depends on the use and disuse of older equipment, mistakes, luck, available capital and labor, and the like, the fact is that invention and innovation today spread more quickly than ever. Symposia and professional associations eagerly pass the gospel along, and no less an authority than George Sarton declared in 1936 that scientific progress was being accomplished in shorter and shorter periods. If the interval between an invention and its adoption is a measure of acceleration, then surely Hart is right. In the eighteenth century, adoption followed invention within a decade or less for almost all the important machines. Somewhat longer intervals appear to have characterized the first half of the nineteenth century. Perhaps more time was needed for digestion. But in the second half of the century about 50 percent of the strategic inventions were adopted within a decade or less; in the first quarter of the twentieth century about 60 percent became viable innovations within a decade; and in the second quarter the ratio rose to 70 percent. Such swift change is not merely a matter of degree, as some writers contend, for, as Norbert Wiener once remarked, the difference between a fatal dose of strychnine and a medicinal one is also a question of degree.

But to suggest that technology manifests an internal drive to accelerate by no means implies a smooth and balanced growth pattern. Development and change are not linear. For many years, even decades, after the Industrial Revolution's take-off, handicrafts subsisted side by side with the mechanized factory. In fact, belief in the values of handicrafts, forlorn as it was, expressed resistance to the machine. At any given time, there were marked differences in the pace at which segments of an economy or an industry were subjected to alteration. In British woolens, for example, the factory system paralleled a still vigorous cottage industry.

This staggered phenomenon was visible in other places and other times: carriage builders (except for Studebaker) did not become automobile manufacturers, nor was the aircraft industry beholden to automobiles. Telephone companies grew alongside the telegraph, and the filming of movies had little to do with the making of still cameras. As Joseph A. Schumpeter has shown, there were Old Firms and New Firms, Innovators and Sticks-in-the-Mud, and the greatest likelihood was that one was ready to bash in the head of the other. Meanwhile, those unfortunate enough to be working in industries made moribund by rivalry were cast aside to live out their lives in utter desperation. The hand-loom weavers did not go to work in the new factories: they were simply left to rot in misery.

That such developments can create structural distortion seems undeniable: the case histories of the defense and space industries in America offer some contemporary evidence. Here is an important and relatively new sector of the economy, dependent mainly on the largesse of the government, whose technology has virtually no relationship to what the rest of the country does. Drawing on exotic materials, these industries employ high-cost, high-specification methods that require parts to be assembled in dust-free, vibrationless plants with devices and components constantly tested, temperature and humidity carefully controlled, and precision machinery of the kind achieved only by computer calculations. The scientists and engineers who work in these companies manifest habits that are sharply different from those in the usual mass-production plants. Involved in building prototypes, they are utterly uninterested in costs: in an ordinary firm they would drive a controller out of his mind. Yet this is one industry into which the bulk of the scientists and engineers have been enticed, and that includes some four million members of the labor force. With a decreasing proportion of the outlay allocated to capital expenditures—the share of the latter in military spending dropped from about 75 percent in 1951 to about 47 percent in 1962—the multiplier effect has fallen to less than two. Meanwhile, the rest of the economy stumbled along with high unemployment, reduced only when the products of these exotic industries were put to use.

With technology, the concept of time became an abstraction and a commodity. Time was money. By 1500, most towns in Europe displayed elegant tower clocks, even though home pieces were available only to the rich. And in the seventeenth century, with the important work of Galileo and Huygens on the pendulum, the clock became one of the first machines to witness the joint venture of science and technology. There is no doubt that the clockmakers contributed much to the shaping of the Industrial Revolution. Precision and accuracy, essential ingredients of modern production, were provided by them. The habits of thought that stemmed from the clock also underpinned the demand for accuracy in weights and measures. Standardization became a categorical imperative: even the requirements of surface and air travel were to be standardized and embodied twice each year in the ritual of the timetable.

Essential to the spread of technology was information, and information meant printing. Again the historian digs back into the past of ancient China to discover its roots. It is not clear from the experts what this tracing proves, for the strategic combinations in printing were not achieved until movable type, oil-based inks derived from the work of painters, type founding, continuous paper-making, and the mechanical press—the idea for which came from the winery—were brought together to form a single complex. Gutenberg's movable type clearly was not enough. Furthermore, books remained an unattainable luxury as long as parchment was the only substance on which to print. Once continuous rolls of paper were made available and type body and end could be held together, universal literacy became a feasible project.

History no longer left anonymous gaps, yet at the same time it was easier to homogenize culture and make the Philistine supreme. The word became omnipresent: it deposited itself behind breakfast eggs; it received vacant stares in the subway; it sustained the coffee break; it became the truth. And with advertising, the major source of income for the newspapers, the beliefs of the dominant class could be decked in objectivity for the easier control of the mass of men who now possessed the last word fit to print.

The components of modern industrialism were gradually finding their proper places. Strategic inventions, no matter when they arrived on the scene, were fitted into the factory, which itself had only to convert discrete production into continuous process to meet the requirements of the twentieth century. Such a process was found in flour-milling, bread-making, and the slaughter of pigs. Industrialization would not have attained the intensity it did without the assembly line and its unbroken flow. Continuous production was implicit in the early factory's organization, and by the 1880's the Cincinnati meat-packers demonstrated how even refractory material, such as hogs, might be processed in a hitchless flow. A continuous, uninterrupted movement from the receiving platform, with quick transfer through all the stages of fabrication to the finished product, became an industrial reality.

Henry Ford got the idea for his assembly line from the butchers. The production of automobiles demanded unimpeded speed: Ford's Highland Park plant, opened in 1910, illustrated how such speed could be attained, for it was indeed an achievement of mechanical art. Scientists may have been sparse in those days, but the technicians more than made up the lack. So skilled had American mechanics become that machine tools were exported to Europe—a case of the pupil surpassing the teacher.

At Highland Park production became a river, fed by tributaries that carried in fenders and doors and wheels while men stood by, pushing it along at greater and greater speed. The apogee of industrialization had been achieved—standardization, interchangeability, continuous flow, and unbearable speed.

Inescapably, the assembly line became a way station on the road to production without men. Humans still had to be employed for tasks the engineers had not yet mechanized. But the search was on for the automatic factory which could function as if it were a set of synchronized watches with split-second timing. Technology was to dispose forever of the need for workers to tend the product-in-process as it gathered shape, from the raw material at the receiving platform to the painting and storing of a finished vehicle. The protest of the worker that the assembly line was a brutal master, driving at inhuman speed, would be heard no longer. Eventually the machine would do the work itself.

Technology was also bound to alter the production function, the relationship of input mix to output. Obviously, the whole business would be pointless unless there were capital or labor savings. That such effects have occurred appears unquestionable. For example, it has been demonstrated that in petroleum refining technical progress has achieved not only an absolute reduction in all input factors but also the greatest relative cutback in labor. From 1913 to 1955, the utilization of labor in this industry dropped in the ratio of 140 to 1; fuel declined in the ratio of 14 to 1; raw materials, 4 to 1; and capital 2.5 to 1. New equipment, improved capacity, high-speed tools, and better layout all contributed to lower capital requirements per unit of output; most authorities suggest that the capital-output ratio has dropped from about three in the 1920's to a little more than one today.

The new technology was quickly assimilated to the forms of business organization that accompanied its development. Ultimately, as Thorstein Veblen was quick to note, business dominated technology. As new sources of energy were discovered and costs of exploitation mounted, much more capital was required than could be supplied by a single entrepreneur or condominium of entrepreneurs. The factory and its costly equipment brought overhead costs to the forefront of economic calculation. Centralization became essential for efficiency. Machine production meant collective effort, for profit could be guaranteed in no other way. Fundamentally, it was all a gigantic transformation in the condition of man, comparable in magnitude to the Neolithic conversion from nomadism to farming. The thrust toward technological change was internalized, creating an irresistible imperative. A tidal wave of mechanization overwhelmed society, flowing from the factory into the home with toasters, tinned foods, and washing machines. Technology became not merely a congeries of instruments to produce goods but also a rigid system that determined in advance the nature of the output and the actions of those who were caught in its complex of wheels. It established ". . . not only the socially needed occupations, skills and attitudes, but also individual needs and aspirations." Technology lost its neutrality: the uses to which it was put became as much part of its drive as were the dynamos, moving belts, and servomechanisms that it comprised.

Man was at the mercy of technology: he was helpless when it failed, even momentarily, as in a great snowfall. The character of work underwent profound and irreversible change: new rhythms were established, severing man from a genuinely close relationship to his environment. Production no longer displayed a communal base. In fact, as man was being exiled from that sphere, he was somehow expected to consume its output, even if he had to mortgage his precarious future to do so. Skill disappeared as an end and virtue in itself: it had been merged into the machine, leaving man bootless in a world he could barely comprehend. Desiccated values and parochial attitudes created faceless personalities ready to leap into the first insane mass movement to come along. The artificial and the ephemeral were enhanced by rationalization and mechanization. Society had been prepared for a new mutation. Sometimes man sought to recapture a sense of self with a weekend camping trip. But technology had become his master, and, as he escaped into the woods, he took the machine with him.

1967

The Uses of Marxism

Even though they may reject his theories, many economists recognize that Marx is a major figure in the development of economic thought. They acknowledge that his effort to look at the economic system in its totality was a relevant one. Marx tried to work out carefully and analytically the relationships between the various social and economic components. He even set up "models," so dear to the hearts of modern theorists. Above all, he dealt with technology, underconsumption, unemployment, and the concentration of capital. These were big questions and Marx sought to supply the big answers. It is true that a number of his answers proved to be wrong. But the fact remains that he was an important economist, if for no other reason than that his challenge to standard doctrine could not be ignored. He was also a keen analyst, and while we may expose his errors, it must be underscored that in his own day he had few peers.

His use of the labor theory of value illustrated his analytical approach. Those socialist thinkers who preceded Marx—Robert Owen, Thomas Hodgskin, John Bray, William Thompson—had wrapped the theory of value in a hard moralistic shell: labor, they said, was being robbed of its own fruit. Marx pointedly denied this by arguing that in reality workers received full value, but that labor's problem stemmed from the fact that it was a peculiar commodity—it always created a value greater than itself—and it was this situation, a built-in imperative of the capitalist system, that remained the basic reality of the economic order.

Marx was able to relate a vast body of empirical data to an abstract model of the economy in a way that few economists in the nineteenth century had been able to match. He could not escape making value judgments, but at least they were explicitly set forth and not obscured by long lines of deduction. Economic questions were approached with an enormous command over the relevant factual data which he hammered into shape with some rather interesting analytical tools. One of these was the "economic interpretation of history"; this did not mean that men are motivoted solely by economic or material considerations but rather that economic situations influenced and helped shape the ideas and institutions of men.

However, it is in the pure economics of his social science (aside from the labor theory of value) that the most useful parts of the Marxian system may be identified. Here Marx tried to demonstrate that value was derived from the socio-economic relationships entered into by men for the purpose of producing means of subsistence, and particularly by the relations between employers and employees.

THE LABOR THEORY OF VALUE

The labor theory of value, which was where he began, stemmed mainly from Ricardo. The theory proclaimed that the value of a commodity was proportional to the quantity of socially necessary labor time included in it. Obviously this held, even in Marx's framework, only under conditions of perfect competition, that is, where there were many business firms competing with each other, and where the actions of any single firm could not affect the market price. Nothing in the Marxian model accounted for the existence of monopoly or other imperfections. From this "model" there flowed surplus value, the excess created by labor over its own worth. It should be noted that labor power, which Marx held to be the sole value-creating process, affected only that portion of the means of production which entered into the final product. This caused a considerable amount of confusion, especially in establishing the rate of profit. In calculating this rate, it is customary to consider total investment in capital. But in Marx's computations only a portion of capital—that part involved in value creation—was included in the calculation. It was not surprising that most economists found it difficult to follow him. Yet when viewing the economic system as a whole, the Marxian definition of the rate of profit made sense. But it made sense only if the economy was not an expanding one, that is, when it was static. When there is growth, when capital expands, the Marxian calculations are simply in error.

Prices and production, according to Marxian categories, can be explained only through a number of assumptions which are most unlikely to exist in a dynamic economy. It is doubtful that all prices, even in a static economy, would reflect the labor incorporated in goods. Moreover, the labor theory of value cannot really operate as a measuring device, surely an important function for such a theory. For example, it suggests that skilled labor is related to unskilled labor as four is related to two; in fact, no such relationship necessarily exists, for it is possible that one kind of labor might not compete at all with other kinds. Another problem is the distinction between productive and nonproductive labor. Marx assumed that bookkeepers and service workers were parasites on productive work; they did not add surplus value to goods. How then are we to account for wages and profits in commercial enterprise? Marx's answer was that these were obtained from the surplus value created in industry. Just how this was done was not clear, but there was the admission that from the "commercial capitalists'" viewpoint, bookkeepers are productive.

The fact is that the labor theory of value had a metaphysical rather than a genuinely economic base. Labor was divided into concrete and abstract labor; the latter supposedly represented the common quality of work *qua* work. While this was never defined precisely, it seemed to be the average of abstract labor embodied in a commodity that provided the standard of measure for value. But this approach simply ignored the question of effective demand. That is, Marx failed to take into account the fact that the value of a product, and therefore its price, depended in part on how many people could afford it and wanted it, and how strongly they wanted it as against competing products.

More specifically, the labor theory of value fails to measure changes in the prices of goods or in productivity, and it is impossible to fit empirical material into its framework. Output has risen over the years despite a reduction in man-hours, and even recourse to the famous "socially necessary labor time" phrase fails to rescue the theory, which is essentially unverifiable. We must conclude that the labor theory of value fails as an analytical tool. If it works at all, it can do so only under conditions of perfect competition and under the assumption that labor is the sole factor of production. The glaring unreality of such a premise is self-evident.

THEORY OF ECONOMIC DEVELOPMENT

Yet despite the labor theory of value, many parts of the Marxian economic corpus can still stand. It is a remarkable body of doctrine which incorporates numerous effective devices for explaining the internal drive of the capitalist economy and for sketching the long-range direction of its movement.

This characterization may be demonstrated more clearly when we leave behind the metaphysics in the early sections of *Das Kapital* and go on to the problem of circulation and accumulation of capital. These were perhaps the most spectacular parts of his doctrine, for they represented in a fundamental way a theory of economic development. This fact is underscored by the central theme—the social relationships that govern the use of capital. Since these were rooted in the wage system, capital as a relationship implied that the worker did not own the tools of production.

Such relationships underpinned the circulation and reproduction process. Technically, industries were divided into those supplying new means of production, those which provided workers with the means of subsistence, and those whose output consisted of luxury goods to satisfy the consumption of capitalists. The production of each was divisible into variable capital (wages), constant capital (that part of total capital used in production), and surplus value. In all three groups surplus value might be consumed or reinvested. If investment was the course to be followed, surplus value again became either variable or constant capital, in which case part of the output was to be exchanged against goods of the other sectors. For example, the capitalists' problem was to discover how the continuous reduction of labor requirements affected economic growth, accumulation, and the changing structure of capitalism. English history provided Marx with many striking illustrations for his analysis. The industrial revolution offered the first occasion where fixed rather than circulating capital was accumulated. Against this backdrop, wealth could be measured by buildings and machinery rather than by stocks of goods in warehouses. Heavy, fixed equipment became the hallmark of a new order, and accumulation was associated with an increasing proportion of constant capital in the total complex.

These dynamic changes demonstrated to Marx the need for a more complicated model of circulation. This he built in the "expanded reproduction" scheme which revealed how capital was augmented. We know that not all of the surplus value available to capitalists was consumed: some portion was invested for the express purpose of enlarging the total stock of capital. This implied the need to create more means of production than was necessary to replace used-up constant capital. More variable capital was also needed for the workers. The analysis of expanded reproduction then went on to depict the combinations and permutations that were possible between variable capital, constant capital, and surplus value. The latter was now distributed to additional variable capital, to more constant capital, and to ordinary consumption for the capitalist. But what happened was that the constant capital in the producer goods industries increased faster than the output of consumer goods, and the disproportion in the economic structure became more and more evident. Equilibrium could be maintained only if both the producer and consumer goods industries were able to expand jointly. According to Marx, this was quite unlikely.

Another way of looking at this question is to say that in the case of an ever-increasing stock of capital, investment can occur only when the market itself keeps expanding. If savings are less than what is required for ordinary investment, capital is apt to become scarce with pressure on resources as the likely result.

Of course, the situation is somewhat more complicated than this, since new capital might be unused or merely substituted for earlier, older capital.

In an expanding economy, productive capacity increases in consonance with income. The required ratio for stable economic growth is established when the rate of increase in capacity equals the rate of increase in income. But simple offsets to savings are not enough to maintain a "growing equilibrium," for in fact investment must always exceed saving. The economy must behave like an Einsteinian universe, constantly expanding at an accelerated rate. But should investment fail to meet these conditions, excess capacity would soon ensue, giving rise to deflationary conditions. It appears unlikely that a continual expansion is indefinitely sustainable.

Surplus value was for Marx the instrument of accumulation of capital resources, such as factories and machinery. It was the rate of saving out of surplus value that governed investment; the pace, however, was set by the competitive drive to defeat one's rivals in the marketplace. It is easy to understand why such a factor as the speed at which surplus value was extracted by the capitalist was viewed by Marx as important. Of course, this element was related to what is now called productivity, and for Marx it was the very element that swelled the available total of surplus value. Now, accumulation meant an increased demand for labor; but if the demand for labor in a dynamic capitalist order was increasing, how could one account for misery and unemployment? Here Marx dragged in the *deus ex machina* of the industrial reserve army, unemployed surplus labor, which presumably kept growing as the proportion of labor utilized in production declined. Wages in the long run were supposed to be determined by the size and effectiveness of the reserve army. Under the most favorable conditions, the increase in capital equipment might take place without changing the ratios of constant capital to the total used in production. That is, more capital could call forth more labor. If there were no such changes, then the division of the national income was not subject to "inexorable" processes, and it was possible for a society to decide how to distribute its income. In short, even the Marxian system could be an affluent one.

Under these conditions Marx admitted the possibility of a rise in the absolute level of wages. But he did suggest that the relative share would decline. For though real wages might rise, they were unlikely to rise proportionately with productivity. Yet modern experience has indicated a contrary trend, for the possibility of wages increasing in consonance with productivity has been demonstrated much too often to make the Marxian proposition a valid one. In many industries the drop in labor's share that might have been occasioned by technological change has been overcome by increases in productivity. Many economists have offered data to show that the share of wages in income moves in ways that Marx would not have thought possible—downward in an upswing and upward in a depression.

Another major argument in the Marxian system was related to the rate of profit. Here Marx looked to the structural organization of capitalism; that is, he did not stress the lack of sales or falling demand as the cause of profit decline, but pointed rather to increases in constant capital or what he called the rising organic composition of capital. It was really a matter of simple arithmetic: if the rate of surplus value was constant, then with an increasing ratio of capital to labor, the rate of profit was bound to fall. This was troublesome to the capitalist, for the more he invested, the lower his rate of profit. Only through more intense work, speed-up, or by depressing wages below the value of labor power could declining profit rates be halted.

But Marx seems to have some difficulty in relating the falling profit rate theme to accumulation, for it is obvious that the latter would soon grind to a halt with declining profit rates. Marxists have responded to this question by happily underscoring it as one of capitalism's "contradictions." If, however, the significant relationships had been redefined in a way that permitted a decline in constant capital while productivity was maintained, Marx would have discovered quite another aspect to the problem. The assumption underlying the declining rate of profit was an increasing ratio of constant to variable capital, so that the proportion of surplus value to the totality of constant plus variable capital always had to fall. This implied that the only conceivable technological improvements were labor saving in character. But if investment were of the capital-saving variety, a larger surplus value could be maintained at a constant or even larger proportion to the sum of constant and variable capitals. Such an experience has not been unknown in Western capitalism.

But an alternative way of calculating profit rates is possible: it would appear to be quite reasonable to relate profit to the sale of output and thus ultimately to effective demand. If the latter kept steady on a fairly even keel, then the rate of profit could be maintained without this "internal contradiction."

The values of Marx, nevertheless, may be seen in his emphasis upon technology and the central role of the capitalist. Investment and accumulation were at the heart of what he called capitalist motion. Yet stability could be attained only if economic growth was properly balanced between the producers' and consumers' sectors of the economy—an unlikely contingency by virtue of capitalism's essential nature. The relation of the accumulation or investment process to the distribution of income and mass consumption was clearly delineated.

MARX AND KEYNES

The gap between ordinary economic theory and Marxian theory always has seemed unbridgeable. Marx, who viewed capitalism as a passing phase in history, sought to expose its failings; ordinary doctrine insists that capitalism is solid and permanent. Marx said that interest and profits were merely divisions of exploitative spoils; some economists have called them rewards for astuteness and abstinence. Yet the modifications that John Maynard Keynes introduced into economics in 1936 revealed common roots with Marxism. Keynes showed that it was possible to discuss economic problems with labor as the major or even sole factor of production. He thought that capitalism, unless revived, would founder entirely, and, when it is said that the tragedy of investment is that it leads to crises that are themselves useful, one comes dangerously close to the Marxian conception. In fact, with but a few shifts in definition and some alteration in variables, it is possible to bring Marxian theory quite close to Keynes. For example, the concept of the declining rate of profit may be seen as a manifestation of the declining marginal efficiency of capital, a central concept in Keynes.

Perhaps the closest affinity in the two systems is to be found in the theory of capitalist circulation. The Keynesian version saw breakdown caused by variations in the inducement to invest. Since the latter depended on profits, the actual limit to investment ultimately became the saving-consumption relation. In Marx, it was the rate of saving out of surplus value that governed investment: the pace was set by the competitive urge to beat down all rivals. And, while effective demand as a consideration in determining investment patterns did not enter the Marxian system at all, unemployment and crises were due basically to an insufficiency of accumulation. In Marx, the depression had to await further acquisition of capital before renewed activity could take place.

It can be argued that such a comparison would demonstrate only formal similarities. For whereas Marxians insist that the variables employed in their economic theorizing are implicit in the system itself, Keynes's basic elements are derived from noneconomic psychological factors. Yet it is extraordinary that, despite an antipathetic outlook, Keynes was able to develop a vision of capitalism the mechanics of which approximated Marx's. When Marx spoke of the excess of surplus value over capitalists' consumption as being limited by the expenditure for new producers' goods and foreign investment, he did approach the Keynesian view.

That is to say, in neither system were automatic adjustments a reality. For both, productive techniques were quite significant: to Keynes, long-run investment decisions depended on productivity, a notion not entirely alien to Marx. Both also recognized that the contradiction, to employ the Marxian term, between consumption and production lay at the root of economic crises. Consumption was limited by the kind of income distribution a society developed. This restricted profitability and investment. Counterbalancing factors were the growth of new industries and the compulsion to expand outwardly.

But Marx wanted to go beyond the technical economic variables to what he conceived to be underlying social relations. Searching for the forces that led to the creation of value, he was compelled to conclude that the crucial relationships could be expressed quantitatively through commodity exchange and social ties created by capitalism.

THE SOVIET EXPERIENCE

As might have been anticipated, the Soviet Union has attempted through the years to employ Marxian economics as a model for its system. The effort was bound to fail, for the allocation of scarce resources, even there, demanded a logic that could not be met by Marxist theory. For example, interest charges as a method for pricing capital equipment was a bourgeois prejudice which had no place in a socialist system. Yet, though the state might give enterprises their capital, the supply was not limitless, and even if decisions on allocations were politically motivated, account had to be taken of a certain measure of scarcity. In actuality, interest can be used to guide capital allocation, and as such is a measure of availability.

Furthermore, the Soviets had to make decisions on specific projects and the kind of resources that would be absorbed. While this appeared to be solely an engineering question, it nevertheless had its economic aspects, particularly insofar as it was necessary to decide on the relative share of capital to be applied to a given project.

Russian debate over these matters, beginning in the 1930's, revolved around the problem of efficient capital investment. Some "revisionist" economists thought the guide to decision-making in this area should be similar to "profitability," while the more traditional "Stalinists" rejected all objective cost considerations, for only the planners' wishes counted. Those who argued for "profitability" said that it could be an effective guide to investment. Moreover, they insisted, a relatively simple index was available by relating the ratio of plant profit to invested funds. But the "abolition" of the interest rate, which took place in the 1930's, made capital in effect a free good and led to useless and costly capital intensive projects. Allocation of resources was directed by the planners, who followed the dictates of political leaders. In the late 1930's, most of the participants in the debate disappeared in the purges and the arguments ceased.

But the problem of efficiency and resource allocation still could not be wiped out of existence, and engineers simply selected the technological "mix" which would yield the lowest operating cost. Russian economists again began to flirt with notions dangerously similar to Western ideas. Planners began to discuss "minimum recoupment periods" which would provide additional capital only if savings in current cost allowed them to recapture the added outlay in a given number of years. If this could be interpreted as the ratio of savings to additional capital, then there was in effect a rate of interest. A. L. Luria, a well-known Soviet economist, developed a theory of investment choice in which he discussed the effects of interest rates on the ability of added capital units to "substitute" for future operating costs, virtually arguing that capital should be efficiently allocated.

Some Soviet economists were concerned with working out time rates for the use of capital and raw materials. This analysis could be reduced to the proposition that in weighing alternatives it was necessary to compare the effectiveness of investment in terms of their effects on future output. This again raised the question of interest charges, something the Soviets had officially dismissed as of no significance. "Revisionist" economists suggested that a "compensatory fund" be accumulated as a device for financing new investment, a category dangerously close to interest. They felt that such a formulation would make it possible to evaluate capital investment on the basis of its future annual additions to income as compared with the "interest" charge incurred. In effect, more critical Soviet economists were beginning to bring Western economic ideas into play. They were beginning to struggle with the theoretical problems of investment and were even trying to work outside the closed system imposed by official notions.

Articles appeared on obsolescence, hitherto a contemptible bourgeois notion; criticism of the turnover tax was made; a debate on costs and productivity in agriculture was staged; and the barest beginnings of a critical examination of value and pricing were discernible. In 1958, a huge forward step was taken when the Institute of Economics recommended the use of "recoupment periods" in investment planning. This signalled a virtual restoration of interest in Soviet economic thinking.

The fact that incorrect economic notions have been endemic to Soviet industry has unquestionably resulted in immense waste. The Soviet price system has not fulfilled the job of effectively allocating resources; the entire stress has been on huge projects employing a lot of capital, with the economy wrenched and distorted out of balance. This has not escaped Soviet economists willing to face the difficult facts. Western concepts and techniques in economic thinking have suggested ways of dealing with these problems, and as Wassily Leontief, a Harvard University economist, reported several years ago, there has been some attempt to utilize once-forbidden methods. The Russians even moved to take an inventory of industrial resources for the first time in thirty-four years, which was to include not only an enumeration of facilities, tools, and supplies but which would also list these in terms of cost and price. All this has clearly reflected a new, searching inquiry into the Soviet price system.

Furthermore, a serious effort has been made to employ mathematics in Soviet economic calculations. Hitherto, the use of mathematics in economics was considered an anti-Marxist sin. Leontief reported an awakened interest in input-output analysis and linear programming, mathematical techniques widely used in the West and equally applicable to economic planning. Such techniques make it possible to describe the operations of the whole economy with a series of equations which relate the output of industries to the resources required to produce that output. Every element going into a product can be identified, located, and evaluated, and every output similarly analyzed. L. V. Kantorovich, the Soviet discoverer of linear programming, courageously castigated his colleagues for failing to apply mathematical techniques to economic planning. He argued that officially decreed prices were misleading and charged that Marxian notions were useless in calculating the effectiveness of capital investments. His attack signaled a demand that Soviet planners should use all kinds of techniques in their thinking, including those that bourgeois economists were making available.

Recent Soviet policy aims at replacing at least some aspects of centralized planning by decentralized decision-making. The idea is to offer the factory manager financial incentives to increase his factory's efficiency. Yugoslavia has gone so far as to abolish industry-wide production targets along with the once all-powerful central planning commission. Of course, such trends have been far less drastic in other East European countries.

In any case, the long-term trend in the Soviet Union appears to be toward a form of "market socialism," under which land and factories will be owned by the state, as at present, but prices and production will be controlled by market forces. Enterprises will compete with each other and with foreign firms. Under such circumstances it is evident that standards of ability and efficiency will come to the fore. Nevertheless, it remains to be seen how much the stranglehold of central planners will be loosened. If the new economic reforms, known as "Libermanism," after the Soviet professor who formulated the basic notions, really take hold, the consequence will be more managerial responsibility and more decision-making power in the plants. Under Libermanism, managers are supposed to decide on what to produce, while rewards are to be based on what is sold, not on whether a production quota set by a central planner is met.

For too long, Soviet factory managers were under pressure from above to meet predetermined production goals rather than to satisfy the needs of the Soviet consumer. Today, however, the ideas of Western economists and Soviet "revisionists" are having a serious impact on Soviet and East European economic thinking. There appears to be a significant shift away from Marxist dogma and command planning to a more flexible and rational approach to economic policy. And in this shift, Western "bourgeois" thought has proved to be more useful than Marxian economic doctrine.

1967

On the Road to Socialism

All through history whenever men have found their lives circumscribed by petty meanness and hardship they have dreamed of places where lions and lambs lie down together. This was so when Plato scorned the rabble of Athens for the kingdom of the philosophers, when the brothers Gracchi gave land to the plebes, when Winstanley and his Diggers naively appealed to Cromwell, when Karl Marx unveiled his wrathful apocalypse for the barons of capitalism. Through all these expressions of alienation and revolt there ran the deep thread of escape from an oppressive now into an ordered future which would provide a home for the displaced individual soul.

This, in essence, is the appeal that socialism, whatever its particular shape at the moment might be, has exhibited in Western society. It is seldom realized how effective a force the chiliastic element is in the socialist dream, nor is it known too well that this millennarianism was one of the major sources of the American socialist's enthusiasm. This point is sharply underscored in the symposium *Socialism and American Life* (1952), which, as part of the Program in American Civilization at Princeton University, is now clearly the definitive study of socialism in our time. It cannot be said too emphatically that the contributors, who include among others Daniel Bell, George W. Hartmann, Will Herberg, Sidney Hook, Harry W. Laidler, and Willard Thorp, have done their work brilliantly.

In the early days of modern civilization, when men first began to think seriously of communal living as a new way of getting on with each other, the search for socialism represented a form of atavism. Medieval society had been basically communal: open field tillage and fiefdom emphasized social *structure* in a system where the individual did not win but was assigned a permanent place. This was a paternalism for which the family was clearly the paradigm, one in which the community was supreme and the individual an anonymity. There was no need to seek protective symbols, for like omniscient parents these were part of the social fabric.

However, within the interstices of this placid society there developed a radical element, an economic individualism whose classic political expression is to be found in the Florentine Machiavelli. Private property was defined more rigidly by John Locke and Adam Smith, and economic activity no longer sought to sustain some minimum level of consumption but to expand and burgeon with profit. Companies and partnerships grew and spread outward encircling the globe in a search for materials and customers. The hero in this adventurous thrust of Western man into unknown regions was the capitalist entrepreneur. Rejected by the closed society of medievalism, he patiently and unremittingly carved for himself a new world with new horizons and new gods. He was a revolutionist without theory.

In this economic and political unheaval, the displaced who sought refuge in such projects as Sir Thomas More's *Utopia* were protesting against that revolution. They were turning their faces to the past and were seeking a world sundered beyond repair. This, as Professor E. H. Harbison says in his contribution to the symposium (Chapter 1, "Socialism in European History to 1848"), characterized much of pre-Marxian socialist thinking. It would not be historically incorrect to say that the Utopians were reactionary.

Ironically, the victory of the individualist spirit occurred at a time when the technologies engendered by the Industrial Revolution turned upon individualism and eventually destroyed it. As Karl Polanyi once said, men could not tolerate subjection to the free market; they rebelled against being converted into a commodity and sought a way that would bring paradise on earth in the midst of the bewildering and often misunderstood industrialism.

It is in this context that the sometimes ludicrous, frequently unhappy experiences of the early American utopian settlements must be viewed. Hundreds of religious communist groups sprang up in the nineteenth century, many of them drawing spiritual sustenance from German pietistic sects. They wanted personal salvation by withdrawing from worldly affairs to seek communication with God. Communal life was necessary for survival; led by fanatical, charismatic personalities, they devoutly prepared themselves for the millennium. Since wickedness was of the flesh, they practiced celibacy (except for the Mormons and the Oneida Perfectionists, whose theology justified an opposite attitude), and, with their economies rooted in a kind of local autarky, they sought salvation on their own terms. This was the experience of the Ephrata community in Pennsylvania, the Amana villages of Iowa, and the Rappites.

Some of the longest lived of these pietistic colonies were those of the Shakers, who drew their inspiration from a belief in spiritualism as well as from the revivalist movement and Quakerism. Most of those who accepted the Shaker theology were native Anglo-Saxons who brought to it a powerful Calvinist heritage. Despite the hostility that their peculiar religious dogmas aroused, they were able to win tolerance by their remarkable business acumen. Their theology fulfilled the spiritual needs of those who sought surcease from sin by enforcing a tough ethic of self-denial. Since perfection was a rational problem, said the Shakers, it should be a way of life which would overcome the perpetual relapse into sin. As Stow Persons remarks in his article (Chapter 4, "Christian Communitarianism in America"), it was this search for a practical perfection that drove the Shakers into communitarian socialism.

In contrast to the Shaker communities, the Mormons were unable to overcome the surrounding antagonisms even though their astute combination of individualism and communalism permitted them to practice the capitalist ethic with impunity. It was not enough that polygamy called forth the hatred of others, but in addition, the wealth they created drew to their oasis in the desert "gentile" parasites who would pollute the faith. When Brigham Young established for the second time in Mormon history a communal order, he was clearly motivated by a desire to withstand the pressures of an outside world. Yet Mormon communism was entirely voluntary and those who gave their property to the church were returned as much as they might be able to handle for their own and for the community good.

The most outstanding example of religious communism was the Oneida Community, whose leaders discovered in the doctrine of salvation a spiritual and physical perfectionism that was employed to rationalize a whole set of irregular practices. Engaging in sexual behavior as distasteful to the outside multitude as that of the Mormons, they too were forced to set up isolated settlements. Their type of mixed marriage, which advocated sexual intercourse without regard to formal legal ties on the ground that this symbolized a spiritual liaison, was not, however, an unregulated promiscuity. Constantly supervised, the children of such unions were a charge on the community. Despite the hostility of its contemporaries, the Oneida group was able to sustain itself for a long period of time more successfully than other communitarians because it made a particular effort to meet the economic demands of an industrial civilization. Today, while it no longer remains as a special mode of communal life, it continues a vigorous existence as a manufacturing enterprise. *139461*

Yet none of these communities could possibly succeed, for they were essentially little more than embodiments of a doctrine of personal salvation that sought to build the next world by altering this world's social and economic institutions. Under the impact of a ruthless industrialism they soon degenerated into ecstatic expressions of conversion. Nevertheless, they did encompass the socialist solution for man's ills, for they not only wanted moral and physical perfection, but they wanted this in a collectivity. This implies an acceptance of the notion of man's perfectibility and an urge to overcome the corrupting influence of material things. They insisted also that the struggle to achieve a "socialist" victory must engage the common efforts of the entire group. But it is this conception that American democracy rejected, for the American believes that the individual personality rather than abstract forces is central in history. The universe, says he, is indifferent to the fate of human beings and what must be done to improve man's lot on earth must be carried through by unflagging individual enterprise.

Among the many who sought a new world in those days were persons who rejected both rugged individualism and the chiliastic reaction of the religious utopians. They preferred communal experiments which would be prototypes of a new civilization without supernatural trappings. These were the secularists like Robert Owen and Charles Fourier, who combined in amazing ways hardheaded analyses of society's ailments with naive and frequently fantastic schemes for the reconstruction of human behavior. Owen believed in a system of general education that could with ease mold character through proper environment. This, he thought, was the way to fashion correct attitudes of cooperation and mutual respect. Yet for all his highly successful factory experience in England, his American colonies paid amazingly little attention to matters of economics. A philanthropist disdained by his fellow capitalists, Owen was compelled to take the side of the workers. Like Cabet and Fourier, he was basically a liberal whose philosophy of communal life could be easily accommodated to the American scene. The secular utopians believed in reason as an instrument for the discovery of reality: free speech, free press, and unhampered assembly were fundamental requirements for the successful conduct of community life. There must be a free choice of occupations, they said, and the rights of women and children must be vouchsafed. They were, in the last analysis, libertarians, and, in this sense, they were strongly anti-state.

Perhaps this explains why later socialists, especially the Marxians, opposed the secularist solution. The Marxist is almost invariably an authoritarian to whom the kind of exploratory casualness implicit in the libertarian approach is a violation of historical order. History, he avers, has a precise pattern which is revealed to the true believer only by dialectics. Primitive communism was the Marxian Garden of Eden, and the Fall of man was brought about by the creation of a surplus of goods over which men were bound to fight. The class struggle is Providence, the proletariat is the Chosen People, and Soviet Russia is the Kingdom of God. These notions are the essence of modern "scientific" socialism, which, despite the disclaimers of its devotees, is as much founded on faith as is any eschatology.

In economics, Marx made what is perhaps his most unique contribution. However, Paul M. Sweezy's discussion of Marxian economics in these volumes (Chapter 9, "The Influence of Marxian Economics on American Thought and Practice") is not merely inadequate but heavily biased. Sweezy, as is well known, is considered by many to be the outstanding Marxian economist in this country, but he accepts official doctrine in a shockingly uncritical manner. Marxian economics, it is true, possesses a macroscopic quality that contrasts sharply with standard theory. The view of reality obtained from the latter is as though we were looking through the small end of a telescope. It has an inescapable microscopic quality: the crucial problems are those of atomistic business units which passively react to economic activity rather than participate in it. Marx repudiated this type of analysis and sought the key to an understanding of men in their relationship to each other. He constructed a grand but rough body of doctrine that would permit us to grasp broad sweeps of reality: the crucial problems encompassed whole systems of economy.

Yet this theoretical structure is built on sand. At the very beginning, Marx employs the preposterous notion that specific skills are not essential for theoretical analysis because skilled labor may be easily compared to unskilled labor by viewing both in a single line of work. This comparison can be made because of the supposed existence of abstract labor through which concrete labor is transformed into a social aggregate. The notion of abstract labor is the key to an understanding of the labor theory of value, which is the cardinal principle in Marxian economics. But no empirical evidence has ever been offered to sustain the validity of the idea of abstract labor. In fact, Marx himself evaded the issue. It is one of those axioms that must be accepted entirely on faith; this is the foundation that supports the labor theory of value and the main body of Marxian economics.

Marxian value theory leads directly to surplus value—to the theory of exploitation. The concept of the surplus has long fascinated men because it promises a solution to all the pressing moral, social, political, and economic problems of the day. Its all-embracing character made it attractively facile. Yet its very generality makes it dubious as a method for solving economic problems, for complications may be easily ignored. These arise when an attempt is made to translate value into price terms, something that no Marxian economist has yet been able to do in a logically satisfying way. Joan Robinson, the noted British economist, was quite right when she remarked several years ago that ". . . no point of substance in Marx's argument depends on the labor theory of value."

Whatever substance there may be in Marx's economics is in his theory of effective demand, his theory of crisis and in his concept of the flow of income from one sector of the economy to the others. All of the rest is in essence a kind of theology. The struggle to establish this systematic socialist theology in the United States has its roots in the early history of the Socialist Labor party. Not only was this the first workingman's political body of any significance in this country, but it brought forth, in Daniel De Leon, one of the major theoreticians of the socialist movement. But, as seems typical of all Marxist parties, factionalism and splits characterized its entire history. There is no need here to specify the details of this story: Daniel Bell, a *Fortune* editor, relates in the longest and, in many ways, the most valuable article in the symposium (Chapter 6, "Marxian Socialism in the United States") the fascinating evolution and sorry collapse of socialism in America.

What we are mainly concerned with here is the seemingly inexplicable attraction that Marxism exerted, particularly on the intellectual. During the nineteenth and early twentieth centuries, Europe's rejected intellectuals and workers escaped in large numbers to this continent and many brought with them an old-world allegiance to socialist ideals. Arriving here they often found themselves subjected to an unexpected exploitation which had the effect of regenerating rebellious sentiments. There was created anew the desire to overcome frustration, and despite the predisposition toward a gradualist philosophy that many socialists evinced, there were numerous others who not only advocated a more radical attack but insisted that the working masses must be led by a professional vanguard to bring on the Marxian millennium.

There is no doubt that Marxism, insofar as it exhibited the aspects of a mass movement, made room for the dispossessed of modern society. And insofar as the intellectual was alienated from the environment that spawned him, he found himself drawn to such mass movements. What was wanted was change, any kind of change, so long as it was rapid and even violent. Sacrifice, the need for a new life, and, as Hannah Arendt has said, the fascination with self-effacement became the lodestones of the estranged.

Among the most alienated is the writer. As Joseph Schumpeter once said, he who had the power of the spoken and written word, and yet had no direct responsibility for practical affairs, soon discovered that capitalism did not utilize his talents. There ensued a sharpened sensibility to materialistic pursuits and a loss of belief in whatever values were symbolized by the word "America." Willard Thorp shows in his essay (Chapter 13, "American Writers on the Left") that this was a characteristic reaction of such writers as Edward Bellamy and William Dean Howells. A tradition of the socialist novel in America began to be formed, and from Howells on there ran a clear thread through Jack London, the utopian fiction of the 1880's and 1890's, and Upton Sinclair, down to the *Studs Lonigan* of James T. Farrell.

The most influential literary force during these years was the perceptible leftward movement of writers and artists. They had reacted against the vigilantism of the Palmer raids after World War I, the corruption of the Harding regime, the legal murder of Sacco and Vanzetti, the stock market collapse of 1929, and the rise of fascism in Europe. The most disturbing event, however, was the October revolution in Russia. For some writers, such as John Reed, this was the birth of the City of God; for others, such as Max Eastman, there was a quick revulsion against the inhuman excesses of the Soviet state. Eastman, and many others who followed him, could not accept being placed into uniform and told that artistic creation must advance the cause of the party. For rejecting this class aesthetic, verbal slop was poured over the head of the helpless writer. He was accused of being a formalist, a sectarian, a Trotskyite wrecker, a literary gangster. Not many writers who were concerned with their own integrity could stay for long in such a climate. Yet the Communist party in this country has never ceased its efforts to gather the intellectual into its fold, as witness the prewar Writers' Congress and the postwar cultural conventions.

The Communists could continue this because Marxism provided the intellectual with a specific function; for now direct action and the drive toward revolt could be verbalized. An all-inclusive ideological system was constructed which explained the nature of society, the flow of history, and the formation of personality. Sidney Hook demonstrates (Chapter 8, "The Philosophical Basis of Marxian Socialism in the United States") that so-called scientific socialism came up with a number of propositions that were very attractive. A seemingly naturalistic social theory made new advances in science welcome and, with man defined as a "rational, symbol-using, and instrument-making animal," morality became a culturally determined aspect of behavior. Neither goodness nor evil was considered to be an innate property of humanity.

But the historical materialism which became their methodological byword blinded Marxists to the possibilities of evil under socialism. Since human nature develops only in consonance with the growth of culture, they argued, mankind must always move upward to higher Hegelian levels. Anything that furthers the attainment of such a goal is by the very nature of the dialectical process moral. Furthermore, this mystic dialectic permits its user to anticipate historical situations and to confidently predict their outcome. Ironically, the implicit optimism in this imperative obscured its quality of absolute determinism. It is this that explains much of the insufferable dogmatism of the Marxist. It also explains his fanatical morale, his haste to demand and to render self-sacrifice, his perpetual passion to become a molder of history. It is, as Hook remarks, a rationalization of intellectual terror which needed only political power to achieve the destruction of the human mind.

To this there is opposed, in this country at least, a pragmatic attitude toward historical progress. Americans, of course, have been attracted from time to time to self-centered teleological systems, as witness the ideology of the Puritans. In the main, however, they have been concerned with what takes place in history rather than with the impersonal forces that motivate events. Says David F. Bowers (Chapter 7, "American Socialism and the Socialist Philosophy of History"): ". . . the chief figure in history is man . . . the universe is neither prevailingly hostile nor prevailingly favorable to human history [and] in any case man has the power (provided he uses it intelligently and imaginatively) to improve his fortunes and lot on earth continuously." Thus, while man can control his fate, there is no ultimate goal beyond the horizon toward which he is inexorably driven. In the hands of America's instrumentalist philosophers this attitude was utilized to emphasize individual intelligence and self-reliance while rejecting the collectivist solution. There is in this approach an expressed preference for experimentation, a statement of generalizations in but tentative form, and a highly flexible conception of knowledge as an instrument for the solution of present day problems.

A good deal of this has filtered into the American socialist's credo (as distinguished from the communist, who by now should be acknowledged as only an agent of a foreign power). Yet socialism as a political force has failed in the United States. Part of that failure may be attributed to the socialists' lack of awareness of the ability of political power to destroy. The class angle that was attached to history made angels of proletarians and their putative leaders. The latter, said the socialist, could serve only mankind; it was inconceivable that the urge to exercise power might impel a leader to serve no one but himself. In economics, the socialist became so enamored of sheer size that he overlooked the frightening totalitarian potential inherent in large organizations. Afflicted with a remarkable political naiveté, he saw reflected in all revolutionaries his own integrity; when he met up with the new radical devotees of the Leninist dictatorship his entire élan was so deflated that he could no longer conceive of democracy in revolution. It was something of a shock to have to acknowledge that democratic political procedures might still possess value; it was something of a relief to discover again the ancient truth that revolutions devour their own children.

Revolution and violence are no strangers to the American tradition. John Locke had defended the right to revolt and from the Declaration of Independence to the Emancipation Proclamation a goodly number of our political philosophers agreed with Jefferson's comment about periodically watering the tree of liberty with tyrants' blood. But with the rise of industrialism after the Civil War, the sanctity and stability of economic processes became supreme; revolutionary remarks were no longer appropriate in polite society and the American middle class settled down to the relentless life of accumulating a glittering industrial enterprise. Only underground, amongst the masses of the dispossessed, did there continue a rumble of talk about the seizure of power under capitalism.

To socialists, the revolution was merely the point in history at which they acquired for all time control of the economic system. Some, like De Leon and the German revisionists, thought that constitutional changes through the ballot box would become the major instrumentality for victory, particularly in such advanced countries as England and the United States. Others, like the communitarians, who were deeply concerned with the effect that the employment of certain means has on the ends in view, preferred moral suasion. The communitarians, many of them sincere pacifists, were utterly incapable of thinking in violent terms. Not so the anarchists and the communists, who urged direct action as the means for attaining the good life. This attitude was bound to evoke the sharpest hostility from the rest of society— as witness the Haymarket affair. Most socialists, however, wisely abjure the uses of terror. They prefer parliamentary procedures, though a suspicion was generated after the debacle of the Spanish republic that the defeated capitalists would not readily accept socialist reconstruction. Neither history nor socialist doctrine, however, have provided answers to the question of handling such recalcitrant situations.

The goal of all socialists has been the creation of the classless society where men would no longer be divided. The conquest of nature, the eradication of poverty, and the final attainment of security would create true conditions of liberty. That this would impel radical psychological and social changes is not denied. It would be all to the good, urged the socialists, for production, distribution and administration would be reduced to a series of electronic impulses, freeing man from all the bonds of the ages. But what the socialists were unwilling to acknowledge is that this dream, like that of the millennarians, is utopian. It is a vague and unspecified goal, which, subject neither to verification nor to disproof, provides a comforting refuge whenever immediate political objectives are rebuffed. In the Soviet Union, the classless society is an even more monstrous myth. With it, the egalitarian ideals of early socialism have been perverted, the dictates of the party justified, the rapacious demands of a secret police fulfilled. All that remains of the classless society is a threadbare slogan, not even useful in political campaigns.

The disintegration of the ideal of classlessness exemplifies what has happened to socialism. The difficulty lies in the approximate fulfillment in our own time of whatever aspirations are expressed in the socialist ideology. Orthodox Marxism assumes that so advanced an economy as ours should generate a high level of class consciousness, as in Germany prior to the first World War. But the American promise itself has become a kind of socialism, and whenever our economy functions reasonably well, as at present, even the one-time radical intellectual becomes conservative. The classless ideal is displaced by the unbounded opportunity of America while communism's mythical cornucopia is dissipated by the reality of mass production. To repeat Werner Sombart's phrase (quoted by Mr. Bell): "On the reefs of roast beef and apple pie, socialistic Utopias of every sort are sent to their doom."

In the past, the American worker has always thought of himself as a kind of businessman. To take advantage of his opportunities, to develop a special skill—this allowed him to command a higher price from his employer. If necessary, he could combine with his fellow workingmen in that peculiar American contribution to trade unionism, the craft local. Aside from such matters as wages and hours, he did not look upon his boss as a hated enemy. This was true even of the larger industrial unions which grew out of the economic strife of the 1930's. In fact, there was little in the American scene to create a genuine socialist mass movement. Socialism was always somewhere on the periphery of America.

Daniel Bell suggests that this was because of socialism's inept adaptation to the political requirements of a capitalist society. To become a politician seemed to violate the ethic of socialism; this, it was thought, could be avoided only on local levels, as in Reading, Milwaukee, and Bridgeport. Beyond that, there was either a thoroughgoing rejection of society, as with the chiliasts, or an active subversion within society, as with the communists. Yet to be successful, socialists were required to make some compromise that would fuse their morality with capitalist politics. However, again and again, with Debs and Hillquit and Thomas, socialists avoided facing up to crucial political issues. This was true, for example, when the Spanish workers asked for arms to beat back Franco, when the New Deal initiated legislative reforms, and when Hitler sent his Reichswehr across the European continent. This political infantilism effectively isolated socialists from the mainstream of American politics, which, as Bell reminds us, was becoming a chessboard for power blocs. With trade union officials and industrial captains sitting on government commissions, there was an increasing tendency for the state not only to mediate in economic matters, but to dictate what actions it believed necessary for its own preservation.

In this atmosphere socialists began to urge a "third force," a notion that rejects the dominant ideologies of both communism and capitalism. While this is an educational, not a political factor, and while it does not exhibit the quality of compulsion and drive demonstrated in earlier left-wing movements, it does nevertheless insist that capitalism still has inherent weaknesses as yet unresolved. But it assumes that the correction of these evils must not be achieved at the expense of the individual personality. Its basic philosophic conception is a recognition of continuous change together with a denial of any Hegelian law of progress. It suggests that political factors may have greater relevance for the present world situation than economic ones. It is, of course, entirely committed to democratic methods in politics and, while it deprecates force in international affairs, it recognizes that democracy must defend itself. As Sidney Hook shows, this approach combines pragmatism with the more useful insights of Marxism in an effort to ". . . realize the highest traditions of American democracy." If there is any future for socialism in America, we must agree with Professor Hook that it is these ideas that will embody its basic philosophy.

1952

On the Question of Operationalism

I

It is now a cliché, and no longer an accurate one at that, to describe Paul A. Samuelson as the *Wunderkind* of American economics. It is not accurate because Samuelson is now past the half-century mark; yet he has been producing professional papers and articles as well as popular columns for sundry newspapers here and abroad (not to speak of the frequent revisions of his introductory text) in such profusion that we are apt to think of him as an elder statesman. But when the time sequence is placed into proper focus one must concede that the Samuelson corpus * represents an extraordinarily sustained performance. Although Samuelson does not discount "late bloomers" in economics (*vide* his article on Abba Lerner as a case in point [13]), Samuelson

* *The Collected Scientific Papers of Paul A. Samuelson.* Edited by Joseph E. Stiglitz, Cambridge, Mass., The M.I.T. Press, 1966, 2 vols.

himself illustrates the Schumpeterian dictum—a preanalytic vision of the economic process developed early in life and then carried through in an endless relation of give-and-take between empirical and theoretical work. For Samuelson this has meant the creation of a "grand neoclassical synthesis" combining modern national income analysis with the classical verities enunciated by the founding fathers.

This central view pervades the present collection of papers, whose 1,813 pages of text span the years 1937 to 1964. Its two large volumes, containing 129 articles, comments, lectures, and statements, include virtually all of Samuelson's contribution to modern economic theory, except, of course, the *Foundations of Economic Analysis* and *Linear Programming and Economic Analysis* (the latter authored jointly with Robert Dorfman and Robert Solow). One finds here the well-known articles on revealed preference, the transfer problem, factor price equalization, the pure theory of public expenditure, and the essays on Ricardian and Marxian economics. Included also are some fifteen pieces on purely mathematical topics, as well as the famous discussions of the multiplier, acceleration principle, and income determination. Some articles are published for the first time, known up to now to only an inner circle who were privileged to read them in manuscript; others have been resurrected from generally inaccessible books of essays, dedicated to professors on the verge of retirement, and from other obscure places. The latter include items on the constancy of the marginal utility of income; market mechanisms and maximization; the evaluation of real national income; probability and attempts to measure utility; a neoclassical reformulation of modern fiscal policy rules and principles; substitutability in open Leontief models; linear programming and economic theory; recent monetary controversies; intertemporal price equilibrium; the structure of a minimum equilibrium system; the 1961 Stamp Memorial lecture; a memorandum for the Canadian Royal Commission on Banking and Finance; and the 1962 Wicksell lectures. It is all quite a heady feast.

The task of putting the papers together was undertaken by Joseph Stiglitz, a graduate student, who has done a commendable job of organization. Several of the articles have postscripts redefining Samuelson's present position on the question at issue. Others are essentially predecessors of the *Foundations* or *Linear*

Programming. (Curiously, two articles from *Econometrica,* published in 1941 and 1942, which were later incorporated in the *Foundations,* are also reprinted. One might ask whether the editor did not really gild the lily at this point!) The arrangement, which is topical rather than chronological, provides for five "books": (1) pure theory: consumer's behavior and capital theory (including the papers on Ricardo and Marx); (2) mathematical economics, linear programming, comparative statics and dynamics, and equilibrium systems; (3) trade, welfare economics, and income determination; (4) the theory of public expenditures, fiscal and monetary policy, and political philosophy; and (5) doctrinal history and methodology. Merely listing the categories is sufficient to underscore the broad scope and depth of the Samuelson *opera.* These in many ways represent the essence of contemporary economics; their significance stems not only from the mirror image they present of what has gone on in economics from 1937 to 1964, but also from the enormous impact that Samuelson has had on the way in which economists now think.

II

It would be only fair to indicate my own biases, which are those of an institutionalist who, contrary to popular opinion on institutionalists, happens to have a rather high regard for theory. (After Keynes, who would dare denigrate theory?) But as I have indicated elsewhere, model building as a mode of theorizing needs to provide insights into economics as a *social* science, thereby providing materials for a more general theory of human behavior. I assume that goods and services are not only commodities and performances, but are significantly related to the human actors who control them, and that the relationships between such actors are also economic. Yet such relationships may be infused and even dominated by other, noneconomic considerations, so that rationality and self-interest are not always the prime movers in human behavior. In fact, the noneconomic may provide parameters for the economic; insofar as this may be the case, many of the models of the economist need rather broad amplification.

I further feel strongly that a theory needs to be viewed not only in its own terms, but functionally as well, that it is the responsibility of a commentator to uncover the meaning of a theory for the particular time to which it relates. This is perhaps the most difficult task of all, and particularly so for an approach that has been developed during one's own lifetime. Nevertheless, such criteria, I think, must be applied to Samuelson's total contribution, which is doubtless an important milestone in the intellectual history of economics. Lasting judgments at such close range may be impossible to make, but since I feel that his work will be pondered by students of economics long after most of us are gone, it seems useful to try. Let us then start at the beginning.

The notion of revealed preference was an early Samuelson contribution that is finally being enshrined in the textbooks. (When this occurs danger signals ought to be raised, for often the original idea is then emptied of all subtlety, a fate suffered by many a major economist.) An evaluation of revealed preference at this juncture, however, requires an estimation of Samuelson's methodological approach, a task we shall attempt below. Obviously, any theory of consumer behavior is intended to provide foundations for the law of demand, and in addition, the more sophisticated versions, such as Samuelson's, seek to establish underpinnings for the logic of index numbers. In older formulations the specified utility function, with price given, defined utility as a function of the quantities purchased, so that a continuous, smooth curve was derived. From this one could construct indifference curves and explicate the nature of substitution and income effects. All this is now well known from the work of such writers as Slutsky and Hicks [8] [9] [14]. Stated as simply as possible, Slutsky, for example, held that the lower the price of a good relative to another, the more attractive it would be to a consumer. The ensuing substitution effect would lead to a negative slope in the demand curve of the affected good. But with a lower price, purchasing power was enhanced, leading to an income effect which could cause a shift in the choice of commodities. That is, substitution and income effects were interrelated.

The roots of this rather refined approach may be traced to the nineteenth-century marginalists Jules Dupuit and Heinrich Gossen [16]. Further contributions were made by Edgeworth while others drew refinements from the work of D. Bernoulli as well as the psychologists Weber and Fechner, who thought that a unit of sensation (utility?) was proportional to the original stimulus. So far as the economists were concerned, all this was an attempt to define the shape of the consumer's utility curve. By Slutsky's time, at about World War I, it was evident that Occam's Razor was to be ruthlessly applied: a theory of consumer's behavior was to be evolved that would be free and independent of psychological lumber. The thrust was toward a general theory, but one that would presumably accord with reality.

Yet the ensuing explanation of consumer behavior remained troublesome. While generality might be supplied by the notions of continuity and smoothness (i.e., infinitely large numbers of combinations of goods were posited along the utility curve with continuous first and second order partial derivatives), the argument nevertheless failed to establish a congruence with reality. It was at this point that Samuelson's revealed preference hypothesis seemed to come to the rescue, for if the observed behavior of the consumer fulfilled the basic Samuelson premises then it would still be possible to derive indifference curves and a demand function. The postulates were that a consumer would buy more of a good if such an action would not affect the amount of other goods he could obtain, and that his choices were consistent as well as transitive. In essence, Samuelson introduced the notion of finite differences so that the observing economist was not required to work with instantaneous rates of change.

The theory seemed persuasive enough, except that it assumed a constancy of buying experience that did not appear to accord with the notion of "congruence with reality." Moreover, if the "observed" consumer were an ideal type or representative man, then the extremes of behavior to be found in such an implicit distribution of actors might very well, by their eccentricities, upset the search for generality. Consequently, the rationality suggested by revealed preference can be quite restricted. And since the information the economist seeks can be gleaned only after preference is revealed, it could be difficult to locate a counterpart of the theory's logic in the hurly-burly of an actual marketplace. True enough, many economists accept Hicks's dictum that there is no need to consider whether or not the real consumer acts like the representative man. But if such considerations are indeed to be set to one side, the economist runs the risk of constructing "black boxes" that in the final analysis are otiose. For if demand theory is really to describe human behavior, then the request for congruence to reality is a valid one.

From another standpoint, it would seem reasonable that the observing economist would welcome a way of independently determining the order of preferences in advance of the choices that a consumer makes. Surely this would provide a framework for empirically establishing consistency [3]. Revealed preference, with a logic internal to itself, cannot supply such information, and, as a consequence, it becomes virtually impossible to obtain independent verification of the rules of consumer behavior. For, in fact, consumers may really believe that the price alone makes a good desirable and make their choices accordingly, or the range of choices may be actually intransitive so that the ensuing inconsistencies may indeed obliterate the postulates of revealed preference. Economists may consider such behavior pathological, but then so much of human behavior is precisely pathological.

Furthermore, since revealed preference deals essentially with points, repeated observations over time are required in order to arrive at sensible statements regarding consumer behavior. This presumes that experience has no impact on behavior, a concept rather difficult to digest. Yet given enough observations of what the consumer does, it is argued, we can derive his indifference map: the question that arises is—do we not come right back to the continuity and smoothness assumptions? There are problems then in utility theory that remain unsolved: one is uncertain that a concern for the minutiae of consumer behavior—under what conditions is tea a substitute for coffee vis-à-vis a third good—really adds much to our understanding of what in fact does occur in the market. Perhaps more important, one is not really convinced that the sophisticated mathematics of modern theory really cuts away from psychological roots, for the underlying details of consumer behavior are psychological and sociological as well as economic.

Samuelson does acknowledge some of these difficulties, especially in his 1950 article on integrability: here he speaks of irreversible lag effects, inconsistent preferences for small changes, and the influence of collective or family preferences as important sources of divergent behavior. The theorist, it would seem, is confronted by a dilemma. Once such difficulties are recognized, the empirical verification that would validate a *behavioral* theory becomes moot. Behavior patterns that might supply evidence to confirm or disconfirm a theory must necessarily stem from a kind of metaeconomics. (The term is used here in a somewhat different sense than is found in Samuelson's Part VII, where, for example, the famous "correspondence principle" is described as metaeconomic. Why the mutual relationships of static and dynamic systems form a transcending principle of analysis is not clear.) The appeal to metaeconomics supplies what G. P. E. Clarkson has called interpretive rules that establish consistency between consumer action and theoretical models [3, pp. 96 ff.].

Such rules—transcending principles or "going beyond"—it would seem, offer the most promising techniques for evolving criteria of verification. An investigation of the *decision* to buy may throw more light on preferences than the mere observation of the *act* of buying, which is where revealed preference begins. Consequently, the latter's behavioral terms may or may not be indicated. Have not all the external conditioning elements in choice-making been brushed aside in revealed preference? Does it really tell us how choice is made? Such questions seemingly raise issues of no small interest. For not all goods are subjected to identical evaluation procedures by the consumer, and his expectations regarding price movements do exert some influence upon his behavior. As Jan Tinbergen once remarked in quite another context, many more parameters of conduct are necessary, "most of which have not yet been measured" [2, p. 9n]. Revealed preference appears to suffer, as do most other variants of the theory of consumer behavior, from such limitations. This entire branch of economics may be questioned on the ground that it avoids what Galbraith has called the diminishing urgency of consumption in an affluent society [4, p. 150]. The reduction of consumer desires to terms of preference excludes the possibility that present needs might be fully satisfied in the calculable future.

On the other hand, I do not imply by any means that practical statistical research is in any better condition. Interviewing techniques to probe the mind of the consumer are filled with snares and traps galore, while time series and cross-section studies may either overlook significant variables or deal with so many elements that the whole apparatus collapses. Yet we have gleaned enough knowledge of consumer behavior from the work of Kuznets, Brady, Duesenberry, and others that it may be more fruitful to pursue their line of investigation. Schumpeter once remarked that a theory ought to be a program for research. Insofar as consumer behavior is concerned, it seems dubious that theories such as revealed preference will perform that function. Perhaps economic analysis, as Samuelson said in his 1961 American Economic Association presidential address, does not really have to trouble itself with the state of the real world. This may explain why so many of the models that theorists construct are virtuous for their own sake; yet their often unmanageable mathematical framework must be subjected to a metaeconomics if we are to have a useful social science.

III

Why has economics taken this turn? Here one must examine some methodological questions, an area to which Samuelson has made important contributions. A fundamental issue involves the uses of mathematics in economics. In a paper given at the 1951 meetings of the American Economic Association, Samuelson argued that no distinction should be drawn between mathematical and nonmathematical modes of discourse. While the latter employs literary forms, said Samuelson, it may be argued that mathematics is also a language. In fact, he insisted, mathematics is a language.*

Now, that would seem to be fudging the methodological issue with a bit of poetic license. Mathematics is mathematics, with its own operational rules and logic. It may have had its roots in language and practical usage, but as it flowered, mathematics necessarily had to transcend the limits of direct experience. That is as it should have been, otherwise we would not now possess so powerful a tool. We may teach mathematics by using language, but what other pedagogic device do we have? Those who think that mathematics can be taught with symbols alone, or those who think that economic discourse should be restricted to symbols, might try learning Swahili by the crash Berlitz method.

If economists assume the task of describing, summarizing, and explaining empirical reality, as Samuelson says they must, then the transformation of mathematics in economics from a tool into a fetish will not help. Mathematics may be faster and more convenient in handling deductive inferences than ordinary logic in literary form, but not all practitioners are as good as Samuelson. He

---

* There would seem to be some confusion here between the functions of a natural language and a formal language.

may very well have to paraphrase Marx—*"Je ne suis pas économiste mathématique!"* Indeed, mathematics may have swept the field like an epidemic of measles, as Samuelson says elsewhere, but it can become quite a serious ailment: all too often the very qualitative elements that underpin differences in variables are ignored [5, p. 119]. Having made so strong a case for the mathematical mode, he must take some responsibility for all those lesser lights who now believe that a symbol is the best entrée into the inner circle of expertise. An illustration of the latter situation is a model offered some years ago by a young economist in which national product was described as a function of capital stock services, the rate of use of natural resources, employment, society's fund of knowledge, and the cultural milieu. Stated in literary form, the expressions made sense, but translated into symbols, the cultural milieu became U, presumably capable of being subjected to all the mathematical operations of the calculus. Surely this is carrying an analytical simile to ludicrous extremes. And it goes on all the time.

One supposes that an ability to manipulate symbols expertly gives an economist a feeling of psychological advantage over his confrères who are less expert (on occasion Samuelson is not above such ploys). But that does not mean that they can predict better than anyone else the direction in which the economy will move. One can quote no better authority on this point than Samuelson, who recently noted that as far back as 1961 some of our best model builders had proved beyond a scintilla of doubt that the international payments problem would be solved. Yet the high aggregate demand in 1966 did spill over into international markets, upsetting the expectations for a sufficiently large current-account surplus that would keep us in overall balance.

True enough, mathematical economists have suddenly discovered a welcome mat in the middle and upper echelons of corporations and in the corridors of Washington bureaus, but they still have to speak English. A case in point is Samuelson's task force paper on economic policy prepared for the incoming Kennedy administration in 1960. It is an excellent document, well-reasoned, and carefully delineating the goals, economic targets, and boundaries within which the new President would have to function. It didn't take much knowledge of mathematics to write that paper: its modern neo-Keynesian policy formulations are clearly stated in pellucid English. Perhaps this merely illustrates the high skill and adroitness that Samuelson displays in literary as well as mathematical forms of discourse.

In any case, the mathematically oriented have their present triumph, and future historians may accord to Samuelson a fair share of the credit. But the victory is not entirely costless, since the current fashion stems in many ways from the apparent ease that it lends toward achieving full-fledged professional status. Few students are willing to undertake the task of dealing directly with empirical materials: nor do many arise before dawn to read Locke and Hume on futurity as, say, did John R. Commons. Having acquired a facility with algebra and calculus, it seems easier to construct a model and enter upon an academic career. Unfortunately, the issue of relevance is oftentimes cast aside. Let us be clear about the matter: mathematics can be a good tool in economics and a useful one in checking theoretical hunches. It gets closest to economics when it can deal with data, as say in econometrics, operations research, or input-output analysis. And there are areas—labor economics for one (which does deal with the behavior of the largest part of the population)—where mathematically based theory has but limited usefulness, despite recent efforts in the literature to expand its application. For man is what he is—changeable, irrational, and unpredictable.

IV

From a philosophic standpoint, one suspects that Samuelson would justify his reliance on the mathematical method by an appeal to that variant of positivism he calls operationalism. The latter suggests that every science must issue in a deductive system in which all observed events stem from structural laws involving relatively simple relations. Unfortunately, there is little outside the *Foundations of Economic Analysis* that one can draw upon to summarize Samuelson's philosophic views. In that *magnum opus* he contended that economics must be concerned only with operationally meaningful propositions, i.e., with statements capable of being refuted. This suggests that a concept must be defined in terms of its implicit operations, that a meaningful statement is one in which the operators can supply an answer. Yet that is not the sole method for conducting investigations in economics, or in other social sciences for that matter. There may be intuitive extensions into untrodden territory that do not immediately yield operational propositions [11]. Indeed, it would appear that a good deal of scientific work began this way. Moreover, a purely operational approach unsupplemented by transcending data can stir up enormous difficulties. To employ a sociological illustration, the operationalist may believe that the causal relationship between poor housing and delinquency necessitates an improvement in housing as *the* way of reducing delinquency. The sad fact is that it does nothing of the kind.

More specifically, the reservations expressed here on operationalism are supported by D. E. Gordon's criticism in his review of Samuelson's *Foundations* (*Quarterly Journal of Economics,* May 1955). Samuelson's response is not fully convincing. Gordon had tellingly argued that Samuelson failed to supplement his principles of maximization and dynamic stability with a demonstration that the specified function would not shift unpredictably; that such shifts in the functions were left unexplained; that observed values might be characteristic of a stable function yet not exhibit a stable equilibrium; and that static conclusions do not always require the correspondence principle, that is, may not necessarily be rooted in dynamic conditions. Similarly, Nicholas Georgescu-Roegen [5, p. 59] speaks of qualitative residuals in a preference map stemming from the contrast of alternative choices of two goods and some admixture of such goods. In fact, the latter might be utterly distasteful, thereby upsetting the presumption of proportionality involved in preference theory. But how the latter would be disturbed and the direction of its movement can be established only by a factual investigation, by requiring an appeal to a system of metaeconomics. Or what account would an operationalist take of the impact of new commodities on consumer behavior? Again Georgescu-Roegen says a change in the character of goods does imply a rearrangement of both production patterns and consumer behavior, a factor not easily incorporated in the operational models thus far offered [5, p. 66].

These difficulties issue from the belief that economics has no need to consider questions that might involve value systems or qualitative elements. Many economists believe, neoclassical synthesizers included, that it is entirely possible to create a "science" that abstracts from all human goals. They believe that the semantic significance of knowledge necessarily consigns issues of values or statements about qualitative reactions to the realm of the senseless. A neutral perception of experience is offered, thereby denying that economics might be concerned with matters of values. In effect, there has developed a refusal to concern oneself with any implications other than those specified by a highly restricted model, with the consequence that economists become involved with technique for its own sake. The habit becomes too deeply ingrained to permit any consideration of the metaphysics of purpose.

The central fact in the contemporary world is an evolving, changing industrialism and within that state of immanence the major questions are those that explore man's role in it. We cannot take as given the institutional framework, since it is precisely that which undergoes change and which needs to be examined. Few theoretical economists have been concerned with the process of *becoming* industrialized or with its consequences: such issues are usually set aside by the rule of *caeteris paribus,* under which all facts not immediately relevant to theory are either set aside or dismissed. Granted that a theoretical model seeks to introduce order into the bewildering variety of variables and parameters and granted that an effort is sometimes made to relax restrictive assumptions; nevertheless, there remain numerous variables that never enter the particular model's equations. How often is it that a theoretical truth requires modification by unconsidered facts, facts which at first glance may not suit the theorist's pattern? At this point, the economist ought to display the angle of vision which permits him to look at society in the round. He needs to be that economist *cum* sociologist who disproves Schumpeter's *bon mot* that sociology is the proper occupation of a tired economist.

The operationalist approach suggests an imitation of the physical sciences and presumes therefore an ability to produce positive propositions. But why should we always imitate the physical sciences? They function, it would seem, on a different level of discourse, and we economists ought not feel so guilt-ridden because we then cannot secure the same payoff. Naturally, economists borrow some of the methodology of the physical sciences and their standards of investigation. One does not depreciate such transactions, of course, but let us not suppose that we can duplicate the precision of their results. Society is a highly complex affair, and its components are not so closely and delicately knit that the slightest disturbance will immediately send convolutions gyrating in explosive fashion throughout the whole structure. A good many of the seams that hold us together are rather loosely sewn: there is much give and play and a change in one sector does not always transmit shock waves to the others. Institutional growth and selection are also loose: perhaps this explains the survival of a good many atavistic traits. The attempted application of the methods of physics to a society is a facile escape from the complexities of our social condition. While we need to know what men do, we also need to know the aetiology of their actions, their motivations, their history. Albert Einstein was once asked, "If we have discovered the structure of the atom, why haven't we found a political means to keep the atom from destroying us?" He replied with characteristic wisdom, "It's quite simple. Politics is more difficult than physics." Not all the attributes of the universe can be reduced to space, motion, and mathematics.

It can be argued, therefore, that economic behavior is not quite analogous to physical behavior; to compare one with the other is to commit a serious logical error, for consciousness and the explication of meaning appear in the acts of humans that are not discernible in the movements of models. For the economist this would presuppose a wish to explore *interpretations* of economic actions in a manner that would expose root causes as well as shifts in interrelations. Generally described as the phenomenological approach, this method appears as one well worth the attention of economists.

As a philosophy, phenomenology is by no means an easy one to digest; moreover, the term itself is subject to numerous interpretations. Literally a theory of phenomena, it may refer to an experienced object which represents some deeper reality that confronts us. Without exploring the roots of the concept in Kant, Hegel, Heidegger, or Sartre at this time, we may note that phenomenological philosophers today generally address themselves to "subjective" descriptions in which human considerations are primary. Actions can be understood by applying a generalized principle of connectibility; it then becomes quite possible to derive general statements about economic or social behavior. Hence, objective propositions are entirely feasible, albeit intimately related to the subjectivity from which they stem. Objects, in other words, may be characterized by experience, and become actuality through phenomena generated by the subjective evaluation of facts and material goods. By no means does this reduce everything to mere experience, for theory can still display an independent persuasiveness. In economics we do not deal directly with the relationships that contribute to the social fabric, but rather with "ideal" formulations—price levels, consumption, even index numbers—which nevertheless do not seriously violate facts.

Here, then, it may be possible to achieve what Niels Bohr called complementarity [1], perhaps the most useful antidote to the self-assurance of operationalism. Bohr had observed that when light interacted with material substances two contrasting results could be observed: on the one hand, there was refraction or similar wave-like behavior; on the other hand, light appeared to travel in packets of energy. It was possible to work out a single set of equations based on the idea of complementarity, which could account for both effects. Reality, therefore, could not be fully described solely in terms of one effect or the other: in fact, conceptions that seemed to be antagonistic were reconcilable at a higher level of analysis as aspects of a single reality. Hence, operationalism is to be replaced, or at least modified, first, by probabilistic considerations, and second, by what has been called the ambiguity of complementariness. That is to say, theoretical science is not the only form of scientific knowledge, as, indeed, Georgescu-Roegen suggests, and economics cannot be limited solely to the realm of the measurable.

Essentially, economic phenomena may not be explained always by pure cause and effect, nor are they always linear; they are rather transactions, a phenomenon well understood by John R. Commons. Moreover, in these transactions there can be no certainty; a principle long established in physics, the science economists wish most to imitate. And, if Bohr is correct, then it may be possible to accept seemingly contradictory explanations of economic phenomena on the ground that the analysis of fact must be supplemented by understanding and comprehension. Those who seek to employ complementarity as a method in economics may wish to use behaviorist description not only to derive operational propositions but also as data to help mark off the margins of discourse. But it is important to note that an operational concept or definition does not insure that absolute clarity has been achieved. Georgescu-Roegen recently demonstrated that there are concepts that violate the principle of contradiction, that there are cases in which "B is both A and Non-A," that indifference may not necessarily occupy the ground between preference and nonpreference [5, pp. 22 ff.]. It is in such situations that the idea of complementarity may be most helpful.

Some economists have, perhaps unconsciously, attempted to achieve a measure of complementarity. While it may be too early to judge their success, we may observe that they have sought to weave a web of operational analysis into the tradition of amelioration established by Mill, Marshall, and Keynes. Samuelson may be classified as a leading practitioner of this difficult approach, for, while he has insisted on verifiable theorems, he has conceded that the economist ought to be ready to offer policy proposals that, though reflecting value judgments, do not wander too far from accepted humanitarian standards. Unfortunately, some of the theoretical concepts have skirted close to the edge of emptiness; for example, when consumers' behavior is explained by preferences with the latter defined by observed behavior, the analysis threatens to become circular. The way out seems to be the assumption of a definite commitment by the consumer before a description of his state of mind is possible. This ordering then allows the observing economist to derive welfare propositions from single acts of choice. Yet even as Samuelson has observed, not much of great significance is forthcoming from all this legerdemain. The conclusion that more production of a good might be desirable, or that the same output could be obtained with less input, is admittedly not very striking.

Complementarity also reveals that economics is but one way of examining the totality of human behavior. Traditionally, economics has explored the areas of production and distribution. But goods and services are not merely commodities and performances; they are in a real sense the expressions of human actors who control them and who in turn are controlled by them. Moreover, the relationships which the actors establish between themselves are also economic. And it is the culture arising from these relationships, acting in reciprocal fashion, that determines the movement of society and the fate of man. How the dangers and rewards of existence are to be shared is established in the last analysis by these cultural forms. The material fact of scarcity may be present at the start, but human action makes the material fact a social pattern.

We suggest then that the immanent meaning of economic theory may be grasped by its relations to *praxis*. In this context, verbal meanings and practical goals are often antecedent to logical validity and analytical elegance. Further, if economics is a science of fact rooted in the human condition, it would be necessary to check theory against those events established at the level of connectibility. No simple correspondence should be expected, however, for economic facts are all too often squeezed through the grinder of political policy and social turmoil. But all too often the problem of relevance is ignored, for theory itself is a way of perceiving reality. Unless this perception is achieved, theory cannot perform its primary function—that of guiding empirical inquiry.

V

It is fascinating to watch Samuelson employ his technique, when the occasion demands it, to transcend the limits of his own preconceptions. Here one examines his brilliant dissection of the Friedman formula for model building. Samuelson once wrote to the present writer that it takes an analyst to answer an analyst, and though I am not sure that I would agree, he may understandably offer this piece as the prime exhibit in support of his contention. Professor Friedman, it will be recalled, argued in rather extreme fashion that direct verification of an hypothesis is not an essential ingredient of a model, for if a prediction is not contradicted by events, then the initial set of assumptions is fully acceptable even though there may be no "congruence with reality." Samuelson's rebuttal is extraordinarily powerful, yet essentially a simple one, employing set theory to demonstrate that consequences are contained in antecedent theorizing, which in turn is implied by certain premises, or, as Samuelson would say, minimal premises. By violating this sequence, the Friedman approach improperly admits invalid propositions into analytical discourse.

It is a pity the editor of these papers was unable to include the subsequent debate on this issue [10]. Some sharp words were addressed by Samuelson to his correspondents. (In the author's preface to the *Collected Scientific Papers* Samuelson hopes that he has mellowed over the years. He can be assured that such is not the case. For example, he suggests that those who are uncomfortable with his sort of theory might prefer doctrinal history or labor economics. Since these happen to be my major areas of interest, I could not help but raise my eyebrows at such a quip; did its maker wish to place boundaries around his specialty, keeping out everyone else as a mere poacher?) In any case, the discussion in the *American Economic Review* drifted from the problem of unrealism in theory to the nature of theory itself, with Samuelson emphasizing a search for empirical regularities as a basis for theoretical foundations in economics. So far as this goes, I must opt for the Samuelson position. One cannot quarrel with his statement that the description of empirical regularities provides a basis for prediction or that explanation is a form of description. Yet in a social science such as economics we may still need a measure of looseness not envisaged in strictly operationalist formulations. Physicists have worked for a long time with concepts that were imprecise by present standards, and it is only recently that a "gene" has been "exactly" defined. There are areas of economic and social science that can be usefully explored by methods and concepts that do not completely partake of the Samuelson purview. To be sure, one must seek to improve and advance conceptual foundations; all one asks is a measure of tolerance from the operationalist, who does not yet, I think, have the last word.

Samuelson's versatility is illustrated by his work in some of the newer, more esoteric areas of economic research—game theory, input-output analysis, and linear programming. His contributions to linear programming are fundamental and now form part of the basic literature. On the other hand, he evidently has been less happy with game theory, founding his reservations on a reluctance to accept the notion that utilities are additive. A cardinal concept such as is implied in game theory is "usable," he has contended, only if there is an external measure proportional to the utilities of the players. The latter assumes that utilities can be specified on some scale of intervals, that is, to make them invariant via linear transformations. Samuelson's hesitation is expressed in the paper "Probability and the Attempts to Measure Utility," which has an interesting postscript conceding the possibility of employing the utility concept in this manner, followed by a paper on the independence axiom which would allow for additive properties in certain cases.

Nevertheless, linear programming appears to be the area that has captured Samuelson's attention, mainly, it would seem, because it does permit a numerical specification of the neoclassical synthesis that he has been advocating over the years. This in no way, of course, minimizes his frequent explorations of the interrelationships that game theory and input-output analysis patently exhibit with linear programming. But it is the latter that has been emphasized, most notably in "Market Mechanisms and Maximization," a paper originally prepared for the RAND Corporation, and in "Linear Programming and Economic Theory."

One of the more significant propositions stemming from this work has been labeled the "Turnpike Theorem." It is one of those theoretical formulations that arouse marked interest because it has imbedded in it direct policy implications. A number of writers have offered subtle variants—R. Radner, L. W. McKenzie, M. Morishima [6, pp. 104 ff.]. Samuelson's contribution is to be found in the paper on market mechanisms, as well as in one on capital accumulation and one on balanced growth written jointly with R. M. Solow. These articles are to be supplemented by the discussion of *Linear Programming and Economic Analysis* in Chapter 12. In these papers—particularly the one co-authored by Solow—one finds mathematical demonstrations of the existence and uniqueness of a balanced growth path, the elements of proportionality of the factors involved, the stability of these proportions, and the suggestion that consumption levels are maintainable under the conditions of "turnpike" growth.

It will be recalled that the turnpike theorem, which theoretically specifies the fastest, most efficient path, has its roots in von Neumann's general equilibrium model of economic growth. The latter described an economy in which the production function exhibited fixed, linear homogeneous properties, where all outputs were inputs, where demand functions of the ordinary kind were excluded, and where all input factors were in limitless supply. The objective was to reveal a path describing a constant equilibrium rate of growth under conditions of perfect competition and zero profits. The equilibrium growth path then required money outlays on inputs to be greater than or at least equal to the value of outputs and the current inputs of any item to be less than or equal to the output of that item in the preceding period. As a consequence, only one such equilibrium rate could satisfy the uniqueness and existence conditions and there was a unique value for the rate of interest and the equilibrium rate of growth. Outputs in excess of those flowing from the equilibrium growth rate were deemed to be free goods. And competition insured that there could be only one such sustainable growth rate.

Consumption, in this original formulation, was not part of the model, so that the von Neumann case appeared as a special one within a more general framework. Essentially, as John R. Hicks has shown, the turnpike theorem is a statement about economic planning [7, pp. 201 ff.]. It asks the significant question: what will production plans be, given the initial capital and the future flow of capital, that will enable an economy to reach some future target? Yet, various turnpike models, including Samuelson's, seem to display certain common features that do raise troublesome questions. For one thing, they abstract from the organizational structure necessary to achieve the stated objective (theorists may take this as a "given," but I doubt that this is enough). Secondly, there seems to be no time horizon to which they are addressed, in almost all cases appealing to some vague precept "given enough time." Further, the assumption that surplus goods, i.e., goods in excess of those required for the equilibrium growth path, are noneconomic is much too facile; discarding such goods may place the growth path on a line that varies substantially from the optimum [7, pp. 228 ff.].

The most serious problem, however, is the model's concentration on capital endowments. To be sure, Samuelson has been more aware of this problem than other writers, yet in most instances, the theorem in its various guises has explored the techniques that would maximize "final" capital. Hicks has described planning based on such motivations as stemming from a "war mentality." His characterization may be a harsh one, but the planning philosophy stemming from "turnpike" theorizing does suggest a "crash" technique; adopted by underdeveloped nations, it has had some unfortunate consequences. The paradigm, of course, is the debate over the pace of development that took place in the Soviet Union in the early 1920's. On the one hand, there were advocates of a kind of paced development to account for the output and demand patterns in agriculture and consumption; on the other, there were the devotees of a massive investment program that would achieve a rapid expansion of "heavy" capital goods [15]. The extraordinary burdens that the latter strategy imposed are well known. Reverting to the "turnpike" concept itself, it would appear that Hicks' evaluation is much to the point: the "turnpike" is simply one of several optimum paths and one ought to search for a model that allows for per capita consumption growth.

Samuelson, to no one's surprise, has already done so, though it appeared too late for inclusion in the present volumes [12]. His new theorem suggests that, *given enough time*, a balanced turnpike growth path would provide maximum per capita consumption. That indeed is the rub—what is "enough time"? Given "enough time" even the Soviets, with their unbalanced growth pattern, may evolve a high-consumption economy. Would fifty years be enough time? How, in the meantime, would the projected growth path be influenced, say, by technical change? And what influences would uncertainties generated by time lags or wage rate movements exert on the optimum growth path? These would appear to be but a few of the practical issues from which the theory abstracts.

VI

If I have given the impression that the first two "books," as well as parts of the third, are rather rough going, that indeed was my intention. At times the high powered symbols are handled after the fashion of those British mathematicians who blithely say: "It can be shown that . . ." Yet no doubt the feast is rich enough to whet the intellectual appetites of economists for years to come. The last two books—on public policy and doctrinal history—are lighter fare, though no less challenging. The reader will find here perceptive comments on fiscal and monetary policy, several excellent essays on famous economists (Keynes, Schumpeter, Hotelling, Robertson) and the insightful Wicksell lecture on the state of the American economy. Yet some are not so good: if Beethoven had his Battle Symphony, Samuelson may be forgiven his Stamp Memorial Lecture. Aside from a memorable last sentence (". . . what do they know of economics, who political economy do not know?"), the lecture rambles painfully and succeeds only in specifying a number of economic issues then current without saying much about them.

On the other hand, if I were to choose the best of the group, the accolade would go to the statement prepared for the Canadian Royal Commission on Banking and Finance in 1962. While agreeing that money and credit policies have enormous influence on the course of an economy, Samuelson makes it clear that monetary policy is not the sole mechanism for influencing aggregate behavior. He rejects the notion that adjustments in the supply of money—say 3 percent a year—would be sufficient to provide the automaticity that some economists believe to be desirable, for ". . . choices have to be made pragmatically in terms of the goodness or badness of behavior patterns that result from various kinds of discretionary action." The implication that human action is subject to a decision-making process that is less than completely automatic is well taken. Hence, the attempt to prove a controlling causal proportionality between money supply and aggregate income cannot be convincing. The technical issues involved are so clearly stated that it seems difficult after Samuelson's discussion to defend the quantity theory of money in any of its versions. Says Samuelson tartly, "Optimal stabilization policy must vary with the probability pattern of the system to be stabilized, which makes it rather ridiculous to specify in advance for all times that some particular gadget like 3 percent money-increase-per-year should be adhered to, in season and out of season." The clarity of his distinctions between monetary and fiscal policy makes this essay one of the best didactic pieces in the collection.

I realize that there is much in these volumes on which I have not commented. To do so would extend an already lengthy piece. The essays on Marx and Ricardo are powerful dissections of these systems from the standpoint of modern analysis; the early articles on the multiplier and acceleration remain viable analytical documents; the papers taken from various published symposia on the state of economic thinking are very good reading indeed; and the A.E.A. presidential address stands up surprisingly well, even after a third reading (although I still do not believe that economists should work solely for each other's applause). What the papers in the last two "books" particularly illustrate, as they move toward greater and greater relevance, is that Samuelson's neoclassical synthesis is heavily weighted on the Keynesian side. They represent an elucidation and extension of the best of economic thinking of the last thirty years. It may be premature to put Samuelson into the pantheon of the greats, but there is no doubt that he is knocking on the door.

REFERENCES

1. N. BOHR, *Atomic Physics and Human Knowledge*, New York, 1958.
2. E. H. CHAMBERLIN, *Towards a More General Theory of Value*, New York, 1957.
3. G. P. E. CLARKSON, *The Theory of Consumer Demand*, Englewood Cliffs, 1963.
4. J. K. GALBRAITH, *The Affluent Society*, Boston, 1958.
5. N. GEORGESCU-ROEGEN, *Analytical Economics*, Cambridge, 1966.
6. F. H. HAHN AND R. C. O. MATTHEWS, "The Theory of Economic Growth," in American Economic Association and Royal Economic Society, *Surveys of Economic Theory*, New York, 1965.
7. J. R. HICKS, *Capital and Growth*, Oxford, 1965.
8. ———, *A Revision of Demand Theory*, Oxford, 1956.
9. ———, *Value and Capital*, Oxford, 1939.
10. F. MACHLUP, "Professor Samuelson on Theory and Realism," *American Economic Review*, September 1964, *54*, pp. 733 ff.; P. A. SAMUELSON, "Theory and Realism—A Reply," *American Economic Review*, September 1964, *54*, 736 ff.; G. GARB, A. P. LERNER, AND G. J. MASSEY, "Professor Samuelson on Theory and Realism: Comments," *American Economic Review*, December 1965, *55*, 1151 ff.; P. A. SAMUELSON, "Reply," *American Economic Review*, December 1965, *55*, 1164 ff.
11. A. RAPOPORT, *Operational Philosophy*, New York, 1953.
12. P. A. SAMUELSON, "A Catenary Turnpike Theorem," *American Economic Review*, June 1965, *55*, 486 ff.
13. ———, "A. P. Lerner at Sixty," *Review Economic Studies*, *31*(3), 169 ff.
14. E. E. SLUTSKY, "On the Theory of the Budget of the Consumer,'" in *Readings in Price Theory*, edited by G. J. Stigler and K. E. Boulding, Chicago, 1952, p. 27 ff.
15. N. SPULBER, editor, *Foundations of Soviet Strategy for Economic Growth*, Bloomington, 1964.
16. G. J. STIGLER, "The Development of Utility Theory," in *Essays in the History of Economics*, Chicago, 1965, pp. 66 ff.

1967

PART TWO. AMERICAN INSTITUTIONS: BUSINESS

Businessmen,
the American Revolution,
and the Constitution

For many years now American historians have been offering a view of our past that appears too clean and gilt-edged. Sordid episodes in the story of our economic growth are frequently deleted. There is not a word, for example, about watered stock in one recent recital of the career of J. P. Morgan and the antics of the nineteenth-century "robber barons" are now quaint tales in the annals of capital accumulation. Critical examinations of the careers of businessmen are rejected because they "rob the people of their heroes" and insult the folk-memory of great men. Allan Nevins makes Henry Ford a genius of industrial productivity with very little stress on the sort of factory totalitarianism with which high output was achieved. Any suggestion that there is a relationship between economic motivation and political action is said to more properly belong to the 1930's. History

in recent scholarship has become a celebration of national greatness and a source of "hope and faith, if not charity."

The central question, and the one I should like to illustrate in
this paper, is: can economic perceptions provide some insight
into the nature of the past? It is not so much a matter of merely
reinterpreting the past, an accusation frequently hurled at Charles
Beard, as that of employing the present to *illuminate* the past,
and thereby perhaps vindicate some of the perceptions of economic
inquiry. For example, if present day benefit-cost analysis were
applied to the projects undertaken by businessmen a century or
more ago, it would be doubtful that the results would exceed
unity. Of course, social benefits and costs would have to be included in the equation as well as private elements. The dubious
undertakings, the prodigal use of resources, and the appropriations
of public usufruct for private purposes suggest that economic
development pursued a hyperbolic path in its thrust toward
maximum efficiency and optimum utilization of human capital,
technology, and natural wealth. One supposes that it is a mark
of the extraordinary viability of the American environment, given
the manner in which destruction more than matched creativity in
the Schumpeterian balance, for us to have come this far.

For the present exercise, I have selected two related events in
our history—the American Revolution and the making of the
Constitution—to test whether the Founding Fathers were, in
truth, incredible demigods or ordinary men moved by ordinary
economic motives. May I warn, however, that my analysis at the
moment is more qualitative than quantitative, for which I offer
no apologies. In any case, let us go back a few years prior to the
Revolution. Merchants had come to represent wealth and power
in society. They held their fortunes in land, homes, and securities
in which investments ran as high as £10,000, no small sum for
those days. In addition to a brick home in the city (brick was a
great luxury in colonial days), the merchant was apt to have a
summer home to which to escape during the hot summer months.
His club was the coffeehouse and, while many did not have a
college education, prosperity induced them to send their sons to
Harvard and Yale.

By the time of the Revolution there were a fair number of such
merchants, chiefly in urban centers or river towns. The merchant
was a leisured "capitalist" and a "gentleman," who usually had

married into the family of some other merchant. Since banking
facilities were generally lacking and, with most enterprises, still
operating on an *ad hoc* joint-venture basis, the merchant in effect
became the community's banker. But as events developed in
the middle eighteenth century, the merchant began to sense
what it was he had to accomplish, and he did not hesitate to
call in the lower orders of society to help him demonstrate against
the restrictions of the Crown. In the main, the older, richer
merchant did not want a show of political force: he had his
investments in loans, securities, and rentals and he did not relish
political strife. But the smaller merchant and the artisan were
bearing the brunt of economic change and they were becoming
restless; though at first there was no thought of independence, by
1774 the sentiment for going it alone had become fairly strong.
The colonists began to feel that the business of America was its
own. The war seemed inevitable.

The American businessman had for too long been a law unto
himself: when war came he could not suppress a taste for profit
despite patriotic and ethical precepts. During the many years of
conflict, he was ever ready to take advantage of all the gainful
opportunities proffered by war. He operated alone, or in concert
with partners, acting as wholesaler, retailer, shipper, and banker.
Although kinship relations permeated business relationships, it
was all a kind of conspiratorial game. Deals were matters of
business security and secrecy. Mutual commitment and involvement generally insured the completion of a transaction. As facts
of economic life, all this also represented the laws of nature.

Trading with the enemy was not nearly so heinous an affair
as it might be today: it even had a certain respectability. Some
merchants agreed that since England had to buy overseas anyway,
trade with America would drain her treasure and enrich the one-
time colonists. Planters feared the growth of an agricultural surplus and insisted on overseas sales, even to England. Individual
states vied with each other for prisoner-of-war camps because the
English government sent specie to prisoners. And there was
enough of a demand for English goods to encourage American
merchants to import them: the profit was good enough despite
high prices. Where did the merchants get such goods? From Nova
Scotia or the West Indies or Amsterdam: these places did a
splendid business with Americans.

Merchants who helped provision the armies of General Washington did quite well: they were able to mix private and public business in about equal proportions. It was not uncommon for merchants holding public office to engage in secret deals with others selling to the government. John Brown of Providence delayed building frigates for the government while he busily constructed ships for private purposes. While Robert Morris and his colleagues did not consider that their practices were immoral, most Americans did abhor their sort of antics. Only after the Constitution was adopted was a conflict-of-interest rule introduced into the Treasury.

Provisioning the army was big business. As Superintendent of Finances for the Continental Congress, Morris offered many opportunities to associates and friends to obtain government contracts. Jeremiah Wadsworth and Nehemiah Hubbard served apprenticeships, as it were, under Morris. Profits in West Indian ports rose sevenfold as American agents scrambled for arms and appropriate commissions. Wadsworth had a frigate built, assigning to himself a 5 percent fee. And Dr. William Shippen, head of the Hospital Department, was not above selling hospital supplies for his own gain. Massachusetts suffered little during the war: the illicit trade with Nova Scotia was centered there. William Duer, William Constable, Benedict Arnold, and several others thought to store goods secretly in New York to make a killing when the British would be finally ejected.

The American businessman carried on his affairs as though the fighting had been all for his benefit, and perhaps it was. Supplies were withheld from the army to force prices up; and if the troops were without food, clothing, and ammunition, the businessman's reaction was not so much that he didn't care as that it underscored his concern with the condition of his coffers. Moreover, the individual state governments were unlikely to enforce the law against him.

More important, of course, was the fact that those in control of the government—such as it was—would not tax themselves enough to pay for the war. A major part of the cost of the conflict was defrayed with paper notes, all of which were virtually repudiated, and by bonds, later funded into the national debt to be liquidated by indirect taxes. The heaviest losers were the soldiers, who were paid in notes. No wonder they were so restless after Yorktown.

Robert Morris was at the center of wartime economic activity, but he could not, or would not, distinguish his private affairs from his public responsibilities. When Morris went along with Silas Deane in a privateering venture, the ship was outfitted at government expense. Morris was *the* financial power. According to one historian, his influence was greater than J. P. Morgan's in a later era. Morgan would have had to be Secretary of the Treasury and in control of Tammany Hall to match Morris' power. His price for the Superintendency of Finances was a high one—the unqualified right to run his own business and, at the same time, absolute control of provisioning personnel, and sole contracting authority for the army. It is frequently said that Morris financed the Revolution. Rather, it was the other way around—the Revolution financed Morris.

These were an interesting breed of businessmen—adventurous, hustling, and unconcerned that the future brought no certainty. They were ready to pursue all opportunities for the single objective of making a profit. Ruthlessness was a common attribute: the businessman was anxious to dispose of the last vestiges of mercantilist regulation in order to create the conditions of life in a virgin continent. When protective legislation for American sailors was passed, William Constable instructed his supercargos to feed the crew substandard food and to abuse them mercilessly, all to encourage desertions in Caribbean ports and replacements by foreigners who could be paid less. The conditions of life were to be of the merchants' own making; but it sometimes helped to marry a wealthy widow or into the right family, as indeed was the case with Silas Deane, one of Morris' associates. And the businessman's ambition to become part of the aristocracy could be satisfied by marrying off his daughter to a French count, an achievement finally attained by William Bingham.

Wealthy colonials survived the war quite well. Class distinctions had not been disturbed too much. Many merchants were less upset by monetary depreciation than by the legal tender laws that required them to accept currency at face value. But some of these laws were undergoing repeal. Merchant wealth had suffered little depletion. Gouverneur Morris' claim that merchants had been impoverished by the war was simply not true. The colonies became sovereign states, retaining in the main the same political structure to which they had been accustomed, except for the eradication of a few feudal remains such as primogeniture and the established church. The franchise was broadened somewhat, although prosperity and money was still the chief qualification for voting in most states. The Continental Congress had not been strengthened: it still had to appeal to the states to accomplish what any government needed to do.

Soon the merchant interests found fresh difficulties facing them. Trade discrimination among the states developed and each levied duties on goods brought in from the others. There were figuratively fifty-seven varieties of money in circulation, and boundaries between the states were in continual dispute. The infant manufacturing industries were strangled in their cribs by British dumping after the war, and there was no tariff to protect them. For the merchants, these years bordered on chaos, and eventually they determined to do something about it.

Perhaps more important, a fairly clear-cut political struggle was developing along easily delineated economic lines. On one side were arrayed those of inherited wealth, together with the rich merchant, speculator, former privateer, and army contractor; on the other there were small farmers, artisans, tax delinquents, purchasers of loyalist property who wanted to pay with depreciated currency, and those hampered by a lack of reliable money. All were middle class, but some were well off and others were hurting.

Sentiment for a stronger government developed apace, especially among the merchants. Ironically, their economic philosophy was derived more from Sir James Steuart than Adam Smith, for Steuart's writing advocated, among other things, a strong central government. It was left to Alexander Hamilton to pose the strongest and most persistent arguments for political centralization. His proposal to consolidate and fund the state and national debt ultimately brought speculative profits to many. William Duer and William Constable picked up securities in North Carolina and South Carolina, valued on their face at $1 million, for about $100,000, actually investing but $20,000 of their own. The securities were resold to a Dutch bank for $800,000 and the profit then invested in British bonds. The interest from the latter was used to pay interest due on the original securities in order to make them look good. The gain on this one transaction netted over $600,000. One authority estimates that such pyramiding brought Duer a total profit of almost $5 million. It is sometimes suggested that Hamilton's funding scheme was the only alternative to chaos. Since other refinancing schemes were in fact offered, Hamilton's scheme was somewhat less than godlike. For men of his persuasion, full funding implied a debt rooted in patriotism. As it was, the patriotism turned out to be quite profitable.

To Hamilton, property meant a strong nation and the accumulation of capital. His model for a bank was England's, embellished by the ideas of John Law, a Scottish adventurer who had helped establish the Royal Bank of France. Hamilton's views did not endear him to a public that feared the moneyed interests. But they were shared by businessmen: Robert Morris, like Hamilton, had only contempt for popular government, for the people were driven only by passion and greed! Hamilton's political behavior was clearly conditioned by the commercial and financial interests of the Northern states as well as by a kind of nationalistic impulse. When these groups carried through the Constitution, they engineered, in effect, a counterrevolution, and, while they believed they were defending the nation, they were really behaving like aggressors. A powerful conservative element developed which tried to defeat legal tender demands, sought bank charters, defended the property rights of former Tories, and helped suppress such outbreaks as "Shay's Rebellion." In fact, the latter event was used by conservatives searching for a scapegoat. Rumors flew about that the enemy was within the gates, and men of principle and property were shocked by the outrage which was in reality a minor incident perpetrated by unhappy ex-soldiers.

Conservatives also preferred that the burden of taxation be placed on farmers: for them, the idea of "equality of sacrifice" in taxation was absurd. Hamilton's debt funding was to provide a store of fluid capital, and there was no intention of surrendering any part of it to the public exchequer. By the time funding was actually carried out, only a fourth of the outstanding securities were held by the original buyers. Financiers and speculators had sent their agents all over the country to buy huge numbers of securities at ten to fifteen cents on the dollar. For almost a decade, a market for transactions in securities had been in full swing. There was enough ambition for great wealth among merchants and speculators to create a need for revising the Articles of Confederation.

For the Continental Congress had been stumbling along, a

debating society for delegates to discourse on their views. Then, in February 1786, Virginia, at Madison's suggestion, sent a circular letter to the other states to come to Annapolis to discuss certain commercial issues, the major one being Virginia's irritation at Maryland's control of the Potomac River. However, only five states came: Northern merchant interests distrusted Virginia, disbelieving that cavaliers were sincerely concerned with the welfare of business. Hamilton appeared for New York, but without much hope that the conference's patchwork would succeed. But he came nevertheless, hoping to press for a constitutional convention. The Annapolis conference did issue Hamilton's appeal, but it was worded circumspectly; otherwise, it would have been ignored, and it was directed to the state legislatures rather than to the Continental Congress. It was hoped that such a procedure would insure the "right" sort of delegations to the Constitutional Convention. Thus began what amounted to a *coup d'état*.

All the states except Rhode Island sent delegations, many with instructions to go no further than a revision of the Articles. The states did not reckon, however, with the temper of politicians, who had, in any case, the support of most of the merchants and commercial interests. At first, the Continental Congress ignored the Annapolis resolution; but when the states appointed their delegations, it was endorsed, particularly after George Washington had been elected a delegate by Virginia. Benjamin Franklin was there, well on in years, but neither John Jay nor Thomas Jefferson nor Samuel Adams was present. Patrick Henry refused to go because he "smelled a rat." Washington appeared in his role as "Father of His Country": his very imperiousness was enough to hold recalcitrants in line. When he had been elected president, Gilbert Stuart, the painter, came to do his portrait. He tried to get Washington to relax: evidently, the president's stern mien was not a matter of keeping his dentures in place. "Now, sir," said Stuart, "you must let me forget that you are General Washington and that I am Stuart the painter." Replied Washington coldly, "Mr. Stuart need never feel the need of forgetting who he is or who General Washington is." Only such a man could chair the Constitutional Convention.

James Madison, erudite and bookish, took the only notes available. The delegates straggled into Philadelphia as the convention dragged on for months. Destined to become the "Founding

Fathers," they were practical men, experienced in business, law, and politics. The delegates were a mixed group, but virtually all were convinced that the Articles of Confederation had failed and some were convinced that the states had become useless political entities. They were hardly spokesmen for society at large, however, for their primary concern was to protect their own interests. Although the Declaration of Independence had spoken of popular government, policies back home in the states were set by men of wealth. While tradesmen of the lower middle class could be found in a number of state legislatures, they took their cues from lawyers, merchants, and the wealthy. If the Constitutional Convention was a cross section, it sliced only the upper layers of American society. Each delegate was aware of the ultimate objective, however: otherwise they should not have compromised so often.

And so, shippers, merchants, aristocrats, and their lawyers could write a document that would establish a strong central government, one in which the rights of the lower orders of society were not terribly important. Hamilton would have preferred that the states become administrative districts of the national government, but he did not speak up too often: he too was willing to accept compromise. The common man did not count, for he was a creature of passion, and all evils could be traced to an excess of democracy. The delegates argued about credentials and house rules and the Virginia versus the New Jersey Plan, and established a rule of secrecy. The various interests worked out deals and compromises and, in the end, the writing of the document was given over to a Committee on Detail and to Gouverneur Morris, who had a fine flair for penmanship.

Morris proceeded to take liberties with the text, introducing ambiguities and shading meanings on the ground that a certain gracefulness of language was desirable in so important a document. He even inserted a clause that had been rejected by the convention: seeking to protect the Bank of North America, he wanted to prohibit the states from "impairing contracts." The clause was to have enormous consequences. At one point, he inserted a semicolon that could have altered the meaning of the general welfare clause enough to give Congress virtually unlimited power. It was caught in time.

In the meantime, the new Stock Exchange in New York was

doing a lively business in government securities. When Hamilton's funding scheme went into effect after ratification, speculators gained $40 million. Interestingly, the bill to fund the securities had been momentarily stalled in the House of Representatives. Robert Morris, now a Senator (earlier he had refused to vote for the Declaration of Independence), became angry and confused, while the other speculators in Congress had visions of a collapse in security prices. The price for passage of the funding bill was handing over the site for the future capital of the nation to Virginia and Maryland: the business interests of the North were delighted to trade a swamp on the Potomac for profits in securities. A contemporary description of Senator Morris savagely depicts him as widening his nostrils and flattening his nose like the head of a viper whenever business interests were endangered.

Were there "classes" in those days? Perhaps not in the modern sense; but in 1765 Cadwallader Colden spoke of four groups in colonial society—landed proprietors, lawyers, merchants, and small farmers and artisans. These groups perpetuated themselves through the Revolution, the Critical Period, and the early decades of the Republic. Distinctions among them were based on reactions to the political and economic questions of the day. But the first three tended to coalesce—socially, economically, and politically. They were the "ruling class" held together by a community of interest, often by intermarriage, and apt to cross easily the thin line of social and economic demarkation, despite variations in the details of their outlook.

Such variances and distinctions were evident in the Constitutional Convention, so that the final document stemmed from a series of compromises over issues raised by conflicting interests. It was a document with which nascent manufacturer, merchant, shipper, and creditor could live. The federal government was to control taxation, money, war, commerce, and the Western lands. Ratification was carried through by a minority, despite recent opinion to the contrary. In fact, the whole procedure of ratification —bypassing the Continental Congress, going to the states, calling for special conventions that could be more easily swayed than state legislatures, and the need for action by just nine of the thirteen states—represented a political coup, and for economic reasons. The Constitution intended to advance property rights: small debtors were clearly adversely affected by the new rules of the game. The delegates may have come from a variety of regions, but in the main they sought to escape the commercial chaos of the Articles, and they represented a demand for the protection of property. If a large number of delegates were lawyers, this fact hardly diminishes the influence of economic concerns, for whom did the lawyers represent?

Ratification went to the states rather than the Continental Congress, for with all the difficulties anticipated by Madison, Hamilton, and others, it would still be the easier way. Five states had suffered so much from the turmoil of the Critical Period that they would probably ratify the action of the convention. Only New York, Virginia, Rhode Island, South Carolina, and perhaps North Carolina might try to go it alone. Hence, ratification might just squeeze through. New Jersey was in fairly good condition, but it needed access to the port of New York, and it was being hampered by import duties levied on its goods. Georgia wanted protection from the Indians, and in Connecticut there were enough problems to make the campaign for ratification a resounding success. Only Rhode Island resisted: speculators like Nicholas Brown were trying to manipulate the situation, if not opposing ratification outright.

Universal acceptance represents another tale in the mythology of the Constitution. Madison and Hamilton mounted an intensive campaign in favor of ratification, culminating in the Federalist Papers. Most states had some sort of voting restriction: to imply that universal suffrage, as in New York, meant a broad decision by the populace ignores the nature of the voting process. There were numerous voluntary nonvoters, just as there are today, and many who were lukewarm about ratification simply followed their leaders. As it was, it took all the eloquence of an Alexander Hamilton to defeat the anti-ratification forces in New York.

The fact is that an "economic interpretation" of the framing of the Constitution is still a meaningful one. The Founding Fathers fought each other for wealth and power and in doing so were able to create a myth of the businessman's beneficence and political wisdom, a myth that was to be celebrated for over a hundred years. Only when the noted historian Charles Beard dared to question that myth in 1913 did the patriot become upset. Perhaps Beard's restricted use of the term "economic interpretation" was unfortunate, but it has not weakened the patent fact that economic concerns represented powerful motivations in the formation of the Constitution. In any case, James Madison was quick to acknowledge the strength of economic interests even though noneconomic ones might be present. In the words of John W. Burgess, the Constitutional Convention had perpetrated a "peaceable revolution." John Adams, who was close to the event, remarked: "The federal Constitution was the work of commercial people in the seaport towns, of the slaveholding states, of the officers of the revolutionary army, and of the property holders everywhere."

The Constitution set the conditions for a businessman's civilization. Hamilton's extreme views advocating a constitutional monarchy were abandoned, as well as Madison's suggestion that the national government have a complete veto power over the states. There resulted, rather, what seemed to be a reasonable distribution of power between the federal government and the states. In the final analysis, the Constitution was a document that protected property in its various guises—securities, goods, and slaves. And perhaps events could be shaped in no other way. The businessman, despite a wide diversity of interests, had time to partake of political life, and he made certain that he did so. In local affairs it was quite clear who comprised the governing elite. Money established one's status, and visitors from Europe were quick to note that "the rich blockhead is more considered than the first magistrate."

1967

The American Corporation: Ideology and Reality

Power, like energy, must be regarded as continually passing from any one of its forms into any other, and it should be the business of social science to seek the laws of such transformations.—BERTRAND RUSSELL

In recent years, managerial elites have urgently sought to justify what it is they do. As Wilbert Moore remarked in his *Conduct of the Corporation* (1962), executives have become worried about the merit of their positions, the salaries they receive but perhaps do not deserve, and the fact that finally they are accountable to no one but themselves. They know that they dispose of vast financial resources and that the economic health of workers, stockholders, and suppliers—as well as entire communities—depends on their decisions. Management, says Moore, is in a "moral crisis."

The older ideology, as reflected in the writings of such economists as John Bates Clark or Frank H. Knight, now seems inadequate. Clark had announced that by virtue of marginal productivity, everyone in society received exactly what he earned, while Knight in his theory converted labor into capital, land into capital, and entrepreneurship into capital, so that in the end capital counted for everything. But all this was too abstruse. The "moral crisis" in the corporation demanded a more supple theory, something not so dense as the Clark-Knight system of apologetics nor quite so rigid as Herbert Spencer's Social Darwinism.

The new outlook started a few years back with books by Adolph Berle, David Lilienthal, and Peter Drucker, whose messages were promptly refurbished in *Fortune*. Berle celebrated the soul of the corporation; Lilienthal argued for bigger and better bigness; Drucker turned his lamp on responsibility. And it was amazing how many came away convinced, at least until General Electric, Westinghouse, and a few others stubbed their toes over antitrust.

A major theme in this new ideology has been responsibility. The corporation, it was argued, must adapt itself so as to become a domesticated citizen in the contemporary polity. The corporation's very size and its impact on the economy, we were told, willy-nilly enforced proper standards of social conduct. The manager himself, of course, was only a professional, like the nineteenth-century British colonial officer: he possessed certain skills and placed them at the disposal of the ". . . vast clientele he always serves and sometimes leads." He was a highly trained bureaucrat in the best sense, and cheerfully shared the world's burdens.

Frequently, the rhetoric from which these notions were drawn exhibited a defensive and sanctimonious tone. Yet all too often the mood was shattered by such remarks as that of a burgeoning retail magnate who told a reporter some time ago: "We're not going to pay dividends. To hell with the stockholders." Now, this seems to be a truer picture of corporate decision-making, for it is self-determined in a manner that locates responsibility in a directorate accountable only to itself. Governance in the corporation, to use Richard Eells's term, is reflexive, that is, it turns inward. The shocked recognition of this seems to have been upsetting to some managerial elites.

How else is one to explain the new corporate literature? Saturated with the message of service, the exploration of "constitutionalism" in the corporation, for example, yet manifests enough buncombe to raise questions of dissimulation. The fact is that those who benefit from corporate affairs are those who shape corporate policy. The literature's purpose is largely to deflect criticism. Here, for example, is Richard Eells, one of the more adroit purveyors of the new corporate ideology, writing in *The Government of Corporations* (1962):

> There is no agreement among corporation theorists as to the definition of terms in the chain of responsibility in corporate governance. *Who* is responsible to *whom* for *what,* and *how* is his responsibility to be enforced? Each of the italicized terms is highly debatable today. As to the first term, the "who" in this formula may refer to board or executive group, or to both. As to the second term, responsibility to "whom" raises arguable issues about the relative positions of various groups of claimants . . . as to the third term . . . one gets answers ranging all the way from . . . maximum profit for stockholders, to the more recent multiple demands of numerous contributors-claimant groups, including the claims of the "general public." As to the fourth term, . . . only the most elementary steps to identify ways and means have yet been taken.

The fundamental issue of control is dissipated in a haze of doubt. Those who bear responsibility for corporate decision-making, Eells tells us, cannot be identified. The outcome is to say a corporation does what it does.

Eells, of course, is too astute not to recognize that corporate power must be made to seem legitimate, but his insistence that this requires a "constitution" cannot be validated by parallels with the democratic state, since the corporation hardly can be said to derive its powers from a principle of consent. The fact is that corporate charters are not determined by consensus and in the exercise of authority might does weigh more heavily than right. It is indeed one's location in the corporate hierarchy that determines how power is exercised. To suggest that directors secure their authority from stockholders, or "from society generally," is otiose.

The truth is painfully reached when Eells concedes that corporate decision-makers often ". . . create power for the purpose in hand and [then] seek to legitimate the necessary decisions." Yet sheer power has seemed an inadequate base for the illusion of rationality, and so writers on corporations, Eells included, have employed such notions as the principle of balance: the function of the manager, it has been said, is to weigh the contending claims of stockholder, supplier, union, government, and competitor and to parcel out justice to all. But such a version of business democracy sharply clashes with the concession that power is rationalized in *post hoc* fashion. Surely the manner in which the automobile companies all too often have abused their dealers is a better measure of the "balance" managerial elites have had in mind.

II

A. T. Mason, the noted Princeton law professor, once gave away the whole show, when he said of the welfare state: ". . . [it] must be accomplished under the auspices of competent and efficient business leadership." This seems adequate underpinning for the theme that as long as the corporation is successful, so will the rest of us be. Yet the bitter-end resistance of the big chain stores to the extension of the federal minimum wage law to retail clerks in 1961 suggests how well executives have learned to live with the welfare state.

"Leadership" has become a major preoccupation in the public addresses of such archons of business as Ralph Cordiner, T. V. Houser, and Henry Ford II. (Incidentally, Ford, who has often spoken sternly about corporate men who undermine public confidence, sat stone-faced at a General Electric stockholders' meeting while Cordiner heroically sought to explain away his company's anti-trust conviction.) Loren Baritz has demonstrated in *The Servants of Power* (1960) how much of a fetish "leadership" notions have become among the corporate elite.

But there are still enough executives around who know that the notions of governance, responsibility, and the corporate soul can be overdone. These men, typified by Roger Blough of U.S. Steel, say that the purpose of business is business. They stress the thumbscrew technique in dealing with unions. General Electric, for example, has long practiced through "Boulwareism" a no-nonsense policy that has enabled it to bypass the hundred-odd unions in its plants and virtually dictate bargaining terms. It blends the old paternalism with the new public relations.

Corporate oligarchs have also called into play the behavioral sciences. Personality dynamics, social psychology, and cultural patterns have become weapons in extracting more output from workers. The sense of "togetherness" in the plant that the soft sell may create seems to offer just the right mood to frustrate the efforts of the union organizer. Thus, a study of the psychology of rodents can help the manager to manipulate workers to respond properly to appropriate stimuli.

A more elaborate version of this sort of thinking has been developed in recent years by the so-called organization theorists. These writers, e.g., Kenneth Boulding and Herbert A. Simon, insist that their overarching concern is with scientific objectivity, but their ideas can be used effectively to rationalize functioning of the corporation. In organization theory, the corporation is an archetypal structure whose highly integrated and delicately attuned personal relationships demand the elimination of rivalry. Communication is preferred to command. Information must flow through feedbacks to managerial control units. The corporation is seen as a social analogue to the computer. Not only must the productive process be rationalized and centrally directed; the humans themselves must be converted into carefully regulated units of a rigidly defined hierarchy. Since the organization—in this case, the corporation—is a "cooperative system of human activity encompassing psychological, social, biological, and physical relations inherent in cooperative behavior," no deviation from the oligarch's norm should be permitted. The corporate collective now stands as the perfect paradigm for the domicile of an emmet.

III

The ideological bias involved in these concepts is obscured by an ostensibly neutral or scientific language. The stress placed on manipulative techniques, for example, disguises such issues as the use of hierarchy in sustaining unequal income distribution. Wages and interest are no longer the outcome of social struggles, as in Ricardo or Marx, but rather "inducements" to complete tasks. Administered prices can be justified by such notable objectives as "desirable levels of internal efficiency." That this constitutes private taxing power, as both David Bazelon and Michael Reagan have demonstrated, is simply ignored. With such formulations, organization theory comes close to apologetics.

Sometimes the whole affair has gone round and round in wondrous circles. Loyalty and teamwork increase satisfaction, which enhances participation, which makes inducements larger, which raise the contribution of work, which reflects an increase in willingness, which leads to an acceptance of corporate goals, which implies loyalty. But, of course, the cost of production could be reduced if satisfaction were available at a low level of inducement: more familiarly, how nice to have lower rates of pay. Obviously, this is an important management goal and if organization theory can show the way, so much the better.

These writings—from the work of Mary Parker Follett and Chester Barnard to James March and Herbert A. Simon—offer the corporate archon a more suitable ideology. By stressing common goals for managers, workers, suppliers, stockholders, consumers—anyone who has anything to do with the corporation— the objectives of the archon become the objectives of all. The problem of power created within the confines of the corporation is dissipated, as it takes its benign and equal place alongside all other groups in society.

Now, it is true that organization theorists are not necessarily liable for the uses to which their scientific ideas are put by corporate ideologues. However, there is not only science but an ethic embedded in organization theory, an ethic that cannot be completely disguised by all the game theoretics and mathematical simulation employed by it. The refined logic has by no means dispelled the aroma of those value judgments that stress harmony and corporate cooperation.

Here then is the new ideology. But what is the reality of the corporation? Now, there are tens of thousands of these "institutions" inhabiting the economic landscape, as the *Wall Street Journal* never tires of saying, yet only a few seriously affect society and the economy. While only 6 percent of the corporations reporting to the Internal Revenue Service in 1959 had assets worth over a million dollars, they did account for 70 percent of corporate receipts. The same few corporations supplied the bulk of the economy's jobs and contributed about 55 percent of total national income and almost 70 percent of national income originating in business. All the small corporations and individual proprietorships and partnerships together do not have the impact on our economic and social well-being that a relatively few large corporations have. It is on the latter that the community depends.

Here are some of the giants: General Motors—assets $8.8 billion, sales $12 billion; Standard Oil of New Jersey—assets $10.5 billion, sales $9.3 billion; AT&T—assets $24.6 billion (not counting Western Electric), sales $8.6 billion; Ford—assets $5.1 billion, sales $6.7 billion; Sears, Roebuck—assets $2.5 billion, sales $4.3 billion. All told, there are some fifty names on the billion dollar nonfinancial corporate list for 1961; their sales represent roughly 25 percent of the gross national product. One might broaden the picture somewhat by taking *Fortune*'s 1962 elite list of 500 leading industrials and the top fifty firms in merchandising, transportation, and utilities. Sales for this group totaled $337.7 billion or 65 percent of GNP. (A certain amount of double counting is involved in this arithmetic, but it ought not to reduce the percentage too much. If assets are considered, *Fortune*'s leading corporations, both financial and nonfinancial, may be said to hold perhaps a fourth of the nation's total wealth.)

Such dominant corporations are becoming increasingly important. The elementary fact is that more giants than ever are inhabiting the economic landscape. Fields that were once a haven for small business, such as retailing and service, have been invaded by the giants. In supermarketing, for example, less than 10 percent of the big chains take in 70 percent of gross sales. More and more, the small businessman finds it difficult to stay alive: the share of sales made by corporations with assets under $1 million has been declining steadily since the war—from 19 percent in 1947 to 13 percent in 1955. It is the huge, sprawling business bureaucracies whose decision-makers really move the economy.

IV

How did they get so big? The simplest way would be by an expansion of sales. But this has seldom happened. The most common method for building an industrial empire has been the merger, a device by which business anacondas simply swallow their smaller rivals. Industrial mergers in America came in periodic waves, the first around the turn of the century. Since then, virtually every major enterprise has experienced one or more of these economic fusions. In virtually all instances the motives were purely financial. As one economist put it, ". . . a rising, buoyant securities market made practicable larger and larger units of business enterprise." The archon discovered that really handsome profits might be garnered by selling and buying intangibles, a practice clearly stemming from the changing nature of property itself. And herein lies the reality of the corporation today.

Traditionally, property implied a precise relationship to corporeal objects with an unimpeded right to use, dispose, and bequeath real things. As developed by John Locke and in the thinking of the colonists, property meant freedom; it provided a means of earning a living; it meant independence. It gave a man a base from which to speak his piece, a base that was not dominated by either church or state. And it justified Jeffersonian hostility to the corporation, for the latter had been in the main a Crown agent and carrier of special privilege. Yet, within three decades of the Constitution's adoption, the corporation had won.

Its legal personality assured by the Fourteenth Amendment and the courts, the corporation lent protective coloration to American industry. Incorporation became an inalienable right, requiring but three names and a modest fee to obtain a charter. Businesses of all kinds and sizes assumed a corporate shape. To be sure, one of the chief attractions was limited liability, restricting the financial responsibility of the "owners" solely to their equity holdings. But the major unintended consequence was to transfer the idea of property from things to pieces of paper. This could be done because in jurisprudence the corporation became a *being,* individual and immortal, and presumably able to manage its affairs as a collective entity and to clothe the spirit of man for all time.

In reality, the stockholders did not own the things that comprised the corporation. A share of stock did not give its holder a right to an aliquot portion of physical assets: it only entitled him to some part of the corporate income, provided the managers were willing to part with it. And if one possessed a share in a holding company, an organization whose assets were merely shares of other corporations, what part of the underlying enterprises did one then own? As the corporation grew and expanded, no one was quite certain who owned what. It was transformed into an institution unto itself, in no way responsible to the shareholder.

The latter became less the capitalist and more the speculator whose concern likely was centered on prospective price rises on the stock exchange. The stockholder seldom felt a sense of loyalty to the corporation, for he could always sever his connection by simply selling his shares. True, he could vote at the annual meeting, if he got there, but any notion that this would lead to corporate democracy was rather silly, for scattered security holders, whose interest in actual operations was minimal, could exert no influence on internal corporate matters. In fact, most stockholders willingly turned their votes over to incumbent managers through the device of the proxy.

Consequently, there is no need to search for some external principle to justify control, as Eells does in so painful a manner. Boards of directors exercise power because no one else can. As Bertrand Russell once said: "Where no social institution . . . exists to limit the number of men to whom power is possible, those who most desire power are, broadly speaking, those most likely to acquire it." Power in the corporation is now antecedent to profit. Gains are extracted by virtue of strategic control of productive and pecuniary relations; it is no longer a case, as in classical capitalism, of possessing power because a venture is profitable. It is enough to control an enterprise. As a consequence, the nature of the political process in business has been reversed, a turnabout made entirely possible by the corporate proxy! Originally intended as an instrument of convenience for absentee stockholders, the proxy allowed management to perpetuate itself in office.

V

The new managers also have obliterated the traditional family capitalism of the nineteenth century. Many corporations were once owned by *personal* dynasties: this no longer is the case. The desire to merge and to dominate an industry enforced a turn to the capital markets, resulting for a while in banker-imposed rule. But finance capitalism was surprisingly short-lived, for the new managerial class discovered that with an adequate supply of funds stemming from accumulated profits they could get along quite well without Wall Street tutelage, especially when the corporation itself provided two-thirds of the saving required for investment. (Federal income tax depreciation rules have underpinned a good part of these savings.) Today, it is the paid professional who governs the corporation. In one study of 232 corporate directorates (*New University Thought,* Winter 1962), 58 percent of board members were classified as executives or former officers while financiers of one sort or another represented but 4.5 percent and major stockholders less than 20 percent. It was also evident that the executives had rather small shareholdings in the corporations over which they held sway.

Sometimes a seemingly genuine contest for internal control develops. The solemnity with which these titanic struggles are conducted have all the attributes of a ritualistic dance in which the participants have no freedom to alter preordained motions. The stockholders—allegedly the legal owners—really have little to say about what goes on. The battles for control of the New York Central Railroad, Montgomery Ward, and the Bank of America all looked like political campaigns, with promises of reform, declarations of new deals and new frontiers, and invective against adversaries. Professional proxy gatherers worked like block captains bringing in the vote, while the candidates made grandiloquent speeches.

Power in the corporation, consequently, has little if any relationship to property. Control and expertise are sufficient to legitimate the uses of power. Eells has said quite plainly that knowledge of how a corporation works is a property right which does not demand stock ownership to justify its use. And how right Adolph Berle was when he said that modern capitalism is no longer a system of property relationships, but one rather in which the exercise of power *without* property is the dominant feature. In his words, a relatively small oligarchy of men out of the same milieu, dealing almost always only with each other, and possessing no ownership relation of any sort, represent *the* power center of the corporation. Thus, it is rather a vain hope that the corporation can be "constitutionalized" to make it responsive to the wishes of its "members."

And in fact, it is technically difficult to impose a proper exercise of the corporate franchise. The National City Bank recently listed fifty-six large corporations with more than fifty thousand stockholders each, and twenty-seven with over 100,000 stockholders. Democracy in the ordinary meaning of the word would simply become chaos. The very diffusion of stockholdings makes government in the usual sense impossible. Even the 5 or 6 percent of stock owners who hold the bulk of outstanding shares are too many to effectively manage a corporation, for they still number over a million persons. Thus, despite some concentration in stock holdings, dispersion is sufficient to create a passive attitude. Further, most stock owners are much too concerned with prices on the exchange to be genuinely interested in running a corporation. Besides, such political analogies are false, since shareholders are not the ones governed in a corporation. The governed rather are the direct participants in the economic and industrial activities dominated by the corporation; they are mainly workers and suppliers. It is here that one must begin to talk of democracy in the corporation.

VI

The passive nature of the stockholder, then, allows control to be seized by a managerial corps. Sometimes, more direct devices are employed, as in the case of Sears, Roebuck. In this company, the nation's largest mercantile enterprise, 70 percent of a $750 million pension fund accumulated since 1916 is invested in Sears' stock, giving the fund more than a fourth of the outstanding shares. This is enough to insure absolute control, particularly when the trustees of the fund are appointed by the board of directors of the company itself. It was not until Senator Fulbright questioned this arrangement a few years ago that employees were allowed to vote for "their" pension trustee. But this in no way has disturbed the self-perpetuating character of the Sears oligarchy. Nor do the voting rights given to future pensioners in similar arrangements in Standard Oil, Union Carbide, or the Celanese Corporation affect the continuing control of managerial insiders, for there would have to be some unity of purpose and some sort of bloc voting for a real change to take place. The likelihood of this ever occurring is dim.

Robert A. Gordon demonstrated in his *Business Leadership in the Large Corporation* (1945) that majority ownership was the *least* common mode of control in the larger nonfinancial enterprises. Minority control was most typical in more than half of the cases studied by Gordon, while stock dispersion was so widespread in another 34 percent of the cases that management was able to do quite as it pleased.

Might increased common stock purchases by financial intermediaries—banks, insurance companies, investment trusts, mutuals and pension funds—lead to a new kind of finance capitalism? In fact this is unlikely. True, most of the $30 billion or so of the stockholdings of these institutions are concentrated in a few hundred issues of the "blue chip" variety. But this stems mainly from their search for safety and a good yield. In almost all instances, as Robert Tilove has shown, those who run the "financial intermediaries" usually transmit their proxies to incumbent managements without question. If they dislike what the latter are doing, the stock is simply sold on the exchange. This often does more to rattle a board of directors than a threatened proxy fight.*

Of course, managers frequently do own stock in their own corporations; yet Gordon's data showed that all the members of his boards of directors plus all corporate officers held but about 2 percent of the voting shares in their firms. In only 20 percent of the companies studied did management hold more than 10 percent of voting stock. Mabel Newcomer's *The Big Business Executive* (1955) not only verified Gordon's analysis but revealed that by 1952, corporate executives owned an even smaller proportion of their companies' stock than was the case in the 1930's. This does not mean that officers have no financial stake in their corporations, for 1 percent of $200 million outstanding shares is $2 million, and at a 5 percent yield this brings a neat $100,000 per annum. The executive does indeed have a keen financial interest in his organization, even though he doesn't "own" it. He thus has sufficient reason to welcome the control provided by the modern corporation; when other stockholders try to rebel, he is apt to view their action as a peasant's revolt to be crushed.

This is the reality of the corporation—non-corporeal property, proxies, and the centralization of power. In Michael Reagan's apt phrase, we have now a managed economy in which the central

---

* *The Wall Street Journal* recently reported several instances in which institutional investors voted against management proposals. This by no means suggests a return to finance capitalism. If the disagreement is sharp, the investor sells the stock anyway. Institutional investors have not yet undertaken proxy contests.

question is: for whom is the managing done? Obviously not for those subject to the archon's power. His rule leads rather to a system of commands and internal sanctions which create a tightly-knit operational code. As a result the oligarchs at the top have successfully disenfranchised the mass of stockholders and unless restrained by the countervailing power of a labor union or government agency, are able to injure workers, suppliers and customers. And contrary to John Kenneth Galbraith's belief, such countervailance is not always forthcoming: as in the case of the electrical conspiracy, "countervailance" often occurs after the damage has been done—if at all.

VII

Joseph Schumpeter, like Galbraith, has argued that bigness in industry has been worthwhile. To Schumpeter, the "creative destruction" practiced by large enterprise acts as a stabilizer for the economy, in that it assures a proper return for a sizable capital outlay. Galbraith has said that only oligopoly—an ugly technical word meaning big business—has been best able to use the unmatched technology with which we have been blessed. Further, corporations are the fount of research and innovation. Yet this seemingly persuasive argument stumbles over the fact that about half the important inventions affecting consumer goods since 1900 have come from the brows of independent researchers working without benefit of a corporate laboratory. Air conditioning, automatic transmissions, cellophane, jet engines, and the quick freeze were among those that came from old-fashioned inventors or relatively small companies.

To be sure, a fair amount of industrial innovation does today appear as the product of the corporate milieu. But three-fourths of the federal government's enormous outlay for research and development is paid to industry, with much of it directed toward military application. Although the government supplied 56 percent of research and development monies from 1952 to 1956, 72 percent of the work was done by private corporations; and if one looks at *applied* research, 75 percent of the activity is found in the corporation.

But how meaningful is this vast industrial research, amounting to almost $8 billion? Aside from expenditures for defense—

perhaps half the research and development outlay by corporations
—much of it may be described as glorified waste, the use of
scientific techniques for enhancing corporate gain. Much research
goes into fancy package design raising the cost of an item and
intended primarily to carve out a little monopoly by making the
product unique because it contains some exotic ingredient not
found in rival packages. This is then advanced by furious advertising campaigns. Between 1947 and 1957 advertising outlays
increased 145 percent—from $4.2 billion to $10.3 billion, or equal
to almost 4 percent of consumer spending. Moreover, advertising
and industrial research often are employed to make a perfectly
good product obsolete. This is called "dynamic" obsolescence, and
in such industries as appliances and autos it is conceived to be
the most noteworthy scientific objective.

It is at this point, in its relationships with the consumer and his
family, that the malefic power of the corporation is most clearly
exposed. Here countervailing power is utterly absent. Here producer and consumer are revealed as unequal antagonists. One
possesses unbounded economic horizons; the other is severely
limited in what he can do, dependent on the sale of labor services
and subject to ailment and accident. One produces commodities of
dubious quality; the other must buy what is available. One is a
paragon of efficiency; the other, a backward practitioner in the
art of spending money. One has vast financial resources at its
command; the other, despite the availability of installment credit,
suffers from serious economic disability. One invests in the latest
physical equipment; the other frequently is unable to make proper
provision for human capital. One can build new plants in the
suburbs; the other must accept such services as the city may
offer, and these are usually inadequate. Yet it is the consumer
who is supposed to be the beneficiary of what the corporation
does. In reality, the consumer has long since lost his sovereignty
and his supposed capacity to influence the social and economic
order. Estranged from the sphere of production by technology, he
has long since forgotten what property means, which itself has
been attenuated to the point where it no longer has substance.

Today few persons are able to select alternatives to the estrange-
ment that contemporary economic and political drives impose. Most
of them are found in the upper reaches of the corporation; though
as propertyless as anyone else, they do possess power and can

exercise choice. As C. P. Snow once said in another connection: "One of the most bizarre features of any industrial society in our time is that the cardinal choices [are] made by a handful of men. . . ." And the choice they make frequently signifies disorganization for the great mass of men they seek to control.

1964

Merger and Monopoly
in the United States

The rash of mergers in the early 1950's once again highlighted the problem of monopoly. Quite the most glamorous corporate marriages occurred in automobiles, where the overwhelming strength of Chrysler, Ford, and General Motors forced Hudson into the arms of Nash, compelled Kaiser to embrace Willys, and linked Studebaker with Packard. When automobiles' Big Three got through with their share of the market, the six independents were left with a mere 4 percent of the industry's total output. The ensuing mergers were desperate attempts to hold on to even this small segment of the auto business.

All this represented the crest of the fourth wave of mergers in U.S. history, a fact of which even the literate public did not seem to be especially aware. From 137 in 1949, mergers increased to 822 in 1952 and have since remained close to 800 each year.

The merger is the classic American way of building an industrial empire. In Europe, where the cartel has usually been employed, some concession is made to individual corporate identity. But here businessmen prefer to buy out their rivals, taking over plants and assets *in toto* and fusing disparate enterprises into new and wonderfully complex organizations. Bringing together plants, financial structures, and selling apparatuses, the merger, which is something of an imperative in American capitalism, has largely been made possible by the ineffectiveness of the anti-trust laws. These laws, sufficient for controlling loose arrangements such as trade associations, were unable, until 1950, to place any restraint at all on merger activity. A Clayton Act amendment in that year, yet to be tested in the courts, makes mergers which tend "substantially to lessen competition" legally dubious. Of course, the question of how competition is *not* reduced in an industrial combination may not be an easy one for a jurist to decide.*

The word "merger" is a somewhat vague one: it applies not only to combinations in which two or more enterprises are displaced by a new corporate entity but also to the case in which complementary manufacturing processes are brought together. The steel industry offers a striking illustration: here coal mines, iron ore fields, foundries, and a host of fabricating plants are brought together to provide a continuous manufacturing process from raw material to finished product. The word also has been used to describe common control of such entirely different enterprises as hotels and sugar factories.

The first great merger movement took place from about 1898 to 1904. This was the time when the "trusts" were born, giving the language a generic term for all industrial combinations. The trust, it will be recalled, was the device utilized by the Standard Oil Company. In this combine some forty firms turned over their voting stock to a board of trustees for trust certificates, thus enabling them to control effectively prices and production for the entire group. After it was outlawed by the Supreme Court, a

---

* An illustration of this problem was made available by the recent ruling of Federal Judge W. J. LaBuy in dismissing anti-trust charges against DuPont, General Motors, and U.S. Rubber. Among other things, this distinguished jurist held that there was no proof that DuPont controlled General Motors even though it was at times voting 51 percent of the stock voted at stockholders' meetings.

ready substitute was discovered in the holding company, an invention of several crafty corporation lawyers who convinced the New Jersey legislature that it was not an unreasonable legal device.

The underlying factors in this first merger wave were, of course, more basic. A rapidly growing market for mass-produced goods irrevocably destroyed the century-old grip of local parochial monopolies; markets became national in scope so that a small merchant or manufacturer might no longer expect to retain leadership at home simply because he held a locational advantage. For this he had to thank the fantastic growth of cheap transportation facilities. In addition, technological advances inexorably increased the ratio of fixed to variable costs. The businessman suddenly faced the problem of idle capacity and overhead. The first solution was a price war calculated to destroy his rivals; but this only raised a dilemma, for the ensuing cutthroat competition theatened to wipe out everyone. And so there came a realization that "live and let live" would be the ideal rule. Even better, some thought, would be "living together as one," for then anxieties concerning mavericks who might willy-nilly cut prices could be entirely eliminated.

This first wave of mergers was the greatest in American history and clearly had the most profound impact on subsequent economic growth. An example of the kind of forces that were joined at this time is offered by the spectacular case of the United States Steel Corporation. In 1898, the Minnesota Iron Company, one of the largest iron ore producers in the country, and a large rail and lake carrier as well, merged with Illinois Steel and Lorain Steel to create the Federal Steel Company, which now had 15 percent of the industry's total ingot capacity. A year later, National Steel was formed out of several other firms, making up 12 percent of ingot capacity. In 1900, the Carnegie Company of New Jersey took over the Carnegie Steel Works and the H. C. Frick Coke Company, to come up with 18 percent of national ingot capacity. Then, in 1901, financiers brought all of these together to form U.S. Steel with 45 percent of the industry's ingot capacity. Yet this was not all. Tossed into the hopper were certain fabricators: American Tin Plate Company (itself a merger of thirty-six companies) with 75 percent of the nation's tin plate capacity; American Steel and Wire, combining nineteen companies with 80 percent of total wire capacity; National Tube Company, which had 85 percent of tubing capacity; American Steel Hoop Company; American Bridge Company; Shelby Steel Tubing; and the Lake Superior Consolidated Iron Mines.

After 1904, the American public, giving vent to its traditional hostility to corporate bigness, began to clamor for a breakup of the trusts. Businessmen themselves were calling for a temporary halt in empire building, not merely to digest what they had already absorbed, but also to gather strength for the coming economic storms which broke out in 1907. Then came World War I.

A favorable climate for a second wave of mergers was created by postwar optimism. Professional promoters, discovering that capital was readily available, prepared to turn an easy profit. From 1919 to 1921 mergers were initiated either through holding companies or outright consolidations expressly for the purpose of taking advantage of a bull market in securities. New companies meant new stocks and in a rising market a handsome gain could be easily realized. Insofar as industry itself was concerned, the major motivation for mergers stemmed either from a desire to establish vertical combines, thereby ensuring a regular supply of raw materials, or from a need to rationalize sales and marketing operations.

By 1926, the third wave period, a number of new industries had reached a state of economic maturity: motion pictures, public utilities, radios, automobiles. But the business community did not hesitate to subject them to reorganization, combination and merger. Nor did these cease with the onset of the depression. From 1932 to 1938, according to a Federal Trade Commission report, numerous consolidations continued to take place. But the outstanding feature now was the absorption of small firms by large ones. In the steel industry during this time, firms worth $3 billion in assets swallowed firms worth $217 million; in auto accessories, $377 million in assets took over $28 million; in oil $832 million absorbed $42 million.

Since the end of World War II, the FTC has found that there have been about 700 to 800 mergers a year. Between 1940 and 1947, more than 2,500 firms with total assets of over $5 billion disappeared. The magnitude of this growing concentration may be more strikingly visualized if we realize that this was 5.5 percent of the total assets in manufacturing industry in 1943. Yet all this was merely a prelude to the wave of mergers that reached its peak in the last two years. Large corporations have been literally hunting for new industrial conquests.

Some recent examples: American President Lines purchased control of the American Mail Line for $5 million; Hilton beat out the fabulous William Zeckendorf for control of the Statler hotel chain with an offer of $75 million; Continental Can Corporation bought up five large bag-making factories; the National Lead Company has branched into other metals; Electric Boat got itself into the airplane business by securing control of Consolidated Vultee; Allis-Chalmers took over an engine-making firm, the Buda Corporation; Chrysler bought Briggs Manufacturing Company, an auto body maker, thus strengthening itself while at the same time weakening Packard, a one-time Briggs customer; H. Daroff and Sons, one of the largest clothing manufacturers in the country, obtained control of Botany Mills, a textile concern.

One of the most heralded mergers (but not consummated because of government opposition) was that planned between Youngstown Sheet and Tube and the Bethlehem Steel Company. Had this been approved by Justice Department attorneys it would have created an integrated firm with a capitalization of over $2.5 billion. Underlying the desire for this merger was the abandonment of the once universal basing-point system. This pricing technique enforced a uniformity that was achieved by adding freight charges to the price of steel at some theoretical mill from the latter point to the place of delivery. Thus, a customer in Chicago would pay the same price as a customer at some distant point despite the fact that the mill might actually be in Gary, close to Chicago, since all prices were calculated "as if" from Pittsburgh. In this way, by calculating prices as from an "originating" point plus freight, all firms were able to compete on a roughly equal footing in the same market.

Today, the FOB mill pricing system is used, so that firms are able to develop a territorial advantage. Bethlehem Steel can no longer compete with Inland Steel in the midwest. Production facilities in the industry have become more and more market oriented. But Youngstown Sheet and Tube does own 2.5 million tons of capacity in East Chicago; the proposed merger therefore would have placed Bethlehem Steel on an equal footing with Inland Steel in the Chicago market. This was one of the few instances where the federal government hesitated to approve a merger; and so Inland Steel still has the upper hand in the midwest.

There is little doubt that businessmen welcome mergers. Pious expressions of faith in the Smithian unseen hand notwithstanding, rigorous price competition remains the bane of their existence. Said the *Magazine of Wall Street:*

> Mergers are part of a national trend that demands greater integration and a higher degree of efficiency in operation if our industries are to further develop . . . and supply this nation which within the next five years will have a population of 175 million people who will need and want what industries turn out today along with many new products to be developed by research and made available through technological developments.

The urge to monopolize is not the sole motive drive in mergers. Frequently a profitable firm will buy up unprofitable ones in order to save taxes through balancing acquired losses against accumulated gains. This was a powerful factor in the Kaiser-Willys get-together. In at least 10 percent of the mergers of small firms the tax element is predominant, while this holds true for at least 25 percent of the large firms. In addition, older firms will purchase younger ones in order to take over new inventions and ideas. Retirement often will be something of a factor in merger sales. Yet whatever the immediate reason, the basic acquisitive urge is to achieve a dominant position in the trade. The merger movement is basically a struggle for greater market strength and larger profit, with personal ambition playing a not insignificant role.

Sometimes the motive for a merger is euphemistically described as diversification or the need for having a fuller line of products. Thus, General Mills, a food processor, entered the home appliance field and more recently took over a small sponge manufacturing concern. International Shoe acquired the Florsheim retail chain. RCA purchased Estate Stove, giving it a connection with gas ranges and heaters: these are doubtlessly natural neighbors for TV sets in retail shops. The absorption of the American Broadcasting Company by Paramount might be said to have been an effort to overcome technological competition. At any rate,

ABC was helped immeasurably by the additional capital that Paramount was able to bring into the combine. And so, 600 theatres, six radio stations, and five TV stations joined a network of over 300 affiliates in radio and seventy-six in TV. Avco Manufacturing Company, a creation of Victor Emanuel, one of the country's shrewdest financiers, originally made airplanes, but now it handles household appliances, engines, boilers and castings. While all this vertical integration does improve stock marketability and often enables a firm to secure working capital more easily, it also tends to create monopolistic industrial structures.

The small firm is frequently willing to let itself be hooked because the bait is so attractive. Small firms while having a good saleable product may have insufficient working capital. The merger of General Mills and O-Cel-O, the sponge company alluded to above, is a case in point. The latter, whose annual sales approximated $3.5 million compared with GM's yearly gross of $480 million, was founded by three young men, previously DuPont engineers, who within a few years had built up a fairly respectable business. When they finally allowed themselves to be taken over, they were given 30,000 shares of General Mills stock. This was about 1.4 percent of the total, a significant chunk in a company where the largest single block was but 4 percent. The profit on the deal amounted to $1,700 for every $100 originally invested and was subject to tax at capital gains rates, which are considerably lower than ordinary income levies.

That concentration in industry is intensified by such mergers would seem to be self evident. George Stigler, a fairly conservative economist, said in 1950 that not one steel company had been able to add as much as 4 percent of ingot capacity through attracting new customers, implying thereby that the greatest part of growth was to be explained by merger, consolidation, and asset purchase. This authoritative statement notwithstanding, there have been several studies in recent years which sought to deny this relationship. Two economists, John Lintner and J. K. Butters, have argued in their "Effect of Mergers on Industrial Concentration, 1940–1947" (*Review of Economics and Statistics,* February 1950) that no correlation between mergers and concentration could be demonstrated. Limiting their survey to manufacturing and mining, they concluded that small companies actually did better in mergers than large ones. They admitted that between 1940 and 1947 over 2,500 firms disappeared as a result of mergers, but nevertheless insisted that this form of combination was not an important source of corporate growth. Examining only the size of the companies involved in mergers, they made the remarkable discovery that the percentage growth in assets during the period was smaller for the large companies. To anyone familiar with the mathematics of percentage calculation this should not be surprising, nor is it especially meaningful, for ratios must necessarily be smaller in the group with the larger arithmetical base. What is interesting is the admission by Lintner and Butters that the larger companies were more active in the merger movement: they found that not only was the proportion of companies acquiring one or more outside firms larger in the big company group but that the average number of acquisitions per acquiring firm was higher for the large companies.

As the FTC later demonstrated, the large companies—that is, those with assets over $10 million—accounted for 63 percent of the number of acquisitions and 76 percent of the total amount of assets bought. Furthermore, the Lintner-Butters study was based on data derived only from companies actually involved in mergers, thus omitting the many small firms that had not taken part in the combination movement. This method in effect understated the activity of the large firms by making it seem that a relatively large number of small firms comprised the bulk of merged companies. FTC economists were quite correct when they argued that Lintner and Butters should have related their statistics not merely to the affected firms but to the whole complex of industry. For the 1940–1947 period, the following data suggest a picture quite different from that painted by Lintner and Butters:

Size of Buying Firm	Percent of Acquisitions	Value of Acquired Firms Millions	Percent
Under $5 million	24.5	$ 451.3	13.9
$5–10 million	12.8	330.2	10.1
Over $10 million	62.7	2,473.6	76.0

Would outright prohibition of mergers have any effect? Probably not, for centralized control of prices and production would doubtless be attained in some other manner. American industrial history demonstrates at least this much. The alternative, it is said, is to control mergers through a judicious enforcement of the anti-trust laws. The FTC and the Justice Department assert that they have nipped in the bud dozens of proposed mergers that would have been monopolistic. This is done under the 1950 Celler Amendment to the Clayton Act, which requires that business show that a merger will be in the public interest and will not substantially reduce competition. Yet the simple fact is that aside from an occasional Bethlehem Steel case, present-day mergers continue their merry way.

Under the New Deal, industrial concentration was viewed with a certain amount of undefined horror. Government lawyers said that competition was healthy and monopoly bad for the body politic. This outlook, accepted by the great assortment of liberals that gathered under FDR's banner, created a certain feeling of kinship with the American radical tradition. Soon Thurman Arnold, who in an early book had lightly dismissed anti-trust action as folklorist whimsy, began to wave the big stick. From 1938 to 1941, Arnold, as head of the Anti-Trust Division of the Justice Department, chased monopolies with headlines and large appropriations. He even broadened the traditional approach by pursuing such non-commercial enterprises as the Associated Press and the American Medical Association.

Did all this furious activity ever alter anything? The answer is, no! There is little proof that governmental action reduced concentration in any sensible way; on the contrary, monopoly in the widest sense seems to have increased despite the close concern of the government. All that could be said is that legal action or the threat of legal action influenced the shape that mergers assumed (that is, asset versus stock purchase or outright amalgamation versus integration). Little effect was exerted on prices, output, or employment policy. Whatever the form, there is an undeniable tendency toward control from the center. In many ways, this is due to the legal philosophy that underlies anti-trust; all too often real collusion or behavior close to conspiracy must be demonstrated. Yet price maintenance and restricted production may be achieved without collusion. Price leadership, "moral suasion" and mutual understanding among giant rivals are all acknowledged social forms for obtaining monopolistic control; yet in such instances it is virtually impossible to discover conspiracy within the meaning of the law.

The simple fact is that anti-trust has been a dismal failure. The Sherman Act was emasculated by judicial interpretation; by 1920, it was useless. The Clayton Act fared no better—though how well the teeth that were inserted by the 1950 amendment will work remains to be seen. The only thing that could be said for anti-trust was that it inhibited outright monopoly; business tycoons thought it the better part of discretion to let a few small rivals stay put. Some writers feel that changes in corporation law, taxes, and the patent system may create incentives for industrial giants to disgorge their subsidiaries. Whatever the merit of these notions, they are at best palliatives, since the hardening tendency that the merger movement implies continues unabated.

Whatever shape monopoly may take, the social costs are essentially the same. Mergers, patent control, cartels, price leadership, all tend to create higher prices, a lower level of output, wastage of resources, and excessive profits. Easy entry into an industry, one of the prime requirements of competition, at least in textbooks, is severely circumscribed. The monopolists (if we want to be technical, we might call them oligopolists) will employ whatever means are necessary to keep out newcomers, as witness the attempt of the auto industry to keep out Kaiser-Frazer just after the war. In these ways maximum control of market and production is incessantly sought.

One argument in favor of combination hinges on the ostensible heightening of industrial efficiency. However, if this is to be defined as the lowest possible cost level, then it can be demonstrated that such is not always the outcome. The elimination of troublesome competitors is often motivated more by high profit considerations than by the desire for low cost. In 1947, John M. Blair, a Federal Trade Commission economist, presented fairly conclusive evidence to show that combination did not bring about decreased costs. Whatever gain large corporations made, he said, was in the purchase of materials. This substantiated in the main the arguments of Arthur S. Dewing, a noted economist of the twenties, who showed at that time that profits after a merger were all too frequently lower than for the total of the previously independent companies. And whatever the other advantages ascribed to monopoly, such as specialization or the ability to use by-products, it must be clear by now that these are derived from the technical features of large-scale production, rather than from combination per se.

Nor do mergers necessarily increase economic stability, as Schumpeter once intimated. It is not often realized that this sort of corporate stability frequently becomes rigidity. The burden of excess capacity may make it difficult to adjust to changing economic situations. The reaction to altered conditions is made not through reduced prices but through curtailed production, thereby effectively shifting the burden of the ensuing idle capacity on to that part of the population least able to bear it, while investment possibilities are determined by the shifting strategy of maintaining market control.

Many of these socio-economic phenomena are obscured by the current postwar prosperity. But should the pressures of an exacerbated international political crisis be relaxed, the underlying drives will tend to assert themselves and then the economic sclerosis toward which the current merger movement contributes will be exposed to full view.

1955

The Computer and Management Control

There is no longer any doubt that the computer is an extraordinarily useful device. A product mainly of the postwar era, there are now, according to the counts made by *Computers and Automation,* some 40,000 installations in the United States with about half that number on order. In 1964, there were only about 25,000 computer installations throughout the world: those who would minimize the accelerated growth of computers would do well to contemplate these data.

Not only is the computer useful, it is extraordinarily versatile. No institution required to process thousands of bits of information can really perform well without the computer. No institution such as a large university, or a bank, can function effectively today without all the hardware installations and the accompanying software. To be sure, it is the latter that is of real significance. All we need to know is the capability of the machine, and then it is the job of the institution to get it to work. And the range of work is wide.

For example, computers can be employed to construct models of particular situations and to simulate their conditions, so that management can ostensibly direct its decision-making into channels with an appropriate payoff. We can simulate, for example, consumers' exposure to advertising. Department store pricing methods, site selection for warehouses, sales forecasts, and inventory strategies have all been simulated on computers. How to handle inventories, one of the more volatile elements in the economy, can be quite important to a business. This problem too has been simulated on the machine by playing the inventory game to demonstrate how lead time in ordering and lag time in production can produce either insufficient or excess inventories. Poor inventory strategy for an individual firm can cause losses or worse: surplus inventory can start the economy on a downward spiral. By simulating an inventory system on a computer, the business manager can study specific failures and correct them. In fact, the entire operation of a business can be replicated on a computer: at M.I.T. such replication was done to cover eight years in the life of an imaginary company.

The technique is not always successful: the complex social systems which the simulators have tried to put into the machine must be reduced to relatively simple segments, or they end in a tortuous chain of equations that no one quite understands. The likelihood that a household will buy certain goods thus depends on the extent to which a product is used (heavy users being more apt to manifest larger replacement demand), timing of previous purchases, consumer attitudes, and, of course, advertising. Differences in purchase probabilities for various goods over a given time period have to be estimated and added to the data. And some picture of household characteristics must be attached to the assumptions employed. The computer then calculates the likelihood of certain purchases, and the businessman can decide how to stock his store and when to order from his suppliers.

The advantages of doing these computations on the computer arise, of course, from its great speed. Meat-packers, for example, may want to forecast beef prices six months in advance. But this forecast depends on many factors, including the number of cattle on feed, steer and feed price ratios, and conditions out on the range. To compute all these relationships by hand for a period covering five to ten years, involving thirty to forty elements, would be practically impossible. But in one meat-packing company, it took some 200 man-hours to program the analysis, comprising about thirty statistical series to calculate twelve monthly formulas. The computer takes but a few minutes to scan the data, compare the various series, and then print out the best equation. With forecast errors reduced to 5 percent, the number of cattle to be slaughtered is readily established.

In the office, the businessman has recognized not only that the computer can handle the routine tasks of bookkeeping and storing information, but also that, with its capacity to manipulate information in extraordinary ways, it can affect the manner in which business itself is to be conducted. Those who recognized the potentialities of the computer are likely to become innovators, after the fashion of Schumpeter's hero, for with advanced data processing and "communications techniques" they can move more quickly than their rivals.

Although not all managements have thought it worthwhile to resort to extensive computerized data processing, for such a giant as DuPont there are few doubts. This company, one of the true pioneers in applying computers to data processing, has had some 5,000 employees involved in one way or another in ADP (automatic data processing). Although the figure does not represent much of an increase in such personnel compared with 1959, the company is twice as large as it was then, and the amount of information processed through its computers has increased geometrically. DuPont's computers evidently pay their way, with each tended on the average by some eighteen operators and programmers. Even the engineers spend half their time at the machines.

With increasing automation in the factory, the data that flow from the production floor or the shipping platform must be equally automatic; otherwise, the manager's control is incomplete. Furthermore, such control cannot be retrospective: it must rather be in "real time," simultaneous with the event itself. Communication channels needed by management to direct its operations must keep pace with the rapid changes that take place on the production floor. To solve this problem, the experts have devised remote data-gathering systems that tell plant managers the instant a machine breaks down or the moment a critical inventory item has been depleted. Such a system provides a running account of the number of workers on a given task, the tools they use, and the location and progress of the job at hand. And while the computer is churning out reports on these "events," it automatically generates the information for payroll and billing.

In some operations, notably in defense and space work, production runs are relatively short, so that the factory must be organized as a huge job shop, with as many as 50,000 different job orders in progress simultaneously. To check on the progress of a single job could be a tedious affair. Now, however, the plant manager merely inserts a card with a description of the order into a remote data unit, which sends the information to a computer. The machine then returns a report telling where the job is located in the plant, the number of parts involved, exactly what work has been accomplished so far, and the estimated completion time. It all takes but a few seconds. The system is especially useful in cases in which numerous parts are used in production, requiring substantial inventories. The remote data units keep track of the materials and of parts requirements, making possible drastic cuts in inventory stockpiling.

In petroleum, the men who search for oil no longer wear leather jackets and stand in sand up to their hips. They are "white-collar" workers who, like anyone else tied to a desk, are up to their knees in paper and statistical data. For example, in searching for oil, the history and data on each well are the geologist's main tools. Sometimes there are so many facts on an individual oil well that four or five days may be spent shuffling papers. But now automated data-processing systems for oil wells are available.

At one steel company, IBM equipment handles every number in the company, except possibly the address on the letterhead. This company, a relatively small producer, had computerized its complicated incentive-pay system as far back as 1956, and in 1962 its computer system was advanced enough to explore the cost implications of the revised supplementary unemployment-benefits program and the extended vacation plan negotiated with the union for the entire steel industry. The company's data processing has resulted in better control of inventory; it has also halted the growth of its clerical force.

The technique, based on a "total-systems concept," is essentially a single-entry record file programmed to relate each recorded activity on which it impinges, and to have each event automatically activate the subsequent one. The variables are quite diverse, stemming as they do from mining, transportation, and metalworking, as well as steel-making. If an order comes in from a regular customer—and most orders are "repeats"—only ten variable bits of information have to be entered into the fifty-six-million-character random-access disc file. The other bits are already in storage. The system then makes twenty-one computations: What size ingots? How many for this order? What dimensions for the slabs? When will the space be needed at the mill? Are any slabs in this type already in stock? Is the customer's credit satisfactory? Which salesman got the business? What is the cost per ton? The computer virtually minds everybody's business. It orders raw materials, checks on mill spares, records straight-time man-hours, computes incentives and accumulated vacation time, tells the sheet mill when slabs will arrive, and records the fact that a delay in a certain department is to be attributed to some defective components.

At a major automobile company's headquarters, plants, sales offices, and warehouses used to send one another a million words a day via teletype and telegram. This now archaic system has been replaced by a computer that receives and transmits messages automatically. Under the old system, in which a Detroit communications center relayed the messages, a query from eastern Canada to Vancouver went first to Windsor, Ontario, then to Detroit, from which it was sent to a relay station in Los Angeles, and finally up to British Columbia. It took twenty-six minutes. The electronic system takes thirty-five seconds and eliminates the stopover at Los Angeles. The new way is much simpler and is connected to only twenty two-way simultaneous circuits instead of the twenty-six two-way unidirectional circuits formerly employed. More teletype stations can be hooked onto each circuit, and there are fewer circuits. The computer also supervises some accounting operations. Every seven-thousandth of a second it checks the circuit's condition and reports to a human supervisor. It also records the number of words stations send and calculates the cost to be assigned to each. At another level is a data-processing system based on corporate centralization that would combine the eleven manufacturing groups into three, employing the transmission of 1.6 billion bits of computer data a month between plants. An enlarged memory capacity would store the history of every car sold under the company's five-year or 50,000-mile warranty, so that any sales office would be able to secure within seconds the complete history of any warranted automobile.

A tobacco company utilizes data-processing equipment to deal with inventory management, leaf usage and logistics, smoke analysis, sales data, and credit review. Sorters and account tabulators handle record-keeping for libraries. Magnetic tapes store records of elementary and high school students and digest other educational information. Drug-dispensing charges are kept by computers in pharmacy departments of hospitals. Automatic ticket-punching devices, in which the commuters' rides are validated by sending instruments, speed passenger movement on suburban rail lines. And computers and radio signals coordinate traffic lights to regulate the direction and volume of traffic on different streets at different times of the day. In this system, information on punched tapes is fed into a computer, giving it detailed data on traffic conditions throughout a city. When the morning rush hour starts, the computer sets the signals to allow a rapid flow of traffic downtown. In the afternoon, the signals are reversed. As one expert remarked: "Traffic control is no longer a bunch of lights at an intersection. It's a data-processing system."

Data processing by computer has many more applications, including verifying checks at retail stores, estimating bids for contractors, making decisions on buying policies, forecasting sales, and guiding the complicated steps that must be taken in building a space missile. In check cashing, for example, a request to the computer elicits information on credit ratings, validity of auto licenses, bank reports, and the like. The machine may also have stored information on checking account numbers of people known to be poor risks. To estimate electrical contract bids, an index of 45,000 electrical assemblies is stored in a special unit with data from blueprints. As the required assemblies are checked off with an electrically operated pencil, signals automatically enter the information into the machine. A computer then prepares a summary of costs and a complete bill of materials and labor requirements.

Of course, there have been moments when management's enthusiasm has gone awry. An expediter for a television manufacturer simply threw away his daily tabulation of shipments received because it was always a week old. To obtain current information he had to employ the conventional method of telephoning suppliers and receiving clerks. A purchasing agent in an aerosol company discovered that the ADP reports on purchases that came from the accounting department gave only financial data without the technical descriptions he needed. In an aircraft company, a data-happy programmer issued a performance report on suppliers based on a fancy statistical formula that tied together in one index number prices, delivery records, and quality. No one knew what he or the machine was talking about. These instances, however, are rather rare; in most cases, sophisticated data processing is useful enough to save 50 percent or more in operating expenses. One company cited in the *Harvard Business Review* (March–April 1964) reduced its personnel by 23 percent after installing a computerized system in its purchasing department. By applying ADP to its purchasing operations, another corporation substantially reduced its product costs, enough to come close to its goal of 15 percent cutback. When the purchasing operation consists of repetitive orders of low dollar volume, the computer can take over the entire routine.

Perhaps the most dramatic use to which computers can be put is in the new management tool called PERT (Program Evaluation and Review Technique). This technique was developed during the 1950's as a way of controlling manpower, materials, and facilities in such complicated projects as building space vehicles or nuclear-powered ships. Starting with a joint effort by DuPont and Sperry Rand to work out ways of checking engineering work, it was adopted by the Navy in 1957 as a method of unraveling the intricacies of the Polaris missile project, which involved more than 11,000 subcontractors. DuPont cut the time on certain projects by one-fourth, and Polaris was built two years ahead of schedule by applying PERT. With Polaris, research and development supervisors were never certain which component would be ready first and how it might fit into what already had been done or what still had to be worked on. Essentially, the problem was one of complex scheduling, of fitting certain activities and production and completion dates together in a way that would bring gains in costs and time. For example, shipbuilding is based on numerous small jobs that are interrelated. The pipe fitter cannot run his conduits until holes have been cut through plates; the electrician cannot lay wires until provision is made for cables. PERT is a method for figuring out what will be needed when. Stated this way it sounds deceptively simple, but the steps can be sufficiently complicated and numerous to warrant the use of a computer.

The method employs a network or flow chart to show the movement of materials and the use of manpower as the project moves from one "event" to the next. Such "activities" as the outlay of money, the scheduling of time, and the use of equipment may be plotted, showing at the same time the various relationships that develop among them. Most important, the charting enables one to make time estimates involving each "event" or "activity": at last, the project manager can evaluate the data to calculate a completion time and then relate the activities to the time when he is supposed to deliver the goods. The "critical path" on the flow chart is the longest time it would take to reach the project goal. Upon completion, the whole network looks like a diagram of the nervous system of an exotic animal.

Obviously, it is not difficult to calculate the details when the network is small, encompassing no more than, say, ten or twenty events and activities. One enthusiast drew up a PERT diagram for himself when his wife bore him a child: it took up three large sheets of paper, listing visits to the hospital, purchases of formula ingredients and bottles, arrangements for diapers, and the like. There are small manual disc graphs available to help figure PERT systems for small projects. Designing a diagram or network is something like working out a plane geometry problem: knowing the end result, the expert works backward to discover how to get there.

The sequence of operations is set up in a manner that can be fed into a computer, which in turn enables the whole design to become more elaborate. As the chart shows the estimated time between events, the computer quickly totals the figures for each possible path and even computes alternative time estimates. In complicated construction jobs, some operations are done in parallel rather than in sequence, so that a measure of time overlaps. The computer will take this overlap into account as well. In a sense, it is all similar to planning a party. Food must be ordered and prepared at various points of time, a cake baked, liquor purchased, a maid hired, the hostess' hair set, a table prepared, a closet emptied for guests' coats, and so forth. Like the housewife, the missile-maker may discover that it is more expensive to pursue a crash program than a normal one.

With its initial success, PERT became quite the rage, especially when the U.S. Defense Department and NASA advised their contractors to carry out their obligations along PERT lines. A typical PERT program was the one designed by IBM for the construction of the student-faculty center at Stevens Institute in New Jersey. The network included 1,500 activities, but that was no problem for the computer. It showed which work had to be started each day in order for the project to be completed on time. When a shipment of granite from Norway threatened a month's delay, the new information was added to the computer, which specified which other jobs could be accelerated to ensure that the structure would be completed on time. By using PERT on one of its projects, General Precision Electronics was able to reduce overtime work substantially. General Electric now uses PERT in most of its divisions; Climax Molybdenum schedules its mining operations according to PERT; Olin Mathieson moved an entire division from Baltimore to New York via PERT; and a Colorado hospital has employed PERT methods to plan open-heart surgery. Canadian companies are beginning to apply the technique, and a member of the Soviet Academy of Sciences showed up at an American Management Association PERT seminar in 1963 to learn what it was all about.

PERT planning has been used in the installation of materials-handling systems, ship construction, blast-furnace relining, tool programs, missile-countdown procedures, and computer installations as well. Its proponents consider it an important tool for speeding project completion, controlling projects, identifying problem areas, managing resources, and reporting progress. For some middle-management people, however, it is simply another reporting system; as one builder snorted, "I've been doing that in my head for years." The literature on PERT has become enormous: there are now articles, reports, papers, manuals, and even books on PERT. The Air Force recently estimated that by 1963 there were more than 700 works in the field. The experts now talk of "PERT time" or "basic PERT," the original form that stressed expected time requirements for the whole set of activities, as against "PERT cost" and other "multidimensional" forms, which take into account expenditures, manpower, performance, and other variables. There is also CPM (Critical Path Method), which concentrates on that path in the network that would satisfy time scheduling at the least cost. In CPM, there is less dependence on time-probability calculations, a characteristic of the PERT technique. This feature makes the CPM approach more useful in cases in which the technology and processes are better known.

Variants of the technique have proliferated. SPAR is a way of smoothing out work loads; COMET, employed by the Army Materiel Command, emphasizes scheduling; CRAM, the Air Force's favorite, is totally computerized, with the machine setting the control cycles of "events" and "activities" and purchasing sequences for components and parts; IMPACT is a way of controlling computer systems by estimating programming costs; CRAFT lays out facilities and materials for new plants; and LESS calculates the least cost method for a particular program. And, of course, there are PERT II, PERT III, PEP, PEPCO, and Super PERT. All are ways of turning over the brain work of middle management—those responsible for the operation of factories or sales forces or control of inventory—to the machine. Granted that the major achievement is in the mathematical technique. Yet what need is there for personnel when the computer can schedule production, determine manpower needs, establish tool requirements, set shipping quotas, and assign salesmen to territories? In these areas the repetitive, routine nature of much of the work makes them candidates for a computer program. And these areas are the ones that have been computerized.

Consider the traveling salesman problem. A salesman wants to visit a certain number of cities, stopping once in each city and then returning to his point of departure. Which route will be the shortest, and which will incur the least travel time? If there are only fifteen cities, the number of different routes that could be followed will reach 1.3 trillion. Even with a high-speed computer it would take centuries to evaluate all the possibilities. Yet the machine can be programmed to provide a fairly close solution for a fewer number of cities, which it achieves in a relatively short span of time. The answer is worked out on an IBM 7094 utilizing 4,500 instructions. The method can be applied to such problems as routing cables or wiring or scheduling production "events" as in a PERT problem.

These methods illustrate certain facets of "operations research," the whole range of mathematical techniques developed since the war to guide management decision-making. Most companies with computer installations have concentrated mainly on payroll, book-keeping, and other routine data-processing tasks. Now that these tasks have been mastered and made routine, they—or rather the programmers in charge—are looking for bigger things to do. And the bigger problems generally consist of the kinds of problems just described. Rule of thumb and trial and error are archaic methods for the conduct of business affairs today. The data that now flow out of the machine are sophisticated enough to solve problems that were seldom thought capable of solution. When A. K. Erlang, a Danish mathematician, worked on the problem of waiting lines in military telephony, no one realized that the theory of queuing that ensued might help solve waiting lines at highway toll booths—after the data had been put through the computer. The question of how long it pays to keep spending money pursuing delinquent credit accounts appears as a variation of the World War II submarine-search problem. Sometimes the query to be answered is rather strange—for example, figuring out how to reduce employee consumption of toilet paper (answer: tighten the clips on the side of the roll so that it won't move easily).

The computer offers opportunities for integration that seem unlimited. It has enabled management to reverse the trend toward decentralization, into which it had anyway backed somewhat unwillingly. Now top management can bypass intermediate staff people, for information comes out of the machine so quickly that the president knows a given situation before his divisional chiefs are aware of it. As *Fortune* once conceded, "Whenever a decentralized company has used the computer to automate operations, and particularly when it has installed management information systems, it has willy-nilly found itself behaving more like a centralized company." Although those below top management may object, there is no doubt that the "discreet monitoring of their activities by computer systems makes them more sensitive to the company's goals." At Westinghouse, for example, such "monitoring" led to a reduction of the white-collar working force by some 4,000 people, including not a few middle managers. The reasons are fairly evident: when markets are monopolistic and prices are administered by management fiat, the enormous savings made possible by the computer require more and more centralized control over production, inventories, and sales. Said one economist: ". . . the introduction of formalized decision procedures, incorporating such tools as linear programming and dynamic programming, has tended to centralize the decision-making process [through computers]. . . . In practice the solutions are invariably obtained by centralized computations using algorithms like the simplex method and not by the *tâtonnement* of a market." That is to say, the machine is superior to the market in determining resource allocation.

In 1963, the U.S. Steel Corporation "reintegrated" seven of its divisions into its central operations to reduce costs and "enhance performance." District sales offices were reduced from fifty-three to twenty-eight, and the reduction in salaried employees was estimated at more than 2,000. The production department was to become "more closely knit and compact" to enable plant superintendents "to act promptly in any situation." Research and engineering operations were also consolidated. The objective was to enable the company to react to market conditions in virtual "real time." None of these changes would have been possible without the integrated data-processing system of the computer. Said *Business Week,* reporting on U.S. Steel's new corporate look, "No specific job changes [were] announced, but it's plain that they will take place—literally by the hundreds. It's less plain, but equally inevitable, that there'll be a huge loss of jobs . . . the management fallout . . . will involve dismissal and demotion as well as end many established paths for career growth. . . ."

Among the methods of the corporate official in achieving these objectives of reintegration is one called "systems analysis." A system in this sense implies that all the inputs and outputs of a company are automatically coordinated. For example, a customer's order means a certain assignment of labor and materials and consonant adjustments in inventories and available work force. As the market projection is now made by the computer, all the manager has to do is read the tape and decide what action to take. Furthermore, if the machine is of the problem-solving variety and is properly programmed, it may also suggest what action the manager ought to take. In effect, a "system" permits management to integrate related departmental activities—it can break up little empires in the organization; it extracts policy decisions from what is properly routine work; and it mechanizes manual operations. And the executive may be able to converse directly with the machine through visual-display devices that make it possible to present problems to the machine and get direct answers without having to rely on programmers.

According to the systems analysts, the natural goal for the organization is a single, unified way of handling information. First, the general requirements of an integrated approach are outlined, enabling critical areas of data to be identified. For example, if the transmission of information must employ ordinary communication links like telephone lines, certain problems of competing uses must be solved. Decisions on hardware cost and availability have to be reached. Finally, the organization has to install the system, at which point "people problems," as one computer expert put it, suddenly become urgent. The program must be sold at various management levels and to the work force. Starting with routine administration and personnel, the systems man proceeds to engineering design, product scheduling, and preparation of the input-data method. This provides the executive with an integrated technique of control and monitoring.

An illustration is the system installed by the Hotpoint division of General Electric. Employing magnetic tapes alone, fourteen main subsystems are integrated through thirty-eight interrelated input tapes. The subsystems handle customers' orders, invoices, carloading directives, and the like. The staff comprises six systems managers, with five programmers and four systems-design experts assigned to each. In manufacturing and engineering, the total system was only 20 percent short of completion by mid-1964, yet the whole operation paid for itself by producing useful information the company could not otherwise obtain. This subsystem handles production schedules, procurement, payroll, and standard costing. Furthermore, it keeps track of parts and the appliance models to which they have to be attached. For those appliances that are assembled on the basis of decisions in the shop (rather than being predetermined in the front office), the computer calculates the optimum ratios of work load to the number of workers on the line. By this sort of line balancing, labor utilization has increased from 85 percent of available time to 93 percent.

Does this method pay? According to one report, the Electronic Specialty Company of Los Angeles was converted within nine years from a floundering firm with only a few items on its production line into an $85 million company with a full line of related products by use of systems analysis. Other companies have evidently had similar experiences, with the result that "systems" based on computers are now all the rage. Although 19 percent of capital spending by industry in 1963 went for automation and systems, in some industries the ratio was even higher—26 percent in automobiles, 30 percent in electrical machinery, and 33 percent in glass, stone, and clay. Despite the fact that the experts do not agree on how close industry can come to the total-systems idea, it seems worthwhile to try, particularly when complete monitoring of business activities—automatic control of inventories, production, shipments, payroll, and anything else that can be reduced to mathematical equations—is made more and more feasible. An apocryphal tale is told of one ambitious president who installed such a system, even teaching the computer to simulate his thinking, and was then promptly fired by the board of directors because he was no longer needed. The reality is that the machine can do more things than we are ready to believe. The new "systems" appear essential in view of the huge scope of operations of many companies, the diversified products, the geographic dispersion of plants and officers: only computer-based management systems, it is said, will permit management to bring order out of threatening chaos.

Some companies are rather lax, from a "management science" point of view, in their use of computer technology in that middle managers are allowed to apply the machines as they see fit; in most instances the ultimate objective is control through a single programming staff. The intent is to exert a central discipline on policy production and procedures, particularly over outlays for direct labor and materials costs. Not surprisingly, the effort to centralize via the computer often generates opposition within the organizations, especially from middle managers. Computer programming for control purposes requires a precise statement of function: loose verbal formulations are no longer satisfactory. But when the systems man asks a departmental manager to state what it is that he does, there frequently is resentment, for the detailed questioning is apt to be interpreted as a search for weakness. What was once an accepted, easy adjustment is converted into strains and challenges. The middle manager fears that coordination and integration will curtail his prerogatives. Furthermore, he knows that a computer places him in a glass cage. One reel of tape contains as much information as does a standard cabinet file, whereas several tapes provide all the operating data for a whole division. But these tapes are not under the control of the middle manager; they are stored elsewhere and can tell top management what goes on without the department head knowing anything about it. In effect, the middle manager is bypassed. As one such department chief exclaimed, "My data could be picked up, read, misunderstood, and I could be fired without ever knowing why."

Nevertheless, the top manager is determined to take back the reins of power he had to surrender under the rule of decentralization, and the computer is helping him do just that. In company after company, headquarters specialists have been installed to assist top management in regaining control: technical-information officers, information-retrieval specialists, and product-engineering coordinators digest masses of detailed information flowing out of the computer to keep top management advised in language that it can understand. In essence, then, the computer removes control of operations from the middle stratum and hands it over to a small corps of specialists responsible only to the top, where planning now takes place. Meanwhile, the men in the middle are pushed down. For the fact is that the alteration in middle-management jobs is taking place more rapidly than is the conversion of the skilled machinist into a machine tender. The supervisor and the department head become sergeants rather than company commanders. No less an authority than Herbert A. Simon has asserted that by 1985 it will be technically feasible to replace many if not all the human functions in organizations with machines. The only question to be answered is whether or not, as a matter of economics, it would pay to dispose of all the people at once. In any case, the decision-making process acquires a new transparency through monitoring by the computer and provides for just the sort of coordination desired by management.

In recent years the number of middle-management jobs relative to output has declined. Indicative is the fact that between 1950 and 1960 the average annual increase in white-collar positions was 2.8 percent; in 1963 it was 1 percent. T. L. Whisler, who has studied the impact of automation on management more closely perhaps than anyone else, reports a cutback in one company of managerial posts as a result of computer installation of almost 30 percent. The computer is upsetting functions, displacing managers, and wiping out jobs, says *Fortune,* and consequently it generates fear and resistance even among the highly skilled white-collar men. Yet corporate officials appear reluctant to talk about this phenomenon, as they are reluctant to talk about displacement in the factory. When the Ford Motor Company took over Philco, it reorganized and rationalized the latter's production lines and cut back the number of employees from 27,000 to 20,000, at the same time eliminating many executives who had thought themselves secure. The tightening of the executive lines stems from the new philosophy of centralization engendered by the computer. This process has been going on now for several years in many American corporations. The result is a lesser need for middle-management skills. Certainly, an important function of the intermediate posts has been to provide training grounds for movement up the corporate ladder. But when jobs can be combined or handed over entirely to the computer, there is not much opportunity for management apprenticeships. Remarked one engineering consultant, "The National Science Foundation says we'll need 700,000 more engineers in the sixties, but I'll wager that a fifth of these will be unemployed or out of engineering by 1970, three out of five will be disgusted with their lot because they're not being used fruitfully—leaving only one-fifth actually functioning satisfactorily as true engineers." Added another consultant, "[With] computerized applications . . . we will not need as many people in management positions. . . . Bitter as will be the resistance and fierce the rationalization, the process of elimination of management positions is necessary and will proceed inevitably."

Even the buyer in a department store is threatened by the computer. In late 1964, a management consultant told the National Retail Merchants Association that by 1970 buyers would make no merchandise-control decisions: in fact, there would be no merchandising middle management at all, as the machine would control inventory, assign sales clerks, process credit applications, plan advertising campaigns, and handle accounts receivable and payable. The computer would provide data on sales performances, undertake customer "walk-out" studies, and "peek" into every selling area of the store to evaluate what the employees were doing. Customers would be rated on marital status, education, place of residence, and type of work. And, said the specialist, all of this work would be under a "vice-president for management services" reporting to the top man and possessed of a "rare combination of [knowledge] of retail practices as well as computer systems."

Unconcern with the fate of the middle manager is sometimes justified by saying that more featherbedding goes on in certain management circles than labor ever enjoyed. Because automation leaves little or no genuine decision-making power in the hands of middle-echelon executives, it becomes relatively easy to cut away redundant staff.

To achieve the ultimate objective of control, future systems will no doubt be based on direct visual and voice communications with the machine, that is, there will not even be a need for programmers. Module equipment will provide flexibility and self-correcting programs, and heuristic techniques will permit solutions to be derived for the most difficult problems. It seems evident that the kinds of control systems envisaged by these developments, which will employ information retrieval, direct document reading, simulation, and the like, will require a new corporate structure with management skills converted into mere reactions to a total information processing system. The traditional operations of market analysis, production, sales, and finance will be linked by unbreakable reels of tape.

In the meantime, management must call upon allies to computerize the organization. Electronics engineers, mathematicians, and technicians have been recruited to assist management. To be sure, conflict has often been the consequence. Yet management can exercise control, for once a program is firmly set, anyone with average intelligence, aptitude for logical thought, and in most cases no more than a high school diploma can be trained to operate the computer. Of an average of about fifteen men working on a large installation, no more than three earn more than $7,000 a year, and at most one or two are the "systems" specialists. It is the latter, of course, who give top management the tools for integrated control. Although "old-timers" often express resentment at "change for the sake of changing," the fact remains that the future will see a new generation of computer specialists achieving their goal of total integration—an objective implicit in the science they have learned and the philosophy they voice.

What sort of men are these systems specialists? Fostered by computer manufacturers to facilitate the permanent placement of equipment in industry, they are generally young, ranging in age from the mid-twenties to mid-thirties. They are well educated, with master's degrees in accounting, statistics, civil engineering, and even library science; a fair number of Ph.D. degrees in chemistry, physics, and mathematics also may be found among them. Logical aptitude is the major requirement for their work. As the early accounting-machine operators have moved up in the last decade or so to controllers' posts or out to sales managers' jobs, the new information specialists have begun to occupy the data-processing posts left vacant or opened by advancing technology. They now "systemize" accounting, engage in "operations research," develop technical reports, and have the machine produce parts catalogues, directories, and customer listings. They are thoroughly committed to the computer.

Their knowledge of hardware and software often is baffling to others, and they may be treated with the deference accorded to outside consultants. The systems men want to get things done; they therefore find the most difficult problems to be the inner politics and conflicts of the organization. Furthermore, their closeness to management is apt to generate hostility and resentment; but assured of support they design their own projects, ignore time-honored rules of the corporation, and cut across departmental lines—all to achieve a totally integrated system. And they are more than likely to tell a personnel manager worried about displacement that it's "all none of your business." When social scientists ask about the impact of the changes they have initiated, the systems men reply that "everyone is thrilled with the challenge of automation."

Despite the sometimes serious hassles with others in the organization, the systems men invariably win out, simply because they have the support of the manager. They may not know much about measured-day work or cost accounting and may be more interested in variables, optimums, closed loops, and other recondite problems, but all their efforts enhance control from the top. In fact, in many places what appears to be happening is the development of a new type of manager who is well steeped in systems analysis. Increasingly he replaces the old-style middle manager so that, to use the language of the marketplace, the demand for systems men rises as that for ordinary middle managers falls. It is said that more managerial time can now be assigned to planning and policy-making; the routine decisions are given to the machine. "Problem-solving" becomes the major responsibility of management, and in that problem-solving the need for control is implicit. Indeed, if more problem-solving is undertaken this may very well be the task of those who are replacing middle managers—the systems men. Yet, as we have argued, systems techniques shift the center of gravity in the corporation from middle management to the front office. The work that the former used to do is given over to the machine, which now processes information at a pace fast enough to supply facts on events simultaneously with the events themselves, that is, in "real time." In the last analysis, control of the corporate organization is centralized through the computer in the hands of less than 1.5 percent of the population: the managerial group that constitutes the class of the corporate archon.

One can speculate that, in one sense, the entrepreneurial drive of the old-line middle manager will be displaced by the extension of the firm to larger "systems," encompassing even activity in the public sector. Should such a development take place, more than likely the new manager will find his horizons to be unbounded.

1967

Ideology and Big Business

Writers on the problem of ideology frequently describe it as an expression of a group or class view which gives the individual both an awareness and rationalization of his particular social role. Developing complex ideological systems along these lines was a favorite, often useful pastime in years gone by, but today, as C. Wright Mills tells us in *The Power Elite*, the recent attempts by dominant groups in American society to create an ideology have not really succeeded. The supposed beneficiaries of new ideological structures have preferred to drift along comfortably with a quasi-liberal rhetoric while the "new conservatism" of a Russell Kirk has been not so much rejected as ignored. The hallmark of excellence among the very rich has been, of course, money, while celebrities of the entertainment world are too unstable as a group to be especially receptive to ideology. It has been only among the *Fortune* readership, the acknowledged forum of management, that any interest has been shown in working up an ideology for Big Business.

How successful the managers have been in perfecting an ideology is illustrated by the interesting study* issued not too long ago by four Harvard social scientists. The authors went for their basic material to the public statements of business leaders, to institutional advertisements in *Fortune, Business Week,* and similar places, as well as to the many pamphlets flowing out of the NAM, U.S. Chamber of Commerce, and the CED. From the numerous quotations compiled by them two major strands of ideology may be discerned; the classical and the managerial, which seem to be roughly equivalent to what C. Wright Mills has called "practical" and "sophisticated" conservatives. One might almost describe these as the Henry Ford–J. D. Rockefeller image versus the Henry Luce–Paul Hoffman conception.

The first, though somewhat old-fashioned, exhibits a certain ruggedness in its blunt approach to basic problems. It unambiguously claims lordship over all creation and extols the general beneficence of the profit motive. Material as well as nonmaterial gains are explained by a relatively simple cause and effect sequence; what's good for business is good for all. Charles Wilson's otiose remark about General Motors a few years back varied this theme but slightly. The devotees of this view are not averse to repeating their litany in ritualistic fashion: the American Way of Life yields a high standard of living; there are 135 million radios; we can always outproduce the Russians; economic success is founded in efficiency; business is conducted in a spirit of service; and, above all, these attainments come about because of the System.

We are sometimes so case-hardened to the blandishments of advertising that we tend to forget how dense the underlying ideas are. As one wanders through this wonderful world put together by copywriters one would hardly know that the high level living the American promise has presumably given us has yet to be paid for; or that lots of people still haven't got that far, for they continue to live in what housing experts call "substandard homes"; or that some 22 million *families* have not broken through the lower middle income barrier of $4,000.

* *The American Business Creed,* by Francis X. Sutton, Seymour E. Harris, Carl Kaysen, and James Tobin. Cambridge, Mass., Harvard University Press, 1956.

The "managerial" ideology is a good deal more subtle. The managers wish to obtain the enthusiastic consent of those whom they would control and manipulate. Theirs is the understanding nod rather than the brutal push. For them human relations is the central core of the managerial ideology: managers and workers must learn to get along with *people,* if not with each other. As William Whyte, Jr., has said, the eye must be calm, the manner attentive, the character well rounded, the teamwork efficient, the handshake brisk. The discrete approach helps one to "get there," assuming that "there" is on top. Standardized routines to assure "performance" become substitutes for creative endeavor until conformity is hailed as the paradigm of morality. Thus, ideology celebrates the manipulation of behavior and the groundwork is laid for the enthusiasms of a total society.

The managers concede that the American economy has changed in the last fifty years, but what they see, after the fashion of Adolph Berle and David Lilienthal, is a growing homogeneity in which faceless automatons will be "professionally managed [by] socially oriented corporations." They see the American system as unique (in the older classical version, it is the outcome of a special act of creation), based on fundamental laws of nature. And being natural it is stable. Only "outside" threats tend to upset the even tenor of American economic growth. It is thus a system of original purity completely devoid of history and origin.

In quite sober fashion the authors detail the miasmic output generated by Madison Avenue on behalf of corporate enterprise. Teamwork, competition, thrift, and research are said to be the keys to our economic well-being. (That these slogans sometimes clash with one another does not perturb the ideologues, Sutton *et al.* rightly suggest.) The ideal American enterprise is the small entrepreneur who is really nurtured by a few large corporations. Besides, the big fellows, the ads always imply, had humble beginnings. And the wonderful thing about large firms, say the institutional advertisements, is that each is a happy family. Relationships inside the enterprise are warm, close, personal, and one would no more dare disapprove of them than of motherhood. It's like a football game: "management is the quarterback, and for the good of the whole team, labor should not try to call the signals." (This, from a *Business Week* editorial.)

The authors then go on to review the ideology's concepts of

profit, ownership, authority, competition, and other economic and social notions that keep cropping up in the businessman's lexicon. Nothing in this recitation is really unexpected. Profits are not merely an income but ultimately a symbol of accountability and rational economic calculation. Efficient executive control rather than stockholder risk bearing is the quintessential aspect of the corporation. The good executive prefers common sense to science, shirt-sleeve economics to academic jargon, purchasing agents to statisticians and the *status quo* above all.

But enough has been said to demonstrate the quality of thought implicit in the business ideology. What is of interest now is the *ideology of ideology* which forms the theoretical core of the Sutton book. The authors start with what they call the "unreflective character of thinking," which, while deeply rooted in social modes of behavior, has now become sufficiently hardened to be a matter of habit. The failure to meet sales expectations, the problems of controlling a production line, or the difficulties of dealing with trade unions are seen as merely imperfections in habitual behavior modes which inevitably give rise to psychological strains. Ideology, say our authors, is basically a reaction to such strain, for it is essentially nothing more than ". . . a patterned reaction to the patterned strains of a social role." This is indeed a neat formula: ideology is nothing more than a symbolic outlet for strain. Where social roles involve conflict, ideology provides the necessary system of ideas and symbols which mitigates the rivalry, and it is in this way that it becomes both driving force and balance wheel in the American economy.

Against this theoretical backdrop it isn't hard to explain the content of the dominant economic ideology by the strains generated in the businessman's role. Anxieties and emotional conflict find release in justifications of managerial expertise. This approval converts ideology into a psychological instrument for helping the businessman to sustain his ability to meet the requirements of being a businessman. Madison Avenue's clever ads are intended to assuage the *Angst* of both the copywriter and his client.

Ideology as an instrument of control or as an expression of interest is rejected as a viable theory by the authors, for, they say, an ideology must be motivated and it is primarily in the stress and strain of role conflicts that motivation can be located. But it is rather odd that the desire to control supply, as the economist would put it, should not be a suitable basis for such motivation. The authors also speak of the need for plausibility and legitimation in terms of audience standards. At this point, however, they seem to have come a cropper, since the experience of totalitarian countries would suggest that criteria imposed by authority can almost always make an ideology appear palatable. It is precisely in these countries that ideology as control was developed in more ways than were ever dreamed of in Western sociology. There was an opportunity here for working out a theoretical framework that our authors unfortunately missed. Certainly the historical approach, as employed, for example, by Reinhard Bendix in his *Work and Authority in Industry* (1956), seems a good deal more fruitful. Bendix recognizes that control is a significant factor, if not the major one, in the development of an ideology, and his careful study of eighteenth-century Britain, present-day America, Czarist Russia, and the Soviet satellites supplies ample evidence of that.

It is difficult to understand the authors' reluctance to employ the idea that the legitimation of power is a major basis for ideology. Clearly, the businessman resorts to this mode of justification in order to counteract the claims of persons outside his enterprise. But, say the authors, he keeps telling himself that he is always subject to market forces beyond his control, that he is a single atomistic unit in a world he never made, and that the question of power in this context is not a relevant one. Consequently the entrepreneur cannot justify his role in terms of power and is thereby unable really to establish his legitimacy. Hence, the resort to professionalization of the business role as an alternative way of attaining success.

Surprisingly enough, the three economists who helped the lone sociologist did not see through all this. To employ their own analytical concepts, price makers in a market are clearly more significant than price takers. The former are enterprises able to fix their own prices and to administer them in accordance with the needs of sales strategy, a quite important aspect of the economic order. Surely, this suggests some posture of control. Surely, it would have been relevant to relate the whole ideological apparatus of enterprise to the realities of market behavior rather than to the putative psychological motivation of Chamber of Commerce speech writers.

In fact, the curious thing about the theory of strain is that it is itself a part of ideology, for what it does is to raise the whole body of advertising gibberish to the level of useful behavior. Such an explanation offers a simple solution, since it provides an easy way out in distasteful situations. Whatever the business-man's reaction might be, he is assured an ample supply of aspi-rins by this ideology of ideology. There is really no other function for the system of business beliefs, according to our authors. This assumes, of course, that businessmen are really emotionally dis-turbed by economic rivalry or class tension. But until such can be conclusively demonstrated, it will still be more fruitful to see the problems of ideology in terms of power, interest, and control.

1957

Price Conspiracy:
The Case of General Electric

John Herling, one of our more astute labor reporters, has for years offered, in his famous newsletter, perceptive and often biting observations on the nation's labor leaders. He has also paid frequent attention to the popular pastime known as politics-on-the-Hill. Now, in *The Great Price Conspiracy*,* he takes a look at the business backyard on the other side of the fence and finds a slightly nauseating weed patch.

The major elements in the story of anti-trust and monopoly in the electrical equipment industry, the focus of Herling's fascinating book, are moral corruption and hypocrisy. Here were dozens of leading corporations and hundreds of respected executives who for years advertised to the rest of the nation that their activities were endowed with a kind of ethical responsibility the

* *The Great Price Conspiracy* by John Herling. Washington, D.C., Robert B. Luce, 1962.

fulfillment of which was threatened only by the tax collector and the labor organizer. They reiterated, *ad infinitum,* through ads on TV and in *Fortune* magazine, that their corporations—which by now had mysteriously acquired souls—were infused with a spirit of neighborliness, and that they desired nothing less than the mantle of good citizenship. Corporate objectives were said to be genuine public service within a framework of legitimate competition.

So far as the anti-trust laws were concerned, the corporations insisted, they would not engage in any activity that their lawyers deemed "violative." This at least was the credo of the General Electric company, the major defendant in the electrical monopoly cases. The hitch here, which Herling so well underscores, was that the conspirators never talked to their lawyers, only to their competitors. They thus set prices and decided which company was to sell to whom. Their public pronouncements extolled the virtues of Adam Smith, but their private behavior was rooted in a belief that a controlled market was the quickest road to corporate health.

Transformers, switch gears, circuit breakers, meters, insulators, and turbines—all instruments used in the manufacture and distribution of electric power—were sold by the combine on a rotating scheme devised to maintain what they deemed to be an adequate level of prices and profit. Only this meant gouging other corporations, municipalities, and the federal government. And these business archons and pillars of society knew they were engaged in an illegal conspiracy: they made certain that their gatherings would be held at duck-hunting resorts and other vacation spots, that meetings would be secret and communication Aesopian. They knew, in short, that they were committing a crime.

How the conspiracies were exposed and some of the violators brought to book makes as exciting a story as any Ellery Queen tale. Moreover, the author's superb handling of the numerous details and his effective irony reveal how universal corruption is in our way of life. (Herling notes that twenty out of thirty young middle managers told the Wharton School in a survey that they too would have conspired if told to do so.)

That price-fixing sessions took place without the knowledge and consent of top-level corporate management is incredible. Yet, as Herling demonstrates in delightful undertones, Ralph Cordiner,

G.E.'s chief, hid behind the veil of official corporate policy and, to compound the extraordinary hypocrisy, proceeded to lay blame on deceased associates or vulnerable subordinates. Such colossal gall is reminiscent of a time when one of the old-time robber barons exclaimed: "The public be damned." Some of the companies, of course, were somewhat shrewder. Westinghouse, for example, did not sanctimoniously discharge its culprits but continued their employment in order to retain loyalties.

The entire sordid episode is laid bare in *The Great Price Conspiracy*. Herling deserves an accolade for what patently was not an easy task—interviewing defendants, reading the hearings of Senator Estes Kefauver's anti-trust committee, attending stockholders' meetings (his description of the G.E. session is a gem), visiting company towns, and poring over court records are enough to try the patience of any reporter. Herling went through all this and has produced one of the finest case histories of anti-trust in recent literature.

The book certainly emphasizes an important aspect of industrial organization today: American corporations have not the slightest interest in free enterprise; in fact, they have gone a long way toward creating a private collective comprised of vassals whose function it is to legitimate profit under the rubric of the public weal. All else is myth.

1962

Buyers' Monopoly:
The Case of Sears, Roebuck

I

The purpose of this brief paper is to review the highlights of economic literature pertaining to certain aspects of monopoly behavior, particularly as they relate to situations in which large retailers are able to dominate markets where they are buyers rather than sellers. This is patently the case with such retail concerns are Sears, Roebuck, A&P, and Safeway. But in this paper I shall refer only to Sears.

Economic analysis generally begins with the competitive market. In such situations, there are presumed to be many buyers and many sellers, so many, in fact, that no single business enterprise is capable of influencing either the market at any given moment or the quantity to be sold. Whatever the individual enterprise does, it must accept the going market price, for if it tries to raise its own price it will lose business. If it tries to lower the price, its competitors will react instantly. That is, in such a market the impersonal forces of supply and demand are said to be dominant.

In reality, there are few such markets in the modern economy, for these would presuppose, in addition to a multiplicity of buyers and sellers, full knowledge of market conditions, complete mobility of capital and labor between industries, and easy entry and exit from industries. These technical requirements for perfect competition simply do not exist, except perhaps for a few agricultural products, or in the stock exchange.

The reality is that most sellers are not in a position to sell all they want at the going market price *without* influencing in some way that price. That is to say, there are few industries in which the selling unit, the business enterprise, does not have some impact on market conditions. Thus, in the case of steel, autos, cigarettes, and many other products, there are certain aspects of the selling situation and of the item itself that create deviations from the model of a competitive market. This is especially true in the case of retailing. As we shall see below, it exhibits many attributes of a noncompetitive market.

Theoretically, a single firm in a competitive market is faced by a sales curve, or more technically, a demand curve, which is infinitely elastic. That is, at the given market price it should be able to sell as much as it wants. Geometrically, with quantity on the horizontal axis and price on the vertical axis, the demand curve for the single firm at any stated market price is parallel to the quantity axis.

In this situation, the firm, being but a single small unit in a market of many buyers and sellers, cannot influence market price because its output is only a fraction of the entire market.

This version of market behavior dominated economic thinking for decades. Its most famous formulation was that given by Alfred Marshall, the famous British economist. Increasingly, however, economists came to be dissatisfied with the theory, for they recognized that perfect competition failed to describe the realities of the business world. It was evident that monopolistic behavior on both the buyers' side and the sellers' side is a common feature. Overhead costs and heavy investment in buildings and equipment became major elements in the economy which the older theory could not explain. Business units kept growing larger, yet in ordinary theory the market behavior that resulted—monopolistic in nature—was described more often than not as an exception to the rule. Location, as in retailing, became an important factor in business strategy. Finally, the exception swallowed the rule; such economists as P. Sraffa, Joan Robinson, and E. H. Chamberlin recognized that there is a whole spectrum of market situations, ranging from competition to outright monopoly, that had to be explained.

The central question in analyzing monopolistic market behavior was the kind of demand curve faced by the firm. In the modern business market, the demand curve was no longer infinitely elastic—i.e., parallel to the horizontal axis—but rather it dipped. This stemmed from the fact that a larger quantity of output could not be sold without reducing the firm's price. This "curve" in turn was due to the fact that in the new kind of market—an imperfect one—customers were *not* indifferent about their source of supply. The fact was that now location, packaging, habit, custom, and the like influenced buyers' preferences. The more such elements as these ruled, the more rigid the customers' preference, the more inelastic was the demand curve.

This meant that geometrically the demand curve for the individual firm was apt to be tilted downward. The major theoretical test of the nature of a market then became the degree to which elasticity or inelasticity of demand ruled. In modern imperfect markets, it was likely that inelasticity would predominate. This implied that a firm would have to reduce its price in order to sell more units, and, conversely, that an increase in price would lead to a loss of customers. It also implied a capacity on the part of the seller to control price, for by fixing the level of output and determining price in advance, he could know presumably how many customers he would have.

All this was conditioned by advertising, brand names, trademarks, and product differentiation, creating, in effect, a kind of little monopoly for the seller. This was possible because there weren't many rivals selling *precisely* the same product.

This situation held true for retailing, as was recognized at the turn of the century by Knut Wicksell, the famous Swedish economist. Said Wicksell: "Practically every retailer possesses within his immediate circle, what we may call an actual sales monopoly, even if . . . it is based only on the ignorance and lack of organization of the buyers." More recently, this description of retailing has been supported by the French economist J. Aubert-Krier. The monopolistic features of a retail market are characterized by stress on location as a kind of monopoly in space; service differentiation; a less than perfectly elastic demand curve; stickiness of retail prices; and a heavy emphasis on advertising and selling costs. All this reveals is that the classic competitive market does not exist in retailing, any more than it does in most other fields.

In analyzing the behavior of the firm in an imperfect market, one gets an estimate of total revenue at any point on the sales or demand curve simply by multiplying the number of units sold at that point by the unit price. Of major relevance, however, is the so-called *marginal* revenue, or the increment of total revenue occasioned by the sale of an additional unit of output. Now, price at any point on the demand curve is also equal to *average* revenue per unit, for it is simply total revenue divided by the number of units sold. When additional units are sold under conditions of a declining demand curve, as in an imperfect market, the price or average revenue is necessarily lower. There is, consequently, a loss in revenue on *all* units produced, so that the marginal revenue is less than the average revenue for the relevant range of the curve.

The same kind of analysis applies to costs. As output is increased, the marginal cost, or increment to total cost, diverges from average cost. At first, marginal cost is less than average cost, but as production expands, given the same plant facilities, marginal cost rises and then exceeds average cost. The firm's best position, according to this analysis, is set by the point at which marginal revenue equals marginal cost, for beyond that point expenses increase faster than revenue, while below that point it will pay to sell more because net revenue is added to the total income.

From the theoretical standpoint, a buyer of factor services or inputs should be able to determine his least-cost combination once he knows the prices of the goods or services he requires and has the proper technical information on how to combine the various factor services he purchases. This least-cost combination is generally established at the point where the marginal product of the inputs, or the contribution of the extra unit of input, is proportional to the prices that have been paid for them. For example, a unit of capital may cost ten times as much as a unit of labor. The least-cost formula means substituting low-cost labor for high-cost capital up to the point where the extra product of capital equals ten times the extra or marginal product of labor. The marginal product is a physical concept and is said to exhibit a declining tendency because of the law of diminishing returns. To restate the rule: least cost implies substituting low-cost labor for high-cost capital up to the point where the marginal physical product per last dollar spent on the input is the same for both capital and labor. Thus, if the marginal physical product of capital in relation to its price is greater than the marginal physical product of labor in relation to its price, capital would be substituted for labor up to the point where their marginal physical products would be the same.

This brings us to the key point: the marginal physical product has meaning for the firm in terms of what it can be sold for. The firm is interested in the salability of the marginal output of the factor service. This is called the marginal revenue product. It is the extra dollar brought in when the marginal physical product is sold and is computed by multiplying it by marginal revenue. A firm able to influence the market of the goods and services it buys will know that if it buys less it may be in a position to restrict the price it has to pay. Theoretically, a firm operating in an imperfect market will purchase inputs up to the point where the marginal revenue product, or added revenue stemming from the extra output derived from a unit of extra input, will equal the price to be paid for that input.

This sets the framework for monopsony, or buyers' monopoly. The latter refers to the capacity of a firm to control the prices of the goods and services it buys. Conversely, the vendor's price becomes dependent on the quantity bought as well as on other influences exerted by the buyers. There may be only one buyer in a market (a position that Sears has attained in any number of situations), or only a few buyers. A firm can enjoy a monopsonistic position even though the markets in which it sells its own products are more competitive. In effect, it can operate in markets with different characteristics.

The most extensive analysis of monopsony is to be found in the work of Joan Robinson, the well-known British economist. In such a market, the available supply of input factor services is not elastic, that is, supply does not respond easily or quickly to price changes. In such cases, the marginal revenue product diverges from the average revenue product. This situation provides the basis for the buyer's exploitation of the seller. To the buyer of input service, marginal cost rises faster than average cost, since the more of the input purchased under inelastic supply conditions, the higher the unit price. In principle, the monopsonist buys up to the point where the marginal revenue product derived from the input service equals its marginal cost. But there is a difference between the average revenue product of the input and its marginal cost, the difference being the excess of the average revenue product over the marginal revenue product of the input service. It is this difference that represents the exploitation of the input service by the monopsonist.

The monopsonist buys up to the point where marginal revenue product equals marginal cost. But he obtains a surplus, as it were, defined by the extension of the vertical through the intersection of marginal revenue product and marginal cost up to the point of average revenue product, so that multiplied by unit price, the latter point represents the monopsonist's exploitation of the input factor. The buyer has extracted more value than what has been paid for. Thus, theoretically, a buyer can exploit a seller.

The foregoing may appear to be abstract and theoretical, but it is frequently reflected in the actual behavior of big buyers. Profit, in effect, may be enhanced by limiting the demand for input services. Buyers often are in a position to offer a quoted price for inputs with vendors left to decide whether or not to take the offer. This is illustrated by the method of price-setting in tobacco markets and in the construction industry. In many ways, such practices also characterize the behavior of Sears as a buyer. The large buyer is in a position to offer a certain volume of business in return for price concessions. Or the large buyer takes a significant portion of the vendor's output, so that ultimately the latter has no alternative outlets, becoming dependent on the single large buyer. These are all features of the monopsonistic market situation.

II

A Brookings Institution study (*Pricing in Big Business,* 1958) is instructive as to the aims of various large concerns in market behavior in general, and of Sears in particular. This study indicated that some firms, such as General Motors and DuPont, are concerned with a target return on their investment. Others seek stable prices and margins, or set prices to meet competition. Several, however, including Sears, were described as *seeking to maintain and improve their market positions*. This is rationalized as price consciousness. To expand its share of the market, Sears is said to work ". . . through manufacturers for lower buying prices . . ." The link between price and buying policies was acknowledged to be closer in Sears than in most other large firms. And with the steady increase in volume over the years, the company has followed a policy of reducing its dependence on open lines available from vendors and has contracted more and more for products to be sold under its own label.

This in itself is no indication of monopsony behavior. Rather, one has to examine the manner in which Sears contracts for its supplies in order to ascertain whether or not monopsony in fact exists. The Brookings study indicates that in 1954 there were twenty-two suppliers controlled by Sears by virtue of majority stock ownership. These suppliers made stoves, plumbing fixtures, paints, farm equipment, television sets, and sewing machines. The authors say that such ownership ". . . developed out of certain situations in the past when buying arrangements satisfactory to both existing manufacturers and Sears could not be made on merchandise that Sears believed could be sold in large volume through its outlets." In other words, Sears was interested in obtaining as low a price as possible on the buying side in order to strengthen its objective of securing a large slice of the sales market.

Control of vendors was generally obtained, according to the Brookings study, through the device of extending financial assistance. In 1954, this was the situation in forty-six companies, comprising 109 factories, that did business with Sears. Aside from wholly owned and partly owned sources of supply, influence was also exerted on independent firms which provided Sears with 35 percent of its merchandise through long-term buying arrangements. Monopsony behavior was most evident in these instances, for here the vendor's price was virtually dictated by Sears. In buying from independents, Sears requires that the price it pays shall be a composite of the direct costs of the item plus a portion of overhead and enough of a ". . . profit on the capital investment deemed applicable to the Sears business." In essence, Sears tells the vendor at what price it will buy without regard to the overall business problems of the supplier. Where the vendor is thought to have made a "mistake" in setting its price to Sears, the latter protects itself with a so-called "competitive" clause, which in effect forces down the purchase price to that of other suppliers. From the economic point of view, the "bulk-line" or marginal vendor sets the price for Sears. But this marginal vendor's price is also dictated by Sears. The "competitive" price may result in shaving the vendor's margin, or Sears may step in directly and "suggest" changes in technique or even personnel. In order to carry through this policy, Sears prefers small factories concentrating on production and relying on Sears for a substantial part of their output. This is typically a monopsonistic behavior pattern, enabling Sears to control its sources of supply.

The latter situation applies in such instances as King-Seeley, which has provided Sears with its Craftsman tools and some Kenmore appliances, and the Emerson Company, which has furnished bench saws and arc-welding equipment. Here Sears's "basic-buying" or cost-plus arrangement obtains. Sears is also known to get into the planning, design, and production program of many of its independent vendors. The Brookings study showed that in the "basic-buying" arrangements, the unit factory margin was lower in all cases than comparable figures for competitive firms. The result was that Sears could buy at figures close to those of other distributors even in seemingly unfavorable situations. Thus, in the cases of refrigerators, house paint, and silverplate, to cite a few instances, Sears was able to outsell competitors despite a higher factory cost, simply because it had the monopsonistic power to enforce a low margin on the vendor.

Behavior of this kind is well known in the economic literature. There is some argument as to who is being exploited in such situations—the vendor or the community in general. In any case, exploitation does exist in monopsony in the sense that the buyer attains a value greater than what was paid for. And there is no assurance that these gains are passed on to consumers, as is sometimes argued, especially where the retail monopsonist is in a position to exert pressures on smaller retailers to obtain a higher degree of concentration in the selling market, a clear-cut objective of Sears.

1968

They Came to Hollywood

The history of Jewish enterprise in the Diaspora is largely a history of peripheral industries. Developed by entrepreneurs who were compelled to seek their fortunes in untried pastures, these industries acquired non-Jewish respectability only when their high profits had been well established. During the Middle Ages money-lending and banking were the only occupations open to Jews, and later it was foreign trade that permitted them to display their commercial talents. But these pursuits were viewed with disdain by the populace, and the authorities did not mind letting Jews extract the initial profits. This pattern of industrial development holds true even in America, and the motion picture industry is the classic example.

The motion picture industry is young—its commercial beginnings go back to but 1896—but it has already passed through all the major phases of capitalistic growth. Innovators forcibly took the industry away from unimaginative inventors and promoted it into a fantastic money-maker. Expansions and mergers marked its history during its first three decades, and once financial success was firmly established, Wall Street moved in quietly to capture another bastion for finance.

The potentialities of the motion picture were not recognized by the first promoters and inventors. They were anxious to protect patent rights, and did not seek a mass market. The task of development was undertaken by hard-driving, aggressive nickelodeon operators willing to shoulder the risks of an infant industry. They did their own financing; they wrote their own scripts; they built their own scenery; they developed the films and exhibited the pictures in their own primitive theaters. They had a capacity for work that only those on the periphery of the business world possess. These entrepreneurs were glove salesmen, pharmacists, furriers, clothiers, and jewelers. They were innovators, arrogant and often vulgar, but they knew what the people wanted and they created a form of entertainment within the reach of all. Responsive to the demands of a hungry movie-going public, they created the feature picture and the star system. Their names were Zukor, Fox, Lasky, Loew, Mayer, Selznick, and Goldfish.

In the beginning the movie industry was shunned by respectable businessmen. They thought it a low form of amusement that would only ruin reputations. The public, however, felt no such qualms and demanded more films. Studios mushroomed all over the country, and anyone who could rent or steal a camera became a producer. By 1909, competition had become so intense that the larger manufacturers formed the Motion Pictures Patents Company as a measure of self-protection. Independent producers, however, refused to be intimidated by the patent combine's legal tactics, and economic warfare raged unabated.

The bitter struggle between the patent combine and the independents continued until, in 1914, the MPPC ceased to be a dominant factor. Carl Laemmle had formed a powerful protective association; William Fox, faced with a shortage of films for his theaters, began to produce his own pictures; the Lasky organization became too important to be suppressed. Men of that caliber did not accept easily the restrictive dictates of the early movie monopolists. Leading a shoestring existence, they did not mind an occasional hasty trip to Mexico to avoid an injunction suit.

The need for quick escapes from the patent combine's process-servers compelled the independents to seek movie locations close to the Mexican border. Southern California became the ideal place, for here one found superb replicas of the deserts of Africa and of the wilds of India. Continuous sunshine permitted all-day shooting and cheap labor made mob scenes an inexpensive undertaking.

The experience of the patent combine proved to alert movie entrepreneurs that distribution and exhibition were the keys to absolute control. Adolph Zukor, William Fox, and Marcus Loew began to dispose of their nickelodeons and acquire more dignified theaters. The extremes to which the early magnates went in their search for dignity is illustrated by one of Loew's theater purchases. He bought a closed burlesque house in Brooklyn that had been often raided by the police. When acquired, the building was being used as a storage place by the Salvation Army. The decrepit theater was fumigated physically and morally; for several months it was used by a troupe of Italian Shakespearean actors. Loew then opened it as a respectable family movie house.

Marcus Loew was a conservative businessman in an industry marked by flamboyant extravagance. He started life as a newspaper boy on New York's East Side and by the turn of the century had become a fairly successful furrier. Peep-shows, the latest rage in low-cost, high-profit entertainment, offered a more attractive field, however, and together with Adolph Zukor, Loew began to build a chain of penny arcades. Zukor and Loew were very unfriendly partners; each wanted to run the business his own way. When the firm rented new office space, Loew conveniently forgot to provide his colleague with a desk and chair. Zukor could not overlook the insult to his dignity; he left to become an independent producer of films.

Throughout this early period of growth Loew sought to exhibit a better kind of picture. But he soon found it difficult to obtain good films, for Zukor, his erstwhile partner and now an important producer, stubbornly refused to exhibit in the Loew chain. In 1920, Loew decided to make his own pictures. He bought out a moribund producing company called Metro Pictures, and in 1924 added the Goldwyn Picture Corporation and L. B. Mayer Company. Thus was formed the alliterative MGM, Loew's producing subsidiary.

L. B. Mayer, born in Poland, came to the United States in the late 1890's. A member of the original group of Jewish furriers, jewelers, and nickelodeon operators who built the movie industry, he became MGM's chief. Mr. Mayer's fantastically high salary testified to his shrewd bargaining powers. When Loew wanted to buy his firm, Mayer inserted a profit-sharing clause in the contract —a clause that often brought his yearly earnings close to the half-million mark.

After Marcus Loew's death in 1927, the enterprise was directed by Nicholas Schenck, a hard-headed businessman who followed the conservative practices of his predecessor. Schenck had come to America in 1892 with his brother Joseph, and together they had operated an amusement park at Lake George, New York. One day Marcus Loew came there to show movies, and the Schenck boys were imaginative enough to forget the amusement park game. Nicholas joined the Loew organization and Joseph became a movie producer. Nicholas Schenck soon won the reputation of knowing best where to build theaters. Thus, although the Loew chain was much smaller than the Paramount or Fox group, its income was markedly increased by the fact that about half of its houses were first-run theaters.

It was Adolph Zukor, however, who established the pattern for expansion in the new industry. Emigrating to America with $40 sewed into the lining of his coat, he sought his fortunes in the novelty-fur business. Penny arcades were more exciting, though, and in 1905 Zukor transferred his energies and his $200,000 profit in furs to that outcast branch of the entertainment world. When motion pictures became an important addition to the line of arcade gadgets, Zukor immediately realized the potentialites of the new entertainment form, and they soon became the sole attraction.

Exhibitors in those days had very poor fare to show. Skirt dances, a daredevil ride in a barrel over the falls, or the pounding of surf on the coast of Maine made up the twenty- or thirty-minute program. Zukor wanted pictures that told a coherent story; the unprecedented success of Sarah Bernhardt's *Queen Elizabeth* strengthened this desire. After his split with Loew in 1912, Zukor went into picture production and formed the Famous Players Company.

Within four years he was at the top of a brawling infant industry. Motion pictures in those days were distributed by so-called exchanges. Zukor did business with the Paramcunt Picture exchange, headed by a W. W. Hodkinson. Dissatisfied with the financial arrangement imposed by Hodkinson, Zukor suggested a merger. The former indignantly refused, but he failed to reckon with Zukor's pertinacity. Zukor quietly bought up most of Paramount's stock and within a year was able to oust Hodkinson.

Zukor reasoned that control of the market rested upon control at the source; if the best actors belonged to Paramount, he thought, the exhibitors would be at his mercy. Within a few years Zukor assembled a great collection of talent. Film rental fees increased sharply and block-booking was forced upon the reluctant independent exhibitor.

The latter, however, did not willingly accept this situation. In 1917, several theater circuits formed First National Pictures, a producing company. With their own supply of film, they could exclude competitors' pictures from their theaters. Soon First National had 5,000 members and Zukor began to worry about theaters rather than talent. For two years he watched First National's tactics and then decided that it was time to set up his own distribution and exhibition outlets. Convinced that theaters were a good investment, he sold $10 million worth of securities through Kuhn, Loeb and Company and began to build the Paramount movie chain.

The technique by which a theater circuit was welded was not a soft one. An independent exhibitor was approached and bluntly told either to sell his property or suffer the competition of a newly constructed theater. Independents screamed that the industry was being "raped," but Zukor went his way, disposing of First National's individual members one by one. By 1921, he controlled over 300 movie houses and in 1926 his acquisition of the Chicago Katz-Balaban circuit completely destroyed First National's importance in the motion picture industry.

With more than 1,600 theaters exhibiting the Paramount product, Zukor felt safe in the face of the depression. But the quiet ex-furrier discovered that even so depression-proof an industry as motion pictures could not carry the heavy fixed charges imposed by Wall Street financing. Paramount began to hit the financial reefs and for two years fifty-three assorted law firms, banks, investors' committees, and experts scowled and quarreled over the ailing corporation. Involved in all this high legal bickering were the Chase National Bank, the Royal Insurance Company, American Telephone and Telegraph, and the Atlas Corporation.

Paramount was finally reorganized in 1935. Of the old officers only Zukor and George Schaefer remained; the new board of directors was composed of bankers and real estate men. John Otterson, head of AT&T's Electrical Research Products, Inc. (ERPI), became president.

The early movie pioneers were quite aware of their humble origins, and their thirst for industrial power was perhaps motivated by an unconscious urge to be treated as equals. But not all of them felt it was necessary to create financial monstrosities; some preferred to be known as artistic picture makers. Such a man was Samuel Goldfish.

Goldfish left his native Warsaw at the age of ten and arrived in Gloversville, New York, one year later. At fifteen he began a successful road-salesman career in the toughest itinerary in the glove business. One day he walked into a Herald Square nickelodeon and became fascinated by the notion of owning a theater. He soon discovered that it was cheaper to produce and sell films. Together with his brother-in-law Jesse Lasky, a vaudeville producer, and on a capital of $26,500, he organized the Jesse Lasky Feature Play Company. Goldfish soon acquired the reputation of a man who did things his own way or not at all. When Lasky merged with Zukor in 1916, Goldfish stepped out to create a new production unit. His partners in this venture were the Selwyn Brothers.

The new business was called, after the founders, *Gold Wyn* Pictures. Goldfish thought so well of the title that for the first time in the history of enterprise a man named himself for a corporation: Goldfish became Goldwyn. And despite Zukor's hope that it would fail, the new company became a factor to be reckoned with.

Goldwyn's great contribution to movie-making was his emphasis upon quality. In 1919, he conceived the notion that the key person in production was the writer. Before this a scenario had been nothing more than a rough outline to guide the director. Of course, this elevation of the writer to an important position may have been but a shrewd competitive device turned against Zukor, who had cornered the market in acting talent. Goldwyn hired such writers as Rex Beach, Gertrude Atherton, and Maurice Maeterlinck. While he failed to obtain many usable scripts, he did get a good deal of valuable publicity thereby.

When MGM was formed in 1924, Goldwyn tried to establish himself as production chief. Here, however, he suffered one of his rare defeats and was forced to withdraw. Not at all disturbed by this unfavorable turn of events, he organized another movie company, Samuel Goldwyn, Inc., Ltd. Here he was absolute boss and the responsibility was all his own. He continued to emphasize the quality of his pictures; in no other way could they have been exhibited. Then when the sound film made dialogue an important feature of the movie, Goldwyn's faith in writers was vindicated.

Most producers also tried to duplicate Zukor's tactics. They realized that their pictures possessed value solely in proportion to the number of theaters they controlled. Movie-making could be enlarged only by tapping an extensive market, and the need for a continuous outlet soon overshadowed the processes of production. Distribution and exhibition became the major means of eliminating rivals and of acquiring control of as large a segment of a highly competitive market as one could grasp.

The struggle for the movie market produced gigantic interlocking corporations whose complexity paralleled the complicated corporate structures in utilities, finance, and automobiles. Independents were ruthlessly eliminated; production, distribution, and exhibition became the functions of a few large corporations.

With the battle for theaters increasing in intensity, eastern bankers began to recognize motion pictures as a legitimate enterprise. As Leo Rosten says, Hollywood shifted from the Arabian Nights to Dun and Bradstreet. The bankers, however, could think only of box-office receipts, and this markedly influenced movie-making policy. In the early days producers exercised their ingenuity without any financial inhibitions; but with the advent of big business, Wall Street supervisors replaced the Hollywood genius. The supervisor's job was to protect his employer's investment; players and directors were selected with both eyes on the box office. A motion picture had to have "production value," "picture sense," and "box office appeal." And, of course, the best way of assuring these was to imitate the smash-hit formula of another company. Forced into this orientation, the motion picture as an art form began a steady decline.

Wall Street men as well as Wall Street money entered the movie industry. W. C. Durant, of the General Motors Corporation, and Harvey Gibson, of the Liberty National Bank, became members of the board of directors of Loew's. The DuPonts and the Chase National Bank sponsored the formation of Goldwyn Pictures. The financiers reorganized the larger movie companies and mergers were effected. Soon the public began to recognize the signatures of these new movie-makers.

Into the midst of all this, the sound film broke with an impact that further shook the hold of the old-timers and strengthened that of the financiers. While most industries were prostrated by the depression, the motion picture industry remained financially healthy. Wall Street gazed at this astounding example of economic health and resolved more than ever to secure absolute control.

During the twenties Warner Brothers found itself on the downgrade, for with no controlled outlets of its own even a superior producing company could not live. At that time the Western Electric Company had just developed its first motion picture sound equipment, and of all the leading companies only Warner was willing to try it. Sound had an amazing restorative effect. Warner Brothers became the only movie company, with the exception of Loew's, that was able to survive the depression without financial reorganization.

Mr. Warner, Sr., was a Polish-Jewish farmer who had come to America in 1883 and settled in Ohio. Harry, the oldest son, had started his business career as a shoemaker. Several years later he went to work for the Armour Meat Packing Company. His brothers Abe and Sam had other ideas, however; they toured the country exhibiting their single print of *The Great Train Robbery*. Barnstorming was profitable enough to enable them to buy a nickelodeon in Newcastle, Pennsylvania, where Harry joined them. By 1917 the Warners had developed a successful movie exchange.

That year James Gerard published his *My Four Years in Germany*. With characteristic enterprise Harry Warner secured the screen rights, and the sensational film of Gerard's experiences, grossing nearly one million dollars, made the Warners top-flight producers. This picture also established the Warner Brothers pattern. Their products, generally based upon the events of the day, became what were called topic snatchers.

Hollywood's financial terrain was exceedingly rough, and it needed Waddill Catchings, the ever-optimistic partner of Goldman Sachs, to take the Warners in hand and teach them how to become important movie magnates. Yet were it not for the advent of sound, Warner Brothers would never have reached the top of a brawling, competitive industry.

It was Sam Warner who insisted that the company gamble on the Western Electric sound device. Most of the motion picture firms had refused to have anything to do with the new gadget. Warners obtained an exclusive license to the device, in return for which they agreed to sell twenty-four hundred complete theater sound-equipment systems for Electrical Research Products, Inc., the telephone company's subsidiary. Then came the remarkable *Jazz Singer,* and all the film companies and theaters clamored for equipment. ERPI promptly canceled its exclusive contract with Warner and sold equipment to all comers. Thereafter the telephone remained one of Harry Warner's pet antipathies.

The Warner boys quickly realized that they would have to control their own outlets if they were to stay in business. From 1928 to 1930, they bought as many theaters as they could and with the acquisition of the powerful Stanley circuit reached their goal. Selling debentures and common stock, they built up a chain of over 500 theaters. Music publishing firms, a radio factory, and a lithographing plant were among some of their more curious purchases.

Becoming adept in high finance, the Warners dazzled the most jaded of Wall Streeters by the brilliance of their stock manipulations. During the twenties, stock was sold to an investment-mad public through Renraw, the Warner Brothers' personal holding company. Renraw (the family name written backward) then lent the proceeds, interest free, to Warner Brothers, thus circumventing the bankers. But the Warners always held on to the voting stock—no one was going to tell them how to run their own business.

Radio Corporation of America also tried to market sound equipment for movies, but the field had already been quickly gobbled up by Western Electric. Within a year after Warners proved the practicability of sound pictures, Western Electric had exclusive contracts with 90 percent of the movie firms. The only alternative for RCA was to create its own movie empire. A holding company, the RKO Corporation, was formed, with control divided between RCA, the Atlas Corporation and Rockefeller Center, Inc. RKO Pictures was organized as the producing subsidiary and the Keith-Orpheum theater chain became the exhibiting outlet. Here was a motion picture giant built exclusively by financiers whose sole motive was to exploit a new technological device.

Between 1927 and 1935, the industry was rocked by a struggle to control the patents for sound equipment. ERPI signed long-term contracts with Loew's, Paramount, United Artists, and Universal. Only ninety-five theaters in the country had other than Western Electric reproducing apparatus, while 1,946 theaters had Western Electric equipment. RCA seemed to have been virtually eliminated from the field; only the large RKO chain used its sound devices.

RCA finally filed an anti-trust suit against the telephone company interests, and in 1935 a peaceful agreement was signed to give RCA new rights in the sound-equipment business. This legal battle was in the last analysis fought by the two financial giants of American industry—the Morgan and the Rockefeller empires —who now controlled motion pictures and sound equipment with a monetary sponsorship that assured them a monopoly beyond the wildest dreams of the old Motion Picture Patents Company of 1909.

The famous case of William Fox well illustrates the power of finance in the motion picture industry. Fox held the American rights to Tri-Ergon, a European sound system; this was dangerous competition for Western Electric. Patent-infringement suits and anti-trust charges, however, did not trouble the Fox Corporation. Fox continued to expand and at one time he virtually dominated the motion picture industry in America. But even he could not withstand the determined onslaught of the telephone interests.

Fox was born of Jewish immigrants from Hungary. His father earned a meager livelihood selling homemade shoe polish on New York's East Side. Young Fox started out in a cleaning and dyeing establishment at $17 a week. One day in 1904 he took the $1,600 he had saved and bought a movie house in Brooklyn. From then on he went ahead steadily in the budding industry. One of the first to defy the old patent pool, Fox launched into production and gradually expanded his theater holdings.

In 1927, Fox began to gobble up theater chains; in 1929 he secured control of Loew's and Gaumont British. But these operations required financing, whereupon Halsey, Stuart and Company, an investment banking firm with Western Electric connections, extended the necessary assistance in the form of short-term loans. Then came the 1929 crash. When Fox tried to renew his loans the bankers insisted that he relinquish control of his company. Fox sought aid from other sources, but no other banker seemed willing to oppose the House of Morgan. In the end Fox was forced to sell his holdings to H. L. Clarke, an Insull associate, for $18 million. For a long time the Chase National Bank was the largest stockholder in the Fox films.

The motion picture industry, dominated by the "Big Five" —Paramount, Loew's, Twentieth Century–Fox, Warner Brothers, and RKO—became very much concerned with the competition of television and the resultant impact on the box office. The lush days when any strip of film made money were over. Movie-makers kept insisting that only "high value" entertainment would draw people away from their comfortable parlors into the motion picture houses: high value meant box office appeal.

The most profitable pictures were those that successfully transferred the soap opera to the screen: Universal's Pa and Ma Kettle series, which went on as interminably as the Hardy pictures, brought fantastically high returns. On the other hand, the prestige film became the tail end of a double feature. While cutting overhead costs as drastically as possible, Hollywood made more pictures than ever in an effort to recapture an audience that was now seeking entertainment elsewhere. This in turn reinforced the "sure fire" cycle formula and strengthened the hold of businessmen.

Of the old-timers, few were still in control by the 1950's. Only in Loew's, where Nicholas Schenck still ruled, and in Warner Brothers, did the original Jewish interests still predominate. Of ten Paramount directors, only two were Jewish as compared with twelve out of nineteen in 1927, Twentieth Century–Fox was now controlled by non-Jewish personnel, and even in Loew's the number of non-Jewish officers and directors was greater in 1953 than in 1927.

As in most modern corporations, stock ownership has been widely dispersed in the movie concerns. There were about 15,000 stockholders in Loew's in 1953, and of the twenty largest holders, four were officers. Their ownership, however, was but 4 percent of the stock. Stock ownership in Warner Brothers has also dispersed, as it has in Paramount. The significant element in the financial structure of the movie companies has been the large proportion of borrowed capital.

The history of the movies exemplifies what happens in a now successful, one-time disreputable industry. Jewish entrepreneurs, after demonstrating the hard-headed practicality of their dreams, were compelled to surrender their leadership to financiers. Patent control, debt financing, and a huge investment in fixed capital demanded steady returns. Business conservatism dictated stereotyped products that would assure income; experimentation was too risky. In motion pictures, the one industry that affects educational and cultural values more than any other, this compelled the immaturity to which we have become accustomed.

1953

The High Cost of Eating

Not too long ago, housewives rebelled all over America. Protesting rising food prices, they picketed supermarkets across the country, and as clerks were furloughed for lack of work and the Retail Clerks Union pleaded with homemakers that the high cost of living was not the fault of employees, prices continued their upward march. It was clear from a Harris opinion poll, however, that the main brunt of the housewives' anger was directed toward the big food processors and the middlemen (wholesalers and jobbers). It was they, the ladies said, who were keeping up the cost of table food, and especially the price of meat. But so involved, so complicated has the food business become in America that no such diagnosis can any longer correspond to the realities. Because of these realities, moreover, no easy answers—if any at all—are available to the problems raised by last year's boycotts.

Food is the nation's largest industry. In 1964, somewhere between $80 and $85 billion worth was consumed at the retail

level. The grocery business itself, that part of the industry which reaches the housewife directly, accounts for over three-fourths of the total. There are almost 320,000 grocery stores in the United States—a number of outlets larger than that of all other retailers combined—and together they employ nearly a million-and-a-half people. Food stores range from the huge supermarket resplendent with banners advertising specials and equipped with play areas for tots to tiny *colmados* in upper Harlem whose owners eke out a livelihood just barely above that of their relief customers.
' In the past twenty years, a fantastic increase has taken place in the variety of goods offered for sale in retail food stores. In 1946 there were perhaps 3,000 items from which the housewife might select her daily or bi-weekly package; today almost 8,000 items clutter the shelves. They not only include the usual assortment of canned goods, but also "convenience" items like TV dinners, and numerous gadgets once bought elsewhere (knives, dishes, and hardware). In addition to all those, there is an endless array of cosmetics, drugs, cleaners, waxes, cigarettes, alcohol, kitchenware, curtains, tires, feed, lawn seed, anti-freeze, undershirts, nails, and batteries—items which account for $3 billion of grocery store sales; there are vast amounts of "processed" foods (breads, pre-packaged meats, and frozen foodstuffs) now flooding the shelves; and there are many different packages for the same item (sub-regular, irregular, doubles, economy, and giant). No wonder the housewife is staggered. (A marketing test a few years ago filmed supermarket customers in order to determine the rate at which they blinked their eyes. The theory was that gaudy colors would increase eyelid action. To the surprise of the investigators, it was discovered that the brighter the colors, the lower the blinking rate—the housewives had been paralyzed by supermarket displays!)

Naturally, it all costs money, for much is invested in rotary hoisters, conveyors, chains of bread trays, packaging, advertising, and marketing. And the investment expands as more and more people with more and more money to spend come upon the scene. Thus, between 1929 and 1963 retail sales jumped from $11 billion to almost $60 billion. Since 1911, moreover, per capita consumption of meats and fish has gone up by 27 percent, and of dairy products, by 6 percent (potatoes, however—a dish for the poor—have declined by a whopping 54 percent). Nevertheless, the total effect of the steady increase in sales, along with the parallel expansion in the range of goods offered, has been a decline in the number of stores that the housewife can patronize. In the main it has been the small outlet, the *colmado*, the "mom and pop" store, that has suffered attrition. Today such stores amount to only about 40 percent of the total and they are no longer of any consequence in any local or regional markets.

The cause of this decline is, of course, the supermarket. The origins of supermarketing—in itself a relatively new merchandising method—may be traced to the "combination" stores that cropped up in California during the 1920's when grocery and meat departments were brought together under one roof. Such combination stores, called "cheapies," were usually opened in abandoned warehouses or garages in the slums of the big cities. The King Kullen markets of Long Island, an early "super," went to the outskirts of New York City in the 1930's and called on new suburbanites to come with their cars to buy cheaply in large quantities. Food was displayed in open crates; there was little overhead; and the entrepreneur's objective was a low-margin, high-turnover business. True, all this was started by enterprising independents who were determined to outdo chains like A&P which had secured an initial advantage by volume buying and excellent urban locations. But between the chain and the supermarket stood the ordinary neighborhood grocer, and in the era of self-service and parking lots he could not survive in very large numbers.

Suburbia grew and created a mass market; the automobile provided mass transportation to shopping centers; home refrigeration made possible a weekly rather than a daily trip to the market. And so the grocery business underwent a quiet yet gigantic upheaval, analogous in many ways to that experienced by the manufacturing industries in the eighteenth and nineteenth centuries. Marketers scurried about buying or leasing new locations in freshly built towns as the small neighborhood outlet of 5,000 square feet, which could hardly accommodate a dozen checkout counters, became inadequate to handle the ever-growing traffic. The new supermarket, operated by chains, franchised licensees, or cooperatives, expanded to an average size of 22,000 square feet in 1957; today it is not uncommon to do one's purchasing in a mammoth 55,000 square-foot "giant" super.

The complicated network of distribution channels needed to supply these retailers can only be dimly perceived by the housewife. Behind the retailer, there are wholesalers, brokers, processors, and producers, each of whom plays a role in making prices what they are. Wholesalers, numbering some 42,000, employ another 500,000 persons, who in 1963 were responsible for selling $59 billion worth of goods. Brokers, who are akin in many ways to the *tolkachi* of the Soviet Union, never take physical possession of goods; they merely handle orders and purchases, pieces of paper, and see to it that a retailer gets what he needs on time. There are about 2,000 brokers in the food business; they employ seventeen thousand salesmen who handle thirty thousand different items, and who bring in $13.5 billion annually in sales. Food "processors," from sugar refineries to huge dairy plants to small automated meat-packing installations located in southern towns, number about 14,000. In 1963, they added $21.4 billion in value to the $42 billion worth of raw materials they acquired from producers, who are to be found mainly on the nation's three million farms, some of them literally factories in the field.

Yet even with all these middlemen, the price of food might still have remained within bounds if there were a significant degree of competition in the industry. The reality of the food business, however, is concentration. The "chain-store movement," initiated in 1859 by the Hartfords of A&P, laid the groundwork by which small retailers were forced together under one management. The chains merged retailing and wholesale functions, moved backward into processing to cut costs, and did not hesitate to use "loss leaders" and spectacular specials to draw customers away from rivals and independents alike. By 1930, some 80,000 units had been brought together into one or another form of chain-store— and the grocery business had been brought into the twentieth century.

Initially, of course, resistance to the movement was strong. Some states, such as Louisiana, even tried to tax the chains out of existence. But in the long run the pressures toward integration and consolidation could not be overcome. By 1948, the chains had secured about 35 percent of the retail market in foods; those independent retailers who had been cajoled by wholesalers into joining "voluntary" cooperatives (based on group merchandising, uniform store layout, joint advertising, and private labels) retained another 35 percent; about 30 percent was left for all the others. By 1963, the chains had gobbled up 47 percent of the market, while the "affiliates" or "voluntaries" had 44 percent of what was now a substantially larger industry.

Some of the competitive practices indulged in by the chains have been attacked under existing anti-trust legislation. Between 1950 and 1965, the Justice Department prosecuted fifty-three anti-trust cases affecting retail food companies and obtained convictions or consent decrees in thirty-one of them. Only eleven cases were dismissed and only seven defendants were found not guilty (four cases are still pending). Some of the more spectacular suits involved Safeway, the National Tea Company, Borden Company, General Mills, Kroger, Morton Salt, Ward's, and even the Teamsters' Union and the Kosher Butchers' Association of Los Angeles. Many were charged with conspiracy to fix prices and establish monopolies; others were charged with predatory competition; some with price discrimination (these are all violations of the Sherman and Clayton Acts, and some, of the Robinson-Patman Act). That such suits had to be instigated shows clearly that old-time competition in the grocery business no longer exists.

To be sure, it is still difficult to speak of market domination on a national scale. The product market—the area in which marketing takes place—has, it is true, widened; once the neighborhood or town, it is now the entire region or metropolitan area. From a national standpoint, the twenty largest food retailers increased their share of the market from 1948 to 1958 by only 7 percent. Since 1958, the situation for the so-called national chains has been fairly stable, reflecting an increased growth on the part of regional or statewide chains which, merger for merger, have been matching the pace of A&P, Safeway, and Winn-Dixie.

Nevertheless, the strength of the large national chains is such that in 1963, according to a tabulation by the National Commission on Food Marketing, the top four grocery companies obtained, on the average, half the sales in 218 metropolitan areas, while the top eight secured 62 percent of the sales in these areas. (In 1954, by contrast, the ratios were 45 percent and 54 percent respectively.) Thus, despite rivalry with local outfits—not necessarily on the level of price competition—the nationwide chains have continued to bite off somewhat larger pieces of the market, which itself has been burgeoning. Even though their investments are high, these chains are highly mobile. Able to finance themselves from internal resources, they can close down old stores with alacrity, open new ones, spin off acquisitions no longer profitable, search out new locations, and buy out rival companies. In any one year a national chain like Safeway may shut down fifty stores and open sixty new ones; its flexibility is much greater than the balance sheet would suggest. It is this that enables such chains to hold on to and even expand their markets.

The strength of the chains is revealed in buying as well as selling. They have so thoroughly invaded the supplier's field that one must wonder what they mean when they blame high prices on vendors. For while independent food wholesalers may still occupy a position of importance—there were 2,000 of them in 1963—the decline of their number since World War II has been dramatic: a drop of about 20 percent. More significant, perhaps, is the rather close relationship these middlemen are apt to have with the so-called "voluntary" chains, such as IGA, Red Owl, and Red and White.

The way in which wholesaler and retailer interpenetrate is illustrated by the example of Consolidated Foods. Originally just a wholesaler enforcing "voluntary" affiliation upon independent grocers, Consolidated went directly into retailing in 1952; by 1963, it was the fifteenth largest retailing food chain as well as one of the major "voluntary" wholesalers. The fifteen biggest "cooperatives" and the fifteen biggest voluntaries now have about 34 percent of total grocery sales between them; in 1948 their share was about 12 percent. Another organization, the National Retailer Owned Grocers in Chicago, links some eighty-five "retailer-owned" wholesale cooperatives and coordinates the buying, advertising, and merchandising of its members with its own trademarks and private labels. NROG is actually a holding company with three regional subsidiaries that do the work; their wholesale business totals a huge $2 billion a year. It has become evident to both the Federal Trade Commission and the National Commission on Food Marketing that concentration at the buying end has increased markedly since 1948 and that such concentration is even greater at the point of sale to the consumer.

These tendencies, moreover, have been strengthened by vertical integration, which, through ownership or by contract, links the disparate operations of production, processing, merchandising, advertising, wholesaling, and retailing. The Temporary National Economic Committee, a congressional group investigating monopoly, observed thirty years ago that grocery chains were reaching back to "bridge the entire span between producer and consumer." And, indeed, by 1963, all but five of the forty largest food retail chains were engaged in processing something for the shelves.

These retailer-manufacturers produce over $217 million worth of canned fruits and vegetables, $57 million of frozen foods, $427 million of bread products, $158 million worth of coffee; in some instances they supply as much as 65 percent of their own marketing needs. It is evident that they exert far more control over costs and prices than they are wont to admit.

The most spectacular gimmick used by grocers, and the most pernicious so far as prices are concerned, is the trading stamp. In one form or another, this come-on has been around for years— the Raleigh cigarette coupon and the United Cigar Store ticket being perhaps the most familiar of all early examples. Trading stamps themselves—gummed stickers accumulated by housewives to be exchanged for blenders, towels, electric can openers, hair dryers, and the like—have become the rage among grocers only in the last fifteen years, but the idea goes back to the 1850's when the B. T. Babbitt Company sold soap with coupons. In the 1890's, Shuster's Department Store in Milwaukee thought of gummed stamps and books. Finally, in 1896, Thomas Sperry had the happy thought of establishing a trading-stamp company, and so Sperry & Hutchinson—S&H Green Stamps—was founded. A group of New England retailers was the first to dispense trading stamps as a roundabout way of giving the housewife a "discount." The trading stamp is now big business, and there are many companies doing only this. S&H, the largest of them all, gives away more catalogues than Sears, Roebuck.

The economics of trading stamps is deceptively simple. A ten-cent purchase entitles the housewife to one stamp, so that a completely filled S&H book, for example, represents a total retail expenditure of $120. Now, the average retail value of a book when turned in for redemption is three dollars. Since the cost to the retailer, who buys the stamps from the redemption company, runs between two dollars and three dollars, the most the customer receives by way of a "discount" amounts to 8/10 of 1 percent, and in many cases it is exactly zero. In 1963, the total number of stamps purchased by retailers was 377 billion; of these, some fifty million were not redeemed. Even if we use the figure of $2 per thousand as the cost to the retailer, this would mean that housewives across the nation shelled out $83.3 million for something they never got. If there had been no trading stamps, consumers would have saved all the money spent by retailers for green, gold, or yellow stickers. The only party that gains is the redemption company, for its profits stem not only from the difference between what it charges the retailer and what it pays out in redemptions (usually at 75 percent of retailer costs) but from unredeemed stamps as well. An additional source of profit is the margin between the cost of premium goods and the redemption value of the stamps. It is quite a business.

Why does the retailer give away trading stamps? The original purpose obviously was to draw customers away from rivals; now, however, when everyone is doing it, only the housewife is left holding the proverbial bag. Of course, the grocer still hopes to generate enough volume to cover the cost of the stamps, and if, as frequently happens, this doesn't work out, he simply jacks up his prices. (When A&P began to give away Plaid Stamps in 1964, new sales were not forthcoming and the company's earnings fell.) A good many retailers dislike the whole business and some have ceased handing out trading stamps; others continue for fear they will lose customers.

The National Commission on Food Marketing has hinted rather strongly that trading stamps have been a major factor in the higher prices of recent years. This suspicion is borne out by studies conducted by the U.S. Department of Agriculture, according to which prices in stamp-dispensing stores went up .7 percent in recent years, while in non-stamp stores the increase was .1 percent. Only 30 percent of this difference was recouped by the housewife—in the form of goods she might or might not have needed.

The affluent consumer has not seemed to care much about the slow upward drift in food prices, a drift of about 40 percent since 1957–1959. When food prices increase at the same rate as other goods, the housewife appears to be undisturbed. It is only when the cost of meats, fruits, vegetables, eggs, and dairy products spurts ahead of other items in the household budget that the consumer begins to wonder. In the meantime, food economists offer the usual panoply of reasons for the increase in prices: milk production is down; government support prices for cheese and butter are up; agricultural exports have increased, diminishing the supply for the American people; it costs more to market processed food, an item in great demand by housewives, less willing today to cook.

None of this, however, tells us much about the kind of competition that is actually taking place, all of which is calculated to jack up the cost of doing business, and ultimately the price of food. In the early days, say before 1930, the basic strategy in the grocery business was to give the customer a break. As the chains expanded and added more outlets, it was discovered that savings in bulk buying gave a competitive edge and could lead to lower prices. Efficiencies were introduced into marketing and the housewife really had a lark. Today, however, the rules of the game have been altered: competition is now focused on such matters as store location, "image," the size of the parking lot, number of square feet, types of gondolas, lighting—anything but price. The strategy now is to fix the price of a particular mix of goods to fit a particular geographic location. As a study by the Retail Clerks Union shows, there is very little variation in price within any given area.

The importance of sale items or price specials is similarly exaggerated. Generally, less than 150 of the 8,000 or so items in an average supermarket will be subjected to specials. To suggest that the housewife concentrate on "good buys," as does one food economist, is to ignore the tremendous disadvantage at which the consumer is initially placed. She simply doesn't know. Few housewives travel from store to store to compare prices; for most, there is really no way to determine where prices may be a penny or two lower. And the "special" is in any case not an authentic form of price competition; it is, rather, a gimmick to catch the purchaser's attention.

Aside from the area of private brands, where some price competition still exists, most retailers concentrate on competing not by lowering prices but by increasing the number of items stocked, improving carry-out services, instituting convenient store hours, or dispensing trading stamps. All these devices are geared toward increasing the cost of the market basket. As a consequence, gross margins, which measure the cost of retailing to society, have been drifting upward and will in all probability continue to do so.

Retail operators, of course, are apt to argue that wages are at fault and that payments to employees have outpaced food prices by about 10 percent. They usually fail to add that only six years ago hourly earnings in retailing averaged about $1.40 an hour, and in many places were less than a dollar an hour; thus, the base was rather low to begin with. Costs in retailing are affected by numerous other factors—managerial skill, equipment, size of store, layout, the flow of goods from storage to selling areas, the arrangement of checkout counters, and the like. Studies by the NCFM suggest that costs drop with more effective use of store facilities, and at a rate more than sufficient to offset wage increases. The retail worker, moreover, has become increasingly productive over the years, as is evidenced by the startling rise in sales per worker in grocery stores—from $14,000 in 1929 to $23,000 in 1963 (in *real* dollars). My own studies of supermarket productivity, which were made a few years ago for the Retail Clerks Union, suggest an average annual gain per employee of at least 5 percent. Yet it is difficult for a man to earn a decent livelihood in food retailing—unless the place has been unionized. At average hourly earnings of $1.73 in 1963, a person would gross about $75 a week, hardly enough to sustain a family. Indeed, most employees in retailing find it difficult to obtain a full week's work—a circumstance that occasioned a bitter fourteen-week strike against the chains in Baltimore a few years ago.

In Baltimore, the employers complained that their profits on sales were not more than 2 percent. How, they asked, could they meet the demands of the union? The employers were right about the ratio—if one looked only at the sales dollar. When their profits were computed on the basis of *investment,* however, the normal way of calculating profit ratios, it became clear that the Baltimore supermarkets were enjoying a healthy 14 percent return, far better than the situation in many other industries.

The truth is that while food retailing still employs much human labor, the upward drift in prices cannot be attributed to this factor, for compared to other factors, wages have hardly risen at all. Between 1954 and 1963, total labor costs went up only by 3 percent, while promotion, rent, and heat were up by 40 to 45 percent. Similarly, between 1956 and 1960 sales for food chains increased 17 percent; payrolls were up just over 6 percent. It can hardly be said that the clerk, who earns a pittance anyway, is responsible for the housewives' predicament.

Is, then, the farmer responsible? Are food prices increasing because he is receiving more for his products? It seems not. In 1947, the farmer obtained 51 percent of the cost of a food product; in 1965 his share was down to 39 percent. To be sure, the amount a farmer receives for particular items varies considerably: he is paid 7 cents for the contents of a can of beets, for instance, and about 50 cents for a pound of butter. The difference between what the housewife pays and what the farmer receives can be substantial—in the case of meats it can be as much as 50 percent. But the blame for this state of affairs lies not with the farmer but with chaotic distribution methods. For example, in 1964 it cost 53 cents to bring one pound of butter from the farm to the plant; processing, storage, packaging, transportation, and delivery cost another 13.8 cents, of which only 5.1 cents went for labor; the retailer then added another 7.6 cents, to reach a total of 74.4 cents a pound. Or consider choice beef, for which the farmer obtained 42.4 cents a pound; marketing, processing, and wholesaling added 11.4 cents (of which labor received 3.6 cents); the retailer's margin came to 17 cents, so that the housewife's bill totaled 70.8 cents a pound. The worst situation was perhaps in breakfast cereals, the farm value of which was 4.3 cents a pound; to this figure, transportation, manufacturing, and wholesaling added 30.9 cents (of which advertising alone represented 7.3 cents, a good deal more than labor's 6.5 cents); and with a retail margin of 6.4 cents, the housewife had to pay 41.6 cents. Hence, one can no more place the blame for high prices at the farmer's doorstep than at the door of labor.

The significant economic element in food marketing remains the continuous upward movement of gross margins in retailing. Between 1949 and 1965, the increase in gross margins was 28 percent. For some chains the rise has been even greater: Safeway up 73 percent; Kroger, 40 percent; Acme, 36 percent. At least for the calculable future, food prices are apt to rise, according to the Agriculture Department's food marketing report for November 1966. The cost of marketing services will also probably rise, said the report, with most of the increase passed on to the consumers; this conclusion has been supported by investigators for the House Agriculture Committee. No wonder the housewife rebels.

It is sometimes argued that gross margins have gone up since the 1950's because modern supermarket methods shift the burden of services to the housewife. No longer is a human clerk available to advise her as to which product represents the superior buy; the clerk has been transformed into a "materials handler," stamping prices on canned goods, and the only information he is able to impart concerns the location of the canned beans. In effect, the housewife herself now performs services that at one time were paid for by the retailer. In Switzerland an effort even has been made to have supermarket customers punch their own cash registers (it has not met with much success). The housewife performs more and more tasks—searching the shelves, selecting the items, grinding the coffee, filling the basket—and contributes to the upward drift of margins because she is not reimbursed for her services. Of course, she ought to be paid in the form of lower prices, but in the present context of events, that seems unlikely.

In general, then, the reason for high food prices must be sought in that curious concatenation of affairs which has allowed large corporations to dominate the industry at virtually all levels. The absence of price competition, the conversion of food into articles of manufacture, the shifting of service functions to the housewives themselves, the growth of both vertical and horizontal integration pursued as a matter of corporate expansion, and trading stamps—all have added to the food bill and will continue to do so. In this situation the housewife is no longer confronted by a white-aproned neighborhood grocer ready to serve her, but rather by huge impersonal aggregations of capital whose sole objective is to separate her from the household budget. In this confrontation the housewife cannot win; she may walk the sidewalk with picket signs, protesting the high prices, but when it comes time to feed the family she will enter the door of the supermarket to do her shopping, and pay ever-increasing prices. For she simply has no other place to go.

1967

PART THREE. AMERICAN
INSTITUTIONS: GOVERNMENT

Courage and Economics in Washington

When FDR came to Washington in 1933, he was accompanied by dashing young economists and social scientists ready to remake the government, if not the world. Many were fresh from Columbia University, and quite unlike the Harvard-M.I.T. contingent that now graces the capital landscape, they were naive enough to believe that America's ills could be solved forever by intelligent planning and good will. They had not heard of the realities tough-minded politicians were wont to talk about, and they exhibited just enough brashness to make one think they might really succeed.

Foremost was Rexford G. Tugwell, who liked to shock people with predictions that America would be remade in the image of the New Deal. Accompanying him was Adolph Berle, assuring everyone he knew more about high finance than the bankers. Berle's intellectual partner, Gardiner Means, went to work with imagination and vigor at the National Resources Committee, a sort of precursor to the Council of Economic Advisers. The NRC was the only agency that provided a haven for economic planners and, while an internal conflict between Frederic Delano, the President's uncle, and Charles Merriam made it somewhat impotent, the very idea of central planning in the government was extraordinary.

There were numerous others, all young and intellectually alive and all anxious to rebuild an America seared by depression. Ideas flowed in abundance; Washington was a lively place to be.

A certain parallel to this experience occurred when John F. Kennedy brought his administration to Washington in January 1961. It was thought that the Eisenhower *ennui* would be overcome by a vibrant new generation, just as the New Deal had displaced the confused placidity of the Hoover years. Among economists, especially, there was the feeling that the newer theorists, having refurbished the Keynesian apparatus, would demonstrate how to make an economy move, not at a languid pace but with buoyancy.

Heading the parade was Paul A. Samuelson, perhaps the most brilliant contemporary virtuoso of mathematical economics. Although not an official member of Kennedy's corps of economists, he has great influence. In his middle forties, Samuelson has been rocking his academic colleagues back on their heels with penetrating theoretical analyses ever since his student days under Alvin Hansen at Harvard. He has continued to display his brilliance both at Cambridge and in Washington with self-consciously urbane letters on a variety of economic problems delivered to such serious congressional bodies as the Joint Economic Committee. Yet the Samuelson glow has had difficulty getting through to Washingtonians. The Task Force paper he wrote for Kennedy on economic policy could just as well have been prepared by a less sophisticated Keynesian. James Reston once expressed the town's reaction when he revealed that he had been quite bored by all the split infinitives in it.

Other well-known Cambridge economists among the Kennedy advisers include Walt Rostow and Seymour Harris. Rostow advises on foreign policy, while Harris acts as consultant to the Treasury and more recently has come forth as chief expositor of the political difficulties faced by the Kennedy economic program. Harris' heart has always been with the angels, that is, on the liberal or slightly left side. Yet one can detect in his most recent popular writings a tone of resignation to the harsh requirements of Washington *Realpolitik*. He evidently has tried hard to impress his perhaps old-fashioned New Dealish views on government offi cials, but they keep coming out as pure New Frontier. And New Frontier these days is comprised of one part thought, two parts hope, three parts rhetoric, and four parts political buck-passing.

Before getting down to issues, as Washington jargon puts it, let us complete the roster. Major interest centers, naturally enough, on the Council of Economic Advisers. Established by the Employment Act of 1946, the Council has had a checkered career. Its first chairman, Edwin G. Nourse, who had come from the academically careful Brookings Institution, made it an agency for economic analysis only. Leon Keyserling, considered by some Washingtonians as the economists' version of the china-shop bull, took the Council right into the political arena where he fought vigorously for the policies espoused in his CEA reports. Eisenhower's chairmen, Arthur F. Burns and Raymond Saulnier, virtually turned the Council into the Washington branch of the National Bureau of Economic Research, that is, a purely statistical body which had nothing to say on economic policy.

The present chairman of the Council is Walter W. Heller, a youngish scholar whose forte is tax policy. While Heller has expressed his midwestern distaste for the excesses of contemporary affluence, he does not, like Galbraith, believe that we have achieved the ultimate in production. That much of the conventional economic wisdom remains with him. Nor is he willing to admit that there is a serious gap in public services, as Galbraith has done. Heller has urged rather that private enterprise needs to be given a chance to demonstrate what it really can do—a chance that war, depression, and a defense economy have denied it.

Next door to the CEA is the Bureau of the Budget, headed by David Bell, also from Cambridge. The strength of the Budget Bureau comes not only from its statutory right to trim departmental pocketbooks, but from the fact that it can and does see that presidential orders are carried out. Moving along Pennsylvania Avenue, from the liberals through the moderate Bell, we come to the administration conservatives at the Treasury, where Douglas Dillon rules. Dillon acquired his conservative label not only because he served Eisenhower and successfully talked Kennedy out of tax cuts during the last recession, but also because he can be found generally on the opposite side from the Cabinet's liberal wing headed by Labor Secretary Arthur Goldberg. Yet often it is difficult to distinguish conservatives from liberals in the Kennedy entourage. Dillon, for example, has supported lower interest rates and budget deficits, the accepted way of moderating a recession. But most important, it is to Dillon that Kennedy is apt to turn for guidance, rather than to Heller or Goldberg or Harris.

All of the presidential economic advisers appear to be of one cut—sophisticated, non-utopian, even bland, and very quick to learn the ways of practical politics. None lacks a ready justification for his retreat from "textbook idealism." Such accommodation, we are repeatedly told, is what Washington needs these days. But part of Kennedy's appeal to intellectuals, at least between the summer of 1960 and Inauguration Day, was his apparent sense of history. He seemed able to trace the roots of our difficulties and called for fresh ways of dealing with them. Only a few observers noted that rhetoric is a poor substitute for genuine proposals. The Task Force papers, because they said so little that was really new, left one with a feeling of controlled skepticism.

In economic policy, for example, virtually everyone recognized that the country had been fumbling under Ike. Only the continued impulses stemming from a defense program kept us upright. Yet each postwar recession was successively more intense, each recovery less ebullient, each residue of unemployment larger and tougher to dispel. There was a promise after the elections that vigorous action—a favorite Washington expression—would be taken. But somehow assessments of situations as preludes to judgments got in the way—so much so that even Samuelson had to admit that the adventures in New Frontier economics constituted a "placebo program for recovery." The cocktail party circuit and car-pool riders began to talk about the Third Eisenhower Administration.

A crescendo of criticism of the Kennedy economic program is now evident. Walter Lippmann calls it Eisenhower stuff thirty years younger; Leon Keyserling says more kindly that it falls short of even modest goals; and the trade unions are so restive they must be placated with middle- and high-echelon conferences.

Why this harsh reaction? Quite plainly, the Kennedy Administration has been unable to break the bonds of its milieu. We have now a society in which the ostensible end of ideology is welcomed and in which serious political debate is frowned upon. Existence under Kennedy is unchanged: it is what it was under Eisenhower, homogenized and apathetic. As Jacob Cohen remarked in his dissection of the mind of Arthur Schlesinger, a key Kennedy adviser, movements become merely lobbies on the Hill, and the imperatives of history are transmuted into the art of the politically possible. And unlike the days of the New Deal, it is believed that there are not too many repairs to make. Whenever a high administration functionary is asked, "When will something be done?" the reply is, "Give us some ideas." Now, who elected whom?

It is at this point that former Kennedy supporters are starting to drift. They see the economy's upward movement spending itself. And while economists outside the administration are beginning to hesitate about continued expansion and growth, those in the CEA and elsewhere in government insist upon telling us that the "slowdown is a reaction to the rapidity of the upturn from the previous recession's trough." Haven't we heard this before in the last ten years?

Recently, the CEA asked industry, labor, and university people for comments on a "full employment" model projected for 1963. The model assumed—*nota bene!*—4 percent unemployment as a mark of full employment. Another assumption was a rate of growth in GNP of 3.5 percent a year. On the basis of these and other premises which need not trouble us at the moment, the CEA suggested the possibility of a $600 billion GNP (in constant dollars), of which investment represented $97.5 billion, consumption $382.5 billion, and government outlays $120 billion. As compared to 1961, this would mean a 34 percent jump in real private investment, while consumer expenditure would rise 14 percent and government spending 12 percent. Of course, a 17 percent rise each year in domestic investment is not inconceivable, particularly when we recall the 28 percent increase in 1954–1955, but that was by all accounts an extraordinary year.

At any rate, an investment level of this magnitude implies either a marked shift in income distribution in favor of the business community or greater participation by government. Current data suggest that the total of business net profit after taxes plus the salary, bonus, and related take of upper-income strata recipients is around $105 billion, and might reach $115 billion in 1963. If we assume that about 70 percent of this is saved (Keynes's average propensity), then at best $80.5 billion would be available for investment. (This estimate seems consistent with a capital-output ratio of 3:1, actual productivity gains of 2.5 to 3 percent a year and an annual population growth of around 2 percent.) Consequently, the CEA's 1963 target would require an income flow to "capitalists" about 20 percent greater than the $115 billion suggested above. Of course, if the "capitalists" decided to save more, say 80 percent, then their required income flow could be less and the gap would drop to a manageable $7 billion. But it is unlikely that the "capitalists" would curtail their consumption by a third. What the CEA hasn't made clear is that growth depends not only on investment, but involves as well income distribution, propensities to consume and save, and capital-output ratios. It's a complicated business.

Now we are told that the big problem is the balance of payments in international trade. Here the administration appears to be caught in a bind. Our merchandise balance, the excess of exports over imports, is more than satisfactory, but the over-all balance is awry because of capital outflow and foreign aid. Thus, in 1960, a merchandise gain of $3.8 billion was wiped out by $3.5 billion in capital exports and $2.7 billion in overseas grants. In this situation, an inflation can be really ugly, for increased domestic prices would depress sales of goods to other nations. The conservative solution, which is well received in some Washington quarters, is to place a damper on wage hikes, since this is presumably what causes inflation. Hence the administration's recent cautionary word to industry and the unions. Yet at least 80 percent of the manufactured goods exported by us come from industries in which prices are administered rather than market-determined, in which automation and advanced technology have reduced the proportion of labor in total unit cost. In autos, for example, direct labor per car is between 16 and 18 percent of unit cost, while material represents about half. The rest is overhead and profit. Moreover, internal inflation at the moment does not seem to be a pressing matter. It could be that other considerations, such as the international trade policies of some European nations (West Germany, perhaps), have contributed more to our balance of trade headaches than internal economics.

Protecting the dollar in international trade can conflict with policies for stimulating domestic growth. Caught between this Scylla and Charybdis, the Kennedyites evidently believe that a balanced budget and wage restraints will help them through the political narrows without much loss. The thought seems to be that a conservative fiscal policy will allay the panic supposedly aroused by an unfavorable balance of payments. The administration's treatment of this question reveals the lack of imagination which characterizes its entire economic program.

It is conceivable that further domestic expansion would present its own cure, for prosperity might attract enough of a capital flow to the United States to help overcome the trade deficit. On the other hand, a stumbling economy would hardly prove attractive to foreign investors, especially in the short run. The only ideas that have come up in recent months are the not-so-original "export-more" campaign and a rather wistful plea to our allies not to run away from the dollar. As the *Economist* remarked, the administration's best weapon is speech-making.

In the domestic field, proposal after proposal for stimulating economic growth is whittled down on grounds of political expediency. More energy is spent by Kennedy's economists rationalizing each compromise than in explaining the urgencies of the case. The latter, in itself, as Keyserling bitterly remarked, would be an education for lawmakers. To blame a Democrat dominated Congress for the inability to advance a Manpower Act merely teaches us how to pass the buck. The fact is that a ready willingness to compromise and back down permeates official Washington. The rather weak wage-hour revision was an almost classic manifestation of the habit. The art of the politically possible has been carried to wondrous extremes.

Meanwhile, the Council of Economic Advisers continues to urge the use of general monetary and fiscal policy as the best way to deal with unemployment. Growthmanship, it is hoped, will solve all problems. This evidently takes off from Samuelson's observation that only the warm sun of a rising national income can melt the deep freeze of a depressed area. A fine thought when an economy has been operating at low levels with accumulated excess capacity, it is hardly serviceable when hard-core unemployment continues year after year despite a high GNP. Obviously, the economy itself has been altered: unemployment of the kind

we are now experiencing is plainly *structural*. Industries are shrink-
ing, the labor force is being reshuffled, the economic mix has
changed. These are specific ailments, requiring specific treatment,
but the CEA prefers a generalized approach. One might well ask
whether gangrene can be halted with fresh air.

Tragically, little genuine hard thought is expended in official
Washington these days on the particular steps necessary to deal
with unemployment in the coal, textile, auto, and steel industries,
or how jobs might be provided for those especially prone to loss
of work—the young, the old, the Negro. Some of the labor
economists have been shouting, and rather loudly, but who lis-
tens? Administration advocates point to the depressed-areas bill,
a new minimum wage, expanded social security, a new housing
act, etc., etc. Yet each was diluted in the face of congressional
opposition: it was more important to get *any* law on the books;
never mind a decent one. How else is one to run successfully for
the history books?

1962

Tariffs and American Politics

> *We are suffering from the intolerable competition of a foreign rival . . . in a condition so far superior to our own for the production of light, that he absolutely inundates our national market with it. . . . This rival . . . is no other than the sun.*—Petition of the Manufacturers of Candlesticks, Waxlights, Lamps. By FRÉDÉRIC BASTIAT, nineteenth-century French political economist.

When President Kennedy delivered his State of the Union message, the few paragraphs devoted to Reciprocal Trade were vague, generally puzzling, and in part contradictory. In fact, no one quite knew where the New Frontier, after a year in office, stood on trade and tariffs, except that a liberal posture was being assumed. The Task Force paper on tariffs, prepared when Kennedy came to office, had been kept a state secret; why, was not certain to anyone. When its contents leaked to the *New York Times* in early January, just a week before the speech to Congress, political expediency seemed once again to have guided the administration's thinking. Evidently Congress would not have accepted the program during the administration's first year, and it therefore appeared the better part of political sagacity to keep the whole matter under wraps.

The full program was not unveiled until the end of January, when Kennedy finally sent his tariff message to Congress. Though it did indeed include a host of liberal proposals, for the main part it was devoted to rationalizing the need for wiping out trade restrictions. All this is well and good—but it presumably had occurred to no one that a great public debate over the whole past year, and not merely prior to the legislative discussions, might have strengthened the President's hand. It is more than likely, as matters now stand, that Kennedy will suffer defeat on the tariff issue. Here again, to use Hans Morgenthau's apt distinction, the methods of the politician were inadequate to a task that required statesmanship.

As anyone who has ever had a decent course in American history knows, more tears have been shed and more teeth broken over the tariff question than any other economic issue in our time. Once again the battle erupts as the administration makes tentative motions toward refurbishing the paste-pot policy which it inherited from past generations. The difficulty in shaping a sensible, cohesive program is undeniable: it demands an economic statesmanship and wisdom that must absorb and allay deep tensions and group conflicts, which, moreover, have the disconcerting habit of shifting with the tides of industrial fortune. The political problem is doubly compounded when the New Frontier comes forth with a readiness to compromise in the face of a curiously increasing protectionist sentiment. Further, the very line-up of forces seems to be veering away from normal anchorages. The South, once the hotbed of free trade, now demands high tariffs. Even the trade unions, long-time defenders of liberalization, have begun to have second thoughts. At the same time, the architects of American policy must assure our overseas allies that we bear them no ill will and that we do really mean to extend the hand of friendliness in trade.

The problem was much simpler a century and three-quarters ago. The imposition of tariffs by the first Congress was merely for the purpose of raising revenues. In the early years of the Republic, all but $20,000 of the $4.5 million of Treasury income stemmed from tariff levies. Up to the Civil War, in fact, over 90 percent of the federal government's receipts came from tariffs. The latter today account for just about 1 percent; other considerations explain their persistence, notably the desire to exclude commodities coming from foreign shores which ostensibly compete with domestic production.

There were indeed early advocates of a protective tariff, the foremost of whom was Alexander Hamilton. Supporters of a firm tariff policy contended that America's young industry could not grow in the face of hot competitive winds from overseas, that protection was essential if we were ever to have a viable economic base. Furthermore, it was argued, wages were higher here than in Europe, and so it was necessary to have a tariff wall in order to protect living standards as well as nascent industries.

These arguments had little effect in an agricultural society whose producers were anxious to exchange farm output for manufactured goods from Europe. It was not until the industries which were developed during the War of 1812 had suffered a severe post-bellum shock that tariff duties began to be pushed upward. Whatever economic troubles afflicted the nation, protectionists were certain to offer the tariff as a sure-fire cure. The question was largely resolved after the Civil War in their favor, for with the agrarian South no longer a political power, the industrial North could move ahead with relative ease to guarantee that trade in the vast new hinterland would become the private province of a now burgeoning American factory system.

The payoff came with the incredible Smoot-Hawley Tariff of 1930. President Hoover's cure for the depression was price maintenance. His overall scheme included high protection for American industries against foreign competition. All this plus persuasion would restore confidence. The task of jacking up the tariff walls was entrusted to Congressman Willis Hawley of Oregon and Senator Reed Smoot of Utah, both fervent protectionists who promptly proclaimed that a self-sufficient and self-contained nation was their objective. No ill winds from a troubled and depressed Europe would disturb America's normality. Hoover used six gold pens to sign the highest tariff bill in our history and remarked that agitation for lower import levies would impede recovery.

The foolhardiness of American policy was underscored as the Depression deepened and nation after nation retaliated with autarky. Import quotas, tariff walls, subsidies, and exchange control, as well as other beggar-my-neighbor policies, became devices for the export of unemployment. World trade went into a tailspin: American imports alone dropped from $4 billion annually to $1.4 billion as exports hit a bottom of $1.6 billion from an earlier high of $4.6 billion. Wherever trade balances were improved, it was generally at the expense of other nations.

The coming of the New Deal brought a fresh look at world trade. Cordell Hull especially was a firm believer in liberalization and tariff reduction, for to him this was a path to recovery and world peace. The country's recent experience conceivably would have opened the eyes of Congress and the business community. Yet when Roosevelt proposed the Reciprocal Trade Agreements Act in 1934, the reaction was explosive. Congressmen did not relish surrendering their log-rolling rights, and the tariff lobby saw to it that the labels "unconstitutional," "dictatorship," and "blank check" resounded from Senate rafters. But the President and his Secretary of State had their way: by June 1934, the new policy was written into law. The President was empowered to enter into agreements with other countries to revise rates, either way, up to 50 percent. Industries claiming injury could secure a hearing from the Tariff Commission.

Hull was delighted beyond description: reciprocal trade adjustment meant a fresh start toward unhampered multilateral trade, and a new kind of internationalism became the official trade philosophy of the New Deal. Within a year reciprocal trade agreements with fourteen nations had been signed; a decade later there were twenty-nine reciprocal trade agreements on the Federal Register.

That reciprocal trade alone could by no means solve the problems of the Depression was clear to all but free-trade visionaries. The world's shortage of American currency, known as the dollar gap, persisted after the war. Nations began to resort to currency and exchange controls as the experience of the thirties threatened to repeat itself. It required a forced-draft economic growth in Western Europe to bring trade to a high pitch, sufficient to allow the relaxation of controls.

The Reciprocal Trade Act itself has never been a long-range affair. Congress simply would not relinquish all of its prerogatives. The act was renewed eleven times after 1934, and only after painful legislative squabbles. Still, tariffs *were* reduced: prior to the first enactment in 1934, duties averaged 50 percent ad valorem; from 1936 to 1940 they averaged 39 percent; from 1941 to 1945 they were 32 percent; from 1946 to 1960, 16 percent; and since 1950, import duties have ranged between 11 and 13 percent. Reciprocal trade legislation, it can be said, did accomplish its initial purpose.

If tariff adjustment has gone this far, why the fuss now? After all, it is argued, foreign trade is but a small part of the gross national product: in 1960, imports represented about 3 percent of GNP, exports only 4 percent. Half our imports are raw materials and semi-processed goods which we do not produce. And it has been estimated that total abolition of our tariff structure might increase imports by some $4 billion. That is to say, foreign competition at a maximum would account for well under 1 percent of the gross national product. However, arguing this way overlooks the fact that American foreign trade represents one-sixth of world commerce. Anything that threatens to reduce this share cannot be taken lightly.

It might be a matter of slight concern for those whose economic vision is circumscribed by purely domestic interests, but foreign trade, small as it is in relation to the billions of GNP we produce, does make a contribution to our well-being quite out of proportion to its numerical weight. There are any number of essential raw materials purchased from other nations, such as chrome ore, without which the American economy would stumble. Moreover, a world of multilateral trade becomes a specialized world, with each country contributing to the welfare of others. Each offers for sale what it most efficiently can produce, and ultimately, perhaps, an approach might be made to the economists' dream of an optimum allocation of resources.

While this sets forth rather crudely a complex and frequently sophisticated argument, there are also cogent political reasons to justify the sort of program asked for by the administration. With the Common Market established on solid ground, as now seems likely, continued trade restrictions by us would eventually polarize the West. Distinct trading areas could arise, self-contained and severely limited in their dealings with each other. Freer movement of goods, on the other hand, would permit a larger measure of integration and a closer knitting of the political fabric. That this implies a willingness to surrender fragments of sovereignty, in the beginning at least, is self-evident. The gains stemming from such an effort would be well worth the frustration and agony that often accompanies protracted tariff negotiations. The decisive political gain from the administration's standpoint, however, is the fillip its program would lend to the Atlantic alliance.

Further, economic adjustments to price differentials at points across the globe are generally facilitated by freer trade. It was a process of this sort that enhanced our now historic growth pattern: what was true for us conceivably might work also for a world economy, given the desire to construct the necessary international institutions. Unhampered trade, in fact, can act as a substitute for the actual movement of labor and capital across national borders. The underdeveloped nations especially are bound to benefit, for they would then obtain with much less difficulty the foreign exchange so vital for their own upbuilding. One need only think of a Ghana or an Israel to see how urgent a matter this is. And by extending to such countries better terms of trade—i.e., an opportunity to obtain more dollars or pounds per unit of native currency—one secures in effect a more equitable distribution of income between nations.

But, we are told, competitive imports only serve to displace American workers. Now no one really knows how many jobs might be lost as a result of increased imports. The Labor Department has only recently studied the problem, and the conceptual and statistical difficulties with which it has wrestled are enormous. A rough guess suggests that 3.1 million persons depend on the export trade, while 1.4 million jobs stem from imports. The best estimates on displacement, by the staff of the Senate Commerce Committee, indicate that not more than 200,000 jobs would be lost as a result of a genuine free-trade policy. Thus, it is evident that fifteen times as many jobs depend on foreign trade as those that might be lost.

Most authorities are agreed that something new in trade policy is desirable. After all, the bulk of past tariff reductions was enacted prior to the last decade. Decreases since 1950 have averaged five percentage points as compared to thirty-four points before then. It is clear that not much more progress can be made with the restrictions imposed by "peril points," "escape clauses," and item-by-item bargaining.* These limits, first imposed by Congress in 1948, kept reductions to 4 percent in 1955–1958 despite legislative permission for a 15 percent cut. Of the 20 percent cut-back authorized in 1958, only about half will have been used by June of this year. As an AFL-CIO report remarked, tariff adjustments have been held to a snail's pace. The administration has indeed asked for broader bargaining powers, but the President's patent effort to placate congressional opposition with the assurance that "we are not neglecting the safeguards provided by peril points, an escape clause, or the National Security Amendment" has evidently created doubt among overseas friends as to the genuine liberality of his intentions. To quote the *New York Times:* "The European embassies were wondering out loud whether the President was not trying to have his cake and eat it too and how he hoped to avoid an adverse reaction in Britain and the Common Market countries."

The President and his advisers know that obeisance to broad principles will not be enough. Only the kind of pressure that the Executive Office can bring to bear, plus the sustained support of liberal opinion, will secure a meaningful trade bill. Yet to judge by his habitual mode of action and the nature of his congressional opposition, Kennedy will undoubtedly acquiesce cheerfully to a compromise. Acceptable amendments are already being prepared in the White House as a kind of fall-back position. This suggests that the administration's full-blown trade program may be curtailed considerably by the time it gets through Congress. The complete plan—including the five-year period in which to eliminate tariffs on goods 80 percent of which are produced by the United States and the Common Market; the 50 percent reduction on other items; bargaining by broad categories of goods rather than item-by-item; and federal aid to injured industries—will continue to be restricted by escape clauses and peril points. It is on the latter that protectionist forces have focused their attention,

---

* The "peril point," determined prior to negotiations with other nations, prohibits the reduction of a tariff rate below the level at which the Tariff Commission believes an industry will be hurt; the "escape clause" offers relief from import competition if an industry or firm can demonstrate that it has been hurt by a previously negotiated tariff concession.

for they have generally found it easier to deal with the Tariff Commission than with the White House. Representative John Byrnes of Wisconsin, the chief Republican member of the Ways and Means Committee, has his own strategy, namely to accept the administration's "broad objectives" but at the same time to "create a mechanism to avoid serious injury that may occur. . . ." Or the tariff on a particular industry will simply be retained, as in the case of textiles. This, in fact, seems quite likely. It is certain that the protectionist camp will seek the kind of limiting device that will substantially undermine the whole endeavor. And the administration is apt to be trapped by its own version of the escape clause—tariff relief for an entire industry after a negotiated reduction will have revealed injury, and federal loans and retraining have proved insufficient.

The administration's main emphasis appears to be on the enhancement of domestic mobility. In the words of the Task Force paper, ". . . assistance to labor and industry in adjusting to tariff reductions . . ." seems essential to the entire program. Avowedly, trade liberalization might impose temporary and local injury, but this could be overcome by a program of federal loans to finance relocation, tax rebates, retraining of workers, early retirement, more unemployment compensation—in fact, a whole battery of measures intended to help management and labor move out of affected industries into those which are more profitable. Moreover, say administration experts, it is always possible to reimpose tariffs, especially in industries where displacement by competitive imports takes place faster than movement into alternative employment. But this patently does not take into account the fact that the differences in such rates of change would most likely require a continuation of tariffs.

The administration obviously wants to be in a position to bargain more effectively with the Common Market. Should Great Britain join the Inner Six, it is conceivable that economic power may shift back across the Atlantic. An enlarged European economic union would encompass a population of 220 million and a regional output of $245 billion. It would attract a third of the world's exports. And America's share of the latter would approximate, at present levels, $3.4 billion, or a fourth of its shipments of goods overseas. Of course, the initial stimulus for European economic integration came from the United States, but now that a more unified Western Europe appears likely, second thoughts have been expressed at times in Washington, thoughts which protectionists are quite eager to exploit.

Liberals, naturally, do not view the situation with alarm; they urge even closer ties with our North Atlantic neighbors. This is essential, they say, if American goods are not to be excluded by a Common Market external tariff. Since trade with this part of Europe represents about 25 percent of our exports, such a contingency would have a catastrophic effect on our balance of payments, already awry for some time. The President then does need a free hand in making across-the-board tariff cuts: old-fashioned item-by-item bargaining will fail to bring about the kind of trade freedom necessary to sustain a high-pressure world economy. And with American interest in Europe displayed by membership in the Organization for Economic Cooperation and Development, any gesture in the direction of Smoot-Hawley would negate whatever role we might seek in that agency. Furthermore, participation in the latter's monetary pool might help relieve the balance of payments stringency, since additional international liquidity could be made available.

Aware of the difficulties it may face on the Hill, the administration is working frantically to achieve the best possible arrangements under present legislation. For over eighteen months, Howard Petersen, special assistant to the President, and Under Secretary of Agriculture Charles Murphy had sought to obtain mutual tariff reductions with the Common Market in order to guarantee that American agricultural exports, especially, would have easier access to European markets. In turn, the United States was expected to reduce tariffs on certain industrial imports from Western Europe by as much as 20 percent, the maximum allowable under the 1958 Trade Agreements Act. How many items will be included is not yet known, but it is anticipated, for example, that the duty on automobiles might be reduced from 8.5 percent ad valorem to 6.5 percent. Nevertheless, the American negotiators were hampered quite seriously by the peril point requirement, so much so that they were unable to reciprocate on many of the tariff deductions offered by the Common Market representatives, who in turn warned they would not settle for anything less than complete reciprocity. Yet whatever the results attained before June, when the present law expires, they will not be enough for a truly liberal trade structure. Continued congressional resistance will induce the Common Market simply to proceed with its own plans. What this would do for the *esprit de corps* of the protectionist camp is self-evident.

Thus the Kennedy administration must make more than a pretense at a liberal posture: it ought indeed *be* liberal on trade issues. It can hardly afford anything else. And to be able to bargain effectively with other nations it will sorely need the five-year period for which it has asked. Across-the-board, or linear, bargaining would do a better job of loosening trade restrictions than the present tedious item-by-item approach. Elimination of the peril point and escape clauses would make the "most favored nation" policy, which Kennedy is so anxious to pursue, truly meaningful. Under such agreements, a concession to one becomes a concession to all. Thus, American cooperation with the Common Market would by no means imply exclusion of Japan or Latin American nations, and in fact would contribute toward a solution of our own balance of payments problem, for the latter countries purchase a good deal more from us than we do from them.

The entire problem is exacerbated by the balance of payments deficit, which indeed has been with us for quite a long time. In fact, in all but one of the last twelve years, the U.S. balance of payments had to be redressed by an "outflow" of gold. The only surplus year was 1957, when the Suez explosion and a European drought skyrocketed exports of oil and wheat. For the next three years, the balance of payments deficit was around $10.5 billion or $3.5 billion each year. In 1961, the deficit was about $1.75 billion. However, each time the *merchandise* balance, the excess of exports over imports, was more than satisfactory. The overall balance was upset only because of capital outflow and overseas aid commitments. Thus, in 1960, a merchandise gain of $3.8 billion was wiped out by $3.5 billion in capital exports and $2.7 billion in overseas grants. It is anticipated that the 1962 deficit will come close to $2 billion, but only because our import increment may be larger than the gain in exports.

So far as the merchandise balance itself goes, the American position is a good one. From 1958 to 1960, exports advanced more, when compared to the base year of 1950, than either imports or GNP. The often expressed concern that we are being priced out of world markets just is not true. Thus, while wage differences may have been a factor in increased imports of textiles, for example, generally the U.S. has been able to hold its own in world trade. Some of the figures, notoriously bad anyway, suggest a fall in our merchandise balance from 1956 to 1959. But this could be explained mainly by automobile and automobile parts imports, which in 1959 were $450 million greater than exports. Since 1959, however, the merchandise balance has spurted forward in our favor to the tune of almost $5 billion, and it is anticipated that this will continue. In the case of Germany and Japan, slightly unfavorable balances with them in 1959 became favorable ones in 1960.

In addition to monetary controls, which we shall not discuss in detail here, the Kennedy experts see the expansion of exports as one of the primary ways of getting the flow of payments to balance in our direction. Following hard on some Eisenhower gimmicks, the administration is ready to fly "E" emblems from the rooftops of successful exporting concerns; the Export-Import Bank is prepared to insure overseas transactions; tax incentives are to be offered for plant modernization by exporters; and our allies are being encouraged to buy their military hardware from American arsenals and cannon manufacturers.

Administration officials are quite right in their argument that a looser flow of trade would ease the balance of payments deficit, for exports unquestionably would receive further impetus, while there would be less incentive for American firms to export capital by establishing foreign branches. Not all the experts, however, are impressed by such an argument: firms go overseas, it is said, not so much to jump over tariff walls as to assure lower production costs and to be close to overseas customers. But this does not deny the contention that increased employment in the export industries could easily offset losses in the import trades: besides, virtually all the economic injury would take place among inefficient firms, which in any case ought to shift over to other lines of endeavor. American firms have acquired too much fatty tissue of late; the stress and strain of competition would do them a lot of good, not unlike the overstuffed athlete who needs to visit Vic Tanny's. One urgent problem in this complex situation would stem from the tendency for imports to rise faster than exports, and, in the battle to reduce costs, adaptation to newer technologies would be hastened. The burden of the adjustment, in the absence of measures to reduce the pain, would be borne by the work force, and especially young workers who would find it even more difficult to locate jobs.

The President's advisers, nevertheless, are quite confident that tariff reduction would have little if any serious impact on the domestic economy. They estimate that zero tariffs on half of American imports, plus a 50 percent cut in the remainder, would stimulate the importation of goods by about $30 million a year for the next seven years. This represents a minuscule fraction of the $540 billion of GNP we enjoy and is a little over 1 percent of the present level of imports. Moreover, general tariff reduction would sharply stimulate European imports, for nations just entering the stage of affluence usually have a high demand for American goods. The fillip given to output, investment, and productivity seems undeniable.

One of the central arguments advanced by protectionists is that foreign nations enjoying lower standards can produce with cheaper labor. True, American wage rates are higher than anywhere else, but this is not the significant measure with which to compare costs between nations. Much more important are *unit* wage costs, an index which takes into account productive capabilities and the capacity to produce more or less for a given unit of labor. Of course, factors such as exchange rates, delivery dates, local taxes, credit terms, and the like are also important, but unit wage costs clearly predominate. It is the latter which influence international trade, not wage rates. America's higher wages, more complex technology, and greater capital investment make it possible to export goods in which unit wage costs are low: in these items we possess a comparative advantage. Otherwise, it is unlikely that they would flow into world trade channels. The coal industry is a case in point. Although coal wages here are three to seven times higher than those in other nations, American mines out-compete foreign ones quite handily. Advanced technology has been the solution. It takes a very low wage level indeed to overcome these advantages. The textile and clothing industries insist that low wage goods coming from Hong Kong and Taiwan are the bane of their existence. Yet what underlies American difficulties in these industries is the presence of a high labor component, and a not very high degree of economic efficiency.

The fact is that wages in Europe have been increasing more

rapidly than in the U.S. From 1950 to 1958 Common Market wages rose 8 percent as compared to 5 percent here. According to an estimate made by AFL-CIO economists, unit labor costs in the United States rose 5 percent between 1933 and 1959, as compared to 10 percent for West Germany, 27 percent for Holland, and 25 percent for Britain. Only in Italy, Japan, and France did unit wage costs decline during this period. The same report indicated that while steel wages in the United States were five times as high as in Belgium, the total labor cost in American plants was 28 percent of sales as compared to 31 percent for French firms and 36 percent for the Belgian steel industry. Labor cost per unit of sales *was* lower in the United States than in comparable Common Market industries. In a French steel plant, the same number of workers on a six-day week produced half the output of an American plant whose workers were on a five-day week. Even in the case of Japan, where productivity tended to outstrip wage increases between 1955 and 1959, there are indications that wages are catching up. It seems likely that the lower labor cost advantage to which Japan's competitive strength has been attributed will in future evaporate.

Will Kennedy obtain what he says he wants? He now seems to be fighting hard for his program. Briefing sessions are being organized for business groups and labor unions, White House coffee hours are staged for dissident Senators and recalcitrant Congressmen, and friendly lobbyists are urged to help the legislators toe the presidential mark. But the line-up, as it is called in Washington, promises to become a crazy-quilt piece of patchwork. Party lines will intertwine in wonderfully complex ways, following only the principle of "whose ox is being gored." With a new Common Market agreement on agricultural goods, even a midwestern Republican may support the President.

Yet there is some question whether Kennedy will succeed. First, there is no little opposition in Congress to further trade liberalization; second, there is doubt that the administration will really fight for its program. Kennedy's own ambivalence was revealed in his NAM speech in which he assured the nation's assembled entrepreneurs that traditional safeguards would not be destroyed and that the major objective was to increase exports. There are some who think that the administration ought not risk a political fight in an election year and should wait for the next Congress, which might prove more amenable. On the other hand, a year's delay could very well harden congressional attitudes. If the Trade Agreements Act were to expire in June, existing tariff schedules would remain, no further negotiations with other nations would be possible, and the escape clause could then be employed to cancel earlier concessions.

The current year provides a pronounced political advantage for the tariff lobby. It is not at all impossible—in fact it is quite likely —that the still potent coalition of Southern Democrats and Republicans may try to embarrass the President on this issue particularly. Of course, they would be performing a nose-cutting operation for the rest of us, since a liberal tariff bill seems an essential part of our effort to convince the rest of the world that sometimes our deeds do match our creeds. The recession last year did not help matters much either, for in its midst a curious amalgam of know-nothing legislators and frustrated unions began to beat the drums for more protection. Representative C. N. Bailey of West Virginia called for a halt to tariff cuts; the International Brotherhood of Electrical Workers decided to boycott Japanese electronic equipment; the Amalgamated Clothing Workers refused to cut cloth from Japan; the International Ladies' Garment Workers growled about imported blouses; while the Textile Workers Union screamed louder than anyone over job losses stemming from foreign competition.

There seems little doubt that the rather drastic changes in Reciprocal Trade proposed by the administration will arouse a bitter floor fight. Protectionist sentiment in Congress has mounted. Last February, Senator John Pastore of Rhode Island offered a list of suggested quotas, and one month later he and ten other senior legislators met with industry representatives in advance of a series of Senate orations demanding higher import quotas and other restrictions. On the House side, a fifteen-man committee headed by Carl Vinson of Georgia was formed to urge the President that import quotas be increased. Then in April, forty-eight Democrats and twenty Republicans spoke up in the House in support of the Vinson-Pastore position. Even so liberal a Congressman as John Dent of Pennsylvania seems ready to abandon the administration on this issue: it is evident that he cannot evade the pressures of the coal industry. The Republican view was most recently displayed by Senator Prescott Bush of Connecticut and

Representative Powers Curtis of Missouri, who in a joint report issued in January told the Congress that they saw no need to broaden presidential tariff powers. They preferred rather a "new alliance of free nations."

The fight that now seems to be in the making has depressed the Japanese particularly. Osaka textile producers recently told Ambassador Edwin O. Reischauer that the proposed entry fee of 8.5 cents a pound, equal to the raw material cost differential, would hit them quite hard, with serious repercussions on the city's economy. The ambassador was politely advised that there was no use talking about friendship without acting like a friend. It is true that the Japanese are strong competitors in textiles. When imports from Japan hit a high of 143 billion square yards of cotton cloth in 1956, the American government had to persuade Japanese exporters to accept a "voluntary" quota. Interestingly enough, the quota was so high that it has never been exceeded. Other production centers, however, have started to export to our shores in increasing quantities—Hong Kong, India, Spain, Egypt, Portugal, and France. Manufacturing capacity has increased sharply in these countries. It is not too difficult to build a textile industry, and the world demand seems ample enough to justify the investment. Not only do these centers have a labor cost advantage, but more important, they can purchase raw materials at about half of what it costs here, thanks to the federal government's agricultural price support program. So far as the Japanese are concerned, it cannot be said that they have flooded the American market: less than 3 percent of their textile output comes to our shores. The largest part of Japan's production is shipped to other Asian countries.

Nevertheless, so disturbed is the Japanese businessman about the outcome of the American trade battle that it was thought necessary to issue a rather wistful, though convincing, study to prove that purchases by Japan provide 190,000 jobs to American workers. Second only to Canada as a customer, the Japanese do buy a wide variety of goods from virtually every state of the union, including the District of Columbia, where one scrap metal dealer supplies $750,000 worth of junk each year. If the textile industry has been hard hit, it cannot be said that foreign competition was the sole cause. Quite simply, it has been a lagging industry, content to work with existing methods and undergoing competition from such domestic rivals as synthetics, plastics, and paper. It has therefore not shared in whatever growth the economy has exhibited. Still the industry was able to recover from the 1960 slump, with substantial improvement reported in mill inventories and back orders. Sales at retail did pick up last year, especially in home furnishings. About the only sector of the industry which has continued to lag is woolen manufactures.

Another industry involved in the tariff question is oil. Part of its problem, as in the case of textiles, is a domestic phenomenon: compact automobiles use less gasoline. While gasoline demand increased from 6 to 12 percent per annum in the early postwar years, more recently the figure has dropped to about 1 percent. The result has been an increasing number of price wars. Nevertheless, oil producers have jumped into the trade and tariff fray. The argument seems to revolve around imports of residual oil, most of which comes from Venezuela. Not that domestic oil producers care very much: with their refining processes, residual oil is not especially profitable. It has been the coal producer, rather, who has been complaining, and the oil men deem it good politics to help stir the cauldron just a bit.

Thus, the crosscurrents of private and special interests continue to muddy the issues. The National Association of Manufacturers wants a *quid pro quo* for a liberalized tariff and trade bill—to wit, lower taxes. Its president, D. J. Hardenbrook, asserts that American businessmen can expand exports only if the government will "remove the shackles from industry, business, and individuals and release creative and capital forces that would propel the United States into an era of economic and social greatness never witnessed before." Some observers might describe such flights of rhetoric as slightly redolent of polite blackmail: all the NAM wants is a tax reduction of about 25 percent, compensated by a temporary sales tax as the price of cooperation on trade.

There are a few businessmen who are less Bourbon-minded. The Committee for a National Trade Policy does express a liberal view on tariffs. It has advocated for a long time the elimination of the peril point clause so highly valued by protectionists; it would give the President the power to remove certain levies and reduce others by at least half, and it has supported an adjustment program for both workers and industry. But to some of the chemical companies, glass makers, shrimp canneries, cord and twine manufacturers, and toy and bicycle factories, all this seems very much like an invitation to slow suicide. They demand protection, the higher the better. They are ably represented on the Hill by a variety of lobbies. Outstanding among the latter is the Committee on Import-Export Trade, whose representative blandly advised Congress that the import dollar hurt a good deal more than the export dollar. And Senator Goldwater, whose retailing business back home in Arizona presumably sells both imports and exports, announced with a deep sense of shock that not only would we be dragooned into the Common Market, but that Kennedy was conspiring to import foreign workers to displace Americans.

On the other hand, the powerful Farm Bureau Federation would like to see trade liberalized, since their corporate farm members would then have easy access to overseas markets. They know that America's "historic share" of farm exports to Europe would be drastically curtailed, unless an agreement were reached with the Common Market. Fortunately, this has just been done, at least within the framework of the present Trade Act. The Common Market Ministers' Council at long last has worked out its own internal agricultural policy and is now in a position to agree on some additional tariff-cutting with the U.S. Thus, for the time being, a high external Common Market barrier has been avoided, but the coverage on agricultural products remains quite inadequate from the American standpoint. Moreover, the European negotiators are not willing to extend concessions on such major items as corn and wheat until the details of their own agricultural relations are set. Since this will be time consuming, Kennedy will need authority beyond June.

The enigma wrapped in a puzzle will be the attitude of the American labor unions. The labor movement has become almost totally schizoid on the subject of trade and tariffs. Of course, the labor movement generally, and its center on 16th Street in Washington, is emotionally and ideologically committed to Reciprocal Trade, a commitment that was strengthened by its association with the New Deal. Yet some international unions have been impelled to demand a measure of tariff protection for their industries in the belief that this will safeguard the jobs of some of their members.

An alternative approach advocated by a number of unions, notably the United Auto Workers, is described as International

Fair Labor Standards. That is to say, substandard nations should be encouraged to improve their wage levels so that competition based on low earning power would be eliminated. Some observers have been quick to urge that until wage equalization will have been achieved, a tariff should be imposed. Implicit in all this is the notion that exploitation ought not be employed as a competitive device. Now, this is a rather slippery idea, in the sense that it is difficult to say what exploitation is in one nation as compared to another. Comparison of wage levels is perhaps the trickiest of statistical stunts, if in fact it can be done at all. Wages within a given country are indeed related to each other, but only by the most tenuous of lines can they be related to what is paid in other nations. To equate the hourly wages of a steel worker in Japan to those paid in the U.S. proves nothing, for the obvious reason that productivity, prices, and a variety of other factors must be included in the comparison. No one has yet figured out how this might be done. If low wages stem from low productivity, restricting the output of such a nation would hardly be the answer, for only by trading with others would it be possible for improvement to take place. Some labor economists have suggested that tariff reductions be tied to wage increases in the exporting nation. This would represent a kind of international redistribution of income, since it would strip the profit-taker here of some of his protected gains and raise income overseas. An interesting idea, it is doubtful that it would be accepted either by the foreign exporter or his domestic competitor.

The AFL-CIO's approach has been to support the administration's adjustment program, i.e., financial aid to those displaced as a result of tariff loosening. In effect, this would shift part of the cost of import competition to the entire economy, and, as in the case of any economic burden which manifests so generalized a character, it can be justified without too much strain on economic logic. Areas and industries most seriously affected by imports would receive priority treatment under the Depressed Areas Bill, but even if a firm were not in a designated depressed zone, it could obtain assistance if injured by a foreign competitor. All this, says the AFL-CIO, might be supplemented by additional unemployment benefits, early retirement, retraining, and relocation. None of this is very startling and it would perhaps provide a kind of painless attrition and might even create that textbook fiction, mobility of resources. In any case, it is evident that labor's position is mixed, confused, ambivalent.

What is apt to be the final thrust of all these divergent forces? Not an especially happy one, for given the President's predilection for compromise, the weakness or unwillingness of the liberal forces to stage a genuine fight, the growing strength of the tariff lobbyists, the division in the house of labor, and the lack of public comprehension of the issues at stake and their ultimate implications, it seems that an ineffective trade bill may be the outcome. The government will have to live with this sort of business for the next three years, at least, and will have a devil of a time trying to explain it away to our allies.

1962

New Frontier Taxes

Make no mistake about it—the great American economy is stumbling over its feet. Between 1958 and 1962, according to the Council of Economic Advisers, the gap between what we produced and what we could have produced amounted to almost $1,000 per person, a total of $170 billion. Had the economy been operating at full blast, each family in the United States could have enjoyed at least another $4,000 in goods and services.

Virtually all the indices suggest sluggishness: the ratio of consumer expenditure to potential gross national product stands at about 63 percent as compared to 67 percent in 1958; the demand for goods and home construction is about half the potential GNP as compared to 55 to 60 percent in earlier years; and business investment has dropped from 10 or 11 percent of real GNP to only 9 percent. These figures are harbingers of unease—most economists would agree on at least this much.

For one thing, the American consumer does not seem disposed

to engage in relatively more spending than he has in years past. Ever since 1950, the proportion of disposable income spent by the consumer has hovered around 93 percent. There has been no visible increase in spending on durable goods, one of the more popular signs of economic vigor. Interest rates are still too high to help home buying and vacancy rates in rental housing—one of the more recent centers of strength—reportedly have been rising. But most important, industry has been limping along at about 80 percent of capacity for many months now. Even the CEA, which has a penchant for burying distasteful economic signs in verbiage, has had to concede that "in the past five years, total demands have not been adequate to promote rapid growth of incomes." Said the CEA in its last report to the President: "Consumption has not generated the profitable markets needed to stimulate investment; and investment spending has not generated the incomes needed to promote strong gains in consumption."

Why has this been so? One economist, James Knowles of the Joint Economic Committee, has argued that we are suffering from an artificially induced deflation. In effect, said he, a cultural lag has been imposed, for the responses required by the inflation of the 1940's and early 1950's are still being voiced. Tax measures that bore down heavily on expenditures are still on the statute books, although the inflationary threat has long since evaporated. No longer are we in possession of deferred purchasing power such as prevailed after World War II and Korea. Even the international "dollar-gap" exists no more; with the remarkable recovery of Western Europe it has been turned over to the historians to write about.

To these must be added the peculiar development of a compartmentalized economy in which a huge defense and space sector is partitioned off from a relatively affluent portion, and a few tidbits trickle down to the poor. The new exotic war goods utilize proportionately less capital and labor, and their highly specialized shape has less of a multiplier effect than most of us realize. The feedback stimulus flowing from rocket construction and similar enterprises is not nearly so sharp as that which used to stem from steel and autos. In the meantime, the traditional industries turn toward luxury markets patronized by an upper middle class, driving another wedge between the affluent and the dispossessed. All the latter can do now is to press the pants of the wealthy or fill their cocktail glasses or merely wait to be called to dig a ditch.

Perhaps this explains why unemployment last February rose to 6.1 percent of the work force. The total number of unemployed had increased to 4.9 million; as compared to the previous February the unemployed had gone up another 400,000. Moreover, long-term unemployment of fifteen weeks or more was now in excess of one million, while manufacturers' placements of new orders declined.

Thus the need for a massive attack on our economic ills was clearly indicated, yet virtually the only measure the Kennedy administration could dream up was the rather tepid tax proposal. One would think that to really stimulate demand, substantial relief for low-income taxpayers would be offered. The administration may have thought it was doing just this, but the facts seem otherwise, for those with incomes under $5,000 are to be given a 20 percent slice of the tax benefits, while the $5,000–$10,000 taxpayer is to receive a 44 percent share of the cutbacks. This may seemingly sound munificent, but note—tax reductions in the $5,000–$10,000 category come to $165 per tax return as compared to $286 per taxpayer in the $10,000–$20,000 group. Those earning from $20,000–$50,000 would get back $820 per return. The 44 percent figure tossed about by administration experts hardly tells the whole story.

Meanwhile, much legerdemain was applied to corporate levies and so-called tax reforms. For corporations a reversal of normal and surtax taxes was proposed so that the initial impost would be 22 percent instead of 30 percent, with an eventual reduction to the total corporation rate from 52 to 47 percent. The reforms themselves were little more than a potpourri of piddling changes that were unlikely to establish greater equity, a broader tax base or simplified tax administration. The new minimum $300 standard deduction, for example, was meaningful only for those with taxable incomes under $3,000. Greater allowances for charitable contributions made a little loophole larger; already the total of such deductions could build the churches of America more than twice over. Social service agencies, however, are upset because of the 5 percent gross income floor to be placed under all deductions. Real estate operators also are perturbed because this will give home owners smaller deductions. But the one great gap—those mineral depletion allowances on which Texas oil millionaires subsist—Kennedy did not touch. The 27.5 percent gross income deduction from net income was left alone. As a substitute, his tax message offered a series of complicated changes that the Treasury insists would really reduce depletion allowances by a fourth. Maybe so, but with Lyndon Johnson sitting in the Senate, one wonders how far that scheme will get.

The Independent Petroleum Association labeled the rather mild depletion reform as "a drastic setback to national security [and] contrary to the objective of stimulating growth." The United States Chamber of Commerce muttered that the tax cuts for middle-income families were illusory and was promptly advised by Douglas Dillon that it didn't know what it was talking about. The brightest gem in the debate came from the NAM, which remarked querulously that JFK's measures were "over-oriented toward a quick pick-up in economic recovery." Congress thus far has been wary: all the elementary lectures delivered by Kennedy's economics professors appear to have had little effect. Walter Heller argued against puritanism in economics; Willard Wirtz warned of an increase in unemployment; and Kermit Gordon feared that a balanced budget would have dire consequences. (Senator Harry Byrd immediately demanded that he be fired.)

But can tax cuts—at least the kind suggested by the administration—really get us away from the brink of depression? Most of the witnesses testifying before the Joint Economic Committee on Kennedy's economics did not think so. The combination of budget deficits and tax cuts in the first year might reach about $4 billion, so that with a multiplier of 2.5, the total impact might be evaluated at around $10 billion. But the labor force will have increased at the end of 1963 by over one million, and another million jobs will have to be provided to make a real dent in unemployment. The final thrust of Kennedy's tax and fiscal policies might just about equal the wage bill for these increased jobs. Moreover, with at least $90 billion in idle capacity, the likelihood of new capital formation seems dim. With a capital-output ratio of 3:1, perhaps two-thirds of our unused capacity will remain unused, for even if the $10 billion were all spent on consumption, it would call into play not more than $30 billion in capital. Thus, there would be no new investment to make the company approach viability. There simply isn't enough starch in the administration program to keep it standing.

At any rate, the tax program is just another illustration of the administration's record of evasion and compromise on fundamental issues, all disguised as New Frontier dynamics. To give the economy in its present flagging condition an effective boost requires at least double what Kennedy wants to do. Instead we have before us a phased program of $13.5 billion spread over three years, with but a $2 billion tax cut for year one!

Much more important, it would appear, is an effort directly to stimulate activity via urban renewal, area redevelopment, mass transportation, a proper retraining program, and public works of various kinds. Yet the myth of the fiscal cure continues to grip administration experts, with only soft murmurings offered whenever the question of structural change in the economy is raised. The specific proposals I have mentioned are necessary for meeting America's needs, but few in Washington, or elsewhere, seem to care.

Thus, as James Reston recently reported in the *New York Times'* International Edition, the malaise of drift is the most easily discernible note in Washington these days. Power balances power, said he, to the point of paralysis. Radical facts confront both moderates and conservatives and both quarrel with each other as to how best to deny their existence. The JFK philosophy of compromise finally has come to dead rest—neither labor nor management, Castro nor Keating, conservative nor liberal have been placated. Compromise has remained what it really is: low-level politics. It has failed utterly to solve any problem, whether foreign or domestic. As Reston remarked, its sole accomplishment has been to heighten frustration for the President, as indeed for the rest of us.

1963

Demobilization: 1918-1945

When World War I ended, Americans felt that they would return to a life of peace without fear. At the close of World War II, Americans were likewise overjoyed, but their sense of release was tempered by a pressing fear of unemployment. As soon as the surrender of Japan was announced, thousands of persons faced the unhappy prospect of joblessness. According to official estimates, the metal, chemical, and rubber industries would lose 3,800,-000 workers, the munitions industry would discharge 1,000,000 workers, shipyards 600,000, the aircraft industry 1,100,000 and government agencies 400,000. This, it was said, would take place within three months and the great industrial centers would be threatened with mass desertion.

Everyone makes easy estimates of the great numbers that will be unemployed, but few dare to say when and how they will be put back to work. By December, six million persons may be repeating the experience of the 1930's. War production will have been eliminated and peacetime production will still be lagging.

Displaced workers have been asked to register at the nearest United States Employment Service office and employers have been requested to notify the USES of potential work opportunities. War contracts are being canceled with great haste. An estimated $25 billion of surplus goods must be disposed of by the government. There are hundreds of government-financed plants that must be sold or dismantled.

The businessman wants to know whether he will have a free hand to do as he wishes. The farmer seems to be well set, at least for the next two years, for "congressional action provides price support for many commodities for two years after final peace," according to the report of John W. Snyder, reconversion director. Unions, too, want to know where they stand.

Prices, wages, and profits complicate an already tangled situation, and we must find answers to the questions that the returning serviceman will undoubtedly put before us. An American economy trying to find a peacetime level will have to make room for 5,000,000 ex-soldiers and 2,500,000 ex-sailors within a year. Yet, fundamental to all of these seemingly diverse and confusing problems is the major question of devising a peacetime economy that will provide security and jobs for all.

The problem of reconversion is essentially one of releasing war controls in such ways as will lift our economy toward maximum peacetime production. But how are controls to be balanced against the immediate impact of mass unemployment? How are we to balance spending and the small amount of available goods? What taxation policy shall we adopt to facilitate the achievement of a high level of economic activity?

Are there any lessons which we may learn from the 1918 effort to achieve a smooth transition from war to peace? The outstanding feature then was the belief that a laissez-faire policy was best. As a result, 40 percent of the inflationary spiral of that war came after the armistice. Congressional conservatism then approximated conservatism today. But the conversion problem was simpler in 1918: 30 percent of productive capacity then was employed in war work, whereas today 60 percent of our facilities were diverted. Yet demobilization in 1918 was quite chaotic.

Today we are presumably more experienced in planning, but we are just as confused. In 1918, the cry was "return to normalcy." Today, big business says virtually the same thing. Henry Hazlitt, financial writer for the *New York Times,* says, "What is needed is to get business back without delay to its normal peace work. What is chiefly required of the existing war control agencies is that they do not stand in the way of this." Continued controls in industry, he implies, are dangerous.

On November 11, 1918, four million men were under arms, fifteen million were engaged in war work, the government was spending $2 billion each month and prices were twice the level of 1914. In May 1918, the Council of National Defense submitted to President Wilson a memorandum on postwar readjustment which stressed the necessity for balancing the supply and demand for labor. But no adequate preparations were made; there was no staff of experts to suggest what measures might be undertaken. The Wilson administration lagged in preparing for peace; and Congress was even more backward—its members made demobilization a political football. Memoranda flowed in profusion from other government agencies, yet no central reconversion body was ever established. Improvisation was the keynote and laissez faire the leitmotif. There was a feeling of impatience in the air; let business alone and it will do the job. There was an implicit faith in the laws of supply and demand; the rigors of the transition, it was felt, would hardly be noticed. Soon after the armistice, most of the leading wartime economic officials resigned: Walter Gifford, William G. McAdoo, and Bernard Baruch thought their jobs had been completed. How erroneous that attitude really was soon became evident.

The USES was established to provide placement service for the unemployed, but lack of experience made the job difficult. The service was poor and employers failed to cooperate with the agency. In spite of its handicaps, the USES was beginning to do a good job when Congress slashed its funds 80 percent in July 1919. In October 1919, the USES temporarily passed out of existence (it was revived during the depression of the 1930's).

In the World War I reconversion period, the War Industries Board first announced that materials would be controlled to permit a smooth flow; limitations were to be removed gradually. Industrialists were then asked to suggest how controls might be lifted; by January 1919, less than sixty days after the end of the war, all priority restrictions were removed. Business was restored to the care of natural market forces.

Contract cancellation policies were inconsistent; clear and integrated policy might have been helpful, but the problem was complicated by the existence of different kinds of contracts. One provided for termination, another made no such provision and a third was altogether informal. The last type caused many difficulties; the Comptroller General ruled that the government had no obligation in these informal contracts. Thus, about $1.5 billion was tied up until Congress could provide the necessary legislation.

In the meantime, many contractors could not change over to peacetime production. The government told new manufacturers, the "war babies," to find their own peacetime work. By December 5, 1918, cancellations reached the sum of only $2.5 billion; five months after the war, half of the contracts had not as yet been adjusted. No clearance machinery had been prepared and the chaos was astounding.

Some persons suggested the possibility of employing public works to take up the slack in employment, but little planning was done along these lines. On November 18, 1918, it was reported that Baruch had prepared a comprehensive plan for construction; nothing was heard of it afterward. The War Labor Policies Board sent letters to the nation's mayors, suggesting that municipalities might resume public works suspended for the duration. The railroads might have provided an opportunity for federally sponsored work, but the issue of public ownership beclouded matters. A land-settlement plan was advanced by Secretary of the Interior Lane, in which he suggested that state governments buy land for veterans and the federal government supply funds for reclamation and irrigation. Again, nothing was done.

As Army demobilization got under way, and as buyers waited for prices to drop, economic stagnation began to settle on the country. Labor surpluses appeared in industrial centers; by the end of February 1919, unemployment reached the million level. Production receded 26 percent in five months. Yet prices, which dropped from an index of 136 in December 1918 to 130 in February 1919, quickly jumped to 167 in May 1920. The stock market, too, reflected these changes. The paralysis was clearly due to the drop in mass purchasing power and business fear of excess plant capacity. And the only thing President Wilson could do was to convene a Conference of Governors and Mayors in March 1919 to discuss ways and means of combating the post-war depression.

Wilson firmly believed in the efficacy of natural market forces. Yet it was clear that the most important problem of postwar adjustment, the inflation of prices, could not be solved by the restoration of the free market. During the war, businessmen had learned how to cooperate; as unemployment became widespread, planned restriction of production assumed serious proportions. The government had encouraged business to do the very things that had long been prohibited. Industries were organized into trade associations, prices were fixed, output was pooled, markets were divided, distribution methods were established—competition was virtually eliminated. Business transferred the techniques of group control into the postwar period. The idea of cooperation between business, labor, and government was not visualized; business wanted to do things its own way. On the other hand, group action by labor was deprecated as an unsound practice.

An adequate price program would have tried to control the movement and direction of prices. The wholesale price index rose from 68 in November 1914 to 136 in November 1918, an increase of 100 percent. Price inflation brought huge profits to business. Net corporate income rose from an annual average of $3 billion in the period 1909-1912, to $11 billion in 1917. When criticized for profiteering, corporate officers said that they needed reserves to balance losses expected in the postwar deflation. In the meantime, war agencies were disbanded, the President was in Europe and Congress did not show much inclination to do anything about reconversion.

Speculation swept the country, and the high cost of living confounded the authorities. In July 1919, prices rose more than 4 percent; the Railroad Brotherhood, among others, warned that it would take drastic action if prices were not reduced. The only solution that could be suggested was a "work and save" program. The public, in its wrath, turned first against the profiteers and then against labor. Reaction especially encouraged the latter.

The memory of the 1918 reconversion follies now pursues a shadow-like existence. Businessmen are indeed concerned with the disposition of war plants and equipment. M. B. Gordon, vice-president of the Wright Aeronautical Corporation, suggests that we pull the roof off the plants and "let the rain come in." Donald Douglas, of Douglas Aircraft, has a simple postwar plan which consists of "shutting the damn shop up."

The battle over the present reconversion began back in November 1943 when the Truman Committee urged that plans for peacetime production should be started. Some businessmen, however, preferred delay for fear that competitors would have the jump should peace be suddenly declared. In February 1944, Bernard Baruch announced his plan for reconversion, but it was much too vague and placed great faith in the ability of the business community to achieve an orderly transition to peace. In October 1944, the Office of War Mobilization was created to handle the staggering problem of the transition.

The problem indeed seemed serious. Over seventeen million workers were engaged in war production; plant capacity increased during the war, from one-third to one-half; and virtually all of industry was engaged in some kind of war work. About three-fourths of the plants will require some technical as well as economic adjustment; only a small number of plants cannot be employed for peacetime uses. The greatest reconversion problems are to be found in the machinery, aircraft, metals, automobile, and railroad industries. The electrical equipment, tires, chemicals, steel, and building industries face a somewhat less difficult problem.

In 1918–1919, property rights seemed more important than human rights. Today's preparations show that this is again the case. The Revenue Act of 1944 enables corporations to recover losses sustained in postwar years up to the amount of taxes paid in the two war years 1943–1944. The Contract Settlement Act gives contractors exceedingly favorable terms in the settlement of government obligations, and also enables them to borrow on liberal terms pending the disposition of their claims. These are but two examples of concessions obtained by business.

What are the determining factors in the reconversion situation? Businessmen want business, labor wants jobs, and government wants stability. This focuses attention on employment and purchasing power. The pent-up demand for consumer durables—automobiles, refrigerators, washing machines, homes—may provide a stimulus for speedy resumption of peacetime production. This demand, it is said, will be sustained by the $59 billion of war bonds held by individuals. But not all of that can be spent at once. A prolonged period of unemployment and the consequent loss in purchasing power could absorb much of these savings. And shortages of materials, especially in the building trades, may hold back the process of reconversion, prolonging unemployment. Many businessmen, too, are holding back in the hope that all controls will be liquidated.

In the meantime, unemployment increases. It is estimated that 63 percent of the workers in the munitions industry will be seeking other jobs. "How long it will take for the majority of these to be absorbed in civilian production is anybody's guess," was the remark of one anonymous government official. Republic Aviation discharges 25,000 workers, Eastern Aircraft lays off 15,000 workers, and so on, down the line. This, of course, is the outcome of Congress' express directive prohibiting the continuance of war contracts for the purposes of providing employment. This may be justifiable, yet Congress has failed to provide for re-employment.

The business world is just as optimistic today as it was in 1918. Ira Mosher, NAM president, says that fewer than 1,500,000 workers will be out of work for more than thirty days. He expects that $9 billion of investment will be made by private enterprise for rebuilding and re-equipment, and this, he says, will provide sufficient jobs. The Committee for Economic Development, representing the "liberal" wing of big business, anticipates full employment, or its near equivalent, within a year. It asserts that business plans to provide jobs for fifty-four million workers and to increase production 42 percent over the 1939 level. But such arguments may very well be used to prevent planning during the transition.

It seems clear that business' outlook for reconversion is predicated on the assumption that government will do nothing to interfere with business' own planning. That assumption seems substantiated in the report submitted to the President by Reconversion Director John W. Snyder. The report admits that the termination of war will bring severe dislocation and economic shock, but expresses the hope that it will prove temporary. It also concedes that a vast expansion will be necessary, if our peacetime economy is to provide a high standard of living, and that plants engaged in war work are to be released at once. Businessmen are urged to proceed with peacetime plans.

The Snyder report creates the impression that coordinated action *will* be the rule this time. "Meetings with the heads of various war agencies in order to formulate policies and to plan and prepare for reconversion" have been held, it says, and a reconversion working committee has been set up.

Yet reconversion procedures again threaten to follow a trial and error pattern. Mr. Snyder clearly says that he does not propose to set forth a master blueprint "which will rigidly prescribe each move." This promises an unintegrated demobilization, paralleling the experience of 1918–1919.

Munition manufacture is to be halted immediately. Army purchases are to be cut 94 percent; cancellations of Navy contracts will total $9 billion. It is suggested that raw materials may be shifted to peacetime uses at once. But utilization of raw materials will take some time, for plants must be retooled. The Reconversion Director estimates that a full changeover to peacetime production will take from twelve to eighteen months.

One of the most difficult problems of the transition is the disposal of surplus goods. The cost of excess war plants and war goods will approximate the national income of any good prewar year. It is estimated that the total of the disposable goods will come close to $210 billion. Some of America's surplus is overseas and will have to be sold in foreign lands. This may very well be employed as part of our contribution to world relief needs.

Properly handled, surplus property disposal can do much to help achieve a smooth transition to a full employment economy. It can help reduce the national debt and promote production. Prompt release of consumer goods can aid in stabilizing prices. Quick distribution of raw materials will facilitate resumption of peacetime production. Government-owned plants may be used to provide jobs as well as materials for other industries. But all this demands planning and the establishment of some system of priorities for the transitional economy. Business fears these possibilities and prefers a hasty return to a "free enterprise" economy.

Surplus-disposal procedures today are disorganized in spite of the warnings of history and competent authorities. Property disposal is handled by the Treasury Department, the Reconstruction Finance Corporation, the Maritime Commission, the War Food Administration, the National Housing Agency, the Federal Works Agency, and the Army and Navy Departments. General policies are set forth by the Surplus Property Board. Mr. Snyder's report holds out little hope for a more integrated policy. Its outstanding characteristic is its emphasis on a speedy relaxation of government controls. The thought seems to be that this is the best way to achieve reconversion.

Perhaps the expansion of the consumers' durable goods industries and the service industries will provide opportunities for re-employment, says the report. Fortunately, President Truman has gone beyond that vague hope; he has indicated that the Full Employment Bill is the first order of congressional business. In his executive order of August 19, the President stressed the need for sustaining purchasing power and preventing wide price gyrations. The President has announced plans for promoting peaceful relations between business and labor. In his statement of August 16, he proposed that WLB permit negotiations for wage increases and that a conference of business and labor be held to map plans for future relations.

Some consumer rationing has been dropped; gasoline, canned foods, fuel, oil, and stoves have been removed from the rationed-goods list. Tires and autos, meats, fats and butter, sugar, and shoes remain rationed for the present. Mr. Snyder says that a greater supply of textiles and clothing will be made available, since the armed forces will reduce their buying by as much as 75 percent. Yet the National Retail Dry Goods Association insists that clothing shortages will be with us for at least six months. The important point here is that premature relaxation of rationing only serves to place low-income groups at a marked disadvantage in the mad scramble for scarce goods.

The Snyder report concedes that price controls will have to be maintained during the transition. Rents "must remain in force in some areas," it says. But observe how vague this is. What principles are to govern rent-control relaxation? When will an area no longer be a defense-rental area?

Closer examination of transition price controls as outlined by OPA indicates that the weakening process may very well start now. The major job of pricing will be left in manufacturers' hands. An attempt will be made to keep prices close to 1942 levels, but firms with gross sales of less than $200,000 a year will be granted automatic-pricing formulas by which they may police themselves. Price adjustments will be made by OPA offices; thus national policy is sacrificed to local expediency.

The indecent haste to drop all controls ignores the essential factors in orderly conversion—the establishment of a system of priority. A sound reconversion policy should emphasize the production of sorely-needed commodities; that requires careful planning and control. The kind of reconversion we now face is but a duplication of 1918.

It seems safe to say that reconversion may bring a period of recession in spite of business re-equipment and orders for consumer goods. The improvisation policy that Washington seems to be following, once more, will hardly help matters. The Snyder report implies that business alone can restore peacetime prosperity. Reconversion is visualized as an emergency program; no long-range program is advanced. The more liberal aspects of the Snyder report do suggest increased unemployment insurance, higher minimum wages, and some public works. Yet the lifting of all controls seems to be giving business too much of a free hand in this critical time.

1945

Can the United States Reconvert to Peace?

Bedazzled by the way in which the American economy success-fully handled three postwar recessions, many observers have con-cluded that prosperity is now normal and routine, built-in to the system. Not only has the economy become less susceptible, they say, to the kind of cataclysmic collapse experienced in the 1930's, but it may well be that the business cycle has at long last been done away with, at least in our own generation. They point to the supposed fact that the downward cumulative force of a recession was halted time and again by a battery of built-in stabilizers which sustained demand in different parts of the economy. Steep progressive income taxes, unemployment insurance, high-level capital expenditures, and national pattern wage bargaining have all seemingly contrived to keep things going at a bubbling pace.

All this suggests to the new optimists that the affluent economy of the 1950's was totally different in quality from the economy of the 1930's and 1940's, and that the 1960's will continue the happy trends established after Korea. Productive capacity, the ability of the economy to maintain a flow of goods and services, is now almost double the 1929 level and the government presumably is better aware of the need to step in whenever economic events threaten to take a turn for the worse.

With Korea there came an upsurge in private spending, initiating a hectic but good-natured scramble for goods by both business and consumers. There was also a gradual and steady spending program for war needs which threatened to set off another inflationary rush. By 1951, despite the war mobilization, prices leveled off, due perhaps as much to full consumer cupboards as to overstocking in inventories. When in 1953 the economy began to sag just a bit, it was thought that house-building and consumer durables would collapse entirely. But investment by business continued unabated, and with the government lending its support through the guarantee of mortgages, home-buying rose swiftly. Added to this was an unprecedented expansion in capital investment by business, again stimulated by Washington's tax privilege program which provided for rapid depreciation and encouraged businessmen to spend as much as they could.

This was the picture as seen by most economists. Yet in virtually all the analyses I have examined, little credit is given to the enormous expenditures by the federal government on defense and other cold war needs. Ever since Korea, so-called national defense expenditures have approximated 10 percent of the gross national product (GNP) and today they stand virtually equal with business investment as a major factor in keeping the economy on a high level of affluence. Perhaps the best way to demonstrate the impact of national defense on the economy would be to present the relevant statistical data for at least the years 1947 to 1958.

A cursory examination reveals that while GNP rose in the eleven-year period by almost 89 percent and business spending by 26 percent, federal expenditures jumped some 235 percent. The increase in national defense costs went up even more, reaching a level of 290 percent as compared with 1947. These figures are on a current dollar basis; but even if we deflate them for constant dollars (to 1954) to eliminate the impact of price rises, the increases are still stupendous. With a correction for constant dollars, GNP increased 41 percent, while federal expenditures more than doubled, with the national defense portion jumping 166 percent.

Yet during the period, business investments, no matter how computed—that is, on a constant-dollar or current-dollar basis—did not rise markedly in a relative sense. The ratio of business investment to GNP, in fact, has dropped during the eleven-year period. Even in constant dollars, there was a decline in 1958 of 4.5 percent over 1947.

It may be said that the 1958 terminal date is unwarranted, for, taking 1957 as the terminal year, constant-dollar business investment showed a rise of 25 percent within a decade. Nevertheless, the cutback in business expenditures of some $20 billion in 1958 did not appear to have appreciably affected the growth in GNP. The suspicion grows that business investment may have been displaced by government spending, especially for war purposes, as the prime mover in the American economy.

Of course, this has not always been the case. During the nineteenth century and prior to World War I, federal spending was a minuscule portion of total output. But with each war, Washington's responsibility for an ever-increasing portion of the national product grew by leaps and bounds. During the nineteenth century, federal outlays increased from some $10 million per annum to about $400 million by 1900. The War of 1812 and the Civil War pushed federal spending up not merely for the duration of the conflict, but permanently, by 150 percent and 230 percent respectively. After World War I there was a jump of 260 percent. But at no time prior to the present were military expenditures so significant a part of the total flow of goods and services. True, in World War I, spending for guns and military manpower was 16 percent of national output, but it quickly dropped back to less than 1 percent. The present 10 percent figure, however, promises to become the normal level. Military responsibility for its portion of gross national product is now ten times what it was in the 1930's and more than twenty times what it was in the nineteenth century.

Some economists have argued that so vast a program is really no drain on our total resources, since some of the materials and manpower utilized by the military might have remained unemployed anyway. Moreover, they say, the shift from low value sectors, such as farming, to high value products, such as electronics and space photography, helps increase the GNP. Thus, our economy, they say, can only be prosperous when we prepare to blow it all to kingdom come. Perhaps the Pharaohs of ancient Egypt were not so crazy when they built pyramids, nor John Maynard Keynes so mad when he suggested that pound notes be buried in bottles to be dug out by the unemployed.

There is little doubt now that military spending has been extremely stimulating to the whole economic system. With the civilian economy growing at an annual rate of about 3 percent per annum, an additional growth curve was added by government spending to meet the cold war needs. Assuming that the civilian economy was already prosperous by 1930 standards (a $300 billion GNP and sixty million employed) military hardware added that much more gravy. That is to say, war is good. It has not occurred to the experts that with other objectives and other values, the civilian economy might have digested the added GNP without any cramped feelings.

What would happen if military expenditures were curtailed? When the fighting stopped in Korea and military spending was reduced by some $10 billion in 1953–1954, there was a sharp accompanying decline in economic activity. Not so much the size of the reduction but simply the fact that it took place at all was important. It is clear that a decrease in military spending in the kind of economy we now have would depress the level of GNP and, in human terms, create no little amount of unemployment. A successful disarmament program would be of great concern not only to those industries involved in research and development, electronics, aircraft, and the like, but to all the peripheral industries which service them. If the economy functions with a multiplier of three, as seems likely, that is, if one dollar of investment leads ultimately to $3 of GNP, then a 50 percent cut in military spending (or about $22 billion) would imply a fall in GNP of $66 billion. Such a reduction would be catastrophic. Since full employment now requires a growth of about $15 billion in GNP (in constant prices) the public projects necessary to replace military reductions would dwarf all imagination.

Would it be possible to replace military spending with other items? This, of course, always depends on the domestic political climate. But with general government costs, veterans' services, agriculture, commerce, and welfare items about as high as they can possibly go in the present juncture of affairs, it is doubtful that they could absorb what is now spent for cold war purposes. Frankly, where else could we spend $40 billion a year but in the military establishment?

There are some, like Seymour Harris and James Warburg, who feel certain that the economy can adjust to peacetime operations, given certain political conditions. But there is a reasonable doubt that the transition really can be made successfully. For the basic question, as always, revolves about our willingness to look ahead and to plan for the numerous delicate adjustments that would be required to keep the economy moving at high levels. Not only would we have to make up the loss in GNP stemming from military cutbacks, but account would have to be taken of the $15 billion per annum increase in productivity.

A 10 percent reduction in military spending, or roughly about $4 billion a year, would require replacements considerably larger than that sum. Simply enough, the reduction of some $12 billion in GNP (the multiplier effect) would be virtually instantaneous, while the initiation of projects and spending programs to replace military expenditures would require time before the effect of their take-off would be felt. The backwash of a sharp and substantial reduction in the military sphere is more than apt to drown out the salutary impact of a new spending program. A large part of military outlays are direct: pay for soldiers and the Pentagon bureaucracy provides a flow of immediate purchasing power, whereas outlays for bridges, roads, and housing require time in order to exert their beneficial glow upon the economy. I submit that public nonwar spending would have to be considerably larger than the military cutbacks themselves merely to overcome the gaps and time lags that would inevitably arise. Now, add to that the need to absorb the additional goods that can be produced by virtue of greater productivity and the enormity of the job becomes clearly evident.

To repeat, it is doubtful that nonmilitary needs can absorb the full amount of expenditures saved through a disarmament program. Even a vast foreign aid effort, such as suggested by Warburg, could not take more than $5 to $10 billion a year. That would more than double the level of economic assistance now being given to other nations. Is Congress, and the present administration, likely to accept such a program? I doubt it.

True, there is a vast reservoir of social needs that we ought to fill. Both Seymour Harris and John Kenneth Galbraith have told us about the gaps in education, housing, flood control, highways, hospitals, medical services, social security, sanitation controls, urban and suburban transit, and recreation facilities—the list is indeed a long one. Schools are overcrowded and colleges do not know from where the funds for the next decade's operations will come; the lag in housing approximates 750,000 units a year; and our old folks are relegated to the heap of the socially useless with pittances of $70 a month. Between the needs and the desire to meet them there yawns a chasm of political apathy, administrative stupidity, and business intransigence.

As Warburg said recently, how many corporate managers living off the fat of government contracts have given thought to what they might produce should peace really break out? How many plans have been developed for reconverting factories now devoted to defense needs? What thought has been given to providing jobs to those now in the armed services when they will have been released? What, in short, has been done to create quickly the markets necessary to replace $40 billion of defense spending?

The question reduces itself then, not to whether it *can* be done, whether a high speed economy is possible, but rather to whether it *will* be done, whether we have the foresight and wisdom to construct a social and political technique for a quick reversal of economic gears. Basically this is a matter of politics, not economics. It implies a radically new way of accomplishing tasks and a major realignment of political thinking. It means a new vision of society, one willing to undertake measures that will unstintingly provide people with the public services they have so long done without. It means, above all, a reorganization of the lines along which power is disposed; it means, if you will, a new political economy.

1960

Disarmament and the Economy

*We must release the human imagination in order to open up
a new exploration of the alternatives now possible for the
human community; we must set forth general and detailed
plans, ideas, visions; in brief, programs . . . and make these
political issues.*—C. WRIGHT MILLS

Let us suppose that we are on the brink of disarmament. Let us
suppose that minimum deterrence, pre-emptive strike, counter-
force, retaliatory capacity, invulnerability, arms control, escalation, and all the other recondite notions of the cold war have
been relegated by our political leaders to the dusty archives of
history. Let us suppose that Polaris, Minuteman, and Davy Crock-
ett are about to be turned into plowshares or preserved as curious
museum pieces. Then what?

Some say that the result would be nothing short of economic
catastrophe. From 1950 to 1959, $230 billion was spent on weap-

onry. In 1960, $46 billion of federal money went into defense, atomic energy, and space, and the budget for "fiscal 1964" will provide $54 billion for the same purposes. It is estimated that by 1965 well over three million people will be working in defense-related industries, and another four million will be working directly for the government, either in blue denims or uniforms. The argument that our prosperity—such as it is—can be traced to the stimulus of the cold war, and that the continued viability of our economy depends on preparation for war, thus appears to have a good deal of weight behind it. After all, did it not take a huge war effort to rescue us from the Great Depression? As John P. Lewis, the new member of the Council of Economic Advisers, once said: "Short of World War II, no adequate cure ever emerged or was contrived" to haul the economy out of the doldrums of the thirties.

Imagine, therefore, the enormity of the economic problem we would face if disarmament were suddenly to emerge as an imminent possibility. At the moment, 6 percent of the work force is unemployed, and at our skimpy rate of growth, the economy cannot even absorb normal increases in the labor force. How, then, would it be able to provide jobs for the perhaps four million persons who would be released from defense industries and the armed services in the event of disarmament? Many economists even think that the situation would be worse than it appears on the surface. For example, Leo and Betty Fishman, a husband-and-wife team at West Virginia University, suggest that the government, paralyzed by snail-like legislative procedures, would be unable to formulate a quick response and might (as some business troglodytes advocate) use the savings from defense to pay the federal debt. The consequences of this would be dire indeed. Debt repayments would increase the lazy cash of financial institutions and rentiers, and by a well-known Keynesian device called the reverse multiplier, income and employment would tumble head down. Now, suggest the Fishmans, add to the four million already jobless (despite a high-pressure defense effort) another four million released from armament work, plus still another four million discharged because the multiplier is running backward, plus a million newcomers to the labor force, and we are confronted by a total of *thirteen million* persons facing the same conditions that existed in the thirties.

There are, to be sure, other economists who argue that this grim picture is overstated and who rather cheerfully believe that no administration would ever become so rigid as to be incapable of reacting to impending doom. No one, however, doubts that the economic problems attendant upon disarmament would be critically serious, and considering that disarmament is one of the stated goals of our foreign policy, it would be reasonable to suppose that top government bureaus and private research organizations in Washington are at this very moment busily engaged in studying these problems. But the sad fact of the matter is that apart from a few private individuals and a single small bureau—the Arms Control and Disarmament Agency—no one has done more than look at the economics of disarmament before turning away either in bemusement or horror.

The RAND Corporation, that den of powerful minds wrapped in their own assumptions, is casually uninterested. The Council of Economic Advisers assures us that it knows what must be done (merely turn a few Keynesian tap valves) and that it anticipates no real difficulty in educating Congress on the issues at stake. The Peace Research Institute, headed by former Ambassador James Wadsworth, concedes that planning for disarmament is important, but it just hasn't gotten around to it yet. The Institute for Defense Analysis—another RAND-type group—regards the whole question as premature. The Joint Economic Committee staff is aware that grave problems may stem from defense cut-backs, but what can they do when Committee members have other cats to skin? In all of Washington, only ACDA, with its relatively low budget and undermanned research bureau, has issued any sort of report on the consequences of disarmament—and this was prepared by an outsider, Emile Benoit of Columbia University.* Add a few more articles and studies by Benoit, Seymour Melman (also of Columbia), Kenneth Boulding of Michigan, the "country reports" submitted by other member nations to the U.N. expert panel on the economics of disarmament, and a London *Economist* survey, and the list of literature on the subject is virtually complete.

Benoit, Boulding, and Melman have done heroic work in try-

---

* In addition, the ACDA has published the American reply to a U.N. inquiry on the effects of disarmament, a rather detailed memorandum which was included in the U.N. disarmament experts' report of February 1962.

ing to arouse public interest in what could happen in the event of disarmament. The first two writers have been nursemaid and godfather to the Research Program on Economic Adjustments to Disarmament (READ), which recently issued a perceptive and useful symposium on the transition to a complete peace,* and Melman, of course, has been a kind of St. John shouting in the canyons. But there has scarcely been so much as an echo in response. A few private citizens in Connecticut have tried to study the issues: Women Strike for Peace has some local committees at work; the American Friends' Service Committee has published one or two brochures; and here and there a major defense contractor has wondered how to penetrate an ordinary consumer market. In the main, however, the important people simply do not care.

The history of what happened to Senator Hubert Humphrey's report on the effects of disarmament illustrates the sort of attitude that evidently prevails in high places. As far back as 1961, Humphrey had argued in his special subcommittee on disarmament that a study of adjustment problems was essential. The "enormous unfulfilled demand for commodities and labor shortage as well" after World War II and Korea contrasted sharply, said he, with the "substantially satisfied demand and . . . unemployment" today. Consequently, he canvassed some four hundred manufacturers to determine the plans they might have on their desks for conversion to non-military production. The replies were quite interesting: a fair number of respondents deep in defense work called for "an orderly reduction over a reasonable period of time," with "extensive government planning to deal with the economic problems of disarmament." (Of course, it was not clear from the replies whether these companies were prepared to accept directives from a central planning body or merely wanted to shift the cost burden to government.) Interestingly enough, Humphrey's study also revealed an extraordinary concentration of defense contracts, with four firms reporting over one billion dollars in defense business and eight firms reporting from $500 million to a billion.

Yet the report was suppressed. The official story in Washington is that some of the subcommittee members feared it might be used by Soviet propagandists, although Secretary of Defense McNamara saw nothing awry in it. Senator Symington was disturbed

* Emile Benoit and Kenneth E. Boulding, editors, *Disarmament and the Economy*, New York, Harper & Row, 1963.

by the chance that the survey might be quoted out of context to "back up the Marxian theory that war production was the reason for the success of capitalism." Subsequently, both he and Senator Aiken insisted on placing a "confidential" stamp on the document, limiting its publication to 150 copies and burying it so effectively that it is now almost impossible to turn up a copy. Humphrey argued in vain that public understanding of the issues was at stake, that most of the data had been shared with the U.N. experts in any case, and that a number of copies already were circulating among sundry federal departments and on the Hill. Finally, on October 5 of last year, irritated beyond words at his colleagues' behavior, Humphrey exploded in the Senate, giving away the major conclusion of the report.

There are, then, several schools of thought on the economics of disarmament. First, we have the uninterested, which includes most of the agencies that ought to be interested. Then there is the self-interest school, which includes certain industrialists who prefer Pentagon projects but are not unwilling to enjoy a slice of arms control and disarmament funds. Senator Humphrey, on the other hand, is a leading spokesman for the "we-can-do-it-but-let's-not-be-stupid-about-it" group—small, fortunately articulate, and probably making the most sense; here we may include the Melmans, Benoits, and Bouldings. The extreme worriers are typified by the Fishmans. And finally we have the "let's be rational" school, exemplified by William Royce of the Stanford Research Institute, who argues tautologically that the industries now engaged in making missiles or electronic components will have little difficulty under disarmament if they find something else to do, and who further intimates that since the Russians can't be trusted to keep an agreement, all planning for disarmament must be predicated on a slow process of transition with phased reductions stretched perhaps over a decade.

The assumption of a phased reduction in arms, while attractive mainly for reasons of *Hochpolitik,* is on other grounds open to serious question. The London *Economist,* in its well-documented survey, makes a cogent argument for a changeover period lasting no more than two years. The quicker the changeover, says the *Economist,* the less likelihood of error would there be. Also, rapid disarmament would have a more salutary psychological impact, for the exhilaration of an unarmed peace might generate its own momentum. But most important, what Thomas Schelling calls the "reciprocal fear of a surprise attack" would necessitate a crash program on both sides to prevent the old escalation from starting up again. All this means that planning must be done *now,* careful planning, both macro- and micro-economic in character.

Apart from everything else, forethought would ease the anxiety voiced by many who still remember the chaos of 1918 and who know that we were only saved from a similar chaos in 1945 by an extraordinary pent-up consumer demand and a population explosion of rare dimensions. The anticipated deflationary impact of reduced federal budgets was obliterated after World War II in an orgy of spending, the likes of which had seldom been witnessed in human history. Today, however, there is no storage bin of unsatisfied demand; consumer debt, at $61.4 billion, is almost six times what it was in 1947; unemployment is running at the rate of 6 percent of the civilian labor force; and one-sixth of those working are on part-time hours. And to make matters worse, today's defense industries, utilizing exotic materials and esoteric production systems, are virtually inconvertible coin. When disarmament comes they may simply have to be junked. *This is the key problem: today's defense industries do not manifest the sort of relationship to the rest of the economy that was characteristic of earlier defense and war efforts.*

It appears, therefore, that nuclear disarmament involves a new and strange structural situation: conversion will not be a matter of searching for fresh consumer markets. The old task of discovering new work for facilities temporarily diverted is no longer the core of disarmament adjustments, for time and technology have made the present defense industries less and less transferable to alternative uses. There is one consolation which could ease the reconversion process: our putative affluence might be sufficient to carry the burden, so accustomed have we become to sudden obsolescence. But the people, several millions of them—where would *they* go? How much *human* obsolescence can our society bear before it cracks under the strain?

But our story is moving ahead too quickly. The economics of disarmament is divided into three parts: conversion, stabilization, and expansion. The problem of human obsolescence belongs to part three—where growth in the industries comprising the civilian economy would presumably take care of it. First, however, we have to worry about conversion, which means rearranging the commodity mix to satisfy a new kind of public and governmental demand, and next we have to concern ourselves with stabilization, i.e., the prevention of unemployment and deflation. Then, and only then, do we start worrying about expansion and growth.

One way of making a comprehensive study of how resources might be shifted about in the event of disarmament is to construct an input-output table, a device that determines how much of the output of all other industries is needed by every single industry to produce a unit of its own. Such a table can yield a complex statistical matrix showing how men and resources may be moved about in response to a given level of final demand. What would a matrix of this kind reveal about disarmament? The answer, as it happens, has already been given by Wassily Leontief, the originator of input-output analysis, and Marvin Hoffenberg, in the April 1961 issue of *Scientific American*. Leontief and Hoffenberg argue that the 2,000 workers and 6,000 servicemen who would be released for each $100 million reduction in arms spending could not be totally absorbed by the private business sector. For one thing, reconversion would create its own bottlenecks: if a heavy road-building program were undertaken, for example, cement shortages might delay the effort, while industries once committed to defense (such as electronics) would wither on the vine for lack of sales. In other words, a proper reallocation of resources is a long-run affair, and in the absence of planning, economic deficiencies would plague the body politic. Yet the matrix also revealed that a 20 percent reduction in military outlays during the first stages of disarmament could increase employment, *provided* the savings were applied to pressing civilian needs.

However, observations such as these are based on large calculations that can be completely upset by the actions of individual business firms. A few years ago, Seymour Melman asked a number of companies how they were preparing for disarmament. One concern replied that the abolition of defense work would be catastrophic—it obviously had never dreamed that its subsidized sales might one day peter out. An engineering research firm with 25 percent of its contracts in defense was candid enough to say that it would simply fire 25 percent of its employees. An electronics manufacturer with half his production geared to the military refused to even weigh the question. And so it went. William Royce, the SRI disarmament expert, has in effect complained that industry can plan only if it knows the direction in which the federal government intends to move—if, that is, it knows something about the proposed curtailment of weapons systems and the programs for space exploration, and knows whether Washington will grant patent protection to new industries stemming from defense work. In short, will the Great Underwriter—as David T. Bazelon calls the federal government—guarantee civilian markets as it has guaranteed military markets? Will there, perhaps, even be lucrative contracts for disarmament itself?

This last possibility is not farfetched. The capital outlay of a test-ban inspection system has been estimated by Melman at approximately $1.7 billion. An international radar network for disarmament inspection with machines installed on land and ships would cost initially about $10 billion, while annual operating expenditures have been calculated at $600 million. Aerial reconnaissance would require another $420 million. All told, these expenditures might reach well over $12 billion, with $1.5 billion needed each year for maintenance and operation. There is not much here as compared with the arms race, but it is something on which to fall back.

And indeed, the scent of these dollars has already begun to waft toward the defense companies. Recently *Business Week* reported that Bendix, Raytheon, and General Telephone and Telegraph were very much interested in the "potentiality of arms-control hardware contracts." In late 1962 Bendix even went so far as to stage a conference on the subject, and the odd mixture of tough thinkers from RAND, Pentagon officials, academicians, electronics manufacturers, and the first secretary of the Soviet Embassy led one observer to describe the session as resembling a meeting of Temperance ladies held in a bar.

No doubt contracts for "disarmament hardware" would ease the burden of adjustment, for to judge by one analysis, existing defense industries would have a devil of a time penetrating ordinary civilian markets. James McDonagh and Steven Zimmerman, two young engineers, discovered that in the airframe industry only once in the years between 1950 and 1955 did a major company sell as much as 30 percent of its product to civilian customers. That, as McDonagh and Zimmerman put it, "the sales and marketing experience of the industry" should "in some respects" be "quite limited" is not surprising, for defense firms (most of whose industrial capacity stems from government subvention anyway) know how to politic and bargain with one big customer only. And this is not quite the same thing as knowing how to carve out a slice of domestic sales.

Where could the airframe industry—to take it as a representative example—go for nondefense business after disarmament? Commercial aircraft? That would bring in a mere $168 million a year, hardly enough to pay expenses. Prefabricated homes? With a potential of one and a half million units annually, the industry might secure $850 million a year. If there were bridges to build or if rapid transit were revived (a genuine need today), perhaps another $400 million or so a year could be recaptured. Yet even with all of this, only 58 percent of the airframe industry's present sales capacity would have been replaced. Thus, assuming a constant relationship between sales and employment, over 200,000 employees would have to be dismissed.

While after World War II many aircraft manufacturers shifted half-heartedly to canoes and power boats and stainless steel caskets and subcontracted for musical instrument manufacturers,* today firms like General Dynamics, skilled only in high-cost, high-specification operations, would have great difficulty in adapting successfully to big-volume, low-cost, low-quality production. There is little opportunity to apply modern techniques of military production—techniques that require parts to be assembled in dust-free, vibrationless plants with devices constantly tested, temperature and humidity carefully controlled, and precision machinery of the kind achieved only by computer calculations—to normal factory methods. For such concerns today, abolition of the cold war means bitter obsolescence—unless a vast space program, or something like it, were to come to the rescue.

Of course, from a purely economic standpoint, the disappearance of these industries would not be a great calamity. Their technology is so special and esoteric that the income they create in other sectors of the economy—the Keynesian multiplier—is considerably less than the amount that stems from the old-line

---

* Some companies were helped by relying on such gimmicks as loss carrybacks to offset past taxes, which enabled them to latch on to more profitable firms—once again the government became an underwriter.

industries. Leontief has estimated that about $42 billion of direct military purchases in 1958 generated another $44 billion of indirect demand—a multiplier of two. But meanwhile, the arms mix undergoes rapid change, and with virtually every alteration in defense strategy (from surface weapons to missiles, from airframes to electronics, from simple logistics to complex "subsystems"), the capital share on military spending goes down; it has indeed moved from about 75 percent in 1951 to 47 percent today. In consequence, the defense industry multiplier is probably a good deal less than two by now.

A further result of the stress on these exotic industries has been the loss of overseas hard-goods markets—machine tools, for example. Moreover, the distorted geographical distribution of defense contracts has influenced the pattern of industrial location in ways that could, in the absence of advance planning, easily result in chaos when cutbacks occur. Many towns in the South rely almost exclusively on military installations—what would happen to Cape Canaveral if disarmament came? In Los Angeles almost 200,000 workers draw pay checks from three aircraft companies. In Wichita, 72 percent of the work force is employed in making planes and missiles. In the states of Kansas, Washington, California, Connecticut, and Arizona, anywhere from 20 to 30 percent of manufacturing employment is in ordnance, electronics, aircraft, missiles, and ships—the leading industries in the military-space complex. Disarmament without planning would unquestionably leave many localities in these areas as destitute as a ghost town in a Western movie.

The National Aeronautics and Space Administration has been admonished several times by Congress to spread its share of the business, but most of it still flows to the West Coast. Of the $2.7 billion NASA spent in fiscal 1963, California received 30 percent, while 28 percent went to three Southern states, and only 1 percent to all of New England. The Pentagon explains—and with some justice—that its contracts must be placed where prior investment had been made in research and where the higher skills for the new weaponry can be found. Thus, the increasing need for technical competence and scientific components intensifies the insulation of the defense sector from the rest of the economy. This, perhaps more than any other single factor, has impeded genuine growth.

In a 1962 *Harvard Business Review* article, Robert Solo of the National Planning Association demonstrated that since 1920 research and development expenditures have increased at a phenomenal rate, rising 400 percent in relation to national income, while output per man-hour in the economy as a whole has steadily hovered around the old norm of a 2 to 4 percent gain per annum. Hence, he argued, not only has there been no perceptible relationship between R&D and economic growth, but the latter may have been inhibited by just the sort of research demanded by the military. Missiles and shooting for the moon may heighten our sense of international prestige, but they add little to the ordinary goods and services needed by an expanding population. Even worse, defense and space research is a parasite on the rest of the economy, for it feeds upon some of the best talents of society. The old-fashioned scientist who might have invented a gadget that could increase output per capita is now an engineer on a team project constructing a component for the trigger of a space vehicle.

Military technology, in short, has moved farther and farther away from industrial research, to the point where the possibility of communication between them has all but disappeared. How, asks Solo, can such skills as preparing a research proposal or designing space instruments or planning "component development" be transferred to production for the civilian markets? Of course, there have been some cases of successful transfer, as with PERT —a computer system—and Telstar. But these are exceptional. There are few, if any, civilian counterparts for nuclear warheads, supersonic planes, and the rare materials that go into spaceships. The very habits of the scientists and engineers involved are wrong for civilian production. They are concerned only with performance—"tell the front office to worry about the cost"—and they are accustomed to producing prototypes of machines while eschewing standardized methods. *The inescapable conclusion is that spillover from defense to civilian life is almost nonexistent.*

We pay a rather handsome price for this strange non-Keynesian situation. The military budget in fiscal 1963 was $51 billion; for fiscal 1964 it has been set at $54 billion. The research and development share, though only 8 percent of the total, is essential to the whole complex. The development of weapons systems takes three-fourths of military R&D funds, while research in engineering, physics, biology, and the like absorbs the balance. Not surprisingly, the scientific community has become utterly dependent on government largesse; in 1961, over 75 percent of electronics scientists and engineers were working on projects paid for by the federal government.

What can happen when sudden cutbacks are made without proper planning was brought home vividly when the Skybolt missile was eliminated from our arsenal not long ago. Douglas Aircraft, the prime contractor for this weapon, dismissed about 4,000 workers, and another 5,000 jobs being supplied by subcontractors were placed in jeopardy. Yet all Douglas could think of to do was protest the Defense Department's decision, arguing that Skybolt should be kept on because it would save billions in taxes by extending the life of the B-52 bomber and Britain's Vulcan II.*

Few of the companies working on missiles and communications meet contract cancellations with anything more than public hand-wringing and telegrams to their senators. Sometimes they get a congressional investigation started. Meanwhile, the workers are sent packing to the unemployment insurance offices. In 1957, for example, the Navajo missile was abruptly removed from the Pentagon's weapons arsenal and two days later some 10,000 persons had to scrounge for other jobs as some $680 million went down the drain. Similarly with Regulus II, a submarine missile; the boron high-energy fuel for supersonic jets; the P6M Seamaster jet seaplane; and the atomic-powered airplane, shelved after a decade's work. The psychological and economic shock to the communities involved has finally set the Pentagon to thinking about the "potential economic impact of procurement efficiencies," and unofficial hints are now going out to localities unduly dependent on federal contracts.

The burden of planning the changeover, then, goes by default as well as necessity to the federal government. Nevertheless, there are business diehards who still insist on laissez faire. Richard Raymond, a General Electric spokesman, urges reliance on the free market with "bold risk decisions to take advantage of conversion opportunities as they arise," without grasping the rather elementary notion that government may have to create such op-

---

* The idea of trying short-range commercial jets did occur to Douglas as well, but typically it was a year behind the British Aircraft Corporation, which already had been selling them to American airlines.

portunities. The *Magazine of Wall Street* proposes a National Reconversion Committee comprised of leading business and retired executives to arrest the onslaught of government zealots. About the millions of Americans who live in abject poverty, and who can only be helped by massive outlays of monies for public needs, such ideologues have nothing to say. Yet the two documents mentioned above that were prepared under the aegis of the Arms Control and Disarmament Agency, by revealing the usual backlog of starved public services, indicate what might be substituted for arms. Housing could absorb $33 billion over a period of years; mass transit might account for $9 billion over the next decade; and resource development $8 billion a year. At least $10 billion a year could be used to improve the educational system. Additional expenditures for health services, better social security schemes, retraining and relocation, area redevelopment, and adequate foreign aid would take care of the rest (and without rushing into space); in fact, the total could easily pass what is now spent by the Pentagon, NASA, and the AEC.

But how does one venture upon these programs? What are the specifics? At what points in the economy do we mark off the starting lines? Difficult as it seems, the problem is not intractable, for there are institutions and organizations in our society which could be used to initiate the new peace. Public corporations such as TVA, local housing authorities, state road commissions, and urban renewal agencies—all could be put to work the moment a disarmament agreement were signed. Despite the acknowledged deficiencies of some of these bodies, their accomplishments might be surprising enough to make us ashamed of the neglect they have had to bear while we have been wrangling our way to the edge of extinction.

All this, to be sure, could only take place in what economists call a proper fiscal environment, which means an environment created by tax cuts and budget deficits. But these would have to be of sizable proportions—much larger than the piddling sums of the present tax and budget program—to correct the combined effects of defense cutbacks and a stumbling economy. The tax cut alone ought at the very least to be $10 billion in the first year of disarmament; with the dual multiplier-accelerator evaluated at 3.7, this would probably yield $37 billion in GNP, enough to initiate the readjustment process with ease.* However, since in a lagging private sector accumulated idle capacity tends to impose restraints on any exuberance stemming from fiscal maneuvers, the tax cut might have to be substantially larger than $10 billion to do an adequate job.

Disarmament, then, need not result in economic catastrophe: the necessary economic knowledge is at hand for dealing with the problems that would arise. What remains to be created is a sense of urgency in high places over the need to prepare *now,* and an awareness throughout our society that with proper planning and forethought, disarmament would be an economic contingency to be welcomed, not a disaster to be feared.

1963

* The multiplier indicates how much new GNP will stem from a given amount of investment; the accelerator measures the response of investment to additional consumer spending. These processes are, of course, interrelated; the Joint Economic Committee recently estimated the multiplier at 2.5 and the accelerator at 1.2.

Economic Annals of the 1950's

I

Judged by the number of people who were working, the almost
unbelievable level of incomes and the total output of services
and commodities, 1953 was by far the most prosperous year in the
already fabulous history of recent years. The ability of the nation
to produce a vast flow of goods remained a most glittering wonder
for the world today.

As the year ended, virtually all economists were called upon
to make their learned diagnoses and perhaps to offer predictions
of even better things to come. Many were not averse to describing the economic future still encased in numerous shades of
cheerful colors. Only one—and a non-American at that—suggested that the rich flow of material wealth would soon dry up.
Colin Clark, an Australian and director of Oxford University's
Statistical Institute, whose pronunciamentos are usually displayed

in dark hues, has opined that all is not well with the American economy.

Writing in the *Manchester Guardian* in November 1953, Mr. Clark asked: "Is it not possible that [the Americans] are playing on the edge of an atomic pile which may get out of control?" He suggested that a collapse, of the proportions suffered in the early 1930's, may come about through overexpansion of our economic plant: overbuilding of houses, for example, may be a particularly exacerbating factor. More important would be the curtailment of inventory holdings, for when the goods on the shelf are too great in relation to sales, orders tend to be reduced. Most American economists are disturbed neither by the over-building of houses nor by the allegedly harmful effects of inventory changes. Nevertheless, there does exist the possibility, says Mr. Clark, of a cumulative drop which, once started, would be difficult to reverse. The fact of the matter is that inventory cut-backs do mean a reduction in buying from middlemen and manu-facturers, even though retail sales may continue fairly high. That this may mean fewer jobs is attested to by current employment figures.

During the last few years, reductions in inventory holdings were counterbalanced by exports, large government expenditures, or the sudden overt, tangible expression of some latent demand in other parts of the economy. Suppose none of these corrective elements were present now? Certainly a chain reaction making 1929 seem relatively mild would ensue. Once such violent eco-nomic forces were loosed, no amount of tax rebates or public works would be able to halt the accelerating deflationary pres-sures. The so-called built-in-stabilizers—unemployment insurance, social security, fiscal controls—would be woefully inadequate shel-ter for the coming storm.

Mr. Clark notes a remarkable parallel with the experience of two-and-half decades ago. Economic activity held up until the third quarter of 1928, when the first weakening signs were ob-servable: in the fourth quarter the downward slide began to pick up momentum. Unemployment rose in early 1929 and was quite heavy by the next year. In these early stages, continues Clark, business investment was fairly high and activity in the construc-tion industry had not yet demonstrated any noticeable decline. But costs were rising and the money market was tightening. All these, says Clark, were little things—each by itself not very meaningful for an economic prognosis. But like the proverbial snowball, they inexorably gathered force and size, fused into one huge mass and hit bottom with catastrophic impact. Mr. Clark believes this is what is happening now.

We need not, however, succumb to complete fatalism, says Mr. Clark. Should building costs be reduced by some magic formula, it would be possible to utilize the upward push of a building program to counteract an incipient depression. Furthermore, there is a far greater public awareness of the latent disaster inherent in the American economy than there was 25 years ago. If this recognition of potential disaster awakens us to quick measures, we may avoid a serious depression with all of its attendant costs. But Clark is not very sanguine, for he feels that the political machinery will move too ponderously and haltingly to prove effective. He questions whether Congress would countenance the kind of rise in public debt that a vast public works program implies: Congress, says he quite bluntly, may prefer six or seven million unemployed to initiating a program that might be distasteful in certain quarters.

This is clearly an extreme view: it represents a most pessimistic outlook and foresees little but unrelieved disaster. It is also a minority position, for the reply of most economists to Clark's Jeremiad is "Not yet!" They feel that while the national output may fall somewhat from the 1953 high of $370 billion, the cutback will be no more than 3 percent. Federal expenditures may suffer a net reduction of perhaps $6 billion but, aver Clark's more optimistic colleagues, there will be a substantial increase in state and local government spending, enough perhaps to take up a good part of the slack. Also, pressure from wages and prices will be upward: labor will want a larger part of the income pie, and this will tend to impel further price increases. On the other hand, it is admitted that real wages, what employees will be able to buy with the contents of their pay envelopes, will decline slightly.

Essentially then, the most general attitude is that of limited pessimism. The economists don't even want to use the word "depression," substituting for it the more reassuring one, "recession." Some even go so far as to speak of an "orthodox" or "normal" recession, as if to suggest that collecting unemployment insurance, home relief, or selling apples ought not to be viewed as disturbing phenomena.

The feeling that we are faced with but a mild recession is based on the contention that unemployment will be somewhat less than three million. (The CIO, however, is already citing figures in excess of that: obviously it is a question of how one counts the unemployed.) Furthermore, say the limited pessimists, whatever the level of economic activity in the next year or so, the decline will be a gentle one, gradual in its downward slope and perhaps even firm during the coming summer. As Gabriel Hauge, one of President Eisenhower's economic advisers, said, "We are coming down from an overtime economy which was being used at unusually high rates. [But] with sixty-two out of every sixty-three employable persons at work, with consumer expenditures running at the level they are today, with American business investing $27 or $28 billion a year in plant and equipment, with levels of government expenditure in prospect for reasonably small changes over the next twelve months, one cannot talk about heading into a depression."

Undismayed optimists are, of course, also to be found. Their predictions are based on as many cogent statistics as those of their more dismal brethren and they are equally impressive with the incisiveness of their arguments. George Hildebrand, of the University of California, for example, asserts that our national ouput will rise in 1954 to as much as $384 billion. Believing in the efficacy of a free flow of funds, Mr. Hildebrand thinks that tax cuts and an easy money policy will stimulate consumer spending and business investment. He visualizes increases in the latter of $1.5 billion, in consumer spending of $7 billion and in state and local government expenditure of about $1.5 billion. These, together with tax rebates and adjustments for higher federal spending, mean a significant rise in what economists call the gross national product.

Another daring young man on a flying economic forecast is W. S. Woytinsky, who at least must be credited with seeking to give his prediction a seemingly reasonable theoretical base. Woytinsky argues that the ". . . prosperity enjoyed by this country in recent years has not been a Korean war prosperity . . ." but that it has been part of our normal process of growth. The rise, he argues, of $25 billion in national output from 1952 to 1953 was a most impressive performance—as indeed it was—and while the benefits of this unprecedented gain may have been unevenly distributed, while the farmers may have begun to lose some ground, while we may still be saddled with the usual quota of ups, downs, grinds, and bumps, the fortitude of the American economy has not yet been dissipated. From 1951 to 1953 industrial production rose 9 percent, with most of the gains concentrated in consumer durable goods. The fact that these industries prospered while consumer nondurables—textiles, suits, dresses, shoes—suffered is not at all disturbing, says Mr. Woytinsky, for the shift from soft to hard goods merely demonstrated an irrepressible desire to slake a long-felt need for autos, washing machines, and household appliances.

Of much greater concern, says Woytinsky, is the fact that the growth in output per employed worker has been declining from the average annual increase of 2.5 percent. Since productivity is the foundation stone of economic advancement, it may be possible, he says, that "the superstructure of the economic system may have expanded more rapidly than its technical base." That is to say, the physical capabilities of the economy have not been able to keep pace with the financial and monetary counterparts, so much so that the latter may soon explode like Aesop's fabled frog.

Woytinsky is not so impressed with changes in business inventory as is Colin Clark, despite the fact that expansion of goods-on-the-shelf since 1950 has been about twice what should be consonant with our growing national income. Nor does he feel that there will be much of a shift in producers' goods output, a very significant sector of the economic system. Examining the construction situation, Woytinsky hazards the guess that state and local spending for hospitals and roads will take up the slack engendered by falling private building. But above all else, he argues, the notion that government spending is an important factor in the present economic pattern is a fallacious one. Government, through its high tax structure, has been taking as much out of the income stream as it has been injecting, and therefore the basis for continued prosperity must be sought elsewhere. This, however, is a most surprising statement, for so long as government spending merely takes place the economic machine can keep on rolling. It is the size and forcefulness of the government sector that are important: it must still be remembered that we really did not shake out the depression until 1940, when Roosevelt's defense program demonstrated the patent fact that in a state of economic prostration only vigorous government investment can make revival effective.

Thus far we have been wading through a welter of facts and opinions quite unrelated to any cohesive framework within which to fit them. Understanding requires an hypothesis, or, more technically, a model, that will illuminate and make more meaningful the conglomeration of factual data our economists and statisticians so gleefully collect. Such a model exists. Stemming largely from the theories of the late John Maynard Keynes, it emphasizes that the prosperity of a nation is measured neither by the gold bullion it buries in military forts nor by physical possessions and factories. The latter are assets—the economist calls them "stocks"—from which prosperity can flow in the shape of income. It is this which provides a high level of living, a multitude of autos, spreading suburbias, and other manifestations of economic fat. A large and vigorous flow of income spells good business and good times; when income pours forth sluggishly, there are bankruptcies, misery, and economic headaches.

Normally, the largest part of the income a person or family receives is spent on the ordinary needs of daily living. This is described in the textbooks as consumption. But persons whose incomes differ in size generally spend their incomes differently: the poor family spends most of its meager weekly earnings on necessities—food, shelter, and if any extra cash is available, clothing; the rich can easily provide themselves with more ample quantities of these basic needs and in addition, they can save. (Statistics are available to show that most of personal savings are in the upper income brackets.) Now, if those who save in the United States were to behave as do many French peasants and store their surplus in earthenware pots, the circular flow of income through the economy would be sundered and a depression easily engendered. For what is basic in this pattern is the continuation of the movement of income from one economic sector to another. Fortunately, most of those who save put their excess funds into banks and other financial institutions where they are channeled in various ways into investments.

The older economists—Ricardo, John Stuart Mill, Alfred Marshall—believed that all savings were automatically invested. But they overlooked the seemingly obvious fact that saving and investment are undertaken by different sets of persons and for different reasons. A substantial part of investment is done by business enterprises, especially corporations, while much saving is done by individuals. The latter may put aside money out of income for many purposes: for a more secure old age; for vacations; for the children's education; or even to satisfy unconscious retentive drives. The businessman will invest only if he anticipates a profit: there is no need to build a new factory or install additional equipment unless the larger output now made feasible can readily be sold. This does not imply that business behavior is necessarily more rational than individual behavior, for impulsive action, lack of information, and plain pig-headedness frequently determine business decisions. The volume of investment, consequently, is unpredictable, since there is no way of foretelling the impact that business expectations will have on overt economic action. In other words, there is no assurance that investment will flow smoothly. In fact, the more usual case is investment by spurts, generating a kind of erratic and bewildering movement. New commodities, new demands, new ways of doing things, all play a significant role in the investment process. This was true during the heyday of the railroad and it is true today when autos and airplanes and the urge to own a home are dominant economic factors.

Further, there is no built-in guarantee that investment will at any given moment match the quantity of available saving. If investment fails to absorb all the saving in society, total spending by consumers and business concerns (investment is nothing more than spending by the latter) will be less than the national output. Society will simply have failed to buy back all that it produces. Goods will remain on the shelves, inventories will be curtailed, and production cut back until a new balance will have been struck between saving and investment. But before this is attained, unknown numbers of workers will have been forced onto the labor market to compete with each other for continually fewer jobs. The equilibrium so strangely attractive to economists can be reached, but at a lower level of economic activity and with a floating corps of footloose unemployed.

On the other hand, if people's savings are inadequate to meet the investment requirements of business concerns, expansionary pressure will be generated. This generally is what happens at the bottom of the business cycle trough: although there is little or no saving, some firms feel adventurous enough to seek investment. A slow process is set in motion: the unemployed are rehired, raw materials bought, factory chimneys begin to smoke, and income flows a bit more rapidly. As income rises, some part of it is saved and so long as this keeps pace with the ever-hungry demands of investment, national income will continue to rise. This rather schematic exposition can be reinforced with such recondite notions as the multiplier and the acceleration effect, but it is not necessary to do so here. The significant element in this structure is its inherent instability. But in the case of economic failure, no single businessman may be said to be at fault, for in a society such as ours, perfect unanimity of behavior is unattainable, nor is it desirable. A pattern of economic action that would make investment amenable to easy control is not possible in the private sector of our economy. We must therefore turn to that area where investment can be turned off and on as conditions may warrant. This is government investment.

The high degree of correlation between government spending and national income is not merely accidental. Both theoretical and empirical analysis testify to their intimate connection. In 1929, national income was $87 billion. The federal government spent a little over $1 billion while the states, counties, and municipalities spent over $7 billion. War and depression forged a revolution in these relationships: by 1945, the federal government was spending over $75 billion, mostly on defense needs, while national income went up to almost $180 billion. When government expenditure began to decline in 1948–1949, national income began to show signs of sagging, only to perk up again with the Korean affair. While it is not suggested here that our current high level of activity is due only to the pressures of war, the demands of government must now be conceded to be a significant element in our economy.

Most experts admit that the federal government will pump a good deal less money into the economic system in the coming twelve months than it did in 1953. In the latter year, government spent roughly $78 billion: in 1954, estimates call for an expenditure of $71.5 billion. This decline, together with an estimated increase in the federal "take" of $2 billion, may very well create the setting for a new downturn. Not only will Washington itself be investing less, but it will be drawing off potential spending power.

This demonstrates with a fair degree of conclusiveness the validity of the Keynesian propositions. During the last depression, government spending was never employed to its highest power, so that even by 1938–1939 there were many thousands of unemployed: in that year gross national output had barely risen to $90 billion. Only when FDR initiated his "defend the democracies" politics did national income rise and jobs become plentiful. These may be distasteful facts for us to ponder but they are nevertheless there: defense spending primed the pump in a way that was unbelievable.

Our economy today is apparently going in high gear, and all the top pundits of the nation's press and bright young *Life* editors foresee a wonderful continuation of these happy prospects. The gross national product, they observe, increased 5 percent in 1953 over the previous year; physical productivity seemed to maintain its normal pace (despite Woytinsky's skepticism); personal income, what people have left over after paying taxes, was at $248 billion, the highest in history; consumers bought $12 billion more goods in 1953 than in 1952; in sum, 1953 was the best year yet.

Still, there is a sense of fear pervading the current scene. The gross national product slid down from an annual rate of $372.5 billion in the second quarter of 1953 to $369 billion in the third quarter; industrial production fell fifteen percentage points between February and November; and wholesale prices continued their year-long decline. While labor pushed its wage rate up, pay envelopes kept getting slimmer, for work schedules were being shortened. The number of factory lay-offs this past fall exceeded expectations by 250,000. Unions are so deeply disturbed by the prospect of declining income for their members that they seriously pressed the adoption of an annual wage scheme. When the average weekly factory wage dropped from the March high of $71.93 to $71.02 in November, when the work week declined from 41.7 hours on the average to 39.9 hours at the end of 1953, there was reason for concern about the economic future.

A certain measure of pessimism is discernible also in many of our major industries. That auto buyers are now holding on to their cars a bit longer is a trite observation. The car-buying public is well stocked with late model autos: it simply isn't anxious to buy. Yet the auto industry's capacity to produce is at its highest. The intended solution is a more vigorous advertising campaign, more intensive blasting of the customers' eyes and ears with magic slogans, more buttonholing by salesmen. Promotion budgets have been doubled; "ad" men have been given new tasks and more money with which to do them. The giants in the industry are girding themselves for a real knockdown battle on all the nation's billboards. Autos will have fancier seats, jazzed-up dashboards, transparent hardtops, and more horsepower to waste getting nowhere on crowded roads. But with all of Madison Avenue's skill in coaxing dollars away from customers, auto merchants are still doubtful that they will be able to sell enough cars to keep the factories going full time.

In the steel industry, supply had been catching up with the demand and was ending the strong sellers' market that had lasted since 1950; there too an optimistic outlook was no longer evident. Production at the year's end dropped fifteen percentage points to below 70 percent of capacity, the sharpest year-end drop since 1945. While some of this may be attributed to seasonal factors, expectations are that the steel industry will produce in 1954 about twelve million tons less raw steel than was the case in 1953, when output was about 112 million tons. Although present plans in the industry emphasize a further expansion of capacity, requiring an expenditure of roughly $800 million, a reduction in steel sales will place severe restrictions on such an investment effort.

The difficulties of selling to consumers during 1954 are anticipated also by appliance makers. In their own language, they expect a "shake-out" this year. As a tough sales year wears on, the marginal manufacturer will disappear. In the past, the giant companies, General Electric, Westinghouse, Admiral, and Philco, geared their production to expected sales. This implied a certain level of output regardless of how well or poorly an item did in the retail stores. Now the companies are being more cautious; they intend to review production schedules every few weeks and if sales indicate an oversupply of automatic flyswatters or a lack of consumer regard for Dialatonic Double-View TV, there will be a quick "adjustment" in the factory, one that would doubtlessly require fewer employees.

Perhaps the most important factor in the current economic picture is construction. That building is a vital element in our modern pattern of business gyrations is an undisputed proposition, even among economists, whose capacity for disagreement is notorious. The building cycle, however, is seldom coterminous with the movements of business itself. The result is that when the trough of a major cycle coincides with a slump in building, the inevitable depression becomes severe and prolonged. If a downturn in business occurs when building is increasing the depression is apt to be short and somewhat "orthodox." Thus, in 1929, the conjunction of declining business and a saturation in the building industry was a harbinger of dark days to come.

New construction in 1953 set a remarkable record and in no small measure contributed to the equally remarkable prosperity. New housing starts were about 1.1 million and cost about $11.9 billion. For 1954, these figures may taper off to 900,000 at a cost of $10 billion. New non-residential construction, a catch-all phrase for stores, factories, public utilities, farms, hospitals, and parks, cost $11.3 billion in 1953; in 1954, they will be $300 million less. Highways, sewers, waterworks, public buildings, and other public facilities will drop from $11.1 billion to $10.5 billion. The overall expected decline totals $2.8 billion: in terms of the possible impact on our economy, this is no insignificant figure.

Despite the continued shortage in housing, particularly in suburban areas, demand will be exacerbated by the smaller number of young people reaching marriageable age. The birth rate during the last depression was, as we all know, extraordinarily low and it is the depression baby who is now reaching maturity. There will be fewer new households in 1954 than in any single year in the last decade. The world may be this generation's oyster, as *Life* magazine would have us believe, but the pickings for the rest of us may be getting a little thinner.

The fact is that most businessmen concede that 1954's profits will not match earnings in 1953. Corporate profits in the latter year, at $20.3 billion, were the third highest in U.S. history, this despite taxes of $24.6 billion. Downward pressures will probably push profits to around $19 billion in 1954. While this would be higher than 1952's net of $18.6 billion, it is the declining tendency that disturbs the many businessmen: they are worried about unmoving inventories, contracting order backlogs, narrowing profit margins, declining exports, weaknesses in consumer durables, decreasing defense orders, production cutbacks, and just plain employment lay-offs. These are the warning signals they are watching with ever-increasing attention.

It is perhaps in the realm of money and finance that some of the most meaningful signs are to be found. For example, the demand for loans at the banks is an excellent barometer of future business activity. Normally, there is an expansion of such loans in the fall in anticipation of the Christmas season. In 1953, the usual fall expansion was less than expected. As 1954 began, there was no evidence that the volume of loans would increase markedly over the next few months. A variety of explanations have been offered for this situation, including inventory changes and differences in tax payment schedules. The largest part of the altered loan pattern, however, was due simply to the fact that commodity dealers and food processors borrowed much less heavily from the banks than they did in past years.

Coupled with this condition there has been a rise in financial embarrassments and bankruptcies. Many small and medium-sized companies are having quite a time meeting their obligations. The prospect, according to credit experts, is adjustment through longer payment periods or liquidation. This extreme condition has been most evident among garment manufacturers, textile jobbers, contractors, and converters. True, unseasonable weather has been a potent factor here, forcing a sacrifice sale of retail stocks and in turn making it difficult for textile concerns to move their bolts of goods, but in conjunction with declining general income the situation has been at many points unbearable.

When the farmer too begins to howl then the search for cracks in the American economy must begin in earnest. Once again America is beginning to talk about the farm problem: this is in many ways *the* critical test for 1954. The question is not one of production, for in virtually all crops there is a surplus. The heart of the matter is the price level. Since late 1952, the prices the farmer has been receiving for his output have been on the average below the prices he must pay for equipment, seed, taxes, wages, interest and all the other items that go into his expense bill. The result was that in 1953 farmers retained before taxes only 36 percent of gross income as compared with 39 percent in 1952 and about 50 percent during 1942–1947. This is the age-old "scissors," and the blades have been widening for a long time now.

Complicating the problem is the entire farm price-support program. The farmer has generally felt that he had a right to share in economic progress to the same degree as he did in the period 1910–1914, when farm prosperity was truly extraordinary. To secure this he has not been averse, despite an implacable belief in rugged individualism, to accepting limitations on production in exchange for federal aid. Through the years, a system of commodity loans was developed together with federal purchases of surpluses and an acreage allotment scheme whose purpose it was to limit production to some estimated demand. Incomes were thus guaranteed to the farmer by making sure that prices of selected farm crops would not fall below a predetermined percent of "parity." Parity itself was a mythical price which would permit the farmer to buy the same quantity of goods as he would have been able to buy with what he received for his crops in 1910–1914.

The need for an expanded farm output during World War II led to guaranteed prices at 90 percent of parity, but after the war this system hardened into official policy. Farmers went on producing basic crops while government storage bins filled beyond capacity. Now that farm income has declined some 14 percent below 1951 levels, resistance to altering the rigid formulas has stiffened. Yet some alteration seems necessary, for government is now holding under loan or outright ownership a total of $5 billion in farm surpluses. The net loss last year to the public through disposal of surplus commodities was $61 million. The administration has a real dilemma on its hands, for coupled with the knotty economic aspects there is also in the farm problem a political question which may very well prove explosive.

All the evidence, then, suggests that the American economy has begun to slip. Whether the drop this year will be a precipitous one is hard to say. Should consumers, businessmen, and government—all three together—decide to wait for something better to turn up, they will have, in ironical fashion, created a setting for worse conditions. It is enough now that there is softness in the demand for autos, appliances, and clothing; that business investment will fall about 8 percent; that new housing starts will be about 200,000 units less; that inventories are down, in annual rates, some $4 billion. Holding our own in the face of these trends will be quite a job. Unfavorable psychological reactions by consumers and businessmen may very well be the last trigger.

Those who accept Keynesian principles find the answer not a difficult one: basically, the government needs deliberately to stimulate demand. But this implies, among other things, a further increase in budget deficits. It has been estimated that unless the federal government accepts the idea of a deficit of $20 billion for the next fiscal year, we shall roll steadily on to a depression of 1930's magnitude. If budget balancing continues as the aim of the present administration, if the preference for archaic principles becomes overwhelming, the American people are in for an uncomfortable economic era.

The fact is that the present administration, despite noble presidential platitudes, is heavily addicted to traditional formulas. Mr. Eisenhower, at last making a show of leadership, has submitted his program to Congress. This has been mainly through the State of the Union message and the Budget and Economic Reports; there is also a likelihood of some dozen more special messages. The range of topics in these documents is as impressive as their treatment is appalling: health, housing, natural resources, land policy, highways, agriculture, foreign trade, and labor are discussed with pollyanna-ish equanimity. The policies suggested for these weighty matters do not deviate too far from pre–New Deal contours, and, as one commentator said, some of these might even repeal the twentieth century.

Wherever there might be in these documents a recognition of governmental responsibility for certain welfare problems, the seemingly liberal idea is wrapped up in language that emphasizes the rights of local and state governments. How far these political entities were able to deal with the shock of economic upset was illustrated in the last great depression. How far the present federal government is prepared to deal with similar questions is fully displayed in the President's Economic Report, released at the end of January.

The document itself is a masterpiece of Washingtonian "newspeak." In its refusal to acknowledge forthrightly the impact of government on economics, it is reminiscent of the politics of "normalcy" in the twenties. For example, it admits that the restrictive monetary measures adopted in early 1953 almost caused a depression right then: but this was because the ". . . business and financial community . . . no longer clearly remembered the discipline of monetary management aimed at preventing inflationary booms. . . ." In other words, says the President with disarming self-righteousness, businessmen have no one to blame but themselves for having been frightened by deflationary prospects. Of course, the federal government was later compelled to reverse its policy. Taking undiminished credit for the latter action, the report pats itself on the back with such a resounding whack that one can almost hear the elbow cracking.

The President's Economic Report is simply disappointing; it fails to give one a sense of confidence in the ability of the present administration to deal with conditions of depression. There is a vigorous readiness, as in earlier Republican administrations, to "study the situation." Thus, says the report, one study has shown a ". . . need for developing a continuous inventory of sound projects. . . ." Employment, it goes on gravely, requires employers: their prospects of reward must be sufficient to impel them to assume risks. (Shades of Coolidge!) Government must carefully redraw the lines between public and private activities. And we really don't know what is happening now for ". . . it is impossible to deduce the future from statistics of the present or to infer it from records of the past . . ."—about as artful a dodge as was ever inserted into a presidential statement. The moderate contraction now under way should soon come to a halt; there is a sound price relationship between raw materials and finished goods; business investment should continue high; the housing industry is no longer vulnerable to recessionary influences; and while many consumers admittedly have no resources as a cushion against a decline in income, it is encouraging to note the tendency toward the wider distribution of liquid assets. Thus, we cross one cliché after the other until, to paraphrase a reporter in the election campaign, we come to the forty-eighth platitude.

There is a promise in the Economic Report of flexible policies should the depression really fall about our heads. These are visualized as mainly of the monetary variety—credit controls, debt management, variation of mortgage terms, and tax rebates. But no blueprint shall be offered, says the President, for economic troubles have different causes and we must be ready with different remedies. Perhaps the key remarks are these: "The need for constant vigilance and preparedness does not, however, justify constant stirring or meddling. Minor variations in activity are bound to occur. . . . The arsenal of stabilizing weapons will be drawn upon by the Government boldly, but not more frequently than is required to help maintain reasonable stability." And, as if to underscore this policy of perpetual watchfulness, the report emphasizes that we must avoid a doctrinaire position and be ready to attack on all fronts. With this philosophy the administration may find itself in the position of Leacock's famous rider who, leaping on his horse, went off in all directions at once. How well this would solve a depression remains to be seen.

II

Described by Eisenhower economists as a sideways movement, the downward turn in 1954 was overcome in a relatively quick reaction. Late in the year the major indices began to move up again and by July 1955 it was evident that those who were optimistic and bullish would win out. The automobile and home construction industries outdid themselves. Automotive experts had hoped to dispose of about six million cars during 1955; the public gobbled up 7.5 million. New housing starts were expected to reach about one million; actually, there were about 1.3 million. The gross national product climbed close to the $400 billion mark. Consumers increased their spending by $20 billion—probably accounting for the quick recovery from the 1954 "sideways slip." But to do this, they drew on their saving accounts and bought on the installment plan as they had seldom done before. By the year's end, urban mortgages were 18 percent higher than twelve months previously. At $135 billion, consumer debt was roughly half the disposable income, the highest debt-income ratio ever.

Most of the continued upward movement was in the private sector of the economy. Stimulated by easy terms on autos, houses, and hard goods, sales volume zoomed, business inventories went up (some $4 billion worth), and capital outlays, or expenditures on plant and equipment, hit a record of about $30 billion per annum. During the summer, steel prices went up by $7.50 a ton on the average (after a one-day strike, the shortest in history). General Motors voted a three to one stock split and the federal government began to wonder whether we weren't getting ourselves into a real inflationary situation. The consumer price index began to push up again when everyone thought it had leveled off, while the largest Christmas sales splurge in U.S. history rounded out another wonderful year for the American businessman.

All this should have stimulated some very rosy forecasts for 1956. And there were, in fact, enough economists to say there would be a steady rise in economic activity. A *New York Herald-Tribune* roundup at the beginning of January reported that general expectations were for the GNP to push past the $400 billion mark before spring. This would make 1956 results even better than those attained the year before. The consensus was that prices would advance slowly but steadily despite the likelihood of downturns in automobile production, housing, and farm income. The latter, said the *Herald-Tribune* experts, would be counter-balanced by further investment and a continued rise in consumer spending, especially for services, furniture, and appliances. What this means, they said, is a "rolling readjustment at high levels"; it was evidently felt that rising activity in some sectors might percolate down to depressed activities in others. How this would buy groceries for an auto worker's family was not specified.

Such optimism is seemingly not unfounded. For seven years now, from 1949 to 1955, the securities market has enjoyed a long "bull" career. If the belief that stock prices are a harbinger of things to come has any validity, then surely economic prosperity is everlasting. After all, say the optimists, the market survived at least three major disasters last year: a congressional investigation, an increase in the Federal Reserve discount rates, and a presi-dential heart attack, any one of which, in less resilient times, would have spelled collapse. Furthermore, they continue, business expansion plans will bolster any tendencies for the economy to slacken. The Ford Company, for example, announced a $1 billion investment program for 1956–1958, while General Motors con-tinues to expand operations and earn astronomic profits.

Nevertheless, the majority of economists were cagey. Virtually all were looking for a slight drop in business as the new year started, and most of the arguments were about the extent of the decline. As one commentator put it, prosperity had stopped pro-ducing universal optimism. Many Wall Street experts were recom-mending that traders ought to have enough of a cash balance to allow themselves to bail out without too much hurt should stock prices begin to slide. There were signs that many economists were shifting from a bullish outlook to one of doubt and hesitancy. They were beginning to talk of the possibility of a "stale boom." They were aware, too, that prosperity is like a man on a treadmill and that a "stationary boom" is the one most likely to fall apart, like the fabled "one-hoss shay."

According to one survey, while only 12 percent of the economists whose opinions were solicited felt pessimistic in mid-1955, 26 percent were worried at the end of the year. They were saying that a ceiling had been reached; bottlenecks were going to develop because of insufficiencies of steel, copper, and aluminum; that more factories and more investment would be needed simply to keep the economic treadmill going at the same pace; and that consumer demand might give out before the full impact of capital investment could be felt throughout the economy. Moreover, the farmer hasn't been doing too well, and it was anticipated that the prices he receives for his goods might drop another 2 or 3 percent.

The more pessimistic views are exemplified by the statements of Edwin G. Nourse, former head of the Council of Economic Advisers, who, at a recent national gathering of economists, predicted a drop of 15 to 20 percent in business activity. A decline of such magnitude is indeed frightening, for it could easily snowball into something worse. However, like many of his professional brethren, Nourse tried to sweeten the bitter pill by speaking of a "disinflationary recession." Though there are dangerous soft spots, the economy is strong, he said. Particularly concerned, however, with the over-expansion of credit, Nourse cautioned that mounting boom pressures could explode with serious repercussions.

Consumer credit in 1955 had been about $35 billion, over $4.5 billion more than in the previous year, and virtually all of this was in installment sales. Only about $8 billion of this type of credit was in service and charge accounts. Most of the installment sales increase, of course, stemmed from automobile purchases. The net increase in automotive installment credit was about $4 billion in 1955. However, this does not show just how much was really borrowed by car buyers, since it is a net figure; the total loans to auto buyers must have been at least four times that amount. Not only were more cars being purchased on credit, but down-payments were cut and the repayment period was increased. Add to this what has been described as the "quick-sale," and it is easy to see that there is much water in the fatted calf.

In fact, there had been so much resort to gimmicks and baits and tricks to tie up customers and load them down with kennels, wire fences, carpeting, repair jobs, sewing machines, and disposals that there were some doubts about the *quality* of consumer credit. So heavy has consumer debt become that it appears to be taking about twelve cents out of every dollar. In effect, the expansion of installment buying in 1955 has meant that consumers were borrowing from future income to buy now. Credit extension thus adds to the treadmill character of the economy. It must continue to expand or, at the very least, remain at a level of $35 billion per annum, or demand will drop—unless, of course, consumer income rises sufficiently to make up the difference. But a rise in income of that magnitude does not seem to be in the cards.

All this is somewhat reminiscent of the Veblenian description of economic crises. In his *Theory of Business Enterprise,* Thorstein Veblen had noted that credit extension was a crucial element in the unfolding of the boom and bust cycle. Initially employed as a device for enhancing the profitability of business enterprise, credit became intertwined with the capitalist productive apparatus. It is employed at first to improve and expand plant facilities and to push sales, so that the volume of business will grow. The drive to capture part of the consumer's dollar impels businessmen to resort to credit devices in both purchases and sales. A sense of buoyancy springs up to give the economy a feeling of everlasting prosperity. But soon loan credit begins to exceed in value the underlying real capital and the stage is set for true inflationary pressures. Eventually, concern arises over this discrepancy and creditors either seek new collateral or demand quick settlement. A forced realignment of capital values takes place which, in other than Veblenian terms, might be described as the beginnings of a depression.

In its broadest outlines, much of the present situation might fit into this exposition. We may very well inquire whether we are not really reaching a business cycle *turning point*. This is that critical phase of the cycle during which a variety of factors are joined to enforce an alteration in the *direction* of movement. Expansionary drives may be cumulative and are frequently self-reinforcing, but their action cannot be perpetually upward. Since past experience indicates that prosperity does not go on indefinitely, we are tempted to ask what takes place when the break does occur. Perhaps a theory of cyclical turning points will help explain the present nature of prosperity.

The late Wesley C. Mitchell advanced a classic description of the business cycle. He divided the cycle into two main parts, an expansion and a contraction, each preceded by a relatively short turn, a revival and a recession. If we merely focus attention on the turning point itself, we may begin to see today's reality mirrored in the theory.

In an expansion, costs generally rise. Plant additions and the renewal of contractual obligations on less favorable terms than were obtained before increase the overhead. Operating costs go up as overtime and wage rates climb. Increasing prices allow less efficient firms to remain in the market and take part in the mad rush for goods. Shifting costs of raw material become important factors in jacking up prices and, according to some economists, they are even more significant than the supposed rise in labor costs per unit of output. This expansion is accompanied by increasing credit, along Veblenian lines, as evidenced by the rapidly increasing volume of bank loans during such periods. Interest rates, the price charged by banks for lending money, also rise, but this does not discourage the demand for loans. The supposed conservatism of the bankers seems to disappear as they, too, become optimistic. Cash flows increase as more currency is needed for payrolls and retail buying. Bond prices begin to fall, not so much because interest rates rise, but because investors decide that equity securities—common and preferred stocks—will bring a larger return.

Add to this familiar picture a disturbance in some important industry—for example, autos. There is a reduction in the sales income of suppliers and a cut in wage income. Vendors of food and clothing begin to suffer and they deem it more advisable to pay off accumulated debts than to continue to invest in inventories. Repercussions are felt through the corollary industries, such as machine tools, tires, and glass. If the break is sudden, the shock may be a severe one; if there is heavy involvement with the banks, trouble is doubly compounded by virtue of forced liquidation of credit.

Even without a sudden upset, it is quite conceivable for prosperity to exhaust itself. The primary reason for this seems to be a limitation in available resources and manpower. Bottle-necks begin to spring up at various points; there are insufficient numbers of certain types of skilled and semi-skilled workers; the railroads find it difficult to meet the demands placed on them. Moreover, changes within the structure of industry itself may take place during an expansion which can lead to future disloca-tions; new goods or new ways of producing old goods influence cost conditions and prices and, as the economy expands, these add to the distortions that are built up.

This gloomy outline hardly seems to match the economic ex-perience of 1955. We have witnessed an unparalleled state of well-being. Yet there are words of caution. Says the *First Na-tional City Bank Economic Letter*: ". . . the economy must walk a tightrope—maintaining an uneasy equilibrium at a high level between inflation, on the one hand, and deflation, on the other. . . . It is possible that the real advances during 1955 could give way to illusory gains compounded of rising prices, involuntary accumu-lation of inventories, and overextended credit. The economy does not yet show convincing signs that excesses have reached dan-gerous proportions, nor are they, in any sense, inevitable. But they could develop if we substitute enthusiasm for caution and emphasize prosperity to the extent that we forget its problems."

There are industries whose current activities seem to promise perpetual prosperity. Steel output hit a record of 116 million tons, a 30 percent increase over 1954. Even better, booked orders guarantee that the furnaces will not be cut back for at least six months. The demand for cold-rolled sheets, heavy plate, freight cars, and structural steel continues unabated. What seems to be disturbing steel manufacturers at the moment is the four-year wage agreement which expires June 30, as well as the unhappy prospect that the automobile industry may not buy as much steel in 1956 as it did in 1955. Thus far, however, the demand has been so strong that some of the old furnaces, long retired from active blasting, are being restored to duty. Equipment is being redesigned and production methods altered in an effort to force production up. All this feverish, almost frenetic, activity suggests that the bottlenecks we spoke of are beginning to ap-pear. When these choke off operations, the steel magnates will have a third item to worry about.

The present record is mixed. This too is a characteristic turning-point feature. Soft goods, such as textiles and apparel, have seemingly recovered from the doldrums of the last two years. Textile concerns did about 80 percent better than they did in 1954, despite some severe competition from imports, especially Japanese goods. Increased demand from consumers supplied the necessary fillip for women's wear. But moving over to so basic an industry as railroads, the picture is somewhat different. While the gross return for rails was high, yield on invested capital was a mere 4 percent, something which made bankers and railroad magnates screw up their faces in wry dismay. They complained, also, that the 4 percent gain was overstated because of special accounting devices required by the Interstate Commerce Commission. As a result, the railroads are looking for a substantial hike in rates.

What has kept the economy going, in large measure, has been the continued high peaks in construction. New building, plus repairs and maintenance, represented about 15 percent of gross national product. It was responsible for 15 percent of total employment; this was no small factor in the present prosperity. New housing starts exceeded the million mark for the seventh straight year and seemingly there was no end in sight. However, much of this hectic activity was stimulated by a small or no-down-payment policy, often with a thirty-year financing period. The total amount of mortgage debt outstanding for "family homes" reached over $86 billion last year. This continuous upward pressure upset Washington officials and mortgage terms were tightened. The no-down-payment clause in government-insured housing was eliminated and five years were cut off the financing period. And so, home building, in the last quarter of 1955, began to thin out. Experts expect home building to drop as much as 10 percent in 1956; the more optimistic estimates, such as those made by the F. W. Dodge Corporation, visualize that the slack will be made up by ordinary commercial construction, such as factories, storage facilities, and the like. When they add to this suburban shopping centers, public utility construction, railroads, hospitals, institutions, and other public works, the end seems nowhere in sight. But some questions have to be asked: what happens when family formation slows down (the low depression baby crop has come of age); when building costs begin to press on profit margins; when housing prices exceed the ability of the average wage earner to pay? These are the already visible signs of turning points.

What seems to be taking place in the automobile industry suggests another turning point. The industry had its biggest production and sales binge in 1955, and it would be truly phenomenal should the pace continue into much of this year. There were almost eight million cars produced in 1955, but it is expected that output this year will drop at least 10 or 12 percent. The great record last year was accounted for by excessive pressure on dealers, carnival sales methods, new car bootlegging, and the wildest kind of credit offers. While General Motors, Ford, and Chrysler experienced extremely profitable years, dealer profits remained low enough for many to be forced into bankruptcy. Toward the year's end in 1955, deliveries to dealers were curtailed and inventories began to pile up once more. In December of last year alone, retail deliveries dropped by 155,000 units. By the end of January, car production was about 40,000 units short of expectation. The industry's trade paper, *Automotive News*, expected February to be even worse. This, in the main, affected new models. A downturn so early is not an auspicious harbinger for the coming year. The auto manufacturers are saying that they want it this way because they are planning an early introduction of 1957 model changes. Since these will be presumably radical style changes, it is hoped that demand in 1956 will be stimulated by enforced obsolescence. As this goes on, one begins to wonder whether the frequency of model changes will not have to be stepped up to maintain production. Evidently, the auto industry needs something like this, or a permanent war economy, to keep it going.

The fact of the matter is that income distribution patterns preclude the perpetual continuation of demand at high levels. Income has not been redistributed so widely as some of the more conservative journals would have us believe. True, 30 percent of all families had incomes of $5,000 or more in 1954, as compared with 21 percent in 1948, but the low-income families (under $2,000) still numbered some 9.4 million in 1954. They still represented one-fifth of all families and, according to the Children's Bureau, they had a disproportionate share of the country's children. In addition, the number of families with incomes under $5,000 were ten million more than those with incomes over $5,000, which, according to the Census Bureau, totaled sixteen million. In the President's recent Economic Report there is this note:

> Consumers were of a mind to buy better things and increase their spending. This pervasive attitude combined with the willingness of women and young people to take on jobs so that their families might better approximate the plane of living they wish to attain has been an outstanding feature of recent experience.

Should such families revert to single wage-earner status, many of them would fall below the $4,000 level.

But it is among the farmers that there is the most questioning about prosperity. The farmer contends that while he contributes almost as much to national output as industry, he does not receive a comparable return. The prices the farmer obtained in 1955 for his goods were 7 percent less than the 1947–1949 average, while the prices he had to pay for materials and equipment were up by 12 percent. Net farm income had dropped almost $2 billion since 1947–1949. What makes the farmer even unhappier is the prospect for little improvement in 1956. The Department of Agriculture has again predicted a drop in farm prices of 5 percent, as it did last year. Furthermore, the "modified parity" formula, based on the average of the last decade rather than the old 1909–1914 average, will have the effect of decreasing government price supports by about 5 percent. In addition, acreage allotments will be more stringent and somewhat smaller. Farmers might feed their corn to hogs or cattle, but this is profitable only if animal prices are higher than feed costs. At the end of last year, hog prices in the midwest were about $10.50 per cwt., as compared with feed costs of around $14.00 per cwt. Lower farm income, it was reported, was beginning to be felt generally: farm implements sales dropped and banks were having trouble collecting on loans.

When it comes to farming, however, the total figures may be somewhat misleading. Among the almost half-million American farms, there are about 100,000 large, prosperous "suitcase" farms, really field factories, based on integrated production techniques. They account for over 25 percent of total farm sales and, like all other farmers, are beneficiaries of Uncle Sam's helpful price-support program. At the other end of the spectrum, there are 1.7 million "hobby" farms which have no impact on the market, and a million small poverty-stricken plots, chiefly tenant holdings, which supply about 10 percent of farm output. These are simply too poor to be disturbed by problems of price supports and farm income. It is the two million farmers that supply 60 percent of the farm products that are howling the loudest today. They are, in the main, in the so-called rich midwest; their average annual income approximates $4,000. This may seem pretty fair for the farming business, but since most are heavily mortgaged it is not likely that the return on their investment matches the return in industry.

Perhaps the best place to watch for turning-point characteristics is in the financial market. On the New York Stock Exchange, 1955 was a year of high-volume trading; almost 650 million shares exchanged hands. But, say Wall Street experts, it was a rather thin market. By this they mean that only a small part of all the stocks, approximately 5 percent, was bought and sold. This implies that investors kept their portfolios zipped up and refused to take part in the year's hectic trading.

Coupled with this as a turning-point indicator was the large volume of currency in circulation, which reached record levels at the end of 1955. To some observers this meant that consumer spending at retail levels was also high, as indeed it was. But the $31 million cash supply was also a reflection of tightened credit, for it seems evident that when the Federal Reserve sought to choke off credit, people began to dip into their cash resources. The spending spree continued unabated, so much so that savings banks were perturbed when their deposits did not rise as much as anticipated. Such developments presaged an inflationary situation to which the Federal Reserve reacted with great haste. Rediscount rates, the price charged to member banks for loans, were raised to 2 percent, thus making it more difficult to obtain bank loans. The FHA and VA tightened maturity and down payment terms on insured loans; by October, commercial bank rates had gone up to 3.5 percent, the highest in twenty-five years. By the end of the year, short-term interest rates had begun to overtake long-term rates, closing out an era when money had been "cheap." Nevertheless, the expansion in credit continued, for the banks merely sold their government securities in order to obtain the necessary reserves for lending. The question whether such borrowing and lending was reaching the danger point was being fully debated at the year's end.

Even the President's Council of Economic Advisers seemed concerned about what it described as the challenge of prosperity. They warned that the continuance of general prosperity could not be taken for granted and that alertness to changes in economic conditions and a readiness to modify and adapt policies was essential. It was evident that the President's advisers felt this had to be said now because they too had noted a number of turning-point characteristics. By late spring of 1955, observed the Council, the expanding demand for output, swollen by excessive credit, was already pressing against industrial capacity. It noted that shortages of steel, nickel, copper, cement, plumbing fixtures, lumber, and other materials had become extensive and that many types of skilled labor were scarce. Wages and prices were "beginning to stir." By the end of the year, continued the report, the scope of the expansion in the previous twelve months had narrowed and the pace slackened.

Some observers have argued that all these warnings have a "short-run" character with no substantive basis in the real long-range economic outlook. They point not only to the seasonal nature of the slump in automobile production, but also to the whole battery of built-in stabilizers such as unemployment and bank deposit insurance, a better controlled banking system, and a stronger labor movement. But basically, it is said, there is the simple fact that the kind of garrison economy we now have will probably counteract any sustained drop. Government spending for national defense, now at a rate of about $40 billion a year, is expected to increase, and even assuming that the armed forces will be merely maintained at their present levels, increasing costs for new continental warning systems, guided missiles, atomic-powered carriers, and other wonder weapons will force expenditures upward.

The leverage that this lends to the economic system is undeniable, but is one that rests on an uncertain political fulcrum. Whatever promising long-range conditions develop as a result of spending for war in no way can become internal to the economy itself. In the absence of such "investment," capitalism has a tendency to falter and stumble; what happened in 1949, just prior to Korea, illustrates the argument. Present prosperity seems rooted in the moving sands of profit inflation. Credit and prices seem to have no real basis in current production. The facts of the case are simple: while in the decade before 1952, consumer and mortgage credit rose in proportion to gross national product, the increase after 1952 has been considerably greater. Mortgages were 4.5 times greater than the rise in output; consumer credit increased more than twice as much; and automobile credit went up at least five times more than the national product. We are sitting on top of a boom that has been built up by an unheard of credit expansion. This is a most precarious economic situation. Under ordinary circumstances a limitless expansion would be unlikely. When such a boom does explode its reverberations will be heard for many a year.

III

The interesting thing about the recession of 1958 is that signs of it were visible as far back as 1956. One indication of economic malaise was an enormous credit expansion accompanied, curiously enough, by a slowing down in the rate of economic growth. Physical output seemed, in the main, to be standing still and, in some sectors, even receding. Prices continued to rise while inventory accumulation began to taper off. And these trends continued on into late 1957.

Suddenly capital investments dropped $750 million. In September, production, sales, and personal income declined, continuing to do so on into January. The Federal Reserve Board, discovering that the situation was no longer inflationary but one in which things had to be stirred up, proceeded to reduce the rediscount rate. Workers in manufacturing, construction, and railroads who had been laid off at the year's end discovered that it was not easy to find another job. Real per capita disposable income, which had risen steadily from $1,586 in 1954 to $1,660 in 1955, began to decline. The peak had been reached in 1956 with a figure of $1,713 but by the end of 1957 it had dropped to $1,695.

By mid-January the official figure of unemployment stood at 5.2 percent, the highest level in the last three years. Today [June 1958] the estimates are pressing close to 5.5 million.

Meanwhile, the American public was edified by sounds of reassurance from the White House. The President did not consider the present level of joblessness unbearable. His economists had informed him there would soon be a "pick up" in jobs. He even promised to do something. Some weeks later he had to shift ground; he now told his press conference that it would take some time to stop the recession. But, like his illustrious predecessor of 1928–1932, he preferred to sit it out.

And the professional economists, what were they saying? At first, not much. When "soft spots" developed around September 1957, the majority thought that things might improve in December. By Christmas, when unemployment was really growing, they said we were in a little setback and spring would bring a thaw. In February, they reluctantly concluded that matters could not improve without drastic action.

One group of forecasters meeting at the University of Michigan expected the decline to continue through 1958. The possibility that private investment, a significant part of gross national product, would drop by perhaps 5 percent seemed very important to them. Senator Paul Douglas, a skilled economist, urged tax reductions and the elimination of excises on consumer goods, estimating that as much as $4 billion might flow into the income stream as a result of such measures. Arthur F. Burns called for public works that could be completed in six to nine months. Even the more conservative economists admitted that the contraction was a severe one.

This was a most curious recession, for living costs seemed to climb to new peaks even as the number of unemployed increased. In February 1958, the BLS Consumer Price Index rose to 122.5 from 121.6 at the end of 1957. The explanation for this increase, the largest since the middle of 1956, was said to be frostbitten crops.

There was little reason to expect that the CPI would soon slide downward. Consumer prices are sticky. Generally it is not until reductions at primary levels filter back to the finished product that price declines are visible—and this takes time. But there are indications that the move to lower prices is already on. Some manufacturers have announced reductions; price cuts have been made in fibers, copper products, heating equipment, industrial machinery, farm equipment, and fuels. There have been reductions through such indirect methods as bigger bonuses to dealers, absorption of freight costs, and distress sales. Changes in the CPI or the Wholesale Price Index do not fully reflect the current economic situation simply because they have a built-in lag. Consumer prices in late 1929 seemed virtually the same as in 1928; the drop then did not show up until well into 1930.

Measures of national output, however, have fallen sharply. In December 1957, the Federal Reserve Board's Index of Industrial Production was 2 percent below the November figure. The decline continued into March 1958, when the index dropped to 128 from a 1947 high of 148. The continued drop was attributed in part to curtailments in durable goods production; steel mill operations, which had already declined in December, decreased even further in January and February.

A number of economists believe that if only home building would increase in 1958, the business recession would quickly disappear. Now, building construction is a primary factor in keeping the economy going at high levels. But the fact that construction went up a bit in January does not seem to be sufficient reason for anticipating a sharp upturn now. A close examination of the long-run figures fails to reveal any substantial recovery in construction. While the three-year decline in housing starts was halted last spring, there has been no sign of genuine strength in the industry.

A recession is intensified when it is superimposed on a declining phase of the construction cycle. This is precisely what happened in 1929–1930, and some analysts are asking whether we are not in just that situation today. It is estimated that the decline in building could not be reversed before the early 1960's. Such a conjuncture of declining production and a drop in building construction suggests a troubled economic future.

The fact that we have not had a major contraction in the last decade and a half is not unprecedented. A study of business-cycle data shows that there were intervals of eight to thirteen years without severe contractions following the sharp downswings of 1894, 1908, and 1921. The percentage of unemployment in the civilian labor force today is in fact greater than in the first eight years of this century. Despite our great prosperity, the rate of economic growth has been slower in the postwar era than in earlier periods when there was comparable stability. The kind of fluctuations in business cycles that we have had after the war are not too different from the past. Nor does the absence of a serious postwar deflation demonstrate that the character of the business cycle has changed. The contractions that we have had in recent years have been mild only because of the growth in capital investment stemming from World War II and the tremendous expansion in population and technology. And to these must be added the tremendous level of government expenditures stemming from the cold war.

At the moment, the most serious trouble is to be found in steel and automobiles. Even *Fortune* has had to admit that the automobile industry, with sales last year of over $13.6 billion, is today in a weak position. Now this is really serious, for the earlier recoveries from the 1949 and 1954 declines were triggered by a fantastically huge capital expansion in that industry. It seems that the sales of passenger cars in 1958 will be about 800,000 units less than in 1957—which would mean total sales of under five million cars, or production at about 60 to 65 percent of capacity.

These difficulties, in turn, have had a serious impact on steel, in which reduced buying by automobile manufacturers dampened hopes for the future. Steel operations were cut back so sharply that by March they were at only 45 percent of capacity in all the major steel centers—Chicago, Youngstown, and Pittsburgh.

As one looks about for causes of this most severe of post-war economic declines, the outstanding fact is that the American economy now has too large a plant for current requirements. Quite simply, we are suffering from excess capacity. This seems to be the proximate cause of the present situation. Manufacturing concerns last September estimated that they were operating at about 80 percent of capacity as contrasted with a preferred operating rate of 90 percent. As a result, they planned to reduce capital expenditures by 16 percent in 1958.

Our economy has moved ahead so rapidly with plant capacity that it must now face a period in which sharp reductions in expenditures for investment are to be made. Manufacturers always like to have a bit of excess plant and equipment for elbow room. But too much freedom of this kind is undesirable, for it not only increases the overhead burden on unit output but also indicates an inability to put the plant to work. A general state of excess capacity inevitably leads to a sharp cutback in capital investment and tends to produce a cumulative downswing in production, employment, and inventory.

After World War II, manufacturing enterprises were short of capacity, at least as measured by the then effective demand. Facilities were increased between 1947–1955 at the rate of about 6 percent a year. Then, between 1955 and 1957 capital investment, plant, and equipment jumped 40 percent. This had a direct impact on prices, forcing some up by as much as 20 percent. Since, however, some obsolete equipment was retired from use, the real increase in capacity seems to have been about 10 to 12 percent, a substantial increase nevertheless. But during the same two years, output increased only by about 4 percent—which goes far toward explaining the projected cutback in expansion plans for 1958–59. A recent SEC survey substantiated this analysis by reporting that plant and equipment outlays for the initial quarter of 1958 would be 8 percent below the same quarterly average of 1957.

The administration's monetary and tax policies have contributed not a little to the downward slide. There was, in a sense, a government subsidy to this vast capital expansion. In 1954, special tax privileges were given to corporations, ostensibly to encourage investment. This was done through accelerated amortization of new fixed assets, while taxes on dividends were reduced by a special credit device. Defense-related investments were allowed a rapid five year amortization, as during the war. Yet, while capital investment grew and boomed, *per capita real personal income began to slip as early as the spring of 1956.* From 1955 to 1957 over $100 billion in additional capacity was installed, but toward the end of this period there was a perceptible and growing gap between actual production and the ability to produce.

The administration, expressing deep concern about inflation, proceeded to cut defense spending while the Federal Reserve Board increased its rediscount rate. In the light of these antics, the charge in certain quarters that the administration and the Federal Reserve wanted a recession in order to control labor does not seem so far-fetched. (Washington rumors have it that the administration will do nothing until the UAW wage negotiations are over.) Administration monetary policy has only discriminated against small business firms, small municipalities, and farmers. The larger corporations have been able generally to look upon Federal Reserve controls without much disturbance, for they have their own inner resources for financing. And this fact indicates the futility of the tight money policy followed last year.

Optimistic observers argue that the upturn will come soon because there will be a need to replenish inventories. *Fortune* has repeatedly advanced this view, saying that inventory cycles tend to be brief and self-reversing, unless there is a complete failure in demand. The argument is made that in this downturn, inventory liquidation has run far ahead of the decline in final purchases, so that the upturn ought to come soon. The fact, however, is that in recent months sales declines have outstripped inventory cutbacks. *Fortune's* experts overlook the fact that the automobile and steel industries are running at tremendous excess-capacity ratios—which means that this recession is evidently something more than a simple inventory cycle.

The United States possesses a number of so-called built-in economic stabilizers which, we are told, will modify the effects of the present decline. These include tax cuts, increased spending, subsidies, loans and grants, and guarantees to mortgage companies. We can put public works into operation, support farm prices, and expand unemployment compensation. But are these working? Is the American economy really immune from a depression? While unemployment compensation schemes, insurance of bank deposits and adjustments of the tax rate can help slow a decline, it requires the kind of massive impact which a permanent war economy supplies for the present downward slide to be reversed. Fritz Sternberg once said that we went into the war in 1941 with the Depression still in our bones. This apt remark underscored the fact that only the war program was able to lift us to a high level of production and employment. In the absence of that, a renewal of the huge postwar prosperity would require vast new technological spurts, another burst of population growth, more consumer credit than we now have, a tremendous housing program, and numerous public works. Should some of these factors be lacking, then we may very well expect a serious decline.

The present "dip," the third of the postwar series, is not at all like the ones which occurred in 1949 and 1954. The reduction in investment for new plant and equipment in the third one was too sharp to be overlooked. This is the major difference between then and now. Nor can we assume that the history of the postwar period will be repeated again. The expansion in the private sectors of the economy, certainly vast in 1955 and 1956, has leveled out in 1957.

This does not mean that another depression similar to that of the thirties is in the offing. But it is likely that there may be several years of activity at a level far lower than that to which we had become accustomed in the last four or five years. In saying this, I assume that the long-range economic forces which played so strong a role in the last decade and a half will be much less potent. But, reply some hopefuls, if the economy would only continue the earlier years' prosperous ways, we should wind up in 1965 with a gross national product of perhaps $575 billion, an increase of some $15 billion a year. These estimates, however, assume that the labor force will grow as it has in the past and that capital investment and output per man-hour will show a steady rise as well. Hidden in such prognostications is the belief that government will really step in to help fulfill the promise of American life.

Together with government expenditures, stemming mainly from the permanent war economy, there are said to be several long-range factors which ought to sustain a generally high level of activity in years to come. These are technological improvements which will stimulate business investments, the continued growth of suburbia, a renewal of the recent commodity hunger requiring even more consumer credit, a further leveling of income distribution, and a rise in international trade.

That these forces are still strong and can give the economy a further push seems dubious. Present excess capacities cast doubt on a rise in business investment during 1958 sufficient to start things rolling once more; the economic philosophy of the present administration suggests a desire to cut back on war spending, for budgets must be balanced; the rate of growth in suburbia has clearly slowed down, if one is to judge by trends in house-building; and the new pattern of income distribution is largely a myth, as was shown by Gabriel Kolko. It seems entirely possible that we shall continue to bump along with a higher rate of unemployment and a lower level of economic activity than was customary in recent years.

1954, 1956, 1958

The Dwindling Great Society

There is little doubt that the great society constitutes the most sparkling demonstration of political energy since the first hundred days of Franklin Delano Roosevelt. With each session of Congress, President Johnson, architect of the Great Society, has let loose a barrage of messages and legislative proposals that have dazzled the imagination. Indeed, so striking has the Great Society's domestic program appeared to be that some commentators have suggested that it really represents a social revolution, as dramatic in its implications as the French or American revolutions of the eighteenth century. Is this really the case? I think not.

For the fact is that the President has been astute enough to pick up a number of programs previously rejected and place them into the Great Society's ample basket. With few exceptions they are small, have been given unrealistic budgetary allocations,

and, in the last analysis, are quite unable to reach the goals that
have been set for them.

Social revolutions are not fashioned in this manner. A social
revolution, whether achieved via a Marxian apocalypse or through
a gradual Fabian permeation, does imply a fundamental alteration in political alignments, not in the sense that Democrats replace Republicans, but rather by the entrance upon the political
stage of hitherto dispossessed classes. Thus, if the Negroes in
the South were to gain, permanently, positions of political pre-
eminence, it would constitute one of the pillars of a social revolution in that region. But this has not been the case despite marked
progress in civil rights since the historic Supreme Court decision
on school desegregation in 1954.

The present tragedy is that the coalition of whites and Negroes
that sparked the civil rights movement is falling apart. If the
administration's program constituted a social revolution it might
have expressed concern over the impending collapse of one of
its major sources of support. But white civil rights activists have
moved away from the movement (some find working for the
Great Society in such programs as the War on Poverty more
attractive), and the Negro organizations are at odds with
each other.

Bayard Rustin says that revolutionary change does not connote
violence. I quite agree: it refers rather, in Rustin's words, to
". . . the qualitative transformation of fundamental institutions,
more or less rapidly, to the point where the social and economic
structure which they comprised can no longer be said to be the
same." Rustin adds that such transformation cannot be achieved
in the absence of full employment, abolition of slums, the reconstruction of our educational system, and all the other programs that ostensibly are part of the Great Society's effort.

Yet school desegregation remains largely unfinished business.
In Georgia, one of the more "liberal" Southern states, less than
1 percent of Negro children attend desegregated schools, while
the growing ghetto walls in the North have created more segrega-
tion than there was in 1954, when the Supreme Court outlawed
"equal but separate" facilities. Discrimination is a condition that
the Great Society has not been able to alter.

Some observers suggest that part of our social revolution lies in the redistribution of income that has occurred since the war. They point to the increase in real income from $5,200 per family in 1952 to $6,300 in 1961. Moreover, the figures show that middle-income families benefited more than others. But all that was before the advent of Lyndon Johnson. Further, the pattern of income distribution, according to Herman P. Miller, the Census Bureau's expert, has not been altered since 1944. The highest 5 percent of the families still get about 20 percent of total income, while the lowest fifth obtains about 5 percent. This situation has been unchanged for over two decades.

In addition, the gap between white earnings and Negro earnings is not narrowing, says Miller. The ratio of Negro to white earnings has dropped from about 60 percent in 1950 to about 55 percent today. A year-round full-time Negro worker today earns about $4,000 as compared with over $6,000 for a white worker. During the 1940's, a decade that included World War II, the relative gain in earnings by workers in low-paid occupations was quite rapid—160 percent as against somewhat under 100 percent for professionals. In other words, in those years the man at the bottom had begun to move upward with a fair degree of rapidity. More recently, there has been a reversal. Laborers and service workers have advanced at half the pace of professional and managerial workers. If indeed there was a revolution in income, it all took place long before the Great Society.

What of all the special programs, particularly the War on Poverty? Poverty, of course, is nothing new in Western civilization: it has been around for so long that it has the character of a social syndrome, apparently everlasting and ineradicable. As the economy made advances, there gathered at the bottom of the heap the dispossessed, the disadvantaged, and the untutored to create a layer of deprivation that has resisted half-hearted public and private efforts to deal with it. Many economists and sociologists denied that poverty was a public issue, and not until Michael Harrington in his *The Other America* and Dwight Macdonald in a brilliant piece in the *New Yorker* reminded them that the poor were still around did they agree that an underground of the poor could be uncovered in America.

The origin of the War on Poverty is interesting. Washington legend has it that Ted Sorensen was so moved by Macdonald's article that he urged President Kennedy to read it. This incident led to the proposal in February 1963 that a National Youth Service be established paralleling the Peace Corps that was working so well overseas. Through the months that followed, congressional discussion revolved about the notion of a Domestic Service Corps. Obviously, this was a limited approach, and aware of the feeling on Capitol Hill, the Kennedy administration, always concerned with the politically possible, moved with caution. When Johnson took over the reins of power, it seemed doubtful that much would be done. But in March 1964, hearings on a broader bill started in the House of Representatives. Suddenly, "poverty" had become fashionable. Adam Clayton Powell, chairman of the House Committee on Education and Labor, opened hearings with a flourish and a press release. The administration spoke of poor youth, the aged, the fatherless, the industrially displaced, the rural poor, and the Negro. It was proposed to spend a billion dollars skirmishing along the poverty front.

When Michael Harrington, Paul Jacobs, and others were called to Washington to consult with the new warriors against poverty, they managed to insert the phrase "maximum feasible participation of the poor" into the statute. No one was quite certain what it meant or what would happen. The intent, in all probability, was to insure the maximum employment of the poor in specific programs, and to avoid too much of an overload of professionals in the projects that were contemplated. The civil rights groups, however, soon realized the potentialities of the clause, and they insisted that it was a directive for the poor to originate projects, administer them, and even control them. Here, indeed, were the elements of a social revolution, for such an interpretation, if carried out, would bring into the center of national activity precisely those people who had been pushed out of sight and out of mind.

This was more than local mayors or congressmen had bargained for. Yet they had no real cause for worry: people in the ghetto were not really radical and the whole debate was transformed into one about local autonomy and local control, quite in the tradition of American urban politics. Some mayors, notably in Detroit and New Haven, knew how to use the words "maximum feasible participation" to contain civil rights activists; others, such as Samuel Yorty of Los Angeles, have been less willing to act in the same way. As a result much turmoil has been generated.

To add to the travail, the War on Poverty is so uncoordinated that the energies of its foot soldiers are completely dissipated. One part of the campaign is carried on by the Department of Health, Education, and Welfare, another by the Labor Department, still another is located in the Department of Agriculture. It was thought that community action agencies functioning at local levels would provide a means for coordinating all the work. This was to be done through the "preference" clauses in the statute which directed that the highest priority be accorded to suggestions stemming from these local bodies. Representing both public and private agencies that had previously sought to help the poor, the community action organizations would presumably know better than Washington officials where the skirmishes should be fought.

Unfortunately, the Office of Economic Opportunity set up many local community action agencies much as one would establish a chain of discount houses. The agencies were literally pasted together by choosing in helter-skelter fashion representatives from local welfare institutions, private voluntary organizations, and leading citizens to serve on local boards of directors. Representatives of the poor were added almost as an afterthought, and only because the statute required it. And no matter how many "preferences" the local boards might send to Washington, such directives never really had much force. Top officials in the OEO were unlikely to step on the toes of heads of other departments so that the entire scheme was diluted. At best the "preference" was an expression of local need which failed to establish priorities since each participating agency went its own way.

The Neighborhood Youth Corps moves along without regard to local community action agencies; the Agriculture Department's anti-poverty loan program is handled by its own agents; HEW's efforts lag because the department awaits the action of notoriously slow state and local welfare agencies; and the community action bodies themselves have displayed poor administrative skill. True, there are some solid accomplishments; but, in the main, the Great Society reveals an exasperating uncertainty in prosecuting the war on poverty.

To cap it all, Sargent Shriver has advised the House Committee on Education and Labor that he might cease financing the election of representatives of the poor to community action boards because the turnouts have been so low. But participants in such elections must virtually take a pauper's oath, an action they are apt to resent. In Los Angeles participants had to affirm their poverty and in Philadelphia they were required to specify that they lived in poor areas. Elections that have been held were staged with inadequate advance notice. The consequence was that only 14,000 persons voted in Philadelphia and 2,500 in Los Angeles. No one thought to remind the OEO that the first day of the month was a bad one in a poverty election: it's the one day the poor stay home to receive their monthly assistance checks.

Saul Alinsky, who has done more than anyone in America to organize the poor and to teach them to help themselves, is savage in his criticism of the Great Society's effort to combat poverty. He calls it "welfare colonialism," "supplements," and a "cosmetic cover-up." The administration's approach, he suggests, is a compound of middle-class *noblesse oblige* and zoo-keeping. Alinsky insists that the poor must avoid entangling alliances with the Establishment. Yet Alinsky's does not appear to be a feasible solution, since poverty projects do require "funding." In any case, the Alinsky method would appear to intensify the quandary, especially as the administration is now downgrading its social program in favor of Vietnam.

Look at another facet of the Great Society—the revitalization of Appalachia. If ever a region could be called depressed it was Appalachia; yet not until 1965 was a direct attempt made to deal with its problems. In March of that year, President Johnson signed a bill to provide $1.1 billion in aid to the eleven states of the area—but about 76 percent of it was to be spent over a six-year period on highways and local access roads. The remainder was to be distributed over two years for health centers, soil conservation, land reclamation, water resource development, vocational schools, sewage treatment plants, hospitals, and airports. It was evidently assumed that Appalachia's distress was due to physical isolation and that roads would open the area to the rest of the nation.

Insofar as jobs were concerned, it was likely that not more

than 20 percent of the total man-hours provided by road building and other projects would go to unskilled labor. And since many of the inhabitants lacked construction skills, workers would probably have to be imported from other regions. If the upbuilding of tourism was the objective, the generation of such jobs would have to await the completion of the roads, a goal that was some years away. As was generally the situation in such legislation, federal funds in most instances would require some state or local matching, this in an area where state and local governments were as poor as the inhabitants. In any case, effective area redevelopment might have called for a reversal of the proportions, since the central problem of Appalachia stems from the decay of its entire social overhead inheritance. Individual states' rights are to be protected through representation by governors on the Appalachian Regional Commission. It was hoped that correcting the deficiencies of physical and human resources would draw in venture capital, but curiously the administration seemed bent mainly on improving recreational and educational facilities. Once more an uncoordinated effort was in the offing.

The first mountain dirt was turned at Isom, Kentucky, and Salem, West Virginia, in July 1965 to start construction of the 2,350 miles of "developmental" highways. According to observers, the onlookers seemed more enthralled with the huge yellow earth-moving machinery than they were with the remote benefits that might be brought to their communities in the future. One can anticipate that the federal government and the states will wrangle over the highways planned for the region. They may accept proposals from a "systems analysis," prepared under a $130,000 contract by a private consulting firm which stuffed masses of data into econometric models in order to decide which depressed spot needs the road or hospital. The greater likelihood was that the governors would insist on locations that would return the most in currency of state politics.

Thus, as one moves from one Great Society program to another the inescapable impression is created that it all represents a huge conglomeration of unrelated partial efforts, without a genuine commitment to serious reform or social change. The ultimate consequence of all these programs is their employment to frustrate the confrontation of man to man, of class to class, to allay our concern with the future of the society, to maintain the existing power structure whether in local communities or at higher political levels, and, at best, to provide long overdue reforms in the most modest of ways. One can hardly say that all this constitutes a social revolution. It represents rather a frenetic churning of political skills to contain the aspirations of people long denied a proper place in the scheme of things.

1966

PART FOUR. AMERICAN INSTITUTIONS: LABOR

Portrait of a Labor Leader

The strenuous life does not seem to have left its mark on David Gordin. A Webster panatela, half of which he chews rather than smokes, punctuates his hard, yet not unpleasant, features. Gordin's clothes always fit well—tailored by Billy Taub, they are the penultimate in Seventh Avenue styles; the four pointed ends of a white, hand-rolled handkerchief effectively break the thin vertical pinstripes and his ties show elaborate floral designs. In fact, Gordin, who pronounces his name in the Russian way, Gor*din,* is virtually indistinguishable from the manufacturers he now includes among his many friends.

Mr. and Mrs. David Gor*din* live in a well-appointed five-room apartment on West End Avenue; three months of the year they divide between the Oceanside Hotel at Miami and Gross' Rest House in the Catskills. Gordin is normally an energetic man and his perennial suntan enhances his appearance of good health. Mrs. Gordin is an active member of several ladies' organizations, and during the war has greatly enjoyed wearing her blue-gray home-front uniform.

Mr. Gordin spends his evenings playing pinochle with friends while his wife learns the intricacies of Mah Jongg. To make a killing at cards affords him incalculable pleasure; not infrequently he will convert a weekend in the country into an extended card game. Gordin openly concedes that a comfortable middle-class existence has its points; and he maintains, sometimes a bit over-emphatically, that it is no wise inconsistent with his long history, position, or usefulness as a labor leader.

Manager of his union's joint board, Gordin occupies a strategic position in the middle strand of organized labor's hierarchy. As a top union representative, he is often busy negotiating contracts with manufacturers' associations. Much of his official time, however, is spent talking about inner union affairs with the members of his immediate Joint Board coterie. This little domain of union intimates generally defers to its boss's views, as Gordin himself yields to the opinions of the president of the National General Office. It is not a hard life.

Yet there is a marked uneasiness these days about Gordin. This first appeared when he found it necessary to select Italian- and Spanish-speaking organizers. "In the old days," he says, "I could talk to the people in the shops myself. Now you got to be a regular linguist." Before the Great Depression the union's membership was largely Jewish, but in recent years it has been recruited from all stocks—Italian, Puerto Rican, Negro. Jews today comprise less than a third of the industry's workers. The union leadership may very well change, too. Gordin recognizes the inevitable, and he is not happy about it. "Look!" he will exclaim. He uses the word "look" as a friendly invitation to examine his statements carefully. "The Italians and the others always take their kids into the shops with them. They teach them the trade and make workers out of them. We Jews, when we're workers, we're not really workers. We're middle class and our children have to be lawyers and teachers and businessmen. And don't forget the doctors. So in the end there's got to be change in the trade."

The leadership, Gordin also admits in his more analytical moments, tends to become self-perpetuating and bureaucratic and to develop interests with which the average union member is but little concerned. The rank and file, however, does not seem to be troubled as long as its demands are satisfied. "A union today is like a corporation. The membership is like the stockholders and the officers are like the board of directors. As long as the board of directors pays dividends the stockholders are happy."

Recently the joint board, with the approval of the general office, increased Gordin's salary from $8,500 to $9,500. "The general office boys get more than that," says Gordin. "If the membership didn't think they were worth it, believe you me they would raise a row. But it's not so much the big salaries that count; it's the difference in jobs—that's what changes people." The average worker's life, remarks Gordin, is unfortunately narrow, being restricted to shop and home. The union leader has a broader horizon. "We meet important people, you know. Manufacturers, politicians, writers," he says with a slightly sardonic gleam in his eyes.

When the general office embarked upon an ambitious program of workers' education some years ago, Gordin expressed his doubts. "A union should maybe teach trade unionism, but poetry and how to paint a landscape? Why should we compete with colleges?" The union's educational director tells a story that illustrates the limits Gordin places on education. "Tell me," Gordin once asked him, "what are you going to teach the workers?"

"We'll have classes in labor history . . . English . . . the economics of the industry," was the reply.

"Anything else?" asked Gordin, after nodding his approval of each subject mentioned.

"And we'd like to give classes in parliamentary law," concluded the educational department's representative.

"No, that's not so good," mused Gordin, scratching his head. "Already they are making too many motions."

Gordin is not a florid orator. He speaks simply, punctuating his talks with anecdotes drawn from his long experience in the labor movement. This is effective with small groups, especially when reinforced by the authority of the manager of the joint board. The president of the general office has always recognized Gordin as a masterful organizer. During a wage conference years ago, the employer, exasperated by Gordin's hard-headedness, shouted, "Why are you holding up things just for a drop in the bucket?" Gordin quickly reached for the man's drinking glass, shook a drop of ink into it from a pen and said, "Go ahead, drink it. It's only a drop."

On rare occasions Gordin may be prevailed upon to "fix" things for a friend; a little favor for members of his inner circle helps keep the peace. But in matters of union policy he is strictly on the side of the angels, provided the angels agree with him and the general office. He will listen courteously to small gossip, but he is shrewd enough to discount most of what is whispered into his ear. Gordin can be quite flexible; he has time and again exhibited in internal union affairs a remarkable resiliency. Yet he knows how to be ruthless in order to retain the power that is his—he enjoys power.

Gordin knows little of music, the arts, or literature; but he does know his own industry. His approach to problems is compounded of 90 percent hard-boiled pragmatism and 10 percent uplift idealism. The school of hard knocks, he says, is a great training ground.

Gordin's matter-of-fact common sense is peculiarly flavored with a kind of special realism. In the old country, ideals were essentially protests against the dispossession of the Jews; in a new land of opportunity those ideals faded into the background. But practicality remained and Gordin discovered that he had little difficulty in accommodating himself to the hard-boiled demands of union life. Accommodation gradually permeated all his thought processes; his generally vague feeling for socialism was assimilated with his even more inchoate feeling for Zionism. Gordin's life is a case study in adaptation.

David Gordin was born in the early 1880's in a small Russian village located in the western province of Viebesk. The youngest of four sons, he grew up in the country. *Gospodin* Gordin was a wheat-miller, a rare occupation for a Jew in Old Russia, and David ran about raising pigeons and swimming in the village creek. The Gordins were not as orthodox as most Jewish families and David's education had a decidedly secular bent. He was sent to the nearby *Gymnasium* and his father urged him to prepare for the bar. A Jewish lawyer in Czarist Russia, thought the old man, would really be an accomplishment.

The young man's contact with one of the many revolutionary study circles proved disastrous to his father's bright expectations. The little underground group pretended to be reviewing the latest developments in geological science; actually they staged fiery readings of Kropotkin, Bebel, Plekhanov, and Marx. David joined the Bund, the Jewish section of the Social-Democratic party, and when the millers' union went on strike, David heroically helped picket his father's establishment. "I can still see the old man," muses Gordin today, "standing at the window and pulling on his beard. But I could see also he was smiling at me."

But David soon found himself lodged in a none too comfortable provincial jail. The influence of his family could not prevent David's exile to Siberia, where he was sent to meditate on the revolutionary follies of youth.

David's meditation was not too prolonged; a few months of frigid solitude and he walked out of his Siberian hut. "The Bund, however," Gordin now relates, "had other plans for me. As soon as I get home they decide that I got to go back to Siberia, to Irkutsk, to contact an underground gun runner. And in the middle of winter, too." Gordin speaks of this revolutionary enterprise with great relish, but it seems somehow apocryphal. Members of his family do not recall the incident; they will shrug their shoulders and say, "If Dave says so it must be so." At any rate, the subterranean political life quickly lost its glamor; David began to dream of America. His father approved and supplied him with money for papers and passage, and David eventually found himself aboard a crawling freighter out of Hamburg.

At Castle Garden, wire caging and a babel of tongues greeted him. "So America," thought Gordin, "puts you in jail first." Yet he slept comfortably on his baggage that night, for he knew that his cousin Avremal, who had preceded him here by several years and was doing well, would call in the morning. But it was not until the next evening that Avremal at long last escorted him out of Castle Garden, explaining with much head-shaking that his boss, *a schwartz yor auf em*, had refused to give him the day off.

Avremal's Pike Street tenement flat rudely destroyed Gordin's expectations. He slept on three chairs placed side by side along the kitchen washtubs and covered with an old Russian *perene*, a kind of heavy down quilt. Early the following day Avremal dragged a still aching and protesting cousin off to work to earn his keep. "I got a job waiting for you, you ungrateful hound!" screamed Avremal, disregarding Gordin's protests that he didn't know his cousin's trade.

"Such foolishness. You'll learn, but quick." Gordin did learn and after several months his weekly pay-check reached the handsome sum of fourteen dollars.

"But such shop conditions!" Gordin now exclaims. "The boss kept the fire-escape doors closed so Satan shouldn't tempt us to get a breath fresh air. And the place was five stories up with no elevator. It's a good thing I had a strong heart. You know, it was bosses like that who made the union."

The foremen were petty tyrants and relished their power. If the workers earned too much, piece-rates were reduced. Stiff fines were imposed for minute infractions of factory rules. It was this practice that cost Gordin his first job. "I made a small damage to one of the articles and the foreman began to scream and yelp and tells me that I'm fined two dollars. So I tell him to jump into Central Park Lake. So he yells, 'You're fired!'" Gordin's friends insist that the incident was more violent than that.

His revolutionary ardor re-aroused by this incident, Gordin joined the union. But he soon learned that its leaders were not interested in his designs for a new social order. They were more concerned with strengthening their craft status in the industry and sneered at the newcomers who didn't know what constituted an American trade union. Gordin joined the socialist faction; the radicals insisted through leaflets, at meetings, and in the columns of the *Forward* that the whole trade, skilled and unskilled, had to be organized.

Sweatshop conditions, repressions, and fines created a situation which reached a boiling point in 1911. The socialist opposition finally forced the union leaders to call a mass meeting. "For almost two hours the Old Guard paraded up and down to the platform and talked about our grievances all around in circles." Suddenly one of the young militants asked for the floor. Reluctantly recognized, he hurled a Yiddish tirade at the heads of the old guard and closed with an impassioned plea for a general strike. Pandemonium broke loose and union officers grudgingly acquiesced to rank and file demands. A strike committee composed of local union representatives was formed and Gordin received his first taste of union power. His local unanimously elected him to the strike committee.

The strike dragged on for three months. One day a newspaper reporter told Gordin that the general office had called off the industry-wide strike. An agreement had been reached with the employers' association. "I almost had a heart attack," says Gordin. By two in the morning, the strike committee had prepared thousands of leaflets calling upon the workers to reject the treacherous agreement. "Boy, did I get a real charley-horse from turning the crank of the printing machine," Gordin recalls. "Because the old guard thought they could discredit the socialist faction they make a settlement. And what a settlement!" Virtually none of the workers' claims had been met. The following morning thousands of strikers gathered in front of the *Forward* building on East Broadway to shout their indignation. The strike continued until a more satisfactory agreement was reached, and at the next convention the old guard was immediately voted out of office. In his own local Gordin was elected to the important post of business agent. Thus began the rise of David Gordin.

"Getting the union organized in the trade, you know, wasn't exactly easy," Gordin informs us. "Competition was something fierce. Manufacturers cut prices and the workers got it in the end. And on top of that the worker only wanted to become a boss; a couple dollars, a couple machines, a package of letterheads printed with your name, and you were a manufacturer."

Lack of standardization and seasonal conditions added to the tragic chaos. Union membership too was seasonal. When business improved, the workers went on strike for higher wages and better conditions. The organizer would quickly print a thousand crude leaflets. "What propaganda!" Gordin recalls. "We used to write: 'Murder! The exploiters! The vampires of the working class—the manufacturers! Join the Union! Pay your Dues! Down with Capitalism!' The bosses would sign an agreement, the workers would go back to the shops and then forget to pay their dues. So we had a union without members. Then the wage cuts began all over again—every season like clockwork it was the same old circle."

Gordin's union hobbled along that way for a long time. Most of his energies were spent in urging union members to pay their back dues; special collections to prevent the padlocking of headquarters were not infrequent. Members were always apologizing; the last poker game had been unfortunate or another baby was expected next week.

Organizers, when found talking to employees, were often arrested for obstructing traffic. A worker would be seen speaking to a picket and the next day he was fired: skilled-craft workers were taken home in private cars to prevent their contamination with unionism. Labor leaders were called "crooks" and "reds." The police set up danger zones around strike-bound buildings, and any picket who dared to cross the forbidden boundary was given a free ride to the Tombs.

Employers frequently found refuge in the courts; judges sympathetic to the cause of free enterprise were not averse to granting blanket injunctions against the union. Penalties for disorderly conduct, vagrancy, and contempt were often imposed upon arrested pickets. In one instance, Gordin recalls, the presiding magistrate shouted, "You are on strike against God and Nature, whose law it is that man shall earn his bread in the sweat of his brow."

Organizing campaigns and strikes are costly affairs and Gordin has always carefully scrutinized the expense accounts of his staff. During one strike an organizer came to him with an itemized bill for $700.

"Can't you make it cheaper?" asked Gordin.

"OK, make it $600," replied the organizer.

"No, no. A little cheaper," pressed Gordin.

"All right, make it $400."

"You dog," shouted Gordin as he grabbed the man by the collar, "so you can afford $300 out of your own pocket!" Thus ended the union career of one organizer.

To Gordin a union is only as strong as its treasury. The manifold activities, including organizing, administration, research, and recreation, require large staffs. And the union must always be prepared to face severe emergencies. In its last financial statement, administration and organizing expenses totalled well over $500,000. Net assets were close to $5,000,000, with a cash surplus of about one million. "Some day and maybe sooner than we like to expect," warns Gordin, "we'll be needing a reserve like that."

Gordin's vocabulary, which used to make him sound like a footnote to the Communist Manifesto, is now quite respectable. Forty years ago he believed in uplift unionism; to him trade unions were the carriers of a socialist civilization. Now he feels that the purpose of a union is job protection within a capitalistic framework. When asked to justify the change, he will say, "When a man at twenty is not a radical he has no heart, but if at fifty he is not a little bit conservative he has no head."

Perhaps this shift toward conservatism was accelerated by the violent factionalism that flared up in the union during the twenties. Left extremists began to see unionism as a means for creating a Soviet America.

"Left-wing councils to save the union from us 'labor fakers' were set up. Soon they began to act like a union inside a union; they started collecting dues and even called strikes on their own. Boy, we had our hands full. Everything the general office and the joint board did was betrayal and a sellout. They were a real nuisance."

The general office quickly moved to ex-communicate the left-wing councils for committing the cardinal sin of unionism—the fostering of a dual organization. To isolate the rebels, one infected local was cut in half, but no sooner were the two new locals established than the hydra-headed left-wing appeared in both. Gordin fought the left opposition stubbornly, deploying his forces as skillfully as any municipal politician.

The Trade Union Educational League, the communists' union arm, called for a "united front from below" and urged the comrades to "bore from within." The general office discovered certain officials consorting secretly with Communist party representatives and promptly expelled them. Yet the left-wingers managed to filter back into the union, where they maintained a powerful but futile barrage of invective.

In 1926, the national convention witnessed the final large-scale parliamentary battle between the incumbents and the left wing. If not for the skilled-craft locals' staunch support of the general office, the radicals would have displaced the old hierarchy. The balconies in the convention hall were filled with leftist adherents, booing, hissing, and stamping. *The Daily Worker* published streams of vilification; the entrenched administration were gangsters and stool pigeons, gunmen and *agents provocateurs*.

The old leadership, much to the noisemakers' chagrin, was returned to office. The following year, however, the union was all but wrecked by a strike called and directed by several of the communist-dominated locals, set on making one more display of strength against the general office. The strike lasted for months and when it was finally settled the union had lost virtually all its gains of the previous five years. "That strike finished off the left wing," says Gordin. "The general office and the joint board checked into the way the strike committee ran the show, and out of $3 million spent on the strike they could only account for about a million and a half."

It was during this disastrous strike that the underworld first effectively penetrated the industry. Employers hired professional gunmen to waylay and assault pickets, and the frantic left-wing strike committee retaliated by employing other gangsters. But Gordin himself is not loath to make occasional use of "educational squads." In fact, his earliest introduction to industrial warfare was as a heavy-fisted "educator."

"Look!" exclaims Gordin as he emphatically waves his cigar in the direction of his auditor. "The union has been through plenty violence. Like the time some boss offered me $5,000 and a good job if I would quit the union. We were following his goods to see that they didn't go to non-union finishing places. I told this boss to go jump off the Brooklyn Bridge, and he tells me to watch out. So the next day I get caught early in the morning near the Square by a couple of guys who start beating me up. Oh, what a fight! Well, anyway I knew what that guy meant, I should watch out. But regular gangsters are different. They're leeches, they get hold of you and they don't let go. An 'educational squad' is something else; it's part of the union's defense and at least it's the union's own members."

Racketeers once tried to get a foothold in the industry by securing control of the shippers' local. Partially processed goods were often sent to finishing factories and it was that local's function to see that the products did not go to non-union shops. Although the trade still seemed busy, many metropolitan finishing establishments did not have sufficient orders to keep them alive. Gordin set about gathering evidence. He collected enough facts to prove that the officials of the local were conspiring with underworld elements and unscrupulous manufacturers to have the work sent to out-of-town non-union shops.

The joint board quietly moved in. "While we were meeting at headquarters to pass a resolution seizing the records and premises of the shippers' local we had our man ready at a phone booth near their building, and as soon as the resolution was passed we called him to go ahead. He walked up to the local's offices and slapped the resolution on the manager before he knew what hit him. Of course, they yelled 'unconstitutional' and threatened to sue in the courts, but the jig was up. They were finished and the racketeers were out—at least for awhile."

That was in the twenties; a decade later the gangsters too were organized. Racketeering became a highly specialized business that sold its services to unwilling buyers. An employer would be told that he ought to be "protected" against unionization; the employer did not dare to refuse the service. Union business agents were then asked to cooperate. To spurn the underworld hint meant blackjacks and brass knuckles.

Complete unionization provides the only certain barrier against the racketeering cancer, says Gordin. "As long as an industry is upset some chiseler will hire gangsters to try to get rid of the union. He thinks it will be cheaper for him that way. You know how we finally got rid of the racketeers? We started to organize all the shops, including all the places that bought protection. A strike was called and an 'educational committee' of about a thousand workers went into the district and we cleaned out the gangsters. The whole trade was organized and we haven't had any trouble by rackets since then. At least not too much, anyway."

Gordin's philosophy of collective bargaining is by now standard. "The individual worker is weaker than the boss. What does the worker know about market conditions? Only the union knows that." With collective bargaining, competition at the expense of the worker is eliminated and he is assured an increased share in the benefits of modern technology. "This," Gordin says, "is good for everybody, because then the workers have enough purchasing power to buy back the things they produce." The economics may be somewhat crude, but the argument is plausible.

"Unionization," Gordin continues, "means higher wages and better working conditions. I know from bitter experience. Look, in 1910 the average wage in this industry was about 23 cents an hour. By 1928, in the Great Prosperity, they went up to about 75 cents an hour. True, in the depression we had to take a little cut, but by 1934 the wage rate on the average was back to 70 cents and today it is 96 cents an hour." At this point Gordin becomes really eloquent. "The old-time rotten conditions are ended. Walk into the shops today and what do you find? Good lighting, good ventilation, enough space to move around, decent sanitation. And do you know why? Ninety percent of all the shops in the United States are organized union shops!"

Gordin is proud of his union. Some years ago he met an important industrialist at a national labor-management conference. "Tell me," asked Gordin, "how many people have you got in your organization?"

"Oh, about 12,000," politely responded the industrial captain.

"Hmmph. I got over 20,000 in my outfit," said Gordin, triumphantly.

Two decades ago the joint board offices were located in a Sixth Avenue loft and the noise of the El provided a steady obbligato to the noise inside. Gordin could seldom be found at his desk; he was too busy patrolling the market. Today he is still seldom to be found at his desk, for "there isn't enough to do here." The joint board headquarters now occupy several stories of a large midtown office building and seem, with their tellers' cages, more like a bank than a union office. And the manager's room bears a striking resemblance to that of a bank president: the large oak desk with its carafe, the leather-upholstered chairs, and the group photographs on the walls contrast sharply with the two cubicles and mimeograph machine of thirty years ago.

Gordin's office used to be cluttered with ancient and current copies of trade journals, magazines, and newspapers. He used to believe that a man's importance could be measured by the calculated disorder on his desk. In 1938, he visited Henry Wallace in Washington and observed that there were few papers on the latter's desk. Gordin's office has since been devoid of papers.

Gordin enjoys the respect that his union has so dearly won. He is now an accepted member of the community. His prestige is all the more glittering because of the contrast between his rebel's background and his present mildly progressive political opinions. But you had better not accuse him of having surrendered his socialist faith. He insists that he has merely adapted socialism to the changing tides of history.

One of the benchmarks of that adaptation is Gordin's activity in third-party politics. This is a new field and it has meant even greater prestige. Conferences, caucuses, and mass meetings have broadened his understanding of American life. But Gordin's participation in politics is only in direct proportion to the importance given to it by the general office president. He prefers Jewish philanthropic enterprises because, some cynics suggest, they provide greater opportunity for contact with people of importance. In any case, as a result of his charitable interests, Gordin's consciousness of his Jewishness has been reawakened. He now frequents Jewish restaurants, particularly the Café Royal, where he exchanges friendly banter with *Forward* writers. He is not averse to publicity.

Recently Gordin completed twenty-five years of service as joint board manager, and, as is customary, his little union coterie decided to "throw him a banquet." It was one of the most elegant affairs in the union's history. The general office president paid a glowing two-hour tribute to the guest of honor, who beamed through his cigar at the twenty-dollar-a-plate manufacturers and smilingly acknowledged the greetings of his union brethren. After a glowing peroration the president ended, "And in appreciation of Dave's great contribution to the union we present him with this thousand-dollar bond." The audience applauded heartily and the manufacturers loudly clanked knives against plates.

Gordin arose to express his thanks. He put his cigar away and said, "I'm very happy to accept this token from the boys. Both Uncle Sam and I can make good use of it. We old-timers may seem a little slow now, but we got no regrets. If we had to do it over again we would. You know, middle-rank union people like me are after all not so important like the rank-and-file and the top leadership. But maybe we've made a little contribution to the union, and to America, and maybe we have a right to be a little proud of it." David Gordin seemed just a bit tired as he sat down.

1945

Needle Trades Unionism

The gradual decline of the typical Jewish trade union from the American scene is regrettable. Here was a movement, in origin a remarkably viable blend of European and native elements, that gave to American civilization a unique union organization—an enlightened national industrial union superimposed upon a variety of craft locals. As a by-product it created a union philosophy that paid attention to the educational and welfare needs of its members, as well as to hard-headed "business." And it sought, in varying degrees of effectiveness, to infuse its economic program with political meaning.

Yet there is little prospect that the Jewish union per se will survive. Almost from their inception, Jewish unions, found mainly in the needle trades, have been dissolving by virtue of an unrelenting process of de-proletarianization. The Jewish immigrant, who in the "old country" was a small tradesman, usually became a worker "by cloaks" in the new land. If he did not revert to a small businessman's status—a grocery or candy store were favorites—then the indomitable urge to move upward on the occupational scale would most certainly be expressed by his children. It was virtually an axiom that the sons of the Jewish worker did not go into the shop. Inevitably, the proportion of Jews in the so-called Jewish trades declined: today over 60 percent of the union membership in the clothing and hat industries is no longer Jewish.

It is good then to have available this remarkably informed history of the Jewish labor movement in the United States.* Written by Melech Epstein, a Jewish journalist whose knowledge of the facts comes from a long association with leading trade union personalities, it traces with considerable detail the industrial, political, and cultural history of the Jewish labor movement from its nineteenth-century East European roots to the present. It would indeed be a pity if this movement did not have its historian: Epstein more than adequately fulfills that function, and his story is manifestly the most complete now available in English. And it is always an interesting one, for it tells of a truly heroic adaptation to adversity.

Without his trade union and political organizations, the latter mainly socialist ones, the Jewish immigrant would not have become accustomed within a generation to his new environment. The breakup of the Russian-Polish ghetto, the growth of the *Haskalah*, that exciting period of enlightenment, and the resurgence of peasant pogroms, especially in the Ukraine, sent the Jews in droves to America, the *goldene medina*. Prior to this time, most Jews in the United States had been small traders: generally peddlers, they had moved about the countryside with hand pack or horse and buggy. The mass immigration of the 1880's, however, brought in by the thousands newcomers who worked at sewing machines, flat irons, in cigar factories, or with carpenters' tools, thereby turning a traders' community into a workingman's society.

Many of the newer Jewish workers were tailors who were welcomed to waiting jobs by *landsleit* already established in the trade as bosses or foremen. The ready-to-wear clothing industry was flourishing as never before: a burgeoning prosperity gave rise

* *Jewish Labor in the U.S.A.*, 2 volumes, published by the Trade Union Sponsoring Committee.

to hundreds of unscrupulous employers who set up small shops in tenements and dank lofts; labor-management relations were governed by the law of the fang; and if the worker could not meet the production standards set by the contractor-boss, his reward was the sack and starvation.

People went to work at four in the morning; lateness brought on harsh penalties; very often the worker saved time and rent by sleeping directly on the bundles during the night. Wages, although appallingly low, were depressed still more through the notorious "task" system, wherein the rate of pay was based upon the completion of an entire garment rather than on time or finished pieces.

Such conditions were sufficient to discourage the hardiest of these East European pioneers. Yet the Jewish trade union raised the immigrant out of his earthly agony: it improved his material conditions and gave him a sense of belonging that provided the foundation for an understanding of the values of American democracy. And, in a larger sense, the unions, closely connected as they were with the socialist movement, made American politics meaningful to the newcomer. The election rallies and political campaigns, particularly those famous ones that almost sent Henry George to City Hall and actually did send Meyer London to Congress, were practical laboratories in Americanization. Democratic processes were also absorbed in such organizations as the Workmen's Circle, where meetings, conventions, and campaigns for office paralleled similar events in the unions. There is no doubt but that the Jewish labor movement, together with the Yiddish press and workers' education programs so often sponsored by the unions, was the basis for the rapid Americanization of the new immigrant.

Not the least important factor in this process were the Jewish intellectuals who felt that they had not escaped the whiplash of the Czar's Ochrana to find another hell. To them a union was an institution that gave meaning to life and they were determined to lead their people from the *Gehenem* of the sweatshop to the *Ganeiden* of the cooperative commonwealth. They sought to uplift the immigrant and worked steadily to prevent him from being used as a scapegoat and unwitting strikebreaker. They spoke Yiddish rather than German or Russian so that they might more effectively bring the message of unionism and socialism to the bewildered immigrant. This too brought them closer to the masses.

The Jewish intellectual was able to offer such leadership because he occupied a pre-eminent position among his people. The urgency to get and keep a job—to make a living—destroyed whatever class lines the ghetto had created and in the tumult of the new world the Jew turned for guidance to his men of learning. It was an opportunity that the intellectual fulfilled brilliantly.

However, the Jewish labor movement in this country did not pursue the same pattern set by native unions. Generally, national labor bodies were preceded by the establishment of local craft unions and city or regional central organizations. Jewish unions developed in reverse fashion. Jewish workers were known for their enthusiastic response when it came to a strike, but as soon as a settlement was attained they returned to a condition of singular apathy. Walking delegates spent most of their time urging union members to pay back dues while special collections to raise rent for union headquarters were not infrequent.

The Jewish intellectual, to whom unionism meant the Good Society, was not easily discouraged, but he soon became aware that for his skeptical brethren the movement would have to be built from the top down. The growth of specifically Jewish unions was also facilitated by the prevailing xenophobias which blamed the problems of the exploited on the victims themselves. An anti-immigration campaign began to sprout and was supported by such curious bedfellows as Terence Powderly, Samuel Gompers, and the D.A.R. The Jewish immigrant was singled out as a special scapegoat: he was accused of spreading the sweatshop system, being insanitary, undercutting wages, and creating a flow of cheap labor that threatened American standards. The answer to these canards was given by the Jewish *intelligentsia:* it was to foster a trade union movement that could with dignity take a rightful place in the cohort of American trade unions.

An early creation of the Jewish intellectual was the Jewish Workers' *Verein*, established in 1885. It became, as Epstein says, a focal point for the steadily rising assertiveness of the Jewish worker. It organized trade unions, cooperated in politics with the Socialist Labor party, and worked closely with German *Geverkshaften* groups. But above all, it stressed Americanization: its slogan "Become citizens!" kept urging the Jewish worker to commit himself irrevocably to his new environment. The United Hebrew Trades was also an influential body. Modeled after the national foreign language labor federations, it took as its main purpose the founding of Jewish trade unions. Beginning with compositors, actors, and singers, it expanded rapidly and in four years had twenty-eight unions affiliated with it.

Ideological motivation was of course a major inspiration in unionization. Most Jewish labor leaders at that time were fervent socialists who conceived of a trade union as ancillary to political activity. Jewish socialists had supported Henry George in his ill-starred attempt to capture the mayoralty in 1886 and during this period they also successfully fought off anarchist influence in the unions. In 1887, a number of them formed the Jewish branch of the Socialist Labor party—the famous Branch 8. This became the instrument for drawing Jewish labor into American politics. Meetings and discussions on political and nonpolitical subjects were frequent (cultural topics were always important to socialists).

It was not too long before the Socialist Labor party went into one of its tiresome splits. This time it was a question of political action and trade union tactics. The New York membership favored working within the existing union structure, while their opponents advocated a kind of revolutionary dual unionism. Participation in local elections was also favored by the New York group and in the next local election a slate of Socialists had not yet learned to counteract the vote-buying propensities of Tammany Hall.

Political socialism in America was deeply affected by the advent of Daniel De Leon, who within a year after joining the Socialist Labor party in 1890 became its most outstanding personality. Intelligent, ruthless, gifted with a sharp tongue, he was the epitome of the rigid doctrinaire. His first objective was to capture the trade union movement. Rebuffed by the Knights of Labor, he formed the Socialist Trades and Labor Alliance. This, however, frightened a number of Jewish socialists, for it seemed a harbinger of bloody internecine warfare. Within a year most of the major figures in the SLP left to join with Eugene Debs and Victor Berger in forming the Socialist party.

Jewish socialists were unable to escape all the quarrels and splits. If, as Melech Epstein says, political differences were less marked than in the rest of the labor movement, the personality clashes were more trying. In addition, an ideological adjustment was taking place, for the Jewish radical, though a sharp critic of the economic order, began to stress his faith in democracy.

The Social Revolution was becoming a kind of hopeful prayer which started the day's work but did not really affect the course of historical events. Many of the young intellectuals eagerly seized the educational opportunities that were available in the new land and transformed themselves into doctors or lawyers. It was this unwillingness to make the revolution a permanent career that characterized the Jewish socialist. His socialism was more rooted in Biblical morality than in sociological or political doctrine: the cooperative commonwealth had a chiliastic flavor that transcended questions of factions or party loyalty.

The great crisis in the Jewish labor movement came over the matter of the party press. The older men in Branch 8, loyal to De Leon, controlled the *Arbeiter Zeitung* and the *Abendblatt,* but Abraham Cahan and Louis Miller pressed the fight for what they thought to be a broader representation. Despite attempts to reconcile the De Leon and Cahan forces, the irrevocable split came in 1897 leading to the establishment of the *Jewish Daily Forward.* Cahan became the editor, a position he held (except for four years) until he died in 1951.

During this long incumbency Cahan made the paper a powerful influence in the Jewish labor movement. He conceived the *Forward* as a source of popular socialist information that would command the confidence of its readers. This was a task it unfailingly met. Suffering in its early years a precarious financial existence, it was able within a decade to raise its circulation to well over 70,000. The building in which the newspaper was housed, with its huge electric sign visible from Manhattan Bridge, became the headquarters of expanding activities: one could find there the Workmen's Circle, the United Hebrew Trades, labor union locals, and numerous cultural societies.

Cahan's major contribution to the *Forward*, and perhaps to Jewish culture in America, was his insistence on an easily comprehended Yiddish. Journalistic style in the Yiddish press was then a complex imitation of the involved grammar peculiar to German. Cahan reviewed books and plays in his paper. Virtually every device of modern journalism was employed to make the reader receptive. The *Bint'l Brief* department, a letter-to-the-editor column in which advice on personal matters was solicited, gave readers a close-up of exciting human situations. Modern literature too was brought to the immigrant through endless serializations.

Complementing the trade unions and the Socialist Labor party branches was the Workmen's Circle—the Arbeiter Ring, a fraternal organization whose creation by the rank and file cloakmakers was an expression of a felt need for mutual aid and self-education. Launched in 1892, and finally awarded a charter in 1905 after altering some of its methods to conform with legal requirements, it reached a membership of 50,000 by 1915. Concerned always with matters of health, the Workmen's Circle became known as the "Red Cross" of Jewish labor. It had its problems regarding dues rates and assessments and it was not immune from the usual schismatic conflicts. A so-called "young" group, consisting of Bundists and Labor Zionists, wanted it to adopt a broad educational program with Yiddish schools for children, workers' choruses, and publication ventures. The "olds," a name that referred to organizational rather than chronological age, insisted on maintaining the fraternal character of the Workmen's Circle. The dispute went on for eight years, and when peace was finally achieved in 1917, the "youngs" had won their point but the "olds" kept their control.

Thus, as the Jewish labor movement passed the turn of the century, it began to exhibit a maturity and responsibility that would become a major source of strength in the coming decades. Meyer London successfully challenged Tammany Hall in its own territory. The unions, especially those in the needle trades, undertook arduous organizing campaigns and led strikes bordering on the violent. Labor Zionists and Territorialists began to inject new viewpoints into the ideological maelstrom. This upsurge inspired an outburst of Yiddish literary activity that has not yet been matched in the Jewish community in America. Poets, novelists, and playwrights found an avid audience in the Jewish labor movement.

Such an outpouring of creative writing was no mere transfer from the old country; nurtured in a strange soil, Yiddish literature, particularly poetry, became a means of sustaining the struggles of an apparently helpless folk. Arousing a sense of self-pity, the poets—Edelstadt, Bovshover, Rosenfeld—wrote lyric verse that could be sung as mournful obbligatos to whirring machines. Their output appeared in such journals as the *Freie Arbeiter Stimme, Abendblatt* and the *Forward,* making these papers combinations of literary magazines and people's colleges. Above all, they brought the face of America to the new Jewish ghettos, a face that was as often harsh as it was kindly.

The immigrant's confusion was compounded by the growing barrier between himself and his children. Part of this was of the Jewish parent's own making, for no sacrifice was too great to send his children to high school and college. White-collar work, especially a profession, was the ultimate aim; on no account must a child be allowed to enter the shop. Thus, there was bound to occur a spiritual rift between orthodox parents and radical children, between immigrant fathers and native sons, between trade union elders and a more conservative new generation. This alienation frequently extended to all things Jewish. It was a problem that affected the entire Jewish community as well as its labor sector.

Meanwhile, the trade unions were fighting bitter battles in an effort to strengthen themselves. The ready-to-wear clothing industry was reaching considerable size and importance, but one in which working conditions were thoroughly exasperating. Strikes were led by United Garment Workers' Union locals despite the frowns of T. A. Rickert, UGW president; the latter was more interested in selling the union label to overall manufacturers than in improving working conditions. In 1907, the Boston cloak-makers struck for a fifty-four-hour week and union recognition, and in the same year the reefermakers, or children's coat workers, succeeded in obtaining a fifty-five-hour week, union recognition, abolition of inside subcontracting among pressers, and a free supply of all working tools. Unfortunately, these gains were soon drowned in the flood tide of unemployment that rose steadily with the 1907 depression.

By 1909, the demoralization that hit the Jewish trade unions began to recede. The first to recover from the economic crisis were the shirtwaist makers, a relatively new branch of the needle trades. The workers were in the main idealistic and energetic young women, unafraid of withstanding the combined onslaught of boss and police. At a meeting held in Cooper Union in November 1909, which had been called to consider general conditions in the trade, the young women responded with such impassioned enthusiasm to an almost hysterical speech by one of their number that they immediately voted a general strike. Public response was generous beyond fondest expectations: the Women's Trade Union League and various other citizens' groups came to the aid of the strikers. Within two months the workers had won a fifty-two-hour week, four paid holidays, and improved conditions. This was the action that came to be known as the "Uprising of the Twenty Thousand."

Soon after this incident came the famous "Great Revolt." Led by the New York cloakmakers, it was carefully prepared and enjoyed the complete support of the UHT, Workmen's Circle, and the *Forward*. Its impact was so great that it halted the entire cloak, suit, skirt, raincoat, and ladies' garment industries. The conflict with the employers' association was a harsh one and it was only after several prominent Jewish community leaders intervened that the employers sat down to the bargaining table. The strikers wanted union recognition; the bosses refused and negotiations were broken off. Louis Marshall and Jacob Schiff again intervened and finally the "preferential" union shop—an invention of Louis Brandeis—was accepted.

Brandeis, who had come into the picture as attorney for A. Lincoln Filene, the Boston merchant, was also responsible for the name given to the settlement that followed—the "Protocol of Peace." He conceived of the arrangement as a social innovation that ". . . would lift industrial relations out of the jungle to a civilized plane and pave the way to lasting unity and harmony." While the Protocol was short lived and failed in the long run to bring peace to the needle trades, it did establish a model for industrial relations. It set up a board of grievances consisting of worker-management representatives to hear complaints in the first instance: beyond that, there was a higher board of arbitration in which impartial public representatives had the final say. Although the grievance board was supposed to be the major instrument, in actuality it was the arbitration board that did most of the adjudicative work.

The fact that worker and employer, both sensitive to public opinion, came out of the same East European environment, speaking a common language, explains the initial success of the Protocol. There was in the old country an ancient tradition of arbitration; disputes were settled within the Jewish community itself rather than by the courts of the "goyim." But this was only an apparent victory, for the majority of the employers were not yet ready to surrender the privileges of cutthroat competition. In addition, the young radical labor leader looked upon the agreement as a temporary lull in the unceasing battle of capital and labor. The workers soon began to complain of illegal discharges and refusals to pay for overtime; subcontracting, which had not been covered by the Protocol, began to spread; but above all, the workers did not feel that the Brandeis preferential shop gave them the job security for which they were ever struggling.

The six-year history of the Protocol was a stormy one. The agreement provided for an administrative officer known as the "Chief Clerk," a post demanding the most skillful balancing of employer and worker pressures. It was not long before a violent storm, called the "Hourwich Affair" after the then incumbent chief clerk, was raised over arbitration procedures. The only calm person in this tempest was Abraham Cahan, the *Forward* editor, who at the time coined his classic phrase, *es vet sich alles auspressen*—it will all iron itself out.

While the ladies' garment workers were going through their first large-scale experiment in industrial relations, the men's clothing workers were attempting to establish a union that would really look after their interests. The leadership of the United Garment Workers not only avoided clashes with employers but made no effort to understand the needs of the new union members. The spirited young radical tailors were not too far wrong in their suspicions that Rickert and his conservative fellow officers did not really care for the large influx of immigrant workers.

The first clash between the old guard UGW leadership and the new rank and file came in the Chicago tailors' strike of 1910. A wage cut in the Hart, Schaffner and Marx plant precipitated a wildcat strike movement throughout the industry. Rickert quietly attempted a settlement providing for an open shop, but his action was repudiated by the strikers. Finally, early the next year, an agreement was achieved which included arbitration procedures. The New York market was struck in 1912 and again the UGW leadership demonstrated its incompetence. The conflict between the newer union elements, led by Sidney Hillman and Joseph Schlossberg, and the Rickert forces was now an open one.

The UGW convention in 1914 became the scene of the big battle. Rickert charged that the New York locals had failed to pay the proper per capita dues and used this as a ruse to unseat his opponents. The barred delegates then convened themselves as the "official" UGW. By the end of the year, a special meeting was called to convert the insurgent union into the Amalgamated Clothing Workers of America with Sidney Hillman as president.

The ACWA, although at once attacked as a dual union by Samuel Gompers, head of the AFL, immediately won the loyalty not only of its members but of all the other Jewish unions as well. This sympathetic attitude helped the ACWA break through the *cordon sanitaire* which the employers attempted to build around it. Despite the formality of not admitting ACWA locals, the UHT recognized them as *bona fide* unions. Nonrecognition was the only way in which Gompers could be kept officially happy. However, so far as the Jewish trade unionists were concerned, this was legalistic subterfuge that meant little.

The new union was met by a series of lockouts intended to cripple it. Employer hostility, which was virtually universal, lasted until the United States entered World War I. As was often the case, Chicago was the scene of the bloodiest fights. The 1915 strike degenerated into a conflict between two Chicagos: the employers and police on one side and the ACWA and, interestingly enough, the Chicago Federation of Labor on the other. After three months of violence the strike had to be called off. Nevertheless, the experience gained in these early conflicts was to stand Hillman and his union in good stead.

World War I was a period of troubled soul-searching for the Jewish labor movement. Jews had sufficient reason to welome the destruction of Czarism and even their warm feelings for Great Britain could not change this sentiment about England's ally. In addition, the socialists, to whom the Jewish labor leaders were closest in political outlook, were largely noninterventionist and pacifist. But once the United States had entered the war, there was a marked reversal of feeling. By the middle of 1918, Jewish trade unionists and socialists were openly supporting the war effort, spurred by an abhorrence of Germany's putative imperialism.

On the other hand, Jewish labor's early sympathy for the new regime in Russia was soon dissipated by the excesses of the Lenin-Trotsky government. Most of the Jewish trade unionists had been active in the Bund, Poale Zion, or Territorialists, groups that were anathema to the Bolsheviks. The Soviets proceeded to outlaw these Jewish organizations because they did not lend themselves to communist coordination, and many of the so-called dissidents were dispatched to Siberia. Much of the feeling engenderd by these events was to become a significant backdrop for the later history of the Jewish trade union movement.

In this country, an open-shop offensive, called the American Plan, was instituted in most industries immediately after the war. It was, of course, a naked drive to smash all trade unions. The clothing workers were not exempt from this scheme, and a number of employer attacks on the ILGWU and ACWA ensued. In 1921, the latter was locked out in New York in a struggle that took six months and cost the union $2 million. A brief postwar depression exacerbated the situation. While these adverse conditions affected all organized labor, for the Jewish trade unions the course of events was made doubly troublesome by the advent of the communists.

Melech Epstein's recital of the communists' attempt to capture the unions during the twenties and thirties is the most thorough-going account of this trying period to be found in labor literature. He demonstrates that the socialist movement always had its impatient and romantic radicals who had to be restrained by more realistic moderates. The war experience and the Russian Revolution, however, meant the end of any organizational cooperation between these disparate groups. By 1919, the left wing in the Socialist party began to coalesce, and in the latter part of that year it split away from the SP to form one of the mushrooming communist "parties." In 1921, Moscow ordered the CP and the United Communist party to cease their incessant and often ludicrous name-calling and to merge. With the enforcement of this shotgun wedding, the Kremlin could now turn its attention to the more serious business of winning control of the American labor movement.

The major instrument for this was William Z. Foster's Trade Union Educational League. Foster, a former Wobbly and syndicalist, had set up the TUEL in 1915 as a private mechanism to further industrial unionism. After a visit to Moscow in 1921, he returned a top communist bigwig with instructions to utilize the TUEL as a means for winning key posts in the AFL.

The communists made a special effort to seize control of the needle trade unions; at that time this meant the Jewish unions. It was a carefully planned attempt, and it almost succeeded. The communists were finally defeated, but only after a harsh, bitter, and long struggle that left the unions shaken and virtually bereft of members. The battle within a particular union would invariably begin with the appearance of a left-wing rank-and-file organization. Attached to this there was often an independent centrist group, actually under the control of the communists. Within these factions there would be a TUEL group, consisting of CP members and their followers; then, inside this "educational center" there could be found the party "fraction" or cell which took its direction from the party leaders.

The ensuing civil war in Jewish labor was fought mainly in the ILGWU. Economic conditions in the trade had created hardships for the workers and many of them responded sympathetically to the blandishments of the CP infiltrees. By 1921, the TUEL had established roots in the New York, Philadelphia, and Chicago locals. In 1923, the TUEL secured its first important victory, capturing the executive board of Local 22, the dressmakers. Morris Sigman, ILGWU president, a burly, resolute, and often heavy-handed ex-presser, banned the TUEL as a dual union. The left-wingers were removed from office and at the 1924 convention the General Executive Board of the union forbade its officers to belong to any outside body which sought to interfere in union matters. Clearly aimed at the TUEL, this directive made the left-wingers howl in anguish.

In the midst of this conflict, Sigman attempted to modernize the union's structure. Technological changes had brought about jurisdictional disputes between locals which Sigman sought to correct by merging some of them. An incidental by-product was to squeeze out a few TUEL adherents. This did not deter the left wing, and in 1924 they secured a majority of the executive boards of the three largest locals in the ILGWU. There followed a TUEL victory meeting offering the standard speeches of the communists, who were now brazen enough to call for a Soviet America! This infuriated Sigman and he brought charges against the TUEL'ers for violation of the ILGWU constitution. The ousted CP dominated officials struck back by forming the Joint Action Committee, a virtually independent union which collected dues, issued work cards, and controlled shops. There was no doubt but that the JAC had a strong following.

A temporary peace was patched up and at the next convention in Philadelphia the left wing, defeated by the administration machine, staged a walk-out which, had it been permanent, would have then and there destroyed the ILGWU. The Communist party, however, was not ready to shift its political line; splitting was not yet on its agenda and the union "fraction" was ordered to return to the convention hall.

This struggle for control of the union was a prelude to the violent communist-led cloak industry strike in 1926. As it turned out, this was also the end of the communists in the ILGWU. A tense situation had been developing for some time and efforts were being made to avoid an industrial clash through a special Governor's Advisory Commission set up to study conditions. The commission sided with the union in the latter's efforts to control the jobbers, but it resisted demands for more effective control over the "inside" shop. The left-wing leadership of the New York Joint Board saw no alternative but to strike.

The response to the strike call was complete. Both the left and the right worked together, although the former controlled all of the leading committees, even rejecting Sigman as strike chairman, an unusual procedure. As Melech Epstein points out, the communists might have captured the entire ILGWU had they settled within a reasonable time. But the CP trade union "cadres" reckoned without the party, in which a bloody factional dispute was beginning to shape up. The party bigwigs could not now accept a settlement, for they were determined to out-Bolshevik the Bolsheviks: the conflict was ordered to continue.

Finally, with its burden becoming heavier and with a sense of demoralization beginning to affect the workers, the General Executive Board took over and liquidated the strike. By January 1927, agreements were reached with the employers' association: the struggle had lasted six months and cost over $3 million. Even the employers' security money, almost $800,000, had disappeared. That there had been mismanagement, waste, and possibly corruption was evident, despite the heated denials of the leftists.

Calling for a re-registration of all workers, Sigman ejected leftist officials in New York, Chicago, Boston, and Philadelphia. The communists urged the workers to refuse to enter the "Sigman" union, but most of them went back to the ILGWU. The employers decided that they would do business only with the latter and this too was a blow to the left. Nor could the embattled communists offer a substitute union, for Moscow's line had not yet changed. However, in 1929, a Kremlin *ukase* converted the

TUEL into the Trade Union Unity League, which, contrary to its name, inaugurated a period of dual unionism. The Needle Trades Workers' Industrial Union was launched in 1930, but aside from the furriers it had no real following. The ILGWU had been badly shaken by the 1926 strike: its treasury had been depleted, the membership dispersed. But the most serious problem was the loss of control over conditions and work relations in the trade. And perhaps the most disheartening aspects of the entire episode were the later revelations that the Communist party had utilized the strike as a football between internal factions.

The ILGWU was not the only union afflicted with the communist curse. The conflict among the furriers was just as fierce, but unfortunately the outcome was different. There the left-wing movement was also started in the early twenties, and by 1925 the communists and their friends were able to win enough posts to control the union effectively. In the following year the leftists conducted a general strike in New York, notable for its use of goons and gunmen. Immediately after the strike the AFL replaced the communist-dominated joint board, calling for reregistration. But unlike the ILGWU workers, most of the furriers supported their radical leaders. With this backing the communists were able to withstand repeated attacks on their position.

The victory of the communists in the fur trade might be ascribed not only to the smaller size and compactness of the industry, making control of the market easier, but also to the aggressiveness and ruthlessness of the communist leaders, Ben Gold and Aaron Gross. Gold, an effective speaker, was always able to display in the loudest possible fashion his vast store of hysterical energy. Personally harsh and even cruel to his enemies, he tolerated no opposition. Gross, on the other hand, worked quietly behind the scenes designing the strategy of the left. When the latter was compelled to leave the union for health reasons, the CP sent in Irving Potash, who, as Melech Epstein puts it, soon became a Sancho Panza to Gold's violent Don.

Gold became a top communist potentate: during the depression he was sent to the Lenin School in Moscow, a major Comintern training ground. He returned to this country adept in political maneuvering, and by 1937 he was able to take over the AFL's International Fur Workers' Union. An apt pupil of Stalin, he publicly fumed about the iniquities of capitalism, while privately he spoke gently to the fur manufacturers to place his own henchmen in strategic spots in the trade. Any union member who protested Gold's policies was immediately driven not only out of the union but out of the fur industry itself. This was the full picture of communist victory in the trade union movement.

Leftist strength in the Amalgamated Clothing Workers did not match that among the ladies' garment workers or in the fur union, nor was the struggle there as severe. One mitigating element was the fact that cities such as Chicago and Rochester were just as important industry centers as New York. Furthermore, Sidney Hillman was not averse to playing footsie with the communists if it suited his purposes. After World War I, the nascent communist parties had advocated industrial unionism. This attracted Hillman, for it implied an assault on his arch opponent, the AFL. Also, Hillman held aloof from the *Forward* and SP circles, preferring to associate with churchmen and liberal reformers. This created a certain amount of visible tension between the ACWA leader and Abraham Cahan, whose conception of sound Jewish trade unionism was in large measure conditioned by affairs on East Broadway.

Impressed by what the Russians were trying to do, Hillman helped set up an organization for developing clothing factories for the Soviets. But a falling out between the communists and the Amalgamated could not be postponed for long. In 1924, Hillman refused to support Foster in the presidential campaign, preferring Robert La Follette; by the end of the year the communist papers were leveling their broadsides of invective at the ACWA. But the communists could not make much headway. They had no adequate leadership and were no real match for Hillman and Schlossberg. The left wing again created a Joint Action Committee which was at once outlawed by the union administration. Hillman also possessed in Abraham Beckerman, manager of the cutters' local, an able lieutenant whose conception of union education was based upon an effective wielding of brass knuckles. Hailed by the *Forward* for his elimination of the communists, Beckerman was later to be involved in one of the most sordid episodes in union history.

The labor movement in the United States had frequently been plagued by racketeer infestation. In this respect, the needle trades unions were no exception. Employers had always utilized hoodlums to intimidate strikers, and Jewish garment manufacturers were not unwilling to pursue a similar pattern. In fact, violent strike-breaking prior to the late 1930's was a commonly accepted mode of industrial relations. For self-preservation, the unions countered with their own strong-arm men. As might be expected, some of these young toughs preferred the dangerous life and graduated into the ranks of those gangsters who specialized in selling "protection." Union officers were advised not to approach a so called protected concern: on the other hand, such a firm might be easily double-crossed if the union offered a higher fee.

One of the leading peddlers of protection in the twenties was L'il Augie Orgen, who numbered in his gang of slug-artists Lepke Buchalter and Gurrah Jacob Shapiro. The mobs were constantly carrying on internecine warfare. Gurrah killed Orgen and with his partner Lepke began to move in on both industry and union. Since the ACWA itself was much too large to capture, Lepke reasoned that the cutter and trucker would be sufficient to give him the leverage he needed. The cutters' local had about 1,800 members, and the truckers less than 100. Thus, with control of about 2,000 workers, he could dominate as many as 50,000.

Lepke and Gurrah, who were now part of the notorious Murder, Inc., syndicate, simply moved in on the cutters by making themselves the local's staff musclemen. At the same time, one of their henchmen, Philip Orlofsky, was made manager of the local and he proceeded at Lepke's direct instigation to challenge the ACWA head office. The shrewd racketeer then reached right into Hillman's office by putting pressure on the Amalgamated's chief organizer. The threats were so direct that during one strike it was reported $25,000 passed from the ACWA national office to Lepke.

The New York Joint Board of the Amalgamated also had its racketeer connections. Abraham Beckerman, who had done yeoman work against the communists, was an easy prey for Lepke. When Hillman decided that it was time to move in on Orlofsky in the cutters' local, Beckerman opposed the action. But a surprise descent was made with police protection, the records of the local seized, and the gangsters' henchmen removed. Several months later Beckerman himself was thrown out of the ACWA.

Management too was squeezed by Lepke and Company. Threatening strikes or sabotage, the racketeers extorted anywhere from $5,000 to $50,000 from manufacturers solely for the privilege of conducting an ordinary business. It was later revealed that the garment trucking firms alone gave Lepke $1 million a year for ten years. Often the gangsters would take a large partnership share or even an entire firm. Subsidiary companies were formed to mask the actual illicit control. While Lepke was evading the FBI and the police in the late thirties, he received large sums each week from clothing firms into which he had forced himself.

Soon the stench of racketeering became unbearable. With the election of Fiorello H. La Guardia as Mayor of New York and the appointment of Thomas E. Dewey as special prosecutor, the drive on the racketeers began. The details of this story need not be specified here, but it can be said that today the clothing industry is an example of good labor-management relations.

With the elimination of both racketeer and communist, the needle trades unions were able to pay attention to basic business. The depression had brought about the resurgence of sweatshop conditions; longer hours were becoming common, piecework once again was the chief method of wage payment and responsibility for shop conditions was being left entirely in the rapacious hands of the contractor. The unions started to hit at this situation: the Philadelphia dress strike in 1933 was particularly successful. At that time the New Deal with its NRA and Section 7 offered all unions a brilliant organizational opportunity. The Jewish ones, especially the ILGWU and the ACWA, seized their chance with great avidity. With careful planning and swift action, the ILGWU within a year increased its membership to almost a quarter of a million. The cloak and silk dress trades were fully organized and the work week reduced to thirty-five hours. The more depressed branches of the needle trades, such as undergarments, children's dresses, and knitwear, were organized more effectively with substantial improvement in work conditions. The Amalgamated too began to rebuild itself, moving into the shirt and laundry industries.

It is interesting to note that when the NRA was declared unconstitutional by the Supreme Court in 1935, one of the few industries in which labor gains were maintained was the needle trades, particularly in those divisions organized by the ILGWU, ACWA, and the hatworkers' union. Not only were standards and membership held at previous levels but it was even possible to continue many of the activities of the NRA codes through voluntary employer-union bodies.

There is no need here to review the rise of the CIO in the mass-production industries: the story has been fully told elsewhere. But it is germane to observe that this development did split the American labor movement and, in a sense, the Jewish unions as well. Industrial unionism had always been an issue in organized labor, and when the question was raised at the 1935 AFL convention, both Sidney Hillman and David Dubinsky were among its strongest advocates. But the latter had grave doubts that splitting the union movement was worthwhile, and together with Max Zaritsky of the Hatworkers he never ceased to urge peace between the AFL and CIO factions. When it became clear in 1938 that John L. Lewis intended making the CIO a permanent body, Dubinsky and the ILGWU stepped out: they later returned to the AFL, Hillman remaining with the industrial union group.

During the Roosevelt era, the Jewish unions went in for politics in a way that represented for them a remarkable break with tradition. It was evident in the early New Deal days that trade unionists were the staunchest of Roosevelt supporters. In 1936, the CIO formed Labor's Non-Partisan League, an organization whose purpose clearly was to re-elect FDR. After the overwhelming defeat of the Republicans, some New Dealers began to experience recurrent visions of a third party modeled on the British pattern. The garment workers' union did a fantastic amount of work for the LNPL, particularly in the American Labor party, which had been set up as the New York branch of the League. Again and again, the ALP, with the needle trades unions as its backbone, demonstrated its effectiveness as a political force. But unfortunately this strength was not destined to last: the communists decided to make the ALP their own.

Putting forth a united front, the communists found the ALP made to order for an infiltration campaign. By 1938, they were firmly entrenched in many local ALP clubs, where friction with non-communists was inevitable. The following year, when the United Front expired in the Hitler-Stalin embrace, the American CP shouted that Roosevelt was an imperialist and Dubinsky a fascist. The irritation between communist and liberal was exacerbated. In 1941, the communists again demonstrated their characteristic agility: Germany had attacked Russia; now Roosevelt was an angel and Dubinsky a loving brother. Peaceful relations in the ALP, however, were no longer possible, and in 1944 the *bona fide* trade unionists and liberals let the communists hold on to the ALP and formed as its successor the Liberal party.

Such political activity was something new for Jewish trade unionists. For years, workers had been exhorted to vote only the socialist ticket, for the two capitalist parties were portrayed as but twin versions of the same corrupt gang. Now, Jewish workers were being advised to accept a capitalist candidate as their champion. The amazing thing is that the workers responded with enthusiasm, demonstrating that socialism as a political faith had vanished. What remained was the moral drive that made the socialist creed so attractive to the Jewish immigrant: it also brought the values of the kind of collective effort embodied in trade unionism. The political milieu under Roosevelt permitted the one-time immigrant to play a direct role in economic change. This was very much to his liking, for the Jewish trade unionist, concerned as he was with the practical present, did not exhibit much need for a utopian future. This was true not only of the Jewish unionists, but of the Jewish press, the fraternal bodies, and of the socialist organizations themselves.

Jewish labor did not avoid nonpolitical and noneconomic activities. After World War I, Jewish labor groups participated in the founding of the Joint Distribution Committee. With the rise of Hitler in Germany, the desperate situation of European Jews was highlighted. In 1934, a group of Jewish unions formed the Jewish Labor Committee, whose job it was to gather support for labor victims of the Nazi terror. It helped organize a boycott of German goods and called attention to the dire condition of Jews in Poland. Rescue work was also an important part of JLC activity. Today, JLC, more concerned with the role of Jewish workers in communal affairs, has developed a program of anti-discrimination activity.

It was through instrumentalities such as these that the Jewish labor movement came closer to the total Jewish community. In large centers such as New York or Chicago it was possible to say that Jewish labor and the Jewish community largely overlapped. In the smaller communities, however, where the synagogue remained the center of Jewish life, the secularist outlook of the trade unionist generated a certain amount of hostility. Also, the tendency of the Jewish workers to build their own institutional life served to create additional barriers. But under the impact of depression, war, and rising anti-Semitism, these impediments began to disappear. The creation too of the State of Israel, which became the last good hope for the remnants of European Jewry, helped bring together once implacable ideological opponents.

Murmurings can occasionally be heard among Jewish needle trades workers that they created unions for others. Measured by changes in relative numbers, this is true: Jews are no longer predominant in these organizations. Second- and third-generation Jews have a wider choice of occupation and, discouraged by their parents, they do not enter the trades their fathers followed. Also, technological improvements have affected what the sociologist calls the shifting composition of the labor force: new fabrics, new machinery, new methods of production have impelled a migration of factories away from the large urban centers into the hills of Pennsylvania and Maryland and even further south. There, old native stocks, once accustomed to cultivating a worn-out soil, have been happy to earn a cash wage as workers in the shop.

But where has the Jewish worker gone? Not all Jews are candy store owners or toy manufacturers. Available information seems to indicate that American-born Jewish workers are now in the wholesale and retail trades, electrical appliances and radio, and, primarily, in white-collar jobs: office workers, technicians, government, and the professions. In the larger cities, especially, where a large part of the Jewish labor force is not self-employed, there is a greater occupational dispersion. The result is that the onetime Jewish trade union, in the sense that these bodies had a predominance of Jewish members and exhibited characteristic Jewish institutions, no longer exists.

The leadership of these unions, however, continues to be Jewish. Interestingly enough, the Jewish trade unionist, who was once an ardent secularist, now exhibits a warm identification with things Jewish. In his youth a radical internationalist, opposed to religious trappings as inimical to human welfare and thoroughly hostile to such movements as Zionism, the Jewish labor leader has today altered many of these once fervently held beliefs. He will now often acknowledge that Jewishness possesses certain values of its own and he will find specific Jewish interests in political and social movements which might go beyond the limits of a pure labor outlook. But Jewish union leaders have never utilized their organizations as a kind of ethnic pressure group. The influence they exerted was general rather than one based on special pleading: it was derived in large measure from their remarkable position *qua* labor leaders. Any other approach would have failed and would in the first instance have been rejected as irresponsible.

It is frequently argued that the Jewish labor movement is virtually nonexistent. But so long as there is a perceptible Jewish influence in labor circles, in the sense that there are Jewish leaders and Jewish organizations that act as advocates of Jewish interests in unions, there may be said to exist a specifically Jewish focus in the labor movement.

1953

Organized Labor and Education

Why do unions complain so much about the manner in which economics is taught in our schools? The primary reason is that the standard economics courses offer a highly biased view of the labor movement. Labor's dissatisfaction is also aroused by the fact that high school graduates entering the ranks of unions have little or no understanding of the function of organized labor in our complex society. Even a cursory review of the current state of economic education occasions considerable dismay.

Labor's interest in education is of long standing. As far back as the 1830's, labor organizations campaigned for the immediate expansion of educational facilities. A free, tax-supported school system existed at that time only in certain regions of New England. The agitation of organized labor for equal educational opportunities spearheaded the drive for the kind of school system which later developed in this country.

As John R. Commons reported in his monumental history

of labor: "Wherever the working men organized . . . public education was their first and foremost demand." Invariably the cry was for "republican education"—a phrase that bore a different connotation in the pre–Civil War days—an education that would strengthen democratic institutions and a democratic society.

Trade unions have always considered themselves an integral part of the democratic society, not merely an appendage which enjoys certain rights on sufferance. But, regrettably, economic education today barely recognizes the legitimate role of labor unions in a free society. At best, unions are regarded as barnacles attached to the underside of a free-wheeling competitive society. At worst, they are a cancerous growth to be removed from the body politic.

Is the description exaggerated? Let us consider one example of "good economics teaching" described in a recent study of the Kazanjian Foundation, published by the Joint Council on Economic Education. In a class consisting predominantly of Negroes and Puerto Ricans, virtually all of whom would undoubtedly have some contact with trade unions during their working lives, the students were encouraged to believe that labor unions throw "monkey wrenches" into the "wheels of prosperity."

The teacher proudly reported that his class discussed how the growing insistence of unions on a bigger slice of the income pie impeded the "plowing back of profits." Further, the students were taught that union funds "are not derived mostly from union dues, but come in large measure from company income channeled in by way of employer 'contributions' as required by contracts with the unions." Is it surprising, then, that unions consider that economics courses in many schools impart highly biased information?

Unfortunately, such erroneous teaching is difficult to counteract. Professor Robert Doherty of Cornell University, who recently surveyed a cross-section of high school economics courses, suggests that the situation described above is the rule rather than the exception. The textbooks either say nothing about the workers and their organizations or are woefully incomplete.

Authors of texts appear excessively cautious or display simple-minded notions about unions and their problems. Labor is depicted in most texts as a disturber of the peace, concerned primarily with promoting violence and strikes. Seldom if ever is it pointed out that time lost due to strikes constitutes less than one-tenth of 1 percent of all working time, or that industrial conflicts are usually resolved by peaceful collective bargaining. Professor Doherty further mentions that a great many teachers derive most of their information from the daily press, which is without doubt the poorest source for factual economic information.

The influx of special-interest materials flowing from chambers of commerce and trade associations only aggravates the situation. I have before me one such propaganda tract sponsored by a group of utilities—companies that have flooded the classrooms with all sorts of booklets and pamphlets. Heading the list of topics in this tract is something called the "free-enterprise system." As Professor Daniel Fusfeld of the University of Michigan has pointed out, one is never quite sure what the term "free enterprise" means. In any case, it suggests that government participation in economic affairs is bad. Perhaps the utilities would like to abolish public rate-control agencies. Of course, they never quite say this, but such an attitude is fostered by them.

The irony is that the high school student subjected to this sort of propaganda will in all probability himself become a worker. As a worker he will want to live in a thriving society and will expect the government to exercise its legitimate responsibilities in keeping the economy viable. But as a student he will have been taught the fiction of laissez faire. And what a fiction it is!

Somehow the story of tariffs, land grants, farm subsidies, public works, credit controls, and monetary management is told, if at all, in an utterly sterile fashion, devoid of the vibrant clash of interests that makes economics such an important and exciting subject. The vapid character of economics teaching today merely conveys a sense of complacency about the failures of the classical market: it does not tell students that many observers have reasonable doubts about the effectiveness of the laissez-faire dream.

Economics is a controversial subject because it deals with human attitudes and aspirations. The objectives and goals of different people may conflict and frequently arouse deep-rooted emotional responses. Even the analytical side of economics can stir a heated debate, as, for instance, the wrangle over the causes of unemployment. Surely economics education must admit the existence of divergent views.

We do not impart knowledge by evading issues, by not mentioning the word "unions" in silk-stocking schools or the word "management" in factory districts. It is damaging enough to insulate the student from contesting viewpoints in economics. But to present only one, slanted approach under the guise of universal wisdom merely serves to inculcate a distorted view in the minds of youth and denies to students their right to know. The result is indoctrination worthy only of contempt.

The experience of Professor Fusfeld may be brought to bear on the problems of economics education. He has found that students have been reared mainly on conservative sermons: free enterprise means democracy; government intervention means socialism; inflation is destructive; the federal budget must be balanced; money should be backed by gold; automation will create more jobs. As Fusfeld commented wryly, this is folklore, not economics.

In one social studies class that I observed last year, tensions within a society and between nations were compared to liver ailments in the human body, requiring only magic pills to restore perpetual harmony. Such analogies are not merely false; they give the student an utterly distorted view of the social and economic structure. Worse still, since labor unions are usually blamed for starting all the trouble, they are regarded as microbes which cause disease. Thus a myth-ridden ideological folklore sustains a blinding bias.

Is it too much to ask that the teaching of economics in schools be relevant to the lives of the students and their families? Since so large a proportion of students will be working for a livelihood, shouldn't they learn that a collective bargaining agreement establishes on-the-job rules, spells out work relationships, provides for grievance and arbitration machinery—in short, is something more than a lever for moving up wages?

Ought not students be aware that unions *are* concerned with minimum wage legislation and social security and community services and foreign aid—in short that their vision is just a bit broader than the mere concern with "employer contributions required by contracts"? And beyond these elementary considerations, should not students learn something of the broader economic issues that will affect their futures—"full" employment, economic growth, taxes, housing, government spending, and prices?

Frankly, I have little patience with people who say that high school students cannot be taught these supposedly abstruse concepts or that it is too difficult to counteract the prevailing folklore. I remember years ago witnessing a lesson on housing. To start with, the teacher was thoroughly familiar with the subject. He motivated the students by asking them to describe the kind of home they would build if unlimited funds were available. The tantalizing thought led to an animated discussion of the kinds of housing that could be built. The problems of providing decent homes flowed naturally out of the pro-and-con arguments offered by the students. I could not help feeling that they left the classroom with some sense of the concreteness of economic problems.

But this happened in bygone days, when economics was taught in high schools as a subject in its own right, and the teachers, by and large, had been trained in economics. Then the "Problems of Democracy" people and the history teachers took over and squeezed economics out of the curriculum. It was absorbed into "social studies," a grab bag of items drawn from the news summaries of Sunday supplements. A disinterest in economics was transmitted from teacher to student.

Even worse, the teacher forgot how to teach the little he knew about economics, as genuine instruction was displaced by panel discussions modeled upon television's "What's My Line?" The passive transfer of ideological tidbits supplied by the chamber of commerce became a substitute for a lively relationship between teacher and student.

Given the gaps in understanding and the absence of the broadmindedness so necessary in the teaching of economics, the vacuum has been filled by traditional notions dribbling down from newspapers and such journals as *Time, Life,* and *The National Review.* Economics quickly degenerated into a parade of dull definitions of money and pat descriptions of the Federal Reserve System which have served as classroom soporifics.

The situation is not much better at the university level. I became convinced of this while attending a session on wages, prices, and employment conducted by a professor at a midwestern university. The competitive marginal productivity model was offered as the last word in economic science. Naturally the audience could only conclude that an increase in wages was bound to result in unemployment. That marginal productivity is only one of several demand theories, that it has little applicability in a mixed, oligopolistic, dynamic economy, that it fails as an explanatory device in a monopolistic world, and that there are alternative concepts which are more relevant to the realities of wage-employment relationships, evidently occurred neither to the lecturer nor to those exposed to this time-honored variant of conventional wisdom.

Of course, this sort of approach is endemic in economics itself. The labor economist can register justifiable complaints not only against the high schools, but against those who set the tone of economic thinking—the academicians. A favorite pastime of the latter is to search for constant relationships among "variables" which can then be manipulated to the heart's desire. Such explorations, it is said, make economics a science just like physics.

Thus the rapidity with which money and/or money substitutes change hands during a given period of time, expressed in the well-known equation of exchange, $PT=VM$, is deemed to be a constant, despite an acknowledged variation of perhaps 1 to 3 percent. Constant also is the marginal propensity to consume and the ratio between labor income and national income. The latter, of course, implies that unions cannot do very much about relative wages; hence, they ought to become social clubs or something like them.

Curiously, the wage–national income ratio has varied by about 10 percent over the last few decades, suggesting at least a 25 percent movement in the ratio of labor to nonlabor income. This makes it a rather strange "constant." It is with this sort of straining after elusive gnats that some economists can call for eliminating unions, enforcing free competition, and nullifying income taxes without serious rebuttal, or, as John Kenneth Galbraith has suggested, without injury to their own reputations.

Professor George Stigler of the University of Chicago has said that the way to instill the habits of logical economic thinking in students is to teach them price theory. Accordingly, the only conclusion the student would arrive at in a debate, say, over the shorter work week is that it would be uneconomic and would result in a misallocation of resources. Hence, the pressure of unions to reduce hours is morally wrong and economically harmful.

Curiously, unions have been quite deaf to this argument and have succeeded in reducing the work week by fifteen minutes annually over the last half-century without diminishing productivity or impeding the advancing march of technology. In fact, an excellent argument can be made for a positive relationship between shorter hours and economic growth during those fifty years. But the presentation of alternative viewpoints in economic education appears unacceptable. Interpretations that deviate from the dominant folklore are apt to be denied a hearing.

The shorter work week is rejected on the ground that it would increase production costs. A thirty-five-hour week, it is said, would augment labor costs by 14 percent. But such arithmetic stops short of the total analysis, since labor costs in many industries may represent only a third of total sales. In retailing, labor costs are even lower, often under a fourth of total sales.

Hence, a 14 percent increase in the labor component may work out to a 1 to 3 percent increase in comparison with overall revenues. Considering the insistent drive for greater sales and ever-deeper market penetration, and considering our vaunted productive capacity, such a modest cost increase may be worthwhile. This, of course, is a controversial argument, but then all arguments are controversial—and economics is perhaps the most argumentative of all social sciences.

Is it possible to teach economics in a way that allows for divergent points of view? Of course it is! Consider the approach used in *Labor Management Dynamics,* a high school text developed by the Detroit Board of Education in 1961. The position of the labor movement in American society is set forth in plain words: "The right of American citizens to organize, to bargain collectively, and, if necessary, to go on strike, is well established now. . . ." Or again: "The vastly improved processes in collective bargaining through use of democratic processes are indications of the recognition of the importance of labor unions on the American scene."

The so-called right-to-work debate is presented in parallel columns with the National Association of Manufacturers' views listed on one side and the AFL-CIO's on the other. Seldom can students examine labor's arguments in so balanced a fashion. Normally, the views of management receive the greatest play and teachers seldom offer rebuttals.

In his recent examination of social studies, *Where, When and Why,* Martin Mayer dredged up some really incredible examples of educational atrocities being perpetrated in our schools. In Houston, for instance, teachers may not mention the United Nations because it is "controversial." Elsewhere in Texas, a history book was banned because its cover design, depicting an eagle clutching arrows, might have been mistaken for a hammer and sickle. And in Indianapolis, AFL-CIO materials sent to the school system never arrived at their destination; they were buried at headquarters. I remember, too, a Teaneck, New Jersey, history teacher who was reprimanded for telling his classes about the Revolutions of 1848 because they had to do with something called socialism.

Under these circumstances, organizations like the Joint Council on Economic Education, which are concerned with improving high school economics courses, have an important task to perform. To be sure, a program such as the one undertaken by the Council cannot get far without the cooperation of school administrators. But would it not be worthwhile to convince the administrators that meaningful economic education cannot be attained or omitted by distorting the objectives of million of Americans whose working lives are directly conditioned by the labor movement?

1964

Wage Incentives in the
Labor System

Wage incentives, or the determination of earnings according to the amount of production, have been devices traditionally employed by American management to ensure efficiency and higher output. In the old days, around the turn of the century, and especially in the absence of a trade union, management simply imposed speed-up techniques by demanding higher and higher production norms. This was little more than crude pressure to get as much as possible out of workers at the lowest cost.

Such methods were bound to generate hostility and resistance among the workers, and it was in fact the intolerable conditions engendered by speed-up that became a primary factor impelling employees to create unions, as in the needle trades at the turn of the century and in the automobile industry. Then, during the 1880's, Frederick W. Taylor saw that work methods could be refined and analyzed more scientifically than had been management's wont. He thought this would reduce worker hostility. Always concerned with the time it took to perform a given task, Taylor argued that each employee's work should be planned in advance and that each man should receive precise instructions on how to do his job. When Taylor first offered his proposals, most managers called it nothing more than another piecework device, and it was not until 1903 that he was able to convince his colleagues that his approach was indeed "scientific."

Yet workers saw little advantage in the Taylor system. Experimentation and close observation were used to establish a "proper day's work"—usually defined as the fastest time of the most expert man. It was not a question of what might be *reasonably expected* from a worker, but what he *could* do. Taylor, for example, taught a steelworker to shovel forty-seven tons of pig iron a day instead of 12.5 tons. Each part of the job was outlined, including the size of the shovel, the arc of the swing, the number of steps to be taken, and the rest periods. But while Taylor and others, such as Frank Gilbreth and Karl Barth, were perfectly sincere in their attempts to improve work methods, their efforts spawned a flock of so-called "efficiency experts" who sold their dubious speed-up schemes to industry without regard to the impact it might have on the worker in the plant. Anxious to prove to management how good they were, and equipped with little understanding of the production process and even less of human relationships, they often established standards that were impossible to meet. Frequently, a management faced with intense hostility from its workers would have to yank the "efficiency expert" out of the factory. This experience during the opening decades of the twentieth century made unions look with skepticism upon the efforts of the industrial engineer and his incentive wage plans.

Some of the more typical schemes introduced during the twenties were the Halsey plan, which paid a premium for time saved, but at a decreasing rate as performance improved; the Rowan plan, a variant of the Halsey approach, which provided premium pay in accordance with the percent of time saved; the Gantt Bonus system, which gave outright bonuses to "superior" workers; and the Bedeaux system, which extended extra rewards for output above the standard unit of time. It was to be expected that in practice these would be modified, but in all instances the objective was to enforce higher output for a given time period.

At first the attitude of the unions was divided. Incentives based on piecework had been traditional in such industries as men's clothing, and were accepted by the unions without resistance. But in others—textiles and autos—there was marked opposition to incentive schemes based on a valid fear of the "speed-up" during the depression of the 1930's. The unions viewed this as an attempt to pit one worker against the other, and the threat of unemployment added to their hostility to incentive schemes.

The pressure for increased production was inevitable during World War II. Management, as well as some unionists, believed that incentives were desirable where output could be measured and where job tasks were definable. But when a continuous process was the basic technique of production, as in a chemical plant, wage incentives were difficult to install. And in many trades, the unions continued their opposition to incentive methods: for them, despite the scientific trappings, it was synonymous with "speed-up." Further, it threatened to undermine the spirit of solidarity that the unions had sought to foster among their members. It was not unusual for the "rate buster"—the man who could exceed norms—to be told by his fellow workers to slow down or be ostracized. Where unions (in rubber, machine tools, and steel) adapted themselves to incentive payment schemes, they did so with rather marked reluctance and strong resentment. In other instances, as in the automobile industry, the union was able to eliminate incentive plans among the major manufacturers (although it was not entirely successful in the parts sector of the industry).

Yet the incentive plans that were installed did not always bring the advertised results. While production did increase, incentives did not always reduce unit cost, which was, of course, the more significant factor. Speed in a machine shop, for example, might only increase waste, for as the operator intensifies his work he becomes more liable to making costly errors in tolerance. Changes in methods as well as products and the manipulation of production standards brought considerable dissatisfaction in their wake. By the end of the war, when many firms had to shift to peacetime markets, new standards had to be developed, and in many plants the older incentive plans were simply abandoned. Moreover, shifts to continuous-flow methods were making incentive plans less and less useful, for production was losing its discrete character, making measurement of separate units of work impossible.

By 1958, the wage incentive picture had become quite mixed. In one survey conducted in the middle 1950's, 40 percent of the companies studied reported that they were not satisfied with existing incentive programs, for they had neither increased production nor reduced unit costs. Moreover, many firms were interested in a happy and stable work force, something that incentive schemes made difficult to attain. As a result of the rather uncertain situation, unions were able to obtain revision of various bonus and premium schemes. Piece rate systems were replaced by standard hours methods, and quite often the plan was simply diluted by attaching hourly wage increases to the incentive base rate. In one case, management discontinued its incentive plan under the threat of a strike, only to discover to its surprise that unit labor cost and total unit cost were lower without the incentive. When the union subsequently tried to get back the incentive program, management refused.

But the predominant attitude of the unions has been one of opposition. Experience with inequities, distortion of the wage structure, and the increasing burden of grievances have led unions to distrust the promises of the industrial engineer. As one union organizer put it: "There's more lottery in it than logic. On top of it, they make the job so automatic that a guy begins to daydream. Before he knows it, he's lost a finger." Further, the unions cannot escape the feeling that incentive schemes redound mainly to the benefit of management. In all too many instances, a close relationship may be found between incentive schemes rigorously enforced and poor union-management relations stemming from the pressure exerted on workers. Consequently, in many plants, impossible standards have had to be loosened, with eventual abandonment of the scheme and conversion to hourly or weekly rates.

An example of the difficulties that may develop is the situation in basic steel. Here the incentive structure after the war became quite muddled, with tonnage plans, piece rates, and a variety of other incentive measures creating conditions of marked uncertainty. A good deal of the problem stemmed from the rather loose language of the original 1937 collective bargaining agreement between the United States Steel Corporation and the Steelworkers' Organizing Committee, in which inequities in wage rates were left to local plant adjustment. While subsequent agreement sought to eliminate some local incentive plans and to improve hourly wage rates, the union found that it was accommodating itself more and more to incentive programs. Intertwined with these practices were work rules at local plant sites built into the agreement over a period of years, which were upheld by independent arbitrators called upon to adjudicate disputes to cover crew size, seniority, distribution of overtime, scheduling, layoffs, and such issues as lunch hours. The companies charged that this was freezing inefficiency and waste into steel operations: the union insisted that such work rules were necessary to protect the workers against speed-up and heavy work loads.

In January 1960, the steel strike settlement resulted in the establishment of two committees: one to study local working conditions, with union and management representatives and a neutral chairman; and another called the Human Relations Committee, comprised only of union and company persons. Among other problems, the latter was to study incentive plans in order to work out equitable wage adjustments. The experience in steel clearly indicated that incentive schemes were not the answer to achieving greater efficiency and output and that they were apt to create grievances and complaints. This indeed had been a longstanding contention of the union, and it was finally recognized by management as a valid one.

The steel industry has been the source of another device for heightening output—the Scanlon plan. This was developed by Joseph Scanlon around 1937 to help reduce costs in a mill in which he was the union representative. The plan provides for union-management cooperation in achieving savings. When the plan proved successful in his own mill, Scanlon moved on to the Steelworkers' Union's headquarters to help install the system elsewhere. Later he went to the Massachusetts Institute of Technology, where he worked as a consultant in developing the plan for various companies. Unfortunately, any favorable impact the plan may have had on labor relations while Scanlon was alive and personally supervising its operation appears now to have been dissipated. This is the view of Bertram Gottlieb, the AFL-CIO's industrial engineer, who has had many years of experience in this area. Gottlieb suggests that the work of the M.I.T. group now differs very little from that of an ordinary consulting firm. He cites a recent case in which the company sought to charge theft losses to the accumulated savings. The M.I.T. consultants agreed with management, although the losses were in no way related to the operation of the plan.

Briefly, the Scanlon plan functions on a plant-wide basis on the assumption that teamwork is required for efficiency. This departs sharply from earlier plans which focused attention on the individual worker. Employees, under Scanlon's approach, received the largest part of the labor cost savings resulting from the plan (as measured by the difference between the normal payroll-sales ratio and the actual ratio). For example, if 40 percent of a sales level of a million dollars normally went for wages, and if workers increased their efficiency so that the same sales volume could be produced with a 35 percent wage cost, then a substantial part of the difference, or $50,000, would be paid to the workers as a bonus. The incentive presumably eliminated competition between individual workers and thus induced a spirit of cooperation.

In actual operation the plan elicited suggestions from workers on labor-saving and has made the installation of new equipment more palatable to them. Loafing is resented because lost time is reflected in higher production costs. More attention seems to be paid to the quality of workmanship because spoilage also increases costs. A greater sense of teamwork in the plant is necessary to achieve results. Overtime may be forgone because the premiums involved tend to increase unit production costs. And, of course, the workers acquire a vested interest in successful sales by the company: they may very well object to reduced sales prices since this would reduce the savings to the company and consequently their bonus.

On the other hand, the plan creates problems for the union which may not have been anticipated. For example, there may be a tendency to put seniority rules aside in an effort to assign the most proficient workers to particular tasks. Workers may be encouraged to exert pressure on each other, a reaction that merely shifts the burden of speed-up from management to the workers themselves. Inclusion of nonproduction workers, as is sometimes done in the Scanlon plan, will cause the ratio of salaries to sales to rise rapidly when sales are poor, since costs for this group are relatively fixed. Or the product mix in the plant's production program may vary so that shifts from high-labor-cost items to low-labor-cost items can make the bonus itself fluctuate. Thus, it appears evident that even in this more sophisticated incentive scheme there are intractable problems that may defy solution.

A more recent derivative of the Scanlon plan was the arrangement developed in the 1960 contract between the Steelworkers' Union and the Kaiser Steel Company for the latter's plant at Fontana, California. A long-range committee was established to determine how gains stemming from technological advances should be shared. After three years of study, during which labor, management, and public members sought to arrive at an equitable scheme, a "Share-the-Progress Plan" was evolved. In essence, there is a monthly sharing with employees of all savings in the use of materials and from increased output. Employees receive 32.5 percent of the savings, a share based on the past ratio of labor costs to manufacturing costs. Those employees who are covered by other incentive plans in the company may opt for the cost-savings scheme. Perhaps more important is the protection against loss of jobs or income due to technological change or improved work methods provided by the plan. In fact, many workers at Fontana have said that without such protection they would have rejected the whole idea. Only when the demand for the product declines may layoffs occur, since such situations are covered by supplemental unemployment benefits. Thus, an attempt has been made in this plan to insure a measure of job security in the face of rapid technological change and yet provide incentives for improved methods of production. The arrangement is to remain in force until 1967, at which time the entire program will be re-examined. Although bonus payments in the first few months of the plan's operation ranged from about thirty to fifty cents an hour, it is as yet too early to offer any judgments on its effectiveness. It does illustrate, however, that problems of incentives and productivity can be dealt with in the collective bargaining process.

Nevertheless, most trade unionists continue to have grave doubts about the value of incentive schemes. In 1961, an AFL-CIO resolution characterized incentive methods as "neither accurate, reliable, nor valid." Walter Reuther has argued that such methods are dependent on human judgment and therefore cannot be truly scientific. And Mr. Gottlieb has described some of the ways used by management to set standards as a combination of stopwatch, crystal ball, ouija board, and tea leaves. Further, with the spread of automation and continuous process methods, the work pace is determined quite independently of the man on the line. It is difficult to apply incentives when responsibility for the rate of speed in production is removed from human hands and given to a computer or electronic gauge. As Paul W. Bennington, an industrial engineer, stated the issue, incentives are illogical when operators literally have no control, except perhaps to practice what Thorstein Veblen called the "conscientious withdrawal of efficiency." Additionally, incentive plans play havoc with the natural, normal rhythmic pace at which a man feels he works best. It is a rhythm that is difficult to alter, and efforts either to speed it up or slow it down tend to create situations of tension. Besides, pace-setting seems to be a group phenomenon, called the Hawthorne effect by industrial sociologists after the famous experiment in a Western Electric plant. This experiment suggested that the pace is established without regard to existing incentives, simply because attention is focused on the group under study. From management's standpoint, nonincentives offer greater flexibility in scheduling men and equipment and avoid the unconscious slowdown that occurs when a time-and-motion man comes into the plant with his stopwatch. The latter all too frequently is gulled by good actors, resulting in margins of error of well over 10 percent. In one analysis of performance tests, 57 percent of the studies revealed errors in excess of this figure. And since it is difficult to establish standards for "overhead" workers (those providing indirect services to production), a whole flock of inequities may be created.

Other disadvantages seem almost self-evident: the high cost of maintaining appropriate records; the creation of individual rivalry and even cheating; the abuse of equipment in an effort to keep up high outputs; the high rate of rejects stemming from hasty workmanship; the encouragement of long hours; and the inculcation of an attitude of cynicism simply do not make the effort to install and operate incentive plans worthwhile in American industry. With the deterioration in operation that is apt to set in and the loose standards that develop, an incentive often becomes little more than a lottery, as one engineer put it.

The fact is that incentive schemes are not nearly as widespread as might be supposed. In 1958, incentives in manufacturing industries covered 27 percent of workers; in 1945, the ratio had been 30 percent. According to Mr. Gottlieb, the proportion today is even less. More and more the trend is toward payment for time worked and, in a modern rationalized plant in which it becomes ever more difficult to assign responsibility for particular units of output to any single person, time payment is the only sensible method of compensation.

But, more important, it is increasingly recognized that the stimulation of output demands that attention be paid to elements other than the purely monetary. The work place can have a dehumanizing impact: it can be mindless and exhausting and so create boredom and hostility. What seems necessary now is closer study of *human* relationships in the plant. This is the area to which industrial engineers and sociologists, unions and management are now turning.

1964

Collective Bargaining

Collective bargaining between employers and unions establishes formal rules governing work and conditions of employment. The term applies to negotiations about wages, hours, conditions of work, and fringe benefits, and to the processes by which agreements on these matters are maintained.

In the United States collective bargaining is inseparable from trade unionism. From its inception the trade union movement in the United States has sought recognition from employers so that unions might enjoy the right of representation and might negotiate an enforceable contract, the culminating point in collective bargaining.

In many countries, however, the forms of collective bargaining have undergone considerable change since the Industrial Revolution. For example, in the early days of industrialism in Britain, questions on specific issues were often adjudicated through bargaining between an employer and an employees' committee set up for the occasion. Later, however, the trade union provided the machinery for a collective bargaining procedure that was continuous rather than casual.

Collective bargaining in a given country is shaped by special factors. Because legal, economic, political, and cultural restraints vary from one country to another, each country develops its own particular forms of collective bargaining.

In Britain, trade unions developed freely only after repeal of the Combination Acts in 1824. Nevertheless, it was not until 1871 that unions could utilize so-called coercive weapons, such as a threat to strike, without fear of conspiracy charges. In certain industries, employers took the initiative in introducing such instrumentalities as local boards of conciliation to reduce tension over wage-fixing and to eliminate unions as bargaining agents. Nevertheless, collective bargaining continued to develop in Britain mainly on a voluntary basis. State intervention did occur in both World Wars I and II, when compulsory arbitration was temporarily enforced. Wage councils are also used to establish wages in those industries that are not well organized. The decisions of the wage councils are enforceable by the minister of labor.

In Scandinavia, collective bargaining is more centralized than in the United States. Negotiations in Sweden, for example, take place between the employers' association and the central trade union organization and then filter down to local bodies. Matters of interpretation are referred to a labor court, established in 1938.

In France, government intervention is more extensive. Work conditions are governed by statute, and a national minimum wage may be set by the government.

In African countries, collective bargaining may be found in the oil extraction industry, in mining establishments, on plantations, and among government employees. Although major employers in Africa have not always recognized unions as bargaining agents, management has moved cautiously toward negotiation as a way of reaching settlements.

In Japan, trade unions have resorted to political pressures. Much reliance is placed on legislative action plus an annual ritual of "struggles" to achieve wage gains.

In the United States the chief participants in the collective bargaining system are the employers (represented by managers); unions and their representatives; government officials; and, on occasion, private individuals, such as mediators and arbitrators. Under collective bargaining in the United States, the roles played by participants in governing wages, hours, and working conditions arc explicit and are usually written into a labor-management agreement. Such a document specifies union security and management rights—questions that revolve about the determination of representation and authority.

Central to the agreement is a specification of wages, production standards, and contingent (fringe) benefits. In addition, the agreement spells out grievance machinery, including arbitration procedures. The "bargains" arrived at through negotiations may apply at the level of individual firms, at regional and industrial levels, or at national levels. In a sense, the agreement delineates the ground rules in a geographic and industrial framework.

Prior to the New Deal of President Franklin D. Roosevelt, collective bargaining relationships functioned within a framework of common law and local ordinances. Employers generally did not bargain with unions unless compelled to do so by the union's economic strength. The National Labor Relations Act of 1935—known as the Wagner Act—substantially altered the legal environment of collective bargaining. The Wagner Act protected the worker's right to join a union of his own choice (blacklisting of workers for union membership had been a common practice). It provided election machinery to determine the representative union. It compelled the employer to recognize and bargain with the union selected by the employees. Certain devices that had been utilized to coerce workers were declared unfair labor practices. Although some matters were referred to the National Labor Relations Board (established by the act), it was clear that the scope of bargaining extended beyond wages, hours, and conditions of employment to the whole range of contingent benefits, such as health and welfare programs, retirement, merit ratings, and the like.

The Taft-Hartley Act of 1947 and the Landrum-Griffin Act of 1959 altered somewhat the relationships established between labor and management by the Wagner Act, but basically there was not much change in specifying the scope of collective bargaining. The effect of Taft-Hartley and Landrum-Griffin has been to make more explicit the conditions under which the federal government may inject itself into the collective bargaining process.

Thus, whenever a strike affecting the national interest is threatened, the federal government may impose a cooling-off period. Picketing and secondary boycotts were subjected to further statutory limitations, although in many instances specific determinations still had to be made by the NLRB.

Some writers have described collective bargaining negotiations before a new contract as a "ritual," implying that somehow the results are predetermined and need only be verified across the bargaining table. This appears to be a simplistic view of the process, for collective bargaining has many more attributes of diplomacy in action than the term "ritual" would suggest.

The common practice on the union side has been to establish a negotiating committee composed of union officers and rank-and-file members. If the negotiations are conducted through a local union, a representative of the international union often will be present. Frequently, the international representative, as the union's "professional," will have consulted with the committee well in advance of the negotiations.

For the employers, especially if they are large firms, labor relations specialists or personnel directors often are designated representatives. There may be variations in the composition of the employer side that result in a limited delegation of authority: this condition often develops in multi-employer or employer association bargaining.

Because the union committee must function with provisional authority, it will generally feed back information to its constituency. Initially the union formulates demands to reflect what the members are requesting, assembles data regarding these demands, and publicizes them. Demands may be based on the union's perception of the needs of employees as well as on an attempt to duplicate what some other union may have achieved. The latter has a tendency to create a pattern of bargaining within an industry and even across industry lines. For example, in the late 1950's supplementary unemployment insurance programs spread from the auto workers to the steelworkers. The initial demands obviously tend to represent an estimation of the higher limit of the bargaining situation.

Most companies also actively prepare for negotiations. A purely defensive strategy tends to be negative and may lead to seemingly irreconcilable differences between the parties. The company may want to define the area of bargaining, excluding from negotiations what it calls management prerogatives, such as production and sales policies.

The negotiations customarily take place privately in order to maintain an atmosphere of freedom from external pressure. Seated on opposite sides of a bargaining table, management and labor engage in the sort of strategy that appears to them most effective under the circumstances. A company may adopt a position of resistance or it may assume a more flexible bargaining posture. In some instances, a company has insisted that its first offer is its final offer, but the NLRB declared this strategy to be an "unfair labor practice."

Union negotiators use a number of factors in evaluating their demands. These include improvements in productivity, ability to pay, effects of a wage increase on purchasing power, and wages and fringe benefits paid elsewhere. Productivity increases pose difficult technical issues revolving about measurements. Unions argue that employees are entitled to share in productivity gains. The ability-to-pay issue relates to a company's financial capacity and implies a comparison of profit trends with wage trends. In periods of rising prices, unions point to changes in purchasing power as a relevant factor.

Management, on the other hand, contends that wage increases contribute to further price increases, and implies that price stability is the desirable course. Or the company may insist that gains in productivity stem from improvements in capital equipment and overall production rather than from labor effort. Frequently, the company insists that it cannot afford to pay higher wages, but this contention, under NLRB rules, has to be substantiated by relevant data.

Should an impasse develop, the union's final recourse may be a refusal to work—that is, a strike. Negotiations may cease, perhaps to be resumed under pressure from the government and with the participation of a conciliator. The decision to strike is seldom taken without serious consideration, because heavy costs and risks are involved. To add to its arsenal of bargaining weapons during negotiations, a union frequently will poll its membership on whether to strike or not. Should a strike develop, the objective is to deprive the company of production and force it to come to terms. Such action involves picketing, a form of union activity that has been increasingly limited by government regulations. The restrictions, for instance, include limits on the number of pickets. The ability to maintain a strike depends largely on the union's resources and its ability to extend financial aid to its striking members.

Employers have similar weapons, such as the lockout—simply shutting down the plant. Or in some cases employers may attempt to generate a back-to-work movement among union members to break the strike. Some writers have described these aspects of collective bargaining in military terms: "negotiations," "strikes," and "agreements" appear to have their parallels in "diplomacy," "war," and "treaties." However, in view of the fact that in the United States lost time due to strikes has been about one-half of 1 percent of all time worked in the average year, it appears that collective bargaining is a relatively peaceable arena.

Some strikes have a great impact on matters of public concern. In an interdependent economy, for example, the transportation of food from farmers and processors to central markets is of crucial importance. Nevertheless, not all strikes manifest such effects, and a distinction needs to be made between "public interest" and "public inconvenience." Some writers contend that strikes in such areas as the newspaper field may create only a public inconvenience, because there are alternative sources of information.

In the United States collective bargaining functions through "bargaining units," which may be single-employer or multi-employer in structure. A Bureau of Labor Statistics study in 1956, based on more than 1,700 agreements covering units of 1,000 or more employees, revealed that 68 percent of the agreements, covering 57 percent of the workers, were of the single-employer type. Only a third of the agreements covered multi-employer units. In manufacturing, the percentages for single-employer units are even higher: about 80 percent of all agreements, covering 82 percent of the workers, were with single-employer bargaining units.

An analysis of bargaining units by size made by Neil Chamberlain for the year 1953 showed that the single-employer unit was generally small. Usually a unit consisted of fewer than 500 employees. On the other hand, larger units, both of the single-employer and multi-employer type, although small in number, included the larger part of the work force. Thus units of 10,000 or more covered 30.4 percent of all employees.

Just as employer bargaining units include many small companies and a few large ones, so a similar variation exists on the union side. About 25 percent of the unions in the United States have fewer than 5,000 members. Only three unions—the United Auto Workers, the Steelworkers, and the Teamsters—have more than one million members.

A development in collective bargaining in the 1960's has been described as "coordinate bargaining." The term stems from the electrical equipment manufacturing industry, where eleven AFL-CIO unions negotiated jointly with the General Electric and Westinghouse companies. At G.E., for instance, bargaining had been conducted individually with some ninety unions, mainly on a local basis with local managements. The unions contended that this was a policy of "divide and rule," and that they were weakened further when the policy was coupled with staggered expiration dates for the various contracts. Beginning in 1965, the eleven unions agreed on national bargaining strategy. Protracted negotiations, involving proceedings before the NLRB and in the courts, led in 1966 to contracts at both firms that created a broader form of collective bargaining.

Some writers prefer to call a collective bargaining contract an "agreement," on the ground that an employer does not contract for labor with the union but with employees. The distinction is pedantic, for the essentials of a collective bargaining agreement are those found in the law of contracts. There must be a meeting of minds, acceptance of an offer, and a definite agreement on terms. In addition the subjects covered must be such that the contract does not violate the law. A collective bargaining contract is enforceable in the courts and need not be reduced to writing to be enforceable. The terms "agreement" and "contract" appear to be interchangeable.

Generally the terms of a collective bargaining agreement are written. The agreement spells out the following: the bargaining unit (that is, the job or job categories to which the contract applies); the form of recognition (usually exclusive bargaining rights); duration of contract and date of renewal; labor grades and pay rate ranges; pay steps within grade; crew sizes and work rules; premium pay (overtime and shift differentials); contingent, or fringe, benefits, such as pensions, severance pay, and health and welfare plans; and coffee breaks, holidays, and vacations. Unions also have paid particular attention to seniority clauses and grievance and arbitration procedures.

Unions seek to "police" the contract during its life. For this purpose local union members may elect a shop steward, who derives his authority from the contract. Normally, arrangements are made to allow stewards to leave their work to confer with management and affected employees.

Collective bargaining in the United States operates within a statutory framework embodied in the Taft-Hartley Act and the Landrum-Griffin Act, successors to the Wagner Act. However, many complexities of the law are so interpreted by the NLRB that its decisions do have the effect of law. In Britain, however, the common law, as modified by Parliament, provides the legal background. It is essentially pragmatic and based on notions of fair play. In Western Europe, many rules governing collective bargaining stem from the Napoleonic code, which tends to inhibit in that region the sort of relationships that exist in Britain and the United States. Consequently, unions in France, West Germany, and Italy have stressed political activity as a means of attaining their objectives.

1968

New Views on Labor

I

At the age of eighteen, Paul Jacobs crawled on his belly across railroad tracks to join other strikers converging on a flour mill to drive away scabs who had taken their jobs. At the age of forty, he sat well groomed in a paneled board room arguing with corporate officials for a twenty-five-cent increase in meal allowances for members of his union. Between these incidents, pregnant with the symbolism of our time, Jacobs had experienced enough as an organizer and labor intellectual to wonder why the coin had become dulled and tarnished. His disillusionment is expressed most sharply in the last of the essays collected in *The State of the Unions* (1964), a corrosive lament for collective bargaining which in his despairing view has aged well before its time.

The charges Jacobs levels are not new and, in an objective sense, may be difficult to rebut. He points to the increasing drain on the labor movement imposed by automation and the new technology; the shift in the work force from factory to office, a place notoriously difficult to organize; the persistent Bourbonism of the Boulwares of industry; the desiccation of the beliefs and social energy that impelled the unions, during the thirties and forties; the inability or unwillingness of the unions to settle their own household quarrels; the lack of any genuine political thrust and a preference for coffee hours in the White House; and the alienation of Negroes, liberals, and other one-time friends. The culmination of Jacobs' indictment is that, in this situation, collective bargaining is no longer the instrument it once was, and can no longer fulfill the broad social, economic, and political needs of those it was intended to serve.

Labor leaders are not yet ready to accept this diagnosis, however. Only a few weeks ago, George Meany roared at an AFL-CIO convention that such predictions fall wide of the truth, that labor has lost none of its militancy, that its success could be measured in the dollars and cents of high wages, and that he would gladly let his critics cling to their nostalgia for the Great Depression. He also pinned the curse of automation onto the lapels of management, which he said was racing to produce more with less.

While all this is true, Jacobs would probably reply that current union activity must be viewed in the much broader context he has sought to establish in his articles and essays. Consider the issue of automation. According to Jacobs: "Automation and the *particular* unemployment it brings to a *particular* plant are problems obviously beyond the capabilities of union-management collective bargaining." Even a cursory perusal of all the schemes that have been worked out to date—in meat-packing, coal, machine tools, on the waterfront, in steel—suggests that they merely postpone the proverbial day of reckoning. Automation is a kind of tidal force that neither the unions nor management can control. It has indeed become a social problem that ought to command the attention of everyone, particularly policy-makers in Washington. And yet, despite all the talk and all the fears, no one knows what to do.

Jacobs illustrates this sort of frustration in his well-known essay, "Dead Horse and Featherbird," which tells of the insecurity among printers and airline pilots. Perhaps nothing typifies the devilish complexity of modern industrial relations so much as the situation in those trades. The printers make up "bogus" or reproduction work as a defense against technological unemployment, but their pride of craft impels them to voice a hatred for such nonwork. Often they simply ignore it, let it pile up, and then trade it off for another coffee break. The pilot—a labor aristocrat if ever there was one—wants an extra seat in the cockpit, just in case. He too dislikes "unwork" but given the choice, as Jacobs perceptively notes, between no work and made work, he will select the latter. Trapped by time and technology into doing what he would prefer not to, he rationalizes and quarrels bitterly with fellow unionists for the right to fill the empty seat.

But this is the nature of American life itself, and the unions may very well be a perfect mirror image of it. Thus, while Jacobs says: "The tragedy of American unions isn't so much in their present state as it is in what they could be and aren't," he has the good sense to add: "But then isn't that the plight of America, too?" Unions have in fact become precisely the kind of thoroughgoing business institutions that American workers and the American public wanted them to be. If members do not attend meetings, a fact that Jacobs bemoans, neither do they go to church with any regularity, nor to their lodges, nor PTA's. If membership commitment to unions is tenuous, it is equally so in other organizations.

The unions in this country are not (perhaps to their detriment) adjuncts to political parties as unions were in Europe. They are, rather, service organizations seeking to improve the economic status of their members. In that function they have in the main been successful. Given the values of our culture, unions could not have done otherwise but to create a new middle class, as Jacobs recognizes. Did not David Dubinsky himself exclaim: "What's good for the capitalist is good for the proletariat!" Or as Charles Zimmerman, a Dubinsky aide, told Jacobs: "Union members don't become saints because they take out union cards."

The consequence, of course, has been the phenomenon of James Riddle Hoffa, who boasts of the excellence of his contracts and in the same breath speaks of "my men" and "my business," an attitude that makes it difficult to distinguish between union business and ordinary business. Yet because he ostensibly gives his members what they want, Hoffa is their popular choice—or at least he seems to be. And it is in the Teamsters' President—with his insistence on absolute loyalty, his paternalism, and his fearful determination to crush opponents with as much muscle as possible—that Jacobs sees reflected the behavior of some other labor leaders as well. It is this muscle, he suggests, that other unions would like to exercise through what has been called the "strategic alliance." Part of the explanation of Hoffa, according to Jacobs, is that he is really a James Cagney villain come alive and, like many such dreamland personalities, has become a rather likable culture hero, victorious against all the hostilities of respectable society.

Hoffa's strength and that of the Teamsters, however, appears to stem more from the condition of the trucking industry. Its typical character is the tough, small owner-operator struggling in an economic jungle in which stealing accounts from rivals is the normal way of life. The workers are isolated from their fellow drivers, engaged in dangerous work, harassed by highway patrolmen and, before the union gave them protection, were apt to be stolen blind by employers.

If "Jimmy" takes care of their economic interests, that is all they ask. As far as they are concerned, to do more would be irrelevant. It is not surprising that the Teamsters became the most powerful organization in so chaotic an industry. And the benevolent paternalism, the demand for unwavering loyalty, quite patently stems from such a situation. Nor has the parallel with the needle trades' unions, in the sense that they can dominate an industry which without them would be a morass, been lost on Jacobs.

Again, is this not a reflection of the larger society? If there is distrust of internal opposition in unions, for example, do we not see the same pattern in the corporation? The irony, though, is that the genteel expression of such behavior in the upper reaches of the board-room does not arouse the violent tempers of the editorial writers as do the actions of a Hoffa or, on occasion, a Hayes or a Reuther.

Jacobs is clearly angry. The high expectations he had when he crawled across the railroad tracks have not been fulfilled. He is angrier still when he looks at the lower depths of the work force—the migratory farm hand—and finds that society and the unions have forgotten these people completely. He can hope only for "a revival of the instincts of social compassion and indignation—qualities recently absent from our society, perhaps because it is so difficult for the prosperous majority to identify itself with a destitute minority."

And yet, despite the author's censure of the unions, there are those of us who know in our bones that without them America would be a much more callous place to live. To the worker who must labor all his life, business is the same whether it strives for profit or merely searches for its corporate soul. The laborer is an instrument for achieving success and once management takes him for granted, as it inevitably would prefer to do, there is need for a union to protect him. Even Jacobs would not deny this. But he is an honest man, and he writes the story as he sees it: that some would not always agree with his view of the unions today is another matter.

II

A much more dyspeptic observer is B. J. Widick. His book *Labor Today* (Houghton Mifflin, 1964) is subtitled "The Triumphs and Failures of Unionism in the United States," but one finds no triumphs in its 200-odd shrill pages. All is failure. The book is quite simply a long and painful yawp. This is a pity, for Widick has been around the labor movement a long time now, and he ought to have been able to detect some virtues in that complex, sprawling, and all-too-human set of institutions known as labor unions. Instead he has allowed a personal gripe to becloud his vision, and what he gives us is bile disguised as reportage.

One has only to read the acid portrait of Walter Reuther to realize that the author can no longer write objectively about the union to which he, Widick, gave so many years of service. The chapter on Reuther recounts just about all the hostile comments that might be gathered and exhibits them like dirty linen on a clothesline. The reader who wants a more balanced analysis of what the UAW is doing these days will have to go elsewhere.

At no point, for example, does Widick hint that the union provides protection for the men in the shop against the intoler-

able pressures that management would enforce without it; nowhere does one get a sense of the union's accomplishments in
the plant. And this is so either because Widick is conducting a
vendetta or because he wants the union to be solely a political
institution, which it is not.

This latter demand is certainly legitimate, but it needs to be
placed in a broader context than Widick has been able to provide. For the American labor movement now stands revealed
as the creature of American society. Complaints about unions
as institutions are fundamentally complaints about that society.
Attacks on union affluence must also be attacks on affluence generally. Revelations of union corruption open vents on the corrupt air we breathe. To draw unions closer to what Widick calls
true unionism—a notion he leaves quite vague—calls for considerable recasting of the habits of American thought itself.

Meanwhile we must make do with *ad hoc* politics and maneuvering. This does not mean that there is no sentiment for more
cohesive action. But the building of political awareness, in
Widick's sense, comes slowly and painfully, and as the result of
an intermingling of apathy and enthusiasm, of patching here and
erosion there. Widick refuses to acknowledge this fact of life in
our society, and so behaves like an ideologue who has reasoned
himself into an impasse.

The unions, at least the larger ones, have achieved a position
of relative prosperity, but this in no way makes them the powerful countervailing organizations that Widick, among others, believes them to be. If union leaders have, on occasion, had coffee
in the White House, that does not make them partners in government or enterprise. In their principal arena of action—collective
bargaining—they are apt to be told by government officials to
hew close to the productivity line. This has obviously made a
good many of them unhappy, and since no one really knows what
productivity growth is, the unions must necessarily continue to
press against management. The alleged accommodation between
unions and management, which Widick claims exists, is so un-
real that management, whenever it can get away with it, en-
courages decertification proceedings before the National Labor
Relations Board.

The only time Widick gets close to a genuine problem is in

his discussion of automation. That the unions are stunned and do not know what action to take is scarcely surprising. There are no social restraints on automation. In his desire to be up to date and at the same time to tighten his control over the industrial process, the business archon does not hesitate to utilize new technology to the fullest, and humans are thereby converted into just so much excess baggage.

Yet there is some evidence to suggest that the unions are beginning to react. Delegates at the last UAW convention talked more about shop conditions than about money. The Steelworkers are experimenting with a unique arrangement at Kaiser Steel. The West Coast Longshoremen have tried to provide "cushions" for their regular members. And the Mine Workers have finally awakened to what John L. Lewis' deal with the coal operators has done to them.

The difficulty, to paraphrase A. H. Raskin, is that most of the union-automation schemes take care of those who are in and overlook those who are out. It is therefore imperative for unions to learn to negotiate for both insiders and outsiders. This would, of course, enforce a responsibility broader than the confines of the shop. And along the same lines, unions must again organize the unemployed if a genuine coalition is to be built that will impel government to acknowledge the social consequences of automation. But this takes hard work, planning, thinking, and, most of all, prodding. Whining of the sort to be found in Widick's book won't help.

III

On the other hand, I know of no labor intellectual who is more knowledgeable in the ways of the trade unions than Gus Tyler, Assistant President of the International Ladies' Garment Workers Union. He is, however, a committed intellectual, one who has spent his entire career inside unions (in fact, just the ILGWU). In his book, *The Labor Revolution: Trade Unions in New America* (1967), he offers not only a defense of their action, or inaction, but an attack as well on all those despairing souls who have written off unions as moribund institutions in American life. Yet for all his seeming forthrightness there is something disingenuous about the book; in the final analysis, he has not convincingly answered the complaints of a Paul Jacobs, a Sidney Lens, or a B. J. Widick.

Not that I would agree totally with the latter; I happen to believe with Tyler that unions are still importantly useful and viable organizations. And he may very well be right in his forecast that the surge of unionism among white-collar and government employees will parallel, albeit on a somewhat smaller scale, the outburst of the 1930's. But what is one to make of this comment: "As the old order changes, so does the old guard. A generation of top leaders exits, with about one-third of the high command of the AFL-CIO Executive Council stepping out at one convention (1965); a younger generation steps in. . . ." One can only greet this hallelujah to progress with a raucous snort; those whose memories are still clear (1964–1965 is not that far back) will remember that the old generation of top leaders, men who had been either retired or defeated in their own unions, were most reluctant to step down from the executive council. They had to be pushed out, mainly by a public outcry. It is a fair surmise that George Meany, president of the AFL-CIO, was not overly anxious to see them go—and one old-timer never did leave.

Such a lack of candor pervades the entire book. But this might have been expected, for Tyler is the shrewdest, cleverest apologist the labor movement possesses. He acknowledges that the young militants of the campus are today utterly unprepared for the sort of labor movement we now have, and he is candid in saying that unions have done little to make the intellectual labor-minded. But he does not tell us, really, why this is so. He does not have much to say about the outrageous behavior of certain labor leaders (some of them, to be sure, outside the AFL-CIO) nor does he comment extensively on labor's failure to convey effectively the message of its primary function to the public at large.

My own experience has led me to be less perturbed by plush edifices in Washington and New York, and more by the failure of some *local* leaders to provide services to members. But on that score American unions, by and large, cannot be faulted. Even Sidney Lens, a sharp critic of the upper echelons in unions and head of his own local in Chicago, will insist that he looks after the daily concerns of the rank and file; essentially, it is in the *detail* that the work of unions must be examined. It is in the creation of bargaining agreements, the establishment of health, welfare, and pension schemes, the conduct of grievances, and in the work of staff personnel as lobbyists, researchers, writers, and educators, that the effectiveness of labor unions must be measured. And it is possible to evaluate these activities without the belligerent tone of apologetics in which Tyler so often indulges.

Perhaps the best chapter in the book is that on the political roots of the labor movement. Here Tyler is on solid ground. From a political standpoint, unions not only vent *political* expressions through a craft or industry, but they are involved also in decision-making that affects what people get and what people do. As Tyler says, unions are fraternities, collective bargaining agencies, factions in a political party, and arenas for warring labor barons. The issue essentially is the exercise of power —in a non-pejorative sense. And what indeed is wrong about that? Do not employers and their many trade associations seek power? Does not the military want power? Do not politicians thirst for power? In an acquisitive industrial society, a worker as an individual is helpless: this much history has taught us. If the worker, through unions, reaches to balance the scales somewhat more equitably, it would be difficult to criticize him for the effort. Hence, we ought to have expected that unions would demand legitimation by law, that they would insist on acceptance by a largely hostile society, that they would protect their members in the shop with rules that establish reasonable rhythms of work. Tyler's implication that those who oppose all this merely want to perpetuate exploitative relationships is not far off the mark.

However, Tyler's belief that collective bargaining is so well developed that it can wrestle with such an exacerbating problem as automation is surprisingly ill-informed. He acknowledges that legislative action may be necessary, yet asserts that "the response to the challenge of automation is to be found in skillful collective bargaining." Elsewhere I have dealt with this issue at some length. The evidence convinces me that the unions are as nonplussed as the rest of us by an onrushing technology, and that in many cases they have simply capitulated. There is not much to say of the classic instances of surrender typified by John L. Lewis and Harry

Bridges. Lewis actively sought to push the miner out of the coal fields by giving the "go ahead" signal to mine operators to automate and mechanize at will. From about 600,000 members right after the war, the United Mine Workers Union is now down to about 125,000 members at best. As one labor reporter put it, the union had become "an enforcer for the machine," not worrying much about workers who now have been displaced.

The experience of the West Coast dock workers, led by Harry Bridges, offers a striking parallel. To be sure, those who remain on the docks have access to a $29 million fund that pays handsome retirement benefits. But what of those workers—the "B" men and the casuals—who were simply frozen out by Bridges' automation agreement with the employers? And what of the long-established work patterns that made arduous work more tolerable? The latter no longer exist, for dock work is now a ceaseless flow subjecting workers to the incessant demands of the machine. As events unfolded on the West Coast, the displaced and unemployed dock worker might stare through the windows of the Mark Hopkins Hotel in San Francisco, looking from union leader to management and from management to union leader, not knowing which is which.

The reluctant conclusion is that collective bargaining has not yet been able to respond to the challenge of the machine. George Meany may declare that automation is ". . . rapidly becoming a curse to this country . . ." but this in no way enables the unions in petrochemicals, autos, airlines, printing, maritime trades, machine shops, basic steel, meat packing, and railroads to achieve meaningful solutions to the problems created by advancing technology. In some cases, as in the airlines and railroads, one union simply tries to swallow another. In other instances, as in mining, unions become "ghosts," mere buildings housing a staff and ample treasury, but with few members. Some may not even have the consolation in the sort of survival enjoyed by the Journeymen Horseshoers, whose 290 members are employed at race tracks.

For the fact is that collective bargaining finds the burden of technological change too great to carry, nor was it ever devised to do so. Severance pay, automation funds, early retirement, attrition, and retraining as currently handled are only palliatives, a form of band-aid treatment. The solution, I suspect, must be achieved in another area, to wit through the kind of intervention that will assert once and for all man's mastery over the machine.

Indeed, as Tyler concedes, our economy is undergoing dramatic shifts and with them the shape of the labor force—unionism's constituency—is changing. As he puts it quite succinctly: "A labor force that was once manual, production based, located in the North and Midwest, and containing few women, has become mental, service based, moving to the South and West, and heavily female." Whereas the labor movement once relied on the railroads, building trades, mining, and printing, it must now look to the service trades and employed professionals for growth. Yet the latter thus far have resisted unionism, Tyler's great expectations notwithstanding. When professionals have organized, they have preferred to operate independently of the AFL-CIO, as did the engineers and technicians in Camden, New Jersey. One supposes that this is all right, so long as such groups *function* as unions. Unfortunately, too many of them are dominated by an employer ethos: they have not yet learned that bargaining demands two parties at arm's length from each other. Tyler anticipates that the professional's present conception of himself will give way to the ". . . realities of the industrial discipline." One hopes that he is right.

In a sense, Tyler's book is a good antidote to the personal imprecations of a Paul Jacobs or a B. J. Widick. Yet it would have been better if so many issues had not been slighted or simply ignored: the reluctance of line officers in some organizations to use staff experts as their counterparts in corporations are used; the sudden idealism of a David Dubinsky when his ill-paid organizers dare to form their own employee group; the unwillingness of some unions to develop a leadership corps from within because the composition of their membership has changed; the arrogant affluence of a maritime union leader who sees nothing wrong in living like a nabob; and the not so amusing imitation of a movie tough displayed by a Teamster official all signify serious deficiencies that ought to have been discussed seriously rather than treated as minor blemishes or not at all. When all is said and done, the labor movement must be, like Caesar's wife, above suspicion. Tyler does not demonstrate that it is.

At the showdown, however, it is Tyler who wins the argument, for despite all the strictures leveled at them, trade unions in America have made the material lot of the ordinary workingman, and indeed for all of us, far better than it would have been had they not existed. American unions—made in the image of America—represent an essential countervailance to the extraordinary power that the rest of society can bring to bear on the worker. One only wants to look at these matters through a glass clearly: Tyler's, unfortunately, is somewhat rose-colored.

1964, 1967

On Writing Labor History

The turbulent history of labor was simultaneously the history of America's growth. Yet, Philip Taft, who gives us now the second volume of his study of the American Federation of Labor, *The A. F. of L. from the Death of Gompers to the Merger* (Harper, 1959), has chosen to write virtually without any reference to the crucial social and economic forces that made labor what it is. This is indeed the definitive book on the AFL, but it is not history. It is rather a huge and careful chronicle, drawn from minute books, official proceedings, letters, and other documents. It is scrupulously honest and just as scrupulously dull.

Taft himself comes out of the great tradition of labor history founded by John R. Commons at the University of Wisconsin. Commons, too, was a great compiler of facts, but he sought to explain the development of trade unions as an expression of certain economic, social, and legal impulses. Mr. Taft has not been able to join chronicle-ism to social history as Commons did, and his bare recital of factual material does not allow us to understand the labor movement.

Certainly, the labor movement is in need of understanding today. With so complex a structure and diverse an organization, with so many jurisdictional and legal interconnections and so *seemingly* different an outlook from that manifested by the middle class, with the exacerbating problem of the Johnny Dios, the Becks, and Hoffas, there has been created in the minds of many the image of a clannish interest, hostile to the respectable goals of American society. The real motives of labor, however, conform perfectly to the dominant impulse of American society: the desire for more bread and butter. Why, then, the atmosphere of conflict which has always surrounded the U.S. labor movement?

In the beginning, the American public looked unfavorably on the efforts of shoemakers, cigar workers, carpenters, and clerks to organize and bargain collectively with management. A higher wage was accorded only to those individuals that deserved it; collective demands by a trade union were thought inimical to the interests of the community. Yet the unionization of workers was inevitable. The factory and the nationwide market had begun to displace the domestic system of manufacture and, together with a vast inflow of cheap labor, had created sweatshops, unsanitary conditions, and slums. Demands for justice could be enforced only by the strategic withdrawal of irreplaceable skilled workers.

Any number of labor organizations sought to redress the industrial balance, ranging from William Sylvis' National Labor Union to Terence Powderly's Knights of Labor, but it remained for the AFL to meet the new realities of American industry. The pragmatic outlook of Samuel Gompers was well suited to his time. He fought the labor injunction and the blacklist with admirable courage. He preached worker solidarity and patiently nursed AFL affiliates at a time when Pinkerton agents and corporation lawyers had things quite their own way. (Senator Robert La Follette later produced some seventy volumes of testimony exposing the instruments of terror used by corporations against unions.)

Yet, by the time of Gompers' death, his Federation was stagnating. In Taft's flat phrase, it was "inactive," barely able to hold its own, with only 3.5 million members just before the depression. Only with the New Deal did the climate of opinion shift. With the Norris–La Guardia Act of 1932, which restricted the easy application of court injunctions, the NRA's famous Section 7(a), as well as the Wagner Labor Relations Act, a new institutional framework was created for the unions.

Taft's description of the CIO split in 1936 catches none of the drama of that great crisis, although this is one of the few occasions when he permits himself the luxury of the historian's prerogative. It is "difficult to follow the reasoning of the majority of the members of the AFL Executive Council," he comments. "Confronted with the most serious crisis in its history," the AFL's president, William Green, "could think of nothing better . . . than to find a legal loophole by which the unions of the CIO might be thrown out."

The organization of the mass-production industries—automobiles, steel, rubber, and textiles—was the task of the CIO, which by 1938 had nine national affiliates and thirty-two organizing committees. Membership in organized labor reached ten million by 1941, so that when the war came, powerful unions were able to join with government and management in increasing production, preventing strikes, and helping to reorganize the economy for an unparalleled war effort.

The honeymoon ended with the defeat of Japan. More than forty major strikes broke out between the summers of 1945 and 1946. The end of price control in June 1946 brought an explosion in prices and the cost of living. Wage demands went up, as labor tried to keep pace with rising retail prices. Disaffection in the ranks and continued public exasperation enabled the 80th Congress to pass the Taft-Hartley Act over President Truman's veto. The unions now had to meet new legal barriers: the abolition of the closed shop, strict limits on union shops and the checkoff, permission to the individual states to toss out "union security" under the guise of "the right to work," and, above all, a National Labor Relations Board setup which allowed labor's foes to play havoc with bargaining rights, particularly at the local union level.

In December 1955, as George Meany and Walter Reuther worked to bring together the AFL and CIO, there were predictions of evil aggrandizement, predictions which failed to recognize that labor's new parent body did not possess the control over its affiliates that would make it a "labor monopoly." Nor was it acknowledged that Meany, Reuther, and other labor leaders had long since made their commitments to American capitalism.

With the merger, Taft ends his chronicle. Its detailed descriptions of the various departments of the AFL, and the positions taken by the executive council on sundry public issues, will unquestionably be grist for the mills of future scholars. But the book casts little light on the important issues that face the trade unions: the increasing resistance of management to organization, the problem of corruption, the pressures to pass more restrictive legislation, the unsolved rivalries within the movement itself, and, above all, the quiet upheaval being imposed by automation and the new technology. Nor has Taft been able to impart any sense of the basic motivations of a labor movement; the need to achieve identification, security, a posture of dignity. No history can afford to ignore such issues.

Mr. Taft's next book, *Organized Labor in American History* (Harper, 1964), demonstrates even more clearly that he is an indefatigable burrower among files, documents, diaries, notebooks, old magazines, and other assorted archival artifacts. He has produced in it another enormous chronicle of American labor. For bulk and detail, it stands very well next to his huge two-volume history of the AFL. No doubt it will be an important source for those who want to verify obscure facts about labor's past. But whether it provides a sense of history, or a feeling for the palpable human thrust that seeks to create a movement, is moot.

Professor Taft's industry is prodigious and in some ways quite admirable, but unfortunately he is not able to distinguish between history and chronicle. Organization after organization parades before the reader; the names of sundry officers are listed; the numerous conventions are tabulated and the debates summarized— yet after all the items have been neatly packaged, one still does not really know the place of organized labor in American history.

Unionism's sole function for Taft is in the work place. American unions, he asserts, always have been exponents of "business unionism" and always have eschewed broad programs of social and political change. Curiously enough, his own recitation belies this judgment: the Workingmens' Party in the 1820's, the old AFL's concern with legislation, the Farmer-Labor party after World War I, and the present Committee on Political Education suggest that there is more to trade unionism than the old walking-delegate philosophy. True, Taft has put all of this into his book and more besides, but at no point is he able to reach the essential spirit that moved men to form themselves into organizations for protection against the crushing burdens of an expanding industrialism.

Unions can hardly become viable institutions if they limit themselves *solely* to job issues. There are those who would argue that unions should help meet the broader needs of their members, for only by doing so can they enhance their abilities to organize and to bargain collectively. For it is evident that no line can be drawn between the worker as employee and the worker as citizen, between the union as bargaining agent and the union as social institution.

In fact, there are any number of problems confronting unionism today—such as automation—that in no way can be solved through ordinary "business" methods. Politics affects such matters as minimum wages and labor law as much as it does the decision of a company to resist union demands. And workers willy-nilly must be concerned with taxation, social security, housing legislation, and the myriad of economic questions perennially weighed by Congressmen. Despite the several chapters in his book on politics and legislation, none of this seems of great import to Taft. It is all submerged by a vast flood of isolated facts.

I really don't know why Taft writes this way; after all, he has been publishing books on labor for over thirty years now. Perhaps the problem stems from his insistence on the continued usefulness of the sort of economic history offered by John R. Commons, one of his revered mentors. Commons, it will be recalled, had argued, rather naively, that alterations in market structure underpinned economic change. Thus the development of retail and wholesale markets in the seventeenth and eighteenth centuries, thought Commons, explained how it was that workers were separated from their tools to become mere employees. Eventually, to protect themselves, they were impelled to organize into unions, through which the characteristic market orientation of capitalism could be expressed as pressure for "more and more."

This now archaic interpretation results in a number of curiosities: The Molly Maguires were just a gang of cutthroats and murderers whose actions had no relation to the harshness of their lives in the mines; the early steel unions had been overly militant at the turn of the century; the unions' fear of Chinese immigration stemmed solely from job fear rather than racist sentiments; Taft-

Hartley was a "non-punitive law which scarcely affected the position of organized labor"; and incidents such as the Haymarket riot really had little to do with unionism and the labor movement.

I may be forgiven perhaps one observation: the Retail Clerks International Association—one of the larger affiliates of the AFL-CIO—has had a regular and steady growth since 1944 and now speaks for over 400,000 employees in the white-collar field. In existence since 1888, its history is fairly interesting, at least interesting enough to have been the subject of two recent studies as well as innumerable student dissertations. Yet Taft can find nothing more to say about the RCIA than a slighting reference to an incident that occurred around 1898! My point is this: if the future growth of the American labor movement is to be in the white-collar field, as many contend, then ought not labor historians say something meaningful about union developments in that area?

Taft's book once again demonstrates that the writing of history —any history—requires many more gifts than ordinary *Sitzfleisch*. At the very least the perceptions of the sociologist, economist, and political scientist must be brought to bear on whatever facts are to be exhumed from ancient documents.

1960, 1964

Game Theory and
Collective Bargaining

It is the view of the renowned mathematician John von Neumann, of the Institute of Advanced Studies, who, with the economist Oskar Morgenstern, another Princeton luminary, wrote *Theory of Games and Economic Behavior* (1944), that correct action in business and labor relations is like a shrewd poker play. In fact, say von Neumann and Morgenstern, it is in the mathematical laws governing such games of strategy that answers to the problems created by monopoly, the growth of trade unions, and the increasing power of government may be sought. Since its publication their book has created much intellectual excitement in scientific quarters. Yet it is interesting to note that many of its ideas seem to jibe with those of a nonmathematical economist whose experience was largely in the field of labor relations, John R. Commons.

Commons sought to explore, in his *Institutional Economics* and in his more recent *Economics of Collective Action,* the actual experience of groups by viewing their behavior against a pattern of action and interaction in which factors of chance as well as coercion and bargaining are integral elements. Game theory, on the other hand, sees social action as a problem of general strategy which excludes, in so far as it is possible, the element of chance. While chance in such games as poker and bridge is strong, the strategic factors are more significant, runs the argument. It is from a mathematical study of the latter that we can derive guideposts for an understanding of the behavior of all economic groups.

As a result of more than thirty years of close experience with governmental commissions, trade unions, and public utility rate inquiries, Commons was very familiar with the business of negotiation. Yet he did not clearly understand the elements of strategy implicit in it. In any bargaining procedure, as in any game, the participants do not possess full information regarding the specific moves of the other participants. In game theory, too, this is a critical factor. The fact that complete information regarding the intention of other groups in the economic situation is not available makes the future not only uncertain but ties present actions to future outcomes. The participant would like to know more about what his opponent disposes or he would like to disguise what he himself proposes. Though this appears to be Machiavellian, it is of the essence of strategic behavior.

Lack of information and future expectations were acknowledged by Commons to be important factors in social institutions. The *collective* action of *conflicting* parties is the major theme of economic life rather than the competitive behavior of myriads of individual units. The conflict of interests among groups of workers, consumers, corporations, investors, and farmers was to him the beginning of economic science.

While Commons recognized such action to be the legitimate province for economic inquiry, he did not offer much comment about its specific forms. Game theory, on the other hand, is especially concerned with the structure of the action implicit in strategic situations. It tells us that a player—or a participant in an economic situation—may and, in many instances, should prefer less than maximum "winnings." This is a preference for an optimum position rather than a maximum one; it is defined more rigorously as the one of least gain and it is naturally the most pessimistic one. In many ways, this is akin to Commons' "reasonable" settlement in economic disputes, the one that is acceptable to all the parties involved. Thus, correct strategy in both games and economic behavior may demand a displacement of maximum aims by the best possible ones "under the circumstances."

This does not, however, eliminate all the elements of chance, for one does take a "flyer" with virtually no knowledge of the outcome of a particular play or action. The result may be a great win or a great loss. But this is gambling, and most persons or groups in strategic situations can ill afford the risks that attend such "flyers." Consequently, the middle course is often preferred and for this a theory of strategy is required.

In actuality, game theory is no simple science. Couched in the somewhat abstruse, yet logically precise, mathematical language of combination and sets, it very often defies translation into narrative. It emphasizes the fact that the behavior of groups in a social or economic situation expresses reciprocal relationships. The action of a labor union, for example, has meaning only as it bears upon and is in turn affected by the actions of all employer groups as well as of all other labor groups, just as the play of a hand in poker depends on the exposed and the unseen cards and on what one knows of the playing psychology of his opponents. This reduces itself to saying that strategy depends upon everyone else's strategy. The action in the game is an interdependent one. Yet groups in society, just as players in a game, do not cooperate with each other. In fact, they are in conflict and it is this that provides the motive power for all strategic actions. It is the conflict that creates the interdependence. The similarity here with Commons' theory is a striking one.

Although there is a lack of complete and full information in strategic situations, there does exist a choice of play. Naturally, the skill exercised in making the selection will determine the win. The fact that there is a choice of play introduces what Commons called willingness. Similarly, in social and economic questions there must be an element of willingness if strategic action is to occur. Without going into details, it may be said that the basic rule of choice in games of strategy is random selection. This is based on the assumption that one's opponent is very much aware of what moves are to be taken. The subsequent plays are then clear; all action should be based on the rule of randomization, since this will confound any response by an opponent that is based on an a priori premise as to the course that is to be followed.

If the players adopt this rule, then losses cannot be great: in fact, the most satisfactory balance becomes a minimum maximum—the lowest possible highest gain.

If there are more than two players in a game (in economic situations three or more groups are the general rule), the problem becomes even more complex since coalitions and countercoalitions may be formed. These groupings, which are created whenever the gain to be secured may be enlarged, are bound to be fragile ones, for the desire to prevent any single participant from becoming too powerful will be an ever-present one. Thus, the search for a higher win will be counterbalanced by the need to curtail the wins of all other players.

Many of the ideas developed by John R. Commons fit squarely into these theories. Commons was concerned with transactions as the starting point of economic action. This he defined as contact between two or more groups which possessed elements of futurity, exchange, persuasion, fraud, command, and the like. The total sum—the national income—to be divided at any given moment was fixed, while the composition of the groups contending for this sum was a shifting one. The similarity of this point to coalitions is obvious. In this situation, economic groups or classes seek a maximum of use values, says Commons, with a minimum of input of energy. This can be interpreted as a minimum maximum and clearly involves elements of strategic action.

Where the transaction is dominated by government or management, the elements of bargaining may be reduced without affecting the presence of strategic conditions. However, the range for the utilization of strategy does become restricted. The process is a reciprocal one: while the kind of transaction (bargaining, governmental, managerial) sets the framework for strategical operations, the specific strategy selected has a subtle impact on the transaction itself. Thus, a government regulation restricting the use of certain raw materials creates a new pattern of business behavior (the expediter, the influence peddler, the gray market, and the like) which in turn lays the foundation for other governmental action.

While the compromise which yields a "reasonable" transaction (in the sense that it is accepted for the time being by all the "players") is doubtlessly a precarious solution, some measure of stability is attained through the legal system, according to Commons. Contract enforcement would be an example of such stability. Commons concedes that what is "reasonable" now may not be so at some future date, and that much irrationality is exhibited in the bargaining process. Yet the continuation of this system, in which freedom to develop one's strategy is maintained no matter what errors the individual makes, is essential for the continuation of political rights such as we have known them.

As was intimated, the conflict of social groups may shift to administrative levels. However, strategic behavior is always present on administrative or managerial levels even though its scope may be severely circumscribed, as in wartime. This suggests that central economic planning has a powerful totalitarian potential.

Now, the kind of action with which Commons was concerned was collective action. This becomes society's primary cohesive force. All the economic groups and classes—labor, business, farmers, government—exert powerful pressures on one another, and what each plans to do is influenced by what it is felt the others will do. Such interclass conflict has a centripetal vector. It necessitates the employment of strategic moves, especially when the relations among the groups themselves are subject to perpetual shifts.

It can readily be seen that within such a context the state may easily become an instrument of coercion. It does not take too long for the various groups in society to recognize that in addition to being a player in the economic game, the state can act as dealer and croupier. Control of the state by a specific group or class means control of the distribution of political privileges; in this sense a new strategic factor must be taken into account.

While under certain conditions there may be an attempt made by some of the groups or classes to seize control of the state, most of the groups (at least in our society) have a vested interest in keeping society operating as a going concern. The going concern in the last analysis is a collective expression of groups or individuals and in so far as they partake actively in social and economic events they have an interest in it. Only the totalitarian seeks to destroy this relationship: in the language of game theory, he prefers a one-person game in which the pattern of distribution cannot be disputed. In a totalitarian state the interests of society are presumably identical with the interests of the individual members, and he who controls the state in such a regime dictates not only the "play" but the "win" as well.

In a nontotalitarian setting, however, all groups are accepted as "players" with their individual interests and specific strategies. This is the setting of Commons' "reasonable capitalism" in which bargaining is the major economic process and the transaction the fundamental economic unit. Such a setting was impossible in the nineteenth century, for then the terms of distribution were dictated by groups identified with capital as a class. It required the growth of trade unions that could duplicate in size and organization the strength of business enterprise for a reasonable bargaining level to be attained.

This theoretical approach promises no facile solution for social and economic problems. Society is comprised of infinite complexities, the unraveling of which sometimes defies comprehension. Yet game theory, with its emphasis on elements of futurity and instability, calls attention to the urgent need to sustain in our system an equality of bargaining strength. If the scales shift away from such an equilibrium, the price that most of us would pay can very well be measured in political terms—in the language of game theory, in the loss of the right to be a recipient in the distribution of the winnings. In a sociological sense, it implies the pulverization of the individual and a destruction of personality. This is a cost that clearly makes it worthwhile to maintain balanced bargaining procedures.

1952

Images of Labor in America

The American labor movement is said to be in crisis. With a membership of some eighteen million, and a growth of less than 40,000 since 1958, it has remained virtually stagnant. Yet this by no means implies that the unions did not accomplish what they set out to do. Compared to the two million or so membership of the 1920's, union growth has been extraordinary. Wages have risen sharply in both real and money terms. And despite the doubts of some academic observers, the unions had much to do with that rise. Health and welfare programs, pension schemes, supplementary unemployment insurance, and effective grievance and arbitration procedures have created a sense of belonging and security that workers did not enjoy three or four decades ago.

Yet virtually everyone inside and outside labor now admits that something has gone awry. The proportion of the work force that is to be found in the unions keeps declining, until it is now but 23 percent of the total. A new, hardened generation of employers adopts ideological positions to justify marked resistance to organizing campaigns, while bargaining has become more than mere ritual: it is now rather a tough battle to sustain positions previously announced. Some observers detect, too, a sense of ennui on the union side. No longer do they see the crusading spirit that motivated labor during the first four decades of the century. Labor's very success, its arrival as an accepted member of society, seems to have weakened its once potent social thrust. At least, so say the critics—and friendly ones at that.

The unionists, on the other hand, reply that some of the "objective" factors responsible for their plight are beyond their control. Technological change has cut into the normal habitat of unionism, industrial employment, and they find it difficult to win adherents in white-collar, service, and technical fields. Since 1958, the unions added a scant 36,000 to their ranks, with about 30,000 of them women. White-collar union membership rose by only 8,000. Political opposition and legal restrictions have hampered their ability to reach the unorganized. They have been rejected time and again by a new generation of workers in new industries and new occupations, by government personnel, and by women employees.

But, argue the friendly critics, all this can be overcome with a new élan. It is said that the labor movement needs fresh goals and a new perspective and that these cannot be attained with the ancient and well-worn techniques of "bread-and-butter" organizing and bargaining. The methods of American unions are, of course, pre-eminently pragmatic and have proven through the years that they can secure material gains for the laboring man. The alternatives, uplift or revolutionary unionism, have simply failed in the American environment.

When the AFL displaced the Knights of Labor in the 1880's as America's major labor organization, a victory was sounded for native pragmatism. The Knights, a most curious union, had been founded in the 1860's as a secret society to improve the status and condition of the working man. In their general outlook, the Knights were something of an uplift organization. Not that they eschewed practical aims altogether: the Knights, in fact, sought collective bargaining agreements as much as AFL affiliates did, but there was a greater stress on such things as social legislation and cooperatives than was the case with the more practical-minded trade unionists.

The AFL, on the other hand, was completely absorbed in what

it considered to be the proper business of unions—wages, hours, and working conditions. It not only fought vigorously against attempts by legislatures and the courts to limit collective bargaining, but it resisted with equal force all measures that seemingly competed with the bargaining process—wage-hour legislation, restriction of child-labor, unemployment insurance, safety legislation, and the like. It wanted no competition from any source in its efforts to do what it alone thought was good for the working man.

Inevitably, this was to result in clashes with those who rejected so narrow a view, and especially with the socialists. The latter were ready and anxious to lend uplift to others, while Federation leaders, notably Gompers, accepted as primary the dictum, "God helps those who help themselves." Gompers, not unfamiliar with socialist ideas and outlook, was convinced that only a thoroughly pragmatic strategy would build trade unionism in the United States. He wanted no political identification, distrusted the legislature, and kept intellectuals in what he considered to be their proper place.

This attitude was ably verbalized and rationalized by intellectuals themselves. Thus, John R. Commons, who had done more than anyone else to establish the study of labor as a respectable academic discipline, would urge that the business of unionism should be left to the unionists. While there was need certainly for idealism in the trade union movement, said Commons, it would have to stem from the practical needs and experiences of the workingman. Since unions were essentially interest groups seeking to advance the welfare of their members, the stress was necessarily on job rights and improvements in working conditions. This view was developed even further by a Commons protégé at Wisconsin, Selig Perlman, who observed that the final outcome of American labor's pragmatism had to be the collective bargaining agreement, with political action relegated to a secondary role.

Only "business unionism" could thrive on these shores, said Perlman, because the American community was private-property minded, opportunities for political action were limited, utopianism was alien to the workingman's psychology, and labor solidarity could flourish only in an atmosphere of "bread-and-butter." This meant voluntarism in structure and an emphasis on craft and skills in organization. It meant fostering property rights in the job and a disdain for "ideology." This was all to the good, thought Perlman. The intellectuals who wanted labor to adopt some kind of transcendental vision of the good society simply did not comprehend the rugged realities that faced the workingman. The abstract conception of labor as "mass," rather than as a group of individuals seeking security and status and material advancement, did not meet the requirements of the American industrial situation. Yet we know that intellectuals provided important services for unions. This much Perlman did concede: he only wanted them to abjure their irritating efforts to mold the objectives of the movement, objectives which were best rooted in the actual desires of the worker, who was after all a member of a voluntary organization.

But what next, when the admittedly short-run material purposes had been attained? Labor, or any other movement for that matter, would soon find itself on an isolated plateau. A limited horizon means limited vision, and this in turn blinds one to problems which are transcendental in a most significant sense. The loss of public regard and the evaporation of tactical alliances with social reformers and political liberals have been a rather high cost to pay for sometime corruption, internal disputes, and affluence. Moreover, the stains cannot be washed away by ordinary public relations. So say the critics. They insist, and perhaps rightly so, that worker apathy and the tarnished image can be dissipated only with a new dynamic, one that would be genuinely meaningful for society and the labor movement as well.

The most extreme position, for example, that advanced by Sidney Lens, urges that labor can make fresh advances only if it recognizes the need for more direct political action. The advocates of an independent labor party see it as a kind of third force in American life. They point to the upheaval being created by automation and heightened productivity and ask whether "free enterprise" can be maintained under the weight of a cartelized economy and permanent war spending. Automation has constricted not only labor forces in key industries but has limited as well the capacity for unions to deal with recalcitrant managements. The steel companies can build inventories in anticipation of a strike, and the chemical firms have much fewer workers to worry about than in the past. Corporate power has increased in our society while that of the unions has diminished.

These problems demand, we are told, not the politics of a pressure group but that of a party seeking power. Labor's interests are coterminous with those of society: it must, therefore, begin to exercise more direct influence on national policy than it has hitherto been able to do through mere identification with an administration in Washington. It must become an administration. It must seek to broaden the basis of political democracy by insisting on the rights of all citizens to participate in the franchise, by restoring the mode of organization that once existed under the Wagner Act, by moving political power at state levels from rotten rural boroughs to urban areas, by making Congress a genuinely representative forum.

The more cautious of the commentators reject such a program as visionary, impractical, and utterly utopian. At best they would prefer to see with Gus Tyler a rescrambling of the existing parties to create genuine foci of liberalism and conservatism. A labor party per se is impractical, it is said, because the workingman no longer constitutes a majority of the population, and besides he has a middle-class outlook anyway. Moreover, a third party would only serve to perpetuate conservative elements in Congress, since it would be most difficult to elect candidates representing a pure labor party. So the argument goes.

On the other hand, liberal politics utilizing coalition tactics could recapture the drive and spirit of FDR's New Deal, lending "purpose and cohesion" to the two-party system. Let the conservatives of both parties, now working together in Congress in any case, take a label of their own, while the liberals, supported by labor, would seek to advance their own objectives. Even if a new realignment were unattainable right now, union participation in politics thus far has been realistically related to genuine possibilities and at the same time has expressed aims which have not always stemmed from a desire for higher wages and other job concerns. Unions have been involved, say the pragmatists, in matters which in reality have transcended the immediate.

These more cautious views confirm the pragmatic nature of labor's normal outlook. Tyler, for example, insists that political activity must continue to stress economic demands because "it is the bread-and-butter appeal that ties the dues payer to leadership in unions." This, it may be noted, continues to limit and restrict the function of the trade union, for it implies an accommodation to received values and modes of political behavior. Thus, unions can be defined only as interest groups, coequal perhaps with others, but they certainly cannot be designated as competitors for social and political power.

In any case, the quality of performance to be ascribed to a group, whatever its purview, stems in many ways from the character of its leadership. This is as true of unions as it is of corporations and political parties. In such groups, particularly when they are large and complex, leadership becomes a matter of establishing and rationalizing a line of authority and ultimate responsibility for decision-making. The degree to which leadership can sway rank and file issues other than "bread-and-butter" often does depend on the success with which the goods are delivered. Even then, says the pragmatist, the union leader cannot always move his people along the path he selects, as witness the failure of John L. Lewis to influence the votes of his miners. Yet in the main, it is urged, contemporary leadership in American unions has been successful; it has been able to shape the conditions and terms of employment in the shop; its maneuverability has been rooted in a native inventiveness which has provided gains without resort to state intervention; and it has demonstrated flexibility by utilizing legislative prescription whenever this was deemed appropriate.

But, if all this is true, then why the crisis? Why the inability to grow, the resurgence of employer hostility, the extension of constricting right-to-work laws across the nation, the alienation of liberal allies, the rising concern with internal democracy, the metastasis of corruption, the unwillingness of white-collar workers to receive unionism's message, and the generally disadvantaged position into which labor has been placed in recent years?

Union leaders may speak of an Eisenhower National Labor Relations Board, a McClellan-Goldwater conspiracy, apathy by rank and file, lack of interest among the great unorganized, and, while all of these certainly merit consideration as causes of the crisis, they do not explain the total situation. For one thing, the very voluntaristic structure of the labor movement in America throws up barriers difficult to overcome. The present unresolved dispute between the industrial unions led by Walter Reuther and the building trades is a case in point. As a coordinating body, the AFL-CIO finds it difficult to coordinate. Its Department of Organization can only prod and suggest, but it cannot compel new drives. Power continues to be centered in the international union affiliates, who, like the members of the United Nations, have neither the desire nor the intention to surrender their sovereignty. They fear the kind of centralization, or at the very least, the minimal restructuring that would provide thrust and direction for fresh advance. Moreover, there are few international unions which have taken a new look at their organizing methods. Those which have done so indeed made gains, such as the Retail Clerks and the Communication Workers. But, for most, the ancient techniques are continued and they bring paltry results.

Essentially, the union movement in America needs to add to its historic pragmatism a powerful dose of social idealism. *Ad hoc* legislative pressures do not seem sufficient for the task of providing a cohesive rationale; for the piecemeal approach which is thereby enforced is all too often submerged by the exigencies of the politically possible. The recent revision of the Wage-Hour Law with its half-hearted extension of minimum standards is a classic illustration of the problem. Quite simply, labor needs to develop a social and political image which will be uniquely labor's. This need not imply a third party; it means rather, as Sol Barkin has so well stated, a revival of the spirit of comradeship and an awareness that the requirements of labor as a movement should be the overriding criterion for growth. It means, too, the unfolding of a cohesive program stemming from the demonstrable congruence of labor's needs with that of society. But this must be proven like an exercise in geometry, with logic and imagination. Once the proof has been established, the QED signature attached, program and action ought to follow as a matter of course.

Unfortunately, too many union leaders, at all echelons, have exhibited more self-satisfaction than awareness of the new vistas before them. They did better than well during the war effort; they responded to the Senate revelations of corruption with a code of ethics; they chartered some new unions and expelled others; they have had ample funds to invest in housing projects; they fought the good fight on political fronts; and they may have elected a President. All this has been essential yeoman work, but it does not seem to have added to labor's acceptability in the general community. The answer, according to some observers, lies in the lack of accomplishments outside the area of bargaining and *ad hoc* legislation. One may very well agree with labor patriarch J. B. S. Hardman when he urges that "Labor leadership . . . could do no worse than assigning a task force for the sole purpose of helping society extricate itself from the intellectual swamps in which it manages to land from time to time." Such a task force, we are told, should advance sound social ideas, but it would indeed take some mental effort to qualify for the job, as Hardman wryly added. It does suggest, too, that labor must be alert to its potential role as a balance wheel in the highly complex, delicately concatenated community of interests that now constitutes the social order.

There still remain deserts in our social and economic landscape that demand irrigation—arid depressed areas, rural poverty, and seemingly perpetual unemployment occasioned by the new industrial revolution. Yet their solutions, pragmatic as they may be, need not exclude the theoretical, for one does enhance the other. One can only hope that union leadership will eventually come to recognize the relationship. Unions, despite their obvious commitments to existing values, can take dissenting positions. In the larger society they can at present only influence decisions; they cannot make them. But such influences must be exerted by the strength of their ideas and the conviction with which they are offered in the market place of opinion. And these ideas must demonstrate validity, i.e., a logic and consistency that will reveal their socially moral nature.

All this indeed implies certain criteria for a dynamic unionism in the modern age. As implied above, it suggests a sense of community rather than collectivity. The latter, as Eric Hoffer has demonstrated, provides an amorphous mass in which the individual, oppressed either by a surfeit of material goods or an aimlessness of purpose, can lose himself. Generally, as we know too well, the drive of the collective is a destructive one. In the community, on the other hand, the individual can work with others harmoniously for a common creative end. The trade union movement needs to provide that community for its members, and in doing so it will once more be able to attract those who so bitterly need what it can offer. To accomplish this, the unions must aspire, must be ambitious for themselves, their members, the unorganized, and, above all, must have the kind of humility and courage that comes with the knowledge that theirs is indeed a humane endeavor.

1962

A Note on the Author

BEN B. SELIGMAN was born in Newark, New Jersey, and studied at Brooklyn College, Columbia University, and the New School for Social Research. He was formerly research director of the Retail Clerks International Association and is now Professor of Economics and Director of the Labor Relations and Research Center at the University of Massachusetts. His first book, *Main Currents in Modern Economics,* published in 1962, is considered a standard in the field, and he has since written *Most Notorious Victory: Man in an Age of Automation* and *Permanent Poverty: An American Syndrome,* and edited *Poverty as a Public Issue* and *Aspects of Poverty.* His articles have appeared frequently in scholarly journals and magazines of opinion. Mr. Seligman is now at work on a study of the philosophic foundations of economic thought.